ViZ

INTER-ARTS EVENT

INTER-ARTS
A TRANS-GENRE ANTHOLOGY

The Invention of the unknown demands new forms. —Arthur Rimbaud

Editor: Roxanne Power Hamilton

Design and Production: Mary Gilliana, Emily Michel, Christopher Kyle Wright, Matt Schriock, Evan Rosen, Max McDaniel, Max Elman, and Roxanne Power Hamilton

Cover Art: ©Sky Power. Ikage #26, 2000, Acrylics, scrap metal on panel, 24 x 24"

Cover Design: Brad Presentati

Contributing Designers: Chris Alexander, Wendy Cung, Amy Fletcher, Stephanie Gliozzo, Anna Huff, Erik Oatman, Amber Pittinger, Johnny Plastini, Brad Presentati, Claire Sund, James Walsh.

Assistant Copy Editor: Laura Perkins

Editorial Review Board: Micah Perks, Karen Yamashita

Editorial Advisors: Ron Padgett, Jerome Rothenberg

Credits and Acknowledgements: pp. 249 – 250.

Viz. Inter-Arts is supported, in part, by the following sponsors:
University of California, Santa Cruz:
Porter College Hitchcock Poetry Fund
The Center for Teaching Excellence
The Non-Senate Faculty Professional Development Fund

Information about Viz. Inter-Arts can be found at viz.ucsc.edu

If you would like to support us or inquire about future publications, please write the editor:
Hamilton@ucsc.edu
Viz. Inter-Arts
Kresge College
1156 High Street
University of California
Santa Cruz, CA 95064

Thank you.

Viz. Inter-Arts is distributed by Small Press Distribution
1342 Seventh Street, Berkeley, California 94710-1409
(510) 524 -1668; E-mail: orders@spdbooks.org
http//:spdbooks.org

Printed by Westcan Printing Group in Canada

Copyright 2007 by Viz. Inter-Arts.
All rights revert to contributors.

ISBN: 0-9786215-0-6
ISSN: 1931-535x

Contents

Introduction vi

Event
Dore Bowen: "What is an Event?" 1
Ken Friedman and Owen Smith: "Introduction to Fluxus Event Scores" 2
Fluxus Event Scores: Ay-O, Robert Bozzi, George Brecht, Ken Friedman,
Dick Higgins, Bengt af Klintberg, Milan Knizak, Jackson Mac Low,
George Maciunas, Yoko Ono, Nam June Paik, Mieko Shiomi,
Tristan Tzara, Ben Vautier 3
Dick Higgins: "Synesthesia and Intersenses: Intermedia" 6

Painters and Poets
George Hitchcock: "Events of Our Epoch" 9
George Hitchcock: "A Painter Among Poets" 10
George Hitchcock: "The Gift" 11
Jerome Rothenberg: "Three Poems for Nancy Tobin";
Nancy Tobin: Paintings: *Waiting For Seurat, Dystopia Parkway,
The Best Thing About Sunday* 12

New York School Collaborations
Ron Padgett and George Schneeman: *Bill Bill*;
Ron Padgett and Joe Brainard: *Upside down Nancy* 14
Joe Brainard: *If Nancy were a da Vinci* 15
Bill Berkson and Joe Brainard: *I Love De Kooning* 16
Bill Berkson: "Working with Joe" 17
Bill Berkson and Joe Brainard: "Like Angels, I Can Only Arrive" 19
Bill Berkson and Joe Brainard: from *Recent Visitors* 20
Bill Berkson and George Schneeman: 1970 Calendar 21
Bill Berkson and George Schneeman: from *Ted Berrigan* 22
Ted Berrigan and George Schneeman: *In the Nam…*and *Untitled* 24
Alice Notley and George Schneeman: *Untitled*;
Anne Waldman and George Schneeman: *Will the World Ever* and *Rogue State* 25
Ron Padgett and George Schneeman: "Collaborating with Poets" 26
Ron Padgett and George Schneeman: from *Little Pages of the Snowman* 30
Ron Padgett and George Schneeman: *Water is Clouds*
Bill Berkson and George Schneeman: *Ball/Park* 31
Ed Bowes, Carl Rakosi, and Anne Waldman: *The Menage* 32

Event: Trans-Genre: Poetry and the Inter-Arts
Karen Jacobs, "Transcontinental Poetry Reading" poster 34
Transcontinental Poetry Reading: A Tribute to Kenneth Koch 35
Kenneth Koch: "Twenty Poems" 36
Anselm Hollo: "It Was All Right" 38
David Antin: from "The November Songs" 38
Anne Waldman: "After 'The Simplicity of the Unknown Past'" 39
Ron Padgett: "Traveling with Kenneth" 40
Andrei Codrescu: "Tristan Tzara: for Kenneth Koch" 41
Rodney Koeneke: "Poem" 42

Barbara Guest: "1913" 44
Will Sherwood: Photograph 45
Kevin Killian and Brian Kim Stefans: *The American Objectivists* 46
Trans-Genre: Poetry and the Inter-Arts. A Panel of New Narrative Essays by
Robert Glück, Dodie Bellamy, Kevin Killian, Camille Roy, kari edwards, and Rob Halpern 58
AnneKarin Glass: *Fallen Reeds I* 69

Screen: A Multiplex
Leslie Scalapino and Konrad Steiner: *Delay series* 70
Robert Glück and Dean Smith: *aliengnosis* 74
Larry Kearney: "For Nathaniel Dorsky's *Love's Refrain*" 78
Nathaniel Dorsky: from *Devotional Cinema* 79
Kristin Prevallet: "Spool Speech" 81
Gary Gach: "Screening as Event" 86
Ken Knabb: Situationist International Cartoon 89
Guy Debord (trans. Ken Knabb): from *The Society as Spectacle* 90
Konrad Steiner: "Remarks on Benshi Tradition and Neo-Benshi" 92
Therine Youngblood: "Poetry and Motion" 92
Norma Cole: *Judex*: A Neo-Benshi Script 93

An Inter-Arts Gallery
Paul Hoover: "Performance and Silence" 94
Roxanne Power Hamilton: "And the Beat Moves On—Michael McClure's Musical collaborations" 99
Ray Manzarek and Michael McClure: from *Mulekick Blues* 100
Chris Stroffolino: "The Day the Music Died (To Give Birth To You)" 102
Andrei Codrescu: "Please Don't Wash" 107
Derk Richardson: "Steeling Beauty: The Inventive Instruments of Oliver DiCicco" ... 108
Oliver DiCicco and Mobius Operandi: "Sculptural Music" 109
Mary Kite: "Moon" 110
Sean Finney: "Balthus," "Brassai," and "Popova" 112
Maxine Chernoff: "Who Were They, What Were They" 115
Bob Holman: "Praise Poem for James Siena" 118
Bob Holman: "Praise Poem for James Turrell" 119
Laura Moriarty: "The Targets" 120
Laura Perkins: "Snooze Alarm" 122
kari edwards: from *Iduna* 123
Mary Burger: from "The Man Without Stumps" 125
David Meltzer: "Life on Line" 127

Event: Is Poetry enough? Poetry in a Time of Crisis
Eileen Myles: "Go Flow" 129
Eileen Myles: from *Hell* 130
Juliana Spahr: "Poetry in a Time of Crisis" 131
Rob Wilson: "Dismantling Imperialist Nostalgia on the Pacific Rim…" 133
Heriberto Yepez: "I Am Bush. Poetry and Authority" 137
Heriberto Yepez: "Border Signs" 139

An Inter-Arts Gallery
Stephen Vincent: "The Art of Urban Walking: Ghosts, Images, & Text" 140
Brenda Hillman: "Girl Sleuth" 142
Charles Bernstein: "If You Lived Here, You'd Be Home Now" 143
Jennifer Scappettone: "The Carapace" 144
Sky Power and Roxanne Power Hamilton: "The Bardo of War" 146
Jane Hirshfield: "The Dead Do Not Want Us Dead" 155

Peter Gizzi: "A Telescope Protects its View" 156
Keith and Rosmarie Waldrop: "Comes and Goes" 157
Michelle Tea: from *Rose of No Man's Land* 158
Marie Cartier: from "The Big O Collection" 162
Sarah Schulman: *Art* 163
Jim Elledge: Two poems 165
David Swanger: "Wayne's College of Beauty" 166
Roswell Spafford: "Apple" 167
Will Sherwood: "Bodyscapes" 168
Micah Perks: "What the Thin Ones Eat" 171
Karen Yamashita: from *I Hotel* 172
Michael Palmer: "Una Noche" 178
Carol Snow: "Syntax" 179
K. Silem Mohammad: "End State" 183
Judith Goldman: from *Fatboy/Deathstar/Ricochet* 184
Terry Wolverton: "Twisted Twister Twist" 187
Susan Silton: from "Tornado in a Box" 188
Joseph Lease: "Hanging from a Cloud" 191
Mahmoud Darwish (trans. Rick London and Omnia Amin): from *Now, As You Awaken* 192
Tim Fitzmaurice: from *Golden Year* 194
Jeremy James Thompson: "Tectonic Factura Construction" 198
Edwin Torres: "Transferred Throat" 199
Joan Retallack: "Lost Brief Case Conjecture" 200
Jocelyn Saidenberg: "Don't Touch The Loot" 201

Event: Poetry and its Arts
Norma Cole and Steve Dickison: from POETRY and its ARTS 202
Taylor Brady and Tanya Hollis: "Poetry Jacket" 214

A Bolinas Gallery
Joanne Kyger: "At the Purple Gate Tent Bolinas: My Memoirs" 215
Bill Berkson: "Out" 216
Larry Kearney and Daniel E. Smith: "Earthquake" 217
Stephen Ratcliffe: from *Human/Nature* 220

Jess: a small Gallery
Jess: from *Boob* 222
Robert Duncan and Jess: "Unkingd by Affection" 224
Kelly Holt: "Jesstures" 225

A Youth Gallery
Leslie Hodgkins: "Lesson No. 1" and "The Jar" 226
Amanda Davidson: "Arcana Caelestia" 228
Dan Fisher: "Mustache Attempt" 234
Elizabeth Young: "Rimming the Pacific" 236
Cedar Sigo and Micah Ballard: "Teaching the Young"; "Live at the East" 237
Kyle Kaufman: "Nite Lites" 238
Max McDaniel: "His Fingers Sang" 239

Contributors 240

Credits and Acknowledgements 249

Introduction
for Emma Joy

In the poem this very lighted room is dark, and the dark alight with love's intentions. It is striving to come into existence... a poetry of all poetries, grand collage, I name It, having only the immediate event of words to speak for it. In the room we, aware or unaware, are the event of ourselves in It." —Robert Duncan

Viz. Inter-Arts publishes work that explores the relationship between the arts. In the spirit of inter-arts communities ranging from the Dadaists through the New York School, Black Mountain College, Poet's Theater, New Narrative writers and others, *Viz. Inter-Arts* publishes trans-genre work and encourages the transgression of boundaries between genres. *Viz.* means "namely" or "that is." Aside from resonating with the word "visual," the title seeks to establish a correspondence between genres through collaboration, juxtaposition, and hybridization. For example, poetry, viz., painting. As Jerome Rothenberg has written about contemporary practices, "the arts themselves begin to merge and lose their old distinctions. The action hereafter is 'between' and 'among,' the forms hybrid and vigorous and pushing always toward an actual and new completeness."

Broadsides included. You will find broadsides—digitally reproduced "art posters" combining the work of writers and artists—in an envelope attached to the back cover. Inter-arts work should be liberated and given space to breathe outside the confines of the book. In each envelope, there will be a unique selection of broadsides—kind of like baseball cards, only bigger—by artists and writers such as George Hitchcock; Kenneth Patchen; Lawrence Ferlinghetti and Momo; Joe Brainard and Ron Padgett; Jerome Rothenberg and Nancy Tobin; Clarence Major and Amy Trachtenberg. We hope you collect them all.

The theme of the book is **EVENT**. We sought submissions that elaborate on this theme in either transparent or unexpected ways, or that document, muse on, or *are* events themselves. The treatment of this theme was entirely up to the artists and writers. We wanted everyone to make an event of it.

Viz. Inter-Arts was inspired by a University of California, Santa Cruz event series I organize entitled "Trans-Genre: Poetry and the Inter-Arts" supported by the Porter College Hitchcock Poetry Fund. The first "Trans-Genre" event included Poet's Theater, a panel on New Narrative, films, live music, and the first-ever live web cast "Transcontinental Poetry Reading" honoring Kenneth Koch. From this event, we include readings by David Antin, Anselm Hollo, Anne Waldman, Ron Padgett, and Andrei Codrescu, as well as Bay Area artists and thinkers prospecting at the edge of genre territories, including a Poet's Theater production by Kevin Killian and a New Narrative writers' panel. We also present material from another UCSC event from April 2004: "Is Poetry enough? Poetry in a Time of Crisis," an event that explores what Juliana Spahr has called the special role of poetry in times of crisis, such as the crises evoked by the so-called "war on terror" and the next wave of the "culture war" against queers.

More than an archive of individual events, *Viz. Inter-Arts: Event* is a print publication that seeks to *be* an event. Though you will find documentation of wonderful inter-arts events, such as The Poetry Center's landmark 2005 "Poetry and Its Arts" event, there are many other "galleries" to explore, including the following: *Event:* a collection of Fluxus Event Scores and descriptive essays; *Painters and Poets* includes the work of poet-painter George Hitchcock and collaborations by Jerome Rothenberg and Nancy Tobin; *New York School Collaborations* features work by New York School poets Ron Padgett, Bill Berkson, Anne Waldman, Ted Berrigan, and Alice Notley and visual artists, Joe Brainard and George Schneeman; *Screen: A Multiplex* gathers collaborations between poets and filmmakers, an excerpt from Situationist Guy Debord's ground breaking film, *The Society as Spectacle*, and many other filmic forms, including an introduction to "Neo-Benshi." An energetic mix of cinema and theater innovated by Bay Area writers, Neo-Benshi draws on the revered art of Japanese Benshi: silent film narration. There are other small galleries, including writers and artists from Bolinas, CA.; collaborations between the visual artist, Jess, and the poet, Robert Duncan; and a gathering of young writers and inter-artists. Throughout, you will find inter-arts galleries that mix up the forms and present a wide range of new work and some older pieces by established and emerging writers, artists, and inter-artists.

While organizing a lot of inter-arts events, I've been thinking about the concept of *event* and how an event—which is, by definition, ephemeral and speech-based—could occur in printed language. How can writing *be* an *event* beyond a mere representation of it? The Situationists International were perhaps the most eloquent in speaking of events and situations. Henri LeFebvre, a Situationist, wrote: "Events belie forecasts... they upset calculations... Movement flares up where it was least expected; it completely *changes the situation*... Events pull thinkers out of their comfortable seats and plunge them headlong into a wave of contradictions."

Much artistic work about political events faithfully *represent* the event without shifting our usual repertoire of feelings about a crisis as obviously horrific as 9/11 or the US invasion of Iraq. Sometimes writing that attempts to "make sense" of catastrophe can blunt the edge of the events' actual incomprehensibility. When language plunges us back into the mess or unintelligibility of actual events, the impulse should be to question the calm language of political rationalization. Some language, some poetry, can be a "preemptive strike" on the real terrorism of a rational façade and expose the distance between comforting words and uncomfortable reality.

Through juxtaposition, we hope to create a conversation between genres, themes, and design that conjures the event of their production through the event of reading and looking; as you walk through the inter-connected galleries, taking in the installations and live performances throughout the hallways and rooms of these pages, we hope you will forge new paths between these spaces and become the event of yourself walking through them.

Roxanne Power Hamilton
Founder and Editor, *Viz. Inter-Arts*

Event
Fluxus Event Scores

Dore Bowen

What is an Event?

Most people would agree that an event occurs when an entity comes into its own, passes through time, flowers or dies. Fluxus artists in the 1960s and 1970s used the notion of the event as a framework so that objects might be reinterpreted as states of being. The ramifications of this shift are suggestive (though not definitively so) of a political stance as well. If an object is an event it is not a commodity; if an object is an event it is social and relational; if an object is an event it is open to chance and participation.

In order to accomplish this transformation from object to perception, Fluxus artists relied on an event score structure. The score provides only an initial instruction that must be interpreted and enacted to be completed. For instance, one of La Monte Young's most well-loved scores, *Composition #10 to Bob Morris* (1960), reads simply: "Draw a straight line and follow it." In Paik's *Zen for Head* (1962) the artist interprets Young's composition by dragging his ink-soaked head across the length of a sheet of paper. In doing so, as David Doris notes, "the grand abstract expressionist gesture is turned quite literally on its head."[1] Although reminiscent of a musical score, one can also conceive of the score akin to freeze-dried food—a product that emerged at roughly the same time as Fluxus. Freeze-dried food requires the addition of water, heat, and time. In a similar manner, the score is animated when it is realized in a performative situation.

If the Fluxus score is a minimal instruction, the event is its culmination in time and space. George Brecht coined this term in order to extend John Cage's sound compositions to environments and situations: the word event, he writes, "seemed closer to describing the total, multi-sensory experience I was interested in than any other."[2] The nature of the Fluxus event can best be explained by differentiating it from other forms of performance. Ken Friedman explains:

> There is an important distinction that George Maciunas drew between the sensibility of the happening and the sensibility of the event. He referred to happenings as "neo-Baroque" theater, a phrase that summoned up the elaborate flourishes of European Baroque architecture and music, as opposed to the concentrated, austere focus of Japanese poetry and its architecture which was reflected in the event form that Maciunas termed "neo-Haiku theater." Yoko Ono characterized this work as having an "event bent," while I created a term that caught both the meditation and the humor in Fluxus pieces with the term "Zen vaudeville."[3]

As Friedman notes, the event does not impede upon its content with gestural flourishes and lavish sets. Quite the opposite. Furthermore, as opposed to the happening, Ono notes that the event "suggests something (an idea) to the audience and allows that audience to move in whatever direction one might choose independent of the artist and eventually independent of the suggestion itself."[4] The event is like an experiment that demarcates an area of investigation, but also an open field of possible engagement. The event's lack of closure challenges the sanctioned borders of aesthetic perception by allowing room for elements that are not preordained within the work itself. In this sense the event score structure is, as Cage writes, "like a bridge from nowhere to nowhere and anyone may go on it: noises or tones, corn or wheat. Does it matter which?"[5]

The Fluxus event is, in fact, an alternative mode of aesthetic perception. In order to break from normative, reifying "perceptualism" (and thus allow perception itself to become an object of perception), the Fluxus event introduced an inventive notion of time, what Margaret Morse calls the "here and nowness of production and reception."[6] This conception of time is more properly called *duration*—what philosopher Henri Bergson describes as the time it takes to wait for the sugar cube to dissolve.[7] When a flower blooms, or a sugar cube dissolves, it dissolves in *its* time, in its duration. "The duration lived by our consciousness is a duration with its own determined rhythm," explains Bergson.[8] Martin Heidegger also invokes duration in order to explain the difference between the mechanistic notion of time and his more existential understanding of it; when taking a walk, for instance, "'half an hour' is not thirty minutes, but a duration [*Dauer*] which has no 'length' at all in the sense of a quantitative stretch. Such a duration is always in terms of well-accustomed everyday ways in which we 'make provision.'"[9]

In its incorporation of unrehearsed and often empty moments, the Fluxus event refers to both Bergson's and Heidegger's notion of duration. Fluxus events revolve around the time it takes for things to evolve, but also the "everyday ways in which we 'make provision.'"

A dramatic example of this bi-durational quality of the event is found in Ono's *Cut Piece* (1964). The impact of this performance derives primarily from the tension wrought by two conflicting experiences of duration. In her performance of this piece, Ono sat before the audience, waiting for members to mount the stage and cut away at her dress with the pair of scissors lying on the stage before her.[10] Ono passively allowed this activity to occur to her. Thus, the "time" of the event was not unlike Bergson's description of duration; it is the time it takes for the activity to unfold unto itself, without the aid of an outside intervention or structure. At the same time, as Kristine Stiles notes, since the event is fraught with the anxiety and anticipation that "cutting" implies for both the performer and the participants, *Cut Piece* uncovers "the latent subject/object condition behind the edifice of art and the presumed opaque neutrality of objects." Behind this "opaque neutrality" lies the anxious relationship between "exhibitionism and scopic desires, victim and assailant, sadist and masochist."[11] *Cut Piece* positions the audience within this temporally open-ended yet anxious situation.

By emphasizing duration, the Fluxus event insists that art cannot exclude the ephemeral and quotidian. Hence, the event involves the incorporation of random, unmediated (human and natural) elements into the work. This tendency to incorporate quotidian detritus into the work of art is generally referred to as *concretism*.[12] Concretism might be mundane—as in Daniel Spoerri's "snare-paintings," where the artist attaches the remains of a dinner directly to the table and presents it as a vertical panel—or more abstract and relational, emphasizing the social relationships that constitute the work.[13] For example, Alison Knowles's *Identical Lunch* (ca. 1971) consisted of a series of "performances" in which individuals were invited to participate by following a prescribed menu which consisted of a tuna fish sandwich on whole wheat toast with butter, no mayonnaise, and a glass of buttermilk or a cup of soup of the day, eaten at a prescribed time, at any location.[14] This interest in everyday life resulted in many interesting new formal combinations including ritual ("fluxfests"), community art (Maciunas's Soho loft project), invention (Maciunas's "multicycle"), publishing ventures (the Fluxus newsletters and newspapers), political and theoretical texts (Henry Flynt's political manifestos), commercial art (Robert Watts's stamps, dispensing machines, and "fluxkits"), and entertainment (chessboards, games, "fluxamusement centers").[15] Clearly, the Fluxus event did not end at the gallery wall or the theatrical stage; since the event merges with its environment and is informed by the participation it solicits, it suggests an alternative mode of perception that threatens the notion that art can copy its world.

1 David T. Doris, "Zen Vaudeville: A Medi(t)ation in the Margins of Fluxus," in *The Fluxus Reader*, ed. Ken Friedman (Chicester, West Sussex, England: Academy Editions, 1998), 121.
2 George Brecht, "The Origin of Events," in *Happening & Fluxus*, ed. Hans Sohm and Harold Szeeman (Köln: Koelnischer Kunstverein, 1970), n.p.
3 Ken Friedman, "Getting into Events," in *The Fluxus Performance Workbook*, 6. [Italics mine.] Available at: http://www.performance-research.net/documents/fluxus_workbook_print.pdf (February 2007)
4 Yoko Ono, "Event, Lecture, Discussion," *Film Culture—Expanded Arts* 43 (Winter 1966): 8.
5 John Cage, "Lecture on Nothing," *Silence: Lectures and Writings* (1961; London: Marion Boyers, 1995), 124.
6 Norman Bryson discusses the limitations of an art history based on "perceptualism" in Norman Bryson, *Vision and Painting* (New Haven: Yale University Press, 1983).
7 Henri Bergson, *Matter and Memory*, trans. N. M. Paul and W. S. Palmer (New York: Zone Books, 1991), 205.
8 Martin Heidegger, *Being and Time*, trans. John Macquarrie and Edward Robinson (San Francisco: Harper and Row, 1962), 140.
9 Dick Higgins, "Boredom and Danger," in *A Dialectics of Centuries: Notes Toward a Theory of the New Arts* (New York: Printed Editions, 1978), 46–47.
10 Ono's performance at Carnegie Recital Hall can be viewed in the film of this event by Albert and David Myles (1965). For more information on the film, see the catalogue notes for Ono's *Cut Piece* by Kristine Stiles in Alexandra Munroe and Jon Hendricks, eds., *Yes Yoko Ono* (New York: Japan Society and Harry N. Abrams, 2000), 158–61.
11 Kristine Stiles, Yes Yoko Ono, 158.
12 In his essay "Neo-Dada in Music, Theater, Poetry, Art" (ca. 1962-5), George Maciunas uses the term "concretism" to describe Fluxus's interest in concrete matter rather than an illusionistic symbol of matter. George Maciunas, "Neo-Dada in Music, Theater, Poetry, Art," in *Fluxus: Selections from the Gilbert and Lila Silverman Collection*, ed. Clive Phillpot and Jon Hendricks (New York: Museum of Modern Art, 1988), 25–27; and Janet Jenkins, ed., *In the Spirit of Fluxus* (Minneapolis: Walker Art Center, 1992), 156–57.
13 See Daniel Spoerri, "Development of the Snare-Picture," in *An Anecdoted Topography of Chance*, done with the help of his very dear friend Robert Filliou; and translated from the French and further anecdoted by their very dear friend Emmett Williams (New York: Something Else Press, 1966), 181-84.
14 Hannah Higgins, *Enversioning Fluxus: A Venture into Whose Fluxus Where and When* (Ph.D. diss., University of Chicago, 1994), 105.
15 All these items can be located under the author or, if no artist is indicated, under the title "Collective" in Jon Hendricks, ed., *Fluxus Codex* (Detroit: The Gilbert and Lila Silverman Fluxus Collection and Harry N. Abrams, 1988).

Photograph by Migdalia Valdes

Ken Friedman and Owen Smith
Introduction to Fluxus Event Scores

The earliest Fluxus event scores date back to John Cage's class at The New School where artists such as George Brecht, Al Hansen, and Dick Higgins began to create art works and performances in musical form. One of these forms was the event. Events tend to be notated in brief verbal notations known as event scores. Events are sometimes known as proposal pieces, propositions, or instructions.

The first collections of Fluxus event scores were the working sheets for Fluxconcerts used by artists and composers who performed the works. With the birth of Fluxus publishing, however, collections of event scores soon came to take three forms.

The first form was the boxed collection. These were individual scores written or printed on cards. The classic example of this boxed collection is George Brecht's *Water Yam*. Other boxed collections by single artists presented scores by Takehisa Kosugi, Mieko Shiomi, and Robert Watts.

A second format was the book or pamphlet collection of scores, often representing work by a single artist. Yoko Ono's *Grapefruit* is the best known of these collections, but during the 1960s, the small collections that Something Else Press published in the Great Bear pamphlet series were even more widely known. These small chapbooks contained work by Bengt af Klintberg, Alison Knowles, Nam June Paik, and other artists in Fluxus and intermedia. The highly portable, easily copied pamphlets spread an idea about what art —and performance art— could be to a wide circle of artists and critics interested in new ways of working.

The third format involved large-format collections carrying the work of many artists in neatly typeset columns on a large sheet of paper. The best known of these was the 1966 *Fluxfest Sale Sheet* compiled by George Maciunas as chief editor and publisher of Fluxus. This tradition translated the early concert collections into a new form, including the compilations that Ken Friedman published at Fluxus West in the 1960s, and the Fluxus compilations organized and reprinted by other publishers in the 1970s.

By the 1980s, there were no widely available publications devoted to the Fluxus event scores other than the extensive scholarly collections gathered by Jon Hendricks in books and catalogues.

In 1989, therefore, Ken Friedman assembled the largest single collection of Fluxus scores to date in the *Fluxus Performance Workbook*. In 2002, Friedman, Owen Smith, and Lauren Sawchyn revised and updated the Workbook for a free digital edition published by Performance Research. It is available online at www.performance-research.net/pages/epublications.html. This selection of event scores comes from that edition.

Fluxus Event Scores

Ay-O

Rainbow No.1 for Orchestra
Soap bubbles are blown out of various wind instruments. The conductor breaks the bubbles with his baton.
Date unknown

Exit No.8
The audience must pass through a vestibule where the floor has been covered with inflated balloons prepared to burst on contact.
Date unknown

Robert Bozzi

Choice 3
A piano is on stage. The performer enters wearing a crash helmet. He takes a stage position as far from the piano as possible. He lowers his head and dashes toward the piano at top speed, crashing into the piano with helmeted head.
1966

Choice 9
Two performers fight between themselves using two violins as if the violins were swords, axes or clubs.
1966

Choice 12
Two teams of performers compete against each other by pushing a piano from opposite sides.
1966

George Brecht

Concert for Clarinet, Fluxversion 1
Clarinet is suspendd by a string tied to its center so that it holds it in a horizontal position about 6 inches above the performers mouth. Performer attempts to play a note without using his hands. He should do this either by swinging the reed end down or jumping up to it and catching the reed with his mouth.
1962

Concerto for Orchestra, Fluxversion 1
Orchestra members exchange their instruments.
1962

Concerto for Orchestra, Fluxversion 2
Orchestra members exchange their scores.
1962

Concerto for Orchestra, Fluxversion 3
The orchestra is divided into two teams, winds and strings, sitting in opposing rows. Wind instruments must be prepared so as to be able to shoot out peas. This can be accomplished by inserting a long, narrow tube into wind instruments. String instruments are strung with rubber bands which are used to shoot paper missiles. Performers must hit a performer on the opposite team with a missile. A performer hit three times must leave the stage. Missiles are exchanged until all performers on one side are gone. Conductor acts as referee.
1962

Ken Friedman

Restaurant Event
Dress as badly as possible. Wear surplus store clothes, tattered shoes, and an old hat. Go to an elegant restaurant. Behave with dignity and exquisite manners. Request a fine table. Tip the maitre d' well and take a seat. Order a glass of water. Drink the water. Tip the waiters, busboy, and staff lavishly, then leave.
1964

Christmas Tree Event
Take a Christmas tree into a restaurant. Place the tree in a seat next to you. Order two cups of coffee, placing one in front of the tree. Sit with the tree, drinking coffee and talking. After a while, depart, leaving the tree in its seat. As you leave, call out loudly to the tree, 'So long, Herb. Give my love to the wife and kids!'
1964

Mandatory Happening
You will decide to read or not read this instruction.
Having made your decision, the happening is over.
1966

White Tooth Workshop
Brush your teeth using a different toothbrush for each tooth.
1989

Dick Higgins

Danger Music Number One
Spontaneously catch hold of a hoist hook and be raised up at least three stories.
April 1961

Danger Music Number Nine
(for Nam June Paik)
Volunteer to have your spine removed.
February 1962

Danger Music Number Eleven
(for George)
Change your mind repeatedly in a lyrical manner about Roman Catholicism.
February 1962

Danger Music Number Seventeen
Scream! Scream! Scream! Scream! Scream! Scream!
May 1962

Bengt af Klintberg

Food Piece for Dick Higgins
A rich variety of food has been placed on a table. The performer starts to take food and put it in his mouth, but he drops the food to the floor the same moment it touches his lips. He takes as much food as in a regular meal, but when he has finished all food is on the floor in front of him.
1963

**Orange Event Number 12
(for Staffan Olzon)**
Fill all the drawers of a chest to the brim with oranges and depart for another part of the world.

Milan Knizak

Fashion
Cut the coat along its entire length.
Wear each half separately.
1965

Cat
Get a cat.
1965

Jackson Mac Low

Tree Movie
Select a tree.* Set up and focus a movie camera so that the tree fills most of the picture. Turn on the camera and leave it on without moving it for any number of hours. If the camera is about to run out of film, substitute a camera with fresh film. The two cameras may be alternated in this way any number of times. Sound recording equipment may be turned on simultaneously with the movie cameras. Beginning at any point in the film, any length of it may be projected at a showing.
*For the word 'tree', one may substitute 'mountain', 'sea', 'flower', 'lake', etc.
January 1961 the Bronx

Social Project 1
Find a way to end unemployment, or find a way for people to live without employment.
Make whichever one you find work.

Social Project 2
Find a way to end war.
Make it work.

Social Project 3
Find a way to produce everything everybody needs.
And get it to them.
Make it work.
29 April 1963 the Bronx

George Maciunas

Note on the Graph Scores: The first scores in this section are printed here as a list of words. The way they are to be performed is that a graph chart is set up, with the words running down the side axis. Across the top, numbers are filled in with time designated in blocks of seconds. The score is filled in some manner. Then, when the performance time for each action comes up, that action is performed to generate sound.

Duet for Full Bottle and Wine Glass
shaking
slow dripping
fast dripping
small stream
pouring
splashing
opening corked bottle
roll bottle
drop bottle
strike bottle with glass
break glass
gargle
drink
sipping
rinsing mouth
spitting
Date unknown

12 Piano Compositions for Nam June Paik
Composition No.1 Let piano movers carry piano into the stage.
Composition No.2 Tune the piano.
Composition No.3 Paint with orange paint patterns over the piano.
Composition No.4 Using a straight stick the length of the keyboard sound all keys together.
Composition No.5 Place a dog or cat (or both) inside the piano and play Chopin.
Composition No.6 Stretch the 3 highest strings with a tuning key until they break.
Composition No.7 Place one piano on top of another (one can be smaller).
Composition No.8 Place piano upside down and put a vase with flowers over the sound box.
Composition No.9 Draw a picture of a piano so that the audience can see the picture.
Composition No.10 Write a sign reading: piano composition #10 and show the audience the sign
Composition No.11 Wash the piano, wax and polish it well.
Composition No.12 Let piano movers carry the piano out of the stage.
1962

Solo for Conductor
Conductor enters and takes a deep bow toward the audience. He remains bowed while he performs various acts with his hands at floor level, such as: tie shoe laces, straighten out socks, wipe shoes with cloth, pick up little specks from floor, etc. Performance ends when conductor straightens up and exits.
1965

Yoko Ono

Four Pieces for Orchestra to La Monte Young
(Provisional Instruction. It may be revised by conductor.)
a. Upon first signal from the conductor, each performer begins to rub a dowel, screwdriver or file across the f hole of any string instrument which will be provided for that purpose, or with an eraser on the surface of a wind instrument. Second signal will indicate termination.
b. Upon third signal, each performer peels off a tape taped upon their instrument.
c. Upon fourth signal, each performer tears off a page from the score.
New instructions to these pieces will most likely be provided by La Monte Young during rehearsal.
Date Unknown

Laundry Piece
In entertaining your guests, bring out your laundry of the day and explain to them about each item. How and when it became dirty and why, etc.
1963

Wall Piece for Orchestra To Yoko Ono
Hit a wall with your head.
1962

Lighting Piece
Light a match and watch it till it goes out.
1955

Painting to be Stepped On
Leave a piece of canvas or finished painting on the floor or in the street.
1960

Fly Piece
Fly
1963

Tape Piece I: Stone Piece
Take the sound of the stone aging.
1963

Tape Piece II: Room Piece
Take the sound of the room breathing
1) at dawn
2) in the morning
3) in the afternoon
4) in the evening
5) before dawn
Bottle the smell of the room of that particular hour as well.
1963 Joe de Marco, Gallerie Deluxxe

Nam June Paik

Moving Theater
Fluxus fleet of cars and trucks drives into crowded city during rush hour. At the appointed time, all drivers stop cars, turn off engines, get out of cars, lock doors, take keys and walk away.
Date Unknown

Mieko Shiomi

Smoke Poem
Props: cigarettes, lighters, finest markers
Each volunteer in the audience writes on a cigarette a name of a person whom he hates or doesn't feel sympathetic. In case he has no such person, he may write a name of a fish.
Then they smoke all together.
The detailed facts of this performance should be held in secret from each other.
1966

Tristan Tzara

Vaseline Symphonique, 1921 Fluxversion
Microphone, hands, vaseline.

Ben Vautier

I Will be Back in Ten Minutes
Performer positions a poster on the stage announcing, 'I will be back in 10 minutes!' and goes across the street to have a cup of coffee.
1963

Audience Piece No.5
Tickets are sold between 8 and 9 p.m. At 9 p.m., the announcement is made that the performance has already begun and will end at 12 p.m. At no time is the audience admitted to the theater.
1964

Audience Piece No.8
The audience is told that the next piece is presented in a special area. They are led away in small groups by ushers, taken through back exits to the street and left there.
1965

Audience Piece No.9
Each member of the audience is led individually into an antechamber where they are asked to undress and led into a dark theater. Those who refuse can have their money returned. When the entire audience is seated naked in the auditorium, a huge pile of their clothing is illuminated on stage.
1965

Audience Variation No.1
The audience is all tied up together using a long string. Performers in the aisles use balls of string, throwing string over the heads of the audience to opposite rows of performers. Balls are thrown until all the string is used up in creating a dense web over the audience. Enough string must be used to entangle the whole audience, tying them to each other, to their chairs, etc., making it difficult for them to leave. After this has been achieved, the performers leave the hall. The audience is left to untangle itself.
Date unknown

Synthesia and Intersenses: Intermedia
Dick Higgins

Much of the best work being produced today seems to fall between media. This is no accident. The concept of the separation between media arose in the Renaissance. The idea that a painting is made of paint on canvas or that a sculpture should not be painted seems characteristic of the kind of social thought—categorizing and dividing society into nobility with its various subdivisions, untitled gentry, artisans, serfs and landless workers—which we call the feudal conception of the Great Chain of Being. This essentially mechanistic approach continued to be relevant throughout the first two industrial revolutions, just concluded, and into the present era of automation, which constitutes, in fact, a third industrial revolution.

However, the social problems that characterize our time, as opposed to the political ones, no longer allow a compartmentalized approach. We are approaching the dawn of a classless society, to which separation into rigid categories is absolutely irrelevant. This shift does not relate more to East than West or vice versa. Castro works in the cane fields. New York's Mayor Lindsay walks to work during the subway strike. The millionaires eat their lunches at Horn and Hardart's. This sort of populism is a growing tendency rather than a shrinking one.

We sense this in viewing art which seems to belong unnecessarily rigidly to one or another form. We view paintings. What are they, after all? Expensive, handmade objects, intended to ornament the walls of the rich or, through their (or their government's) munificence, to be shared with large numbers of people and give them a sense of grandeur. But they do not allow of any sense of dialogue.

Pop art? How could it play a part in the art of the future? It is bland. It is pure. It uses elements of common life without comment, and so, by accepting the misery of this life and its aridity so mutely, it condones them. Pop and op are both dead, however, because they confine themselves, through the media which they employ, to the older functions of art, of decorating and suggesting grandeur, whatever the detailed content of their artist's intentions. None of the ingenious theories of the Mr. Ivan Geldoway combine can prevent them from being colossally boring and irrelevant. Milord runs his Mad Avenue Gallery, in which he displays wares. He is protected by a handful of rude footmen who seem to feel that this is the way Life will always be. At his beck and call is Sir Fretful Callous, a moderately well-informed high priest, who apparently despises the Flame he is supposed to tend and therefore prefers anything which titillates him. However, Milord needs his services, since he, poor thing, hasn't the time or the energy to contribute more than his name and perhaps his dollars; getting information and finding out what's going on are simply toooooo exhausting. So, well protected and advised, he goes blissfully through the streets in proper Louis XIV style.

This scene is not just characteristic of the painting world as an institution, however. It is absolutely natural to (and inevitable in) the concept of the pure medium, the painting or precious object of any kind. That is the way such objects are marketed since that is the world to which they belong and to which they relate. The sense of "I am the state," however, will shortly be replaced by "After me the deluge," and, in fact, if the High Art world were better informed, it would realize that the deluge has already begun.

Who knows when it began? There is no reason for us to go into history in any detail. Part of the reason that Duchamp's objects are fascinating while Picasso's voice is fading is that the Duchamp pieces are truly between media, between sculpture and something else, while a Picasso is readily classifiable as a painted ornament. Similarly, by invading the land between collage and photography, the German John Heartfield produced what are probably the greatest graphics of our century, surely the most powerful political art that has been done to date.

The ready-made or found object, in a sense an intermedium since it was not intended to conform to the pure medium, usually suggests this, and therefore suggests a location in the field between the general area of art media and those of life media. However, at this time, the locations of this sort are relatively unexplored, as compared with media between the arts. I cannot, for example, name work which has consciously been placed in the intermedium between painting and shoes. The closest thing would seem to be the sculpture of Claes Oldenburg, which falls between sculpture and hamburgers or Eskimo Pies, yet it is not the sources of these images themselves. An Oldenburg Eskimo Pie may look something like an Eskimo Pie, yet is neither edible nor cold. There is still a great deal to be done in this direction in the way of opening up aesthetically rewarding possibilities.

In the middle 1950s many painters began to realize the fundamental irrelevance of abstract expressionism, which was the dominant mode at the time. Such painters as Allan Kaprow and Robert Rauschenberg in the United States and Wolf Vostell in Germany turned to collage or, in the latter's case, dé-collage, in the sense of making work by adding or removing, replacing and substituting or altering components of a visual work. They began to include increasingly incongruous objects in their work. Rauschenberg called his constructions "combines" and went so far as to place a stuffed goat—spattered with paint and with a rubber tire around its neck—onto one. Kaprow, more philosophical and restless, meditated on the relationship of the spectator and the work. He put mirrors into his things so the spectator could feel included in them. That wasn't physical enough, so he made enveloping collages which surrounded the spectator. These he called "environments." Finally, in the spring of 1958, he began to include live people as part of the collage, and this he called a "happening."

The proscenium theater is the outgrowth of seventeenth-century ideals of social order. Yet there is remarkably little structural difference between the dramas of Davenant and those of Edward Albee, certainly nothing comparable to the difference in pump construction or means of mass transportation. It would seem that the technological and social implications of the first two industrial revolutions have been evaded completely. The drama is still mechanistically divided: there are performers, production people, a separate audience and an explicit script. Once started, like Frankenstein's monster, the course of affairs is unalterable, perhaps damned by its inability to reflect its surroundings. With our populistic mentality today, it is difficult to attach importance—other than what we have been taught to attach—to this traditional theater. Nor do minor innovations do more than provide dinner conversation: this theater is round instead of square, in that one the stage revolves, here the play is relatively senseless and whimsical (Pinter is, after all, our modern J.M. Barrie—unless the honor belongs more properly to Beckett). Every year fewer attend the professional Broadway theaters. The shows get sillier and sillier, showing the producers' estimate of our mentality (or is it their own that is revealed?). Even the best of the traditional theater is no longer found on Broadway but at the Judson Memorial Church, some miles away. Yet our theater schools grind out thousands on thousands of performing and production personnel, for whom jobs will simply not exist in 20 years. Can we blame the unions? Or rents and real estate taxes? Of course not. The subsidized productions, sponsored at such museums as New

York's Lincoln Center, are not building up a new audience so much as recultivating an old one, since the medium of such drama seems weird and artificial in our new social milieu. We need more portability and flexibility, and this the traditional theater cannot provide. It was made for Versailles and for the sedentary Milords, not for motorized life-demons who travel 600 miles a week. Versailles no longer speaks very loudly to us, since we think at 85 miles an hour.

In the other direction, starting from the idea of theater itself, others such as myself declared war on the script as a set of sequential events. Improvisation was no help; performers merely acted in imitation of a script. So I began to work as if time and sequence could be utterly suspended, not by ignoring them (which would simply be illogical) but by systematically replacing them as structural elements with change. Lack of change would cause my pieces to stop. In 1958 I wrote a piece, *Stacked Deck*, in which any event can take place at any time, as long as its cue appears. The cues are produced by colored lights. Since the colored lights could be used wherever they were put and audience reactions were also cuing situations, the performance-audience separation was removed and a happening situation was established, though less visually oriented in its use of its environment and imagery. At the same time, Al Hansen moved into the area from graphic notation experiments, and Nam June Paik and Benjamin Patterson (both in Germany at the time) moved in from varieties of music in which specifically musical events were frequently replaced by nonmusical actions.

Thus the happening developed as an intermedium, an uncharted land that lies between collage, music and the theater. It is not governed by rules; each work determines its own medium and form according to its needs. The concept itself is better understood by what it is not, rather than what it is. Approaching it, we are pioneers again, and shall continue to be so as long as there's plenty of elbow room and no neighbors around for a few miles. Of course, a concept like this is very disturbing to those whose mentality is compartmentalized. Time, Life, and the High Priests have been announcing the death of happenings regularly since the form gained momentum in the late fifties, but this says more about the accuracy of their information than about the liveliness of the form.

We have noted the intermedia in the theater and in the visual arts, the happening, and certain varieties of physical constructions. For reasons of space we cannot take up here the intermedia between other areas. However, I would like to suggest that the use of intermedia is more or less universal throughout the fine arts, since continuity rather than categorization is the hallmark of our new mentality. There are parallels to the happening in music, for example in the work of such composers as Philip Corner and John Cage, who explore the intermedia between music and philosophy, or Joe Jones, whose self-playing musical instruments fall into the intermedium between music and sculpture. The constructed poems of Emmett Williams and Robert Filliou certainly constitute an intermedium between poetry and sculpture. Is it possible to speak of the use of intermedia as a huge and inclusive movement of which dada, futurism and surrealism are early phases preceding the huge ground swell that is taking place now? Or is it more reasonable to regard the use of intermedia as an irreversible historical innovation, more comparable, for example, to the development of instrumental music than, for example, to the development of romanticism?

1981

In 1965, when the above words were written, the intention was simply to offer a means of ingress into works which already existed, the unfamiliarity of whose forms was such that many potential viewers, hearers, or readers were "turned off" by them. The world was filled at that time with concrete poems, happenings, sound poetry, environments, and other more or less novel developments; unless the public had a way of seeing into the work by causing it to stand still for a moment and be classified, the work was likely to be dismissed as "avant-garde: for specialists only." To any dedicated nonspecialist this could be frustrating—one wanted to know well the art of one's time, since one wanted to hear one's own voice or self at work, without the interventions of history and historical judgements; this was art whose horizons would closely match one's own.

The vehicle I chose, the word "intermedia," appears in the writings of Samuel Taylor Coleridge in 1812 in exactly its contemporary sense—to define works which fall conceptually between media that are already known, and I had been using the term for several years in lectures and discussions before my little essay was written. Furthermore, as part of my campaign to popularize what was known as "avant-garde: for specialists only," to demystify it if you will, I had become a publisher of a small press, Something Else Press (1964-1974), which brought out editions of many primary sources and materials in the new arts (as well as reissuing works of the past which seemed to merit new attention—works by Gertrude Stein, the dadaists, the composer Henry Cowell, etc.). It seemed foolish simply to publish my little essay in some existing magazine, where it could be shelved or forgotten. So it was printed as the first Something Else Newsletter and sent to our customers, to all the people on our mailing list, to people to whom I felt the idea would be useful (for example, to artists doing what seemed to me to be intermedial work and to critics who might be in a position to discuss such work). All in all, I gave away some 10,000 copies of the essay, as many as I could afford; and I encouraged its republication by anyone who asked for permission to do so. It was reprinted seven or eight times that I knew of, and it still lives on in print in various books, not just of mine, but where it has been anthologized along with other texts of the time or as part of surveys.

The term shortly acquired a life of its own, as I had hoped. In no way was it my private property. It was picked up; used and misused, often by confusion with the term "mixed media." This last is a venerable term from art criticism, which covers works executed in more than one medium, such as oil color and guache. But by extension it is also appropriate to such forms as the opera, where the music, the libretto, and the mise-en-scene are quite separate: at no time is the operagoer in doubt as to whether he is seeing the mise-en-scene, the stage spectacle, hearing the music, etc. Many fine works are being done in mixed media: paintings which incorporate poems within their visual fields, for instance. But one knows which is which.

In intermedia, on the other hand, the visual element (painting) is fused conceptually with the words. We may have abstract calligraphy, concrete poetry, "visual poetry" (not any poem with a strong visual element, but the term is sometimes used to cover visual works in which some poem appears, often as a photography, or in which the photographed visual material is presented as a sequence with a grammar of its own, as if each visual element were a word of a sentence, as in certain works by Jean-François Bory or Duane Michaels).

Again, the term is not prescriptive; it does not praise itself or present a model for doing either new or great works. It says only that intermedial works exist. Failure to understand this would lead to the kind of error of thinking that intermedia are necessarily dated in time by their nature, something rooted in the 1960s, like an art movement of the period. There was and could be no intermedial movement. Intermediality has always been a possibility since the most ancient times, and though some well-meaning commissar might try to legislate it away as formalistic and therefore antipopular, it remains a possibility wherever the desire to fuse two or more existing media exists. One can avoid it; one can be like Rosalind Krauss, a much respected critic who said in a lecture at Iowa City in 1981, "I am devoted to the idea of trying to bury the avant-garde," which she does by attacking it, ignoring it and its implications, or, even worse, presenting theory as such an end in itself that any sort of artwork becomes, at best, an unimportant appendage to the theory. But there is always an avant-garde, in the sense that someone, somewhere is always trying to do something which adds to the possibilities for everybody, and that that large everybody will some day follow this somebody and use whatever innovations were made as part of their workaday craft. "Avant-garde" is merely a conventional metaphor drawn (in the mid-nineteenth century) from the military, in which an avant-garde moves in advance of the main body of troops. "Avant-garde" is relative, not absolute. A conservative poet can be at least morally avant-garde by moving in the direction of ever-greater integrity and purity, of vividness or metaphor and excellence of line. Others seek to follow, even when they cannot; and thus the metaphor retains its relevance.

But when one is thinking of the avant-garde of forms and media, one is often thinking of artists who, for whatever reason, question those forms and media. They can reject some (e.g., André Breton's predecessors in French dada rejected the novel, and they were avant-garde, while André Breton chose to move toward some kind of novel as a possibility, thus provoking a break between his group, which in due course became the surrealists, and the other—and the new group, too, was avant-garde). They can create others. And often this creation of new media is done by the fusion of old ones; this was very common in the late 1950s and early 1960s, with the formal fusions I have already mentioned. No work was ever good because of its intermediality [1]. The intermediality was merely a part of how a work was and is; recognizing it makes the work easier to classify, so that one can understand the work and its significances.

Further, there is a tendency for intermedia to become media with familiarity. The visual novel is a pretty much recognizable form to us now. We have had many of them in the last 20 years. It is harping on an irrelevance to point to its older intermedial status between visual art and text; we want to know what this or that visual novel is about and how it works, and the intermediality is no longer needed to see these things. Same with visual poetry and sound poetry (or "text-sound," if one prefers that term). In the performance arts, once there was the happening which was close to "events"; some happenings artists did fluxus, and some did not. At least one fluxus artist, Alison Knowles, evolved in her work until she found herself doing what other new artists—many of whom took great pains to distinguish what they were doing from happenings, events, and fluxus—were calling, variously, "art performance" or "performance art." Where do we look for to find the continuity of these? To their intermediality: they are all the same intermedium, a conceptual fusion of scenario, visuality and, often enough, audio elements. But will the intermediality explain the uniqueness or value of the very best of art performance (or performance art)? I think not. Some works will become landmarks and will define their genre, while the others will be forgotten. At best the intermediality was needed to suggest their historical trajectory, to see their sometimes obscure pedigree (as one might use it, with happenings, to point toward the heritage of happenings from dada or futurist manifestations). But if the work is ever to become truly important to large numbers of people, it will be because the new medium allows for great significance, not simply because its formal nature assures it of relevance.

This, then, is the caveat inherent in using the term intermedia: it allows for an ingress to a work which otherwise seems opaque and impenetrable, but once that ingress has been made it is no longer useful to harp upon the intermediality of a work. No reputable artist could be an intermedial artist for long—it would seem like an impediment, holding the artist back from fulfilling the needs of the work at hand, of creating horizons in the new era for the next generation of listeners and readers and beholders to match their own horizons too. What was helpful as a beginning would, if maintained, become an obsession which braked the flow into the work and its needs and potentials. One often regrets the adherence of an artist to a set of dogma: the "movement artist" is a case in point—he adheres to the teachings of his or her movement, long after these have passed their relevance. There is the "late" futurist, the "late" abstract expressionist, the "late" pop artist. To be late in that sense is somehow to create a sort of academicism, good for providing examples to a class ("Okay, class, now this week I want each of you to do a pop art painting"), perhaps useful for heuristic purposes but not likely to open up new horizons for the artist or his viewers, listeners, or readers.

And with this I would leave the matter of intermedia. It is today, as it was in 1965, a useful way to approach some new work; one asks oneself, "what that I know does this new work lie between?" But it is more useful at the outset of a critical process than at the later stages of it. Perhaps I did not see that at the time, but it is clear to me now. Perhaps, in all the excitement of what was, for me, a discovery, I overvalued it. I do not wish to compensate with a second error of judgment and to undervalue it now. But it would seem that to proceed further in the understanding of any given work, one must look elsewhere—to all the aspects of a work and not just to its formal origins, and at the horizons which the work implies, to find an appropriate hermeneutic process for seeing the whole of the work in my own relation to it.

Intermedia

Higgins' "Intermedia Chart" resonates with temporally dynamic sociograms, where human interactions are highly differentiated and radically decentralized and based primarily on the specific needs of a given body, in this case artists. According to a model like this, historic and contemporary experience is diverse, causally flexible and permissive of the as-yet-unknown.

The chart depicts intersections between fluxus and related work and makes no attempt at linear chronology. Fluid in form, the chart shows concentric and overlapping circles that appear to expand and contract in relationship to the "Intermedia" framework that encompasses them. It is an open framework that invites play. Its bubbles hover in space as opposed to being historically framed in the linear and specialized art/anti-art framework of the typical chronologies of avant-garde and modern art.

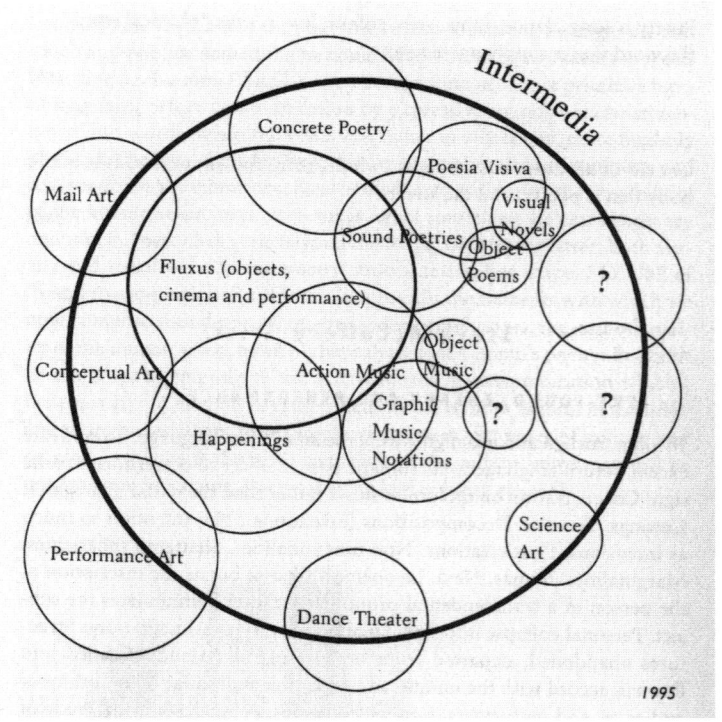

1995

Events of Our Epoch
George Hitchcock

oil is discovered in the crowns
   of hats and is piped
   out of melodious stockings
a symphony somewhat wider than
   Australia
   is performed under Niagara
   Falls to the applause
   of anxious cannonballs
the construction of unemployed
   kidneys is voted
   precedence over
   carrousels & parallelepipeds
elegant hydroponic forests
   of chanterelles
   populate the space
   platforms
kerosene lanterns are hastily
   organized into brigades
   for the conquest of
   Mount Situ-Nervosa
male children whose names begin
   with semi-colons are
   granted
   placentas of cocaine
embalmed deodorized dentures
   are worshipped in
   the Cathedral of spasm
Zeus hurls an immense dais
   in the general direction
   of the prostate gland
access to electro-shock
   therapy is
   limited to
   those under ninety
Congress passes a law
   forbidding
   epaulets on bicycles
the penalty: amputation
   of one's shadow

George Hitchcock: A Painter Among Poets

George Hitchcock's work helps us to see relationships between the arts and between communities within the art and literary worlds. As poet, painter, editor, and teacher, Hitchcock's life work reveals the vital connection between making art and helping others to make their own.

Hitchcock's paintings are seriously playful in the surrealist mode of his poetry. We are happy to include broadsides designed from his poetry and paintings. As a poet, Hitchcock's work and philosophy serve as models for us in our quest to understand how, in Robert Duncan's words, "poetry is an event in language."

> Writing poetry, to me, is always a question of the present moment, so it's where I am right now that interests me… It is moment after moment after moment in which the poet creates something and alters reality in the course of it, which is the beauty of poetry, though nobody recognizes it."
> from interview with George Hitchcock in *Durak*, No. 1

In 1964, George Hitchcock founded the legendary poetry magazine, *kayak* whose motto was "[a kayak] is a small watertight vessel operated by a single oarsman…It has never been successfully employed as a means of mass transport." This may be true, yet *kayak* gave a lift to a whole generation of poets seeking a new way into the literary currents of the 60s.

We are grateful that George Hitchcock is reinvigorating the poetry community at the University of California, Santa Cruz, with his annual support of poetry projects through the Hitchcock Poetry Fund. We are excited that this fresh start is nestled among the visual, performative, musical, film, and digital arts at the University's college of the arts–Porter–where Hitchcock taught for many years. The collaborative possibilities are infinite at these intersections. *Viz. Inter-Arts* plans to explore them and extend them beyond our own generative geography–where the redwoods intersect the Pacific–to you.

Photograph by Debra St. John

"Various Faces," Jorge Hitchcock, 1998

George Hitchcock

"THE GIFT"

Catkins fallen from the alders
float on the water's surface.

The bicycles are leaner. Under the foot-
bridge there are new fronds of fern.

The faces of unknown poets drift
in the sky disguised as plumes of mist.

Spring enters my window
carrying a small bouquet of steeples.

Design by Max McDaniel

Three Poems for Nancy Tobin
Jerome Rothenberg

Waiting For Seurat

waiting for seurat
is not so bad is not

what everybody thinks of
standing in a fish tank

arms akimbo legs too
when the bathers fail to make

the morning's exercise
forsaken all awash

as I am too
but now

the final holiday draws nigh
some sunday afternoon

the chime has chimed
the branches overhang

the crowd of watchers
& it's time

to coax the children
back into the car

to leave the dishes
& the soap behind

the other little friends
so soon departed

still we wait for them
we are the walkers

in the park
& if we fall into the lake

a second time
the acrobats will scoop us out

will whisk us home
like children

neither lost nor found
our bodies & our thoughts

like tiny flecks
& little reckoning

the time it takes
to sink or swim

still bug eyed
half alive

the big bowl broken
waiting for seurat

Nancy Tobin, *Waiting for Seurat*, 2005; Mixed media, 14″ x 8″

Dystopia Parkway

how far he dives
into a sandbox
lights erupting flicker

down a parkway
riding to the Star Hotel
a place to watch

the stars on carpets
sidewalks stitched into a
pure dystopia

as one by one
we dance
for all the children

in the world
my temper will ignite
feed you my flames

a red confusion
opens to the right of us
we raise white fingers

stubby arms
a forest of computer
screens alight

the parkway filled with
phantom windows mothers
can stare out from

their dystopias
more like a fact of life
seeing that nothing

can cohere however
solid are the walls
however bright

soap bubbles floating
over broken glass
the perch deserted where

birds seldom sang
the parkway packed into
a sun box flat

I carry underneath
my coat the memory of where
we all will live

a family of artists
each one with a simple story
resolved to bring it home

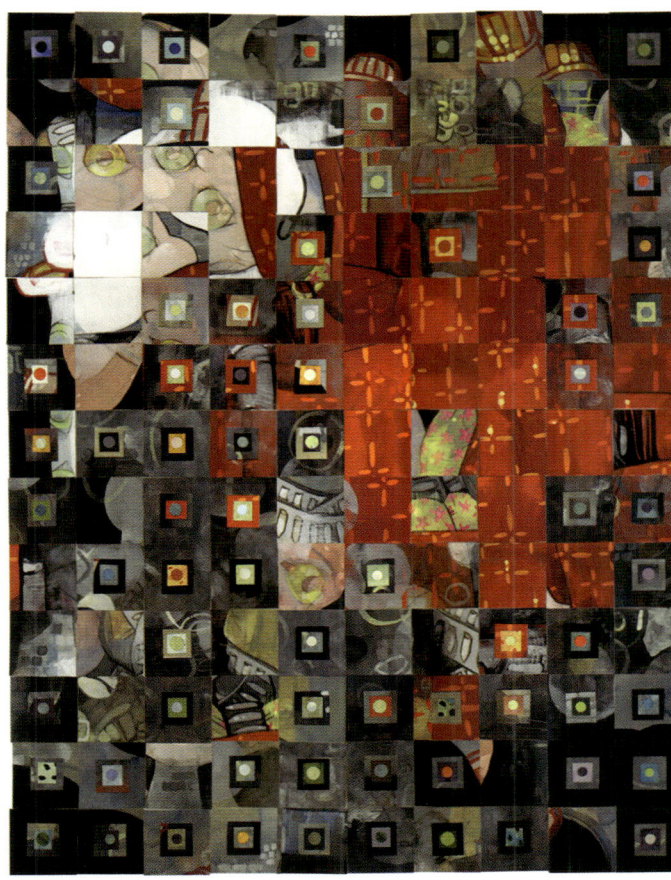

Nancy Tobin, *Dystopia Parkway*, 2005; Painted paper collage, 26.5" x 20.5"

Nancy Tobin, *The Best Thing About Sunday*, 2005; Painted paper collage, 20.5" x 16.5"

The Best Thing About Sunday

is the color
& the next best
how the little folk
find here a place to fly

balloons & kites
skidaddle
rummage among the broken
mother boards

how pink & paper thin
the world appears
to be a field of pinwheels
driven by the wind

& spinning
line on line
& circle into circle
strings cut free

these are the gifts
they bring us these
are what we throw
into the air & see them

flying by
the children's room
a little brighter
walking cockeyed looking

for the wind to stop
then we can find
the best thing about sunday
eggs & eyes

adornments cars that run
on spirits wheels
too precious for the road
a pig that squeals

New York School Collaborations

Joe Brainard and Ron Padgett, *Bill Bill,* 1963; Mixed media, 6" x 4 1/2"

Joe Brainard and Ron Padgett, *Upside Down Nancy*, 1963; Mixed media, 6" x 4 1/2"

What follows is a gallery of collaborations between poets and visual artists from the New York School, first and second generations. Visual artists include Joe Brainard and George Schneeman. Poets include Bill Berkson, Ted Berrigan, Alice Notley, Ron Padgett, and Anne Waldman. Collaborations among these poets and artists covered the gamut from extremely informal to formal, including visual art, spontaneous poems, numerous handmade books (or "bokes"), illustrated poems and books, poetry book covers, and classic volumes of co-authored poetry like Ron Padgett and Ted Berrigan's *Bean Spasms* and Berrigan and Waldman's 1970 book, *Memorial Day*. We also include a poetic tribute to New York School poets Kenneth Koch ("The Transcontinental Poetry Reading") and work that references the work by Frank O'Hara and John Ashbery. The section ends with a tribute to the late Barbara Guest.

Joe Brainard, *If Nancy Were a da Vinci,* 1972; Ink on off-set of da Vinci sketch, 14" x 10 1/4".
From Joe Brainard Collection, Mandeville Special Collections Library, University of California, San Diego.

Joe Brainard and Bill Berkson, Original Artwork for *I Love You DeKooning,* c. 1969; Ink on paper, 11 matted panels, 13" x 10".
From Joe Brainard Collection, Mandeville Special Collections Library, University of California, San Diego.

Working With Joe
Bill Berkson

WHILE working on his open-ended prose masterpiece *I Remember*, Joe Brainard commented: "I feel that I am not really writing it but that it is because of me that it is being written. I also feel that it is about everybody else as much as it is about me. I feel like I am everybody." One great truth about style or character in art is that it is not so much to be pursued or cultivated so much as to be allowed or tolerated as that aspect of the work that can't be avoided. Thus viewed, personality, style, even so-called "meaning" register as inexorable elements, not necessarily the main order of business at all. A certain hankering after anonymity—or generality, anyway—rules the greatest art. As Carter Ratcliff once wrote of Brainard, "His hand has its own, immediately recognizable way of trying to be anonymous."

All art is collaboration. You collaborate with your culture, your language, your reading. Kenneth Koch called Frank O'Hara's poem "Choses Passagères," written in O'Hara's limited French but inspired by a French dictionary, O'Hara's "collaboration with the French language." When Bernadette Mayer says of her writing "It's as if the language wants to say this," she acknowledges the proper relation of matter to genius. Or, as Brainard again put it, giving "advice to a collage maker: 'Do not try to "arrange" your objects; let them help you formulate.'" As an artist, you collaborate with history, the past, the art—poetry, paintings, dance, whatever—that you admire. You don't so much control as work with your materials, which inevitably include yourself, whatever may be your most intimate facts. You collaborate with your peers, either directly (that is, you write works together) or not (that is, by parallel creations you form the work that comes to be recognized as that of a period style, the art of your time). Competitiveness is a form of collaboration. Addressing an audience—conceiving an addressee, a reader or viewer, for the work—you collaborate with that shifting phantasmagoria. Such sociability is what puts the work in the world.

Artistic collaboration between one or more poets, or between poets and other artists (be they dancers, painters, musicians or theatre folk), is often a spontaneous extension of social life. If your friends are other artists, the inclination to make something is likely to become salient in the midst of the most casual occasion. The writing pad gets passed across the room. Some nights in the late 1960s the drop-in work force in George Schneemann's studio was George plus four to six poets deep. There are, of course, more formal, institutionalized projects—but those are usually livres d'artiste, where the text is the starting point for, and eventually incidental to, the creation of a beautiful luxury item, a book of illustrated verse. Artists have illustrated poetry perhaps since poetry was first written down. Image-and-text work certainly goes back at least as far as the Mayans. Botticelli's drawings for a folio edition of Dante's *Divine Comedy*, Manet's responses to Poe and Mallarmé, Picasso's drawings on poets as various as Ovid and Pierre Reverdy—the tradition stretches to the present with Joe Brainard's settings of images to John Ashbery's *Vermont Journal* and to Kenward Elmslie's *Album* and *The Champ*, and more. But the more hands-on variety of such works, by now so familiar, has a much shorter history. "Poem-paintings" and "poem-pictures" or just "collaborations" are some of the terms for the kinds of image-and-text combinations painters and poets together and separately have invented in this century. Foreshadowings of these modes may be found among the group inventions of the Surrealists—Exquisite Corpses made in the 1920s by poets, painters and others, where revelation rather than virtuoso handicraft was the charge. Collage and ready-mades in a sense had already insinuated a kind of a collaborative spirit into modern art. (Ernst's collage novels such as Semaine de Bonté enlisted the tacit collaboration of nineteenth-century dime-novel illustrators.)

In 1957 Larry Rivers and Frank O'Hara were invited to produce a portfolio of lithographs in collaboration for Tanya Grossman of Universal Limited Art Editions. Working together over the next two years in Rivers's Second Avenue studio, they made a set of twelve prints called *Stones*. Rivers recalled the process a few years later in these terms:

> I did something, whatever I could, related in some way to the title of the stone and [Frank] either commented on what I had done or took it somewhere else in any way he felt like. If something in the drawing embarrassed him he could alter the quality by the quality of his words or vice versa... With these images... and his words we were at once remarking about some subject and decorating the stone.
>
> We were fully aware... That Frank with his limited means was almost as important as myself in the overall visual force of the print... Frank without realizing it was being called upon to think about things outside of poetry. Besides what they seemed to mean he was using his words as a visual element. The size of his letters, the density of the color brought on by how hard or soft he pressed on the crayon, where it went on the stone (which many times was left up to him) were not things that remained separated from my scratches and smudges.

O'Hara went on to do other, less formally proposed, collaborations with Norman Bluhm, Michael Goldberg, Jasper Johns and, eventually, Joe Brainard. With Rivers, Kenneth Koch soon followed suit. The '50s and '60s were the prime decades of such wildcat improvisation, the working principles of which, in retrospect, could be set down as three:

- Two or more people working on one or more surface at a time in the same room.
- Given a degree of impersonal "otherness" (or what William Burroughs more arcanely called "The Third Mind")—simply put, more, and more varied, information goes into the mix.
- Participants have no expectations—there's a tacit agreement that the result may be a desultory mess—but there is a strong sense of obligation, again sociable, to keep one's end up. (Brutal undercutting, rash obliteration and every other form of one-upupmanship—each has its place.)

Commenting on the 1950s poetry-and-jazz collaborations, Frank O'Hara wrote to Gregory Corso (March 20, 1958): "I don't really get their jazz stimulus but it is probably what I get from painting... that is, one can't be inside all the time, it gets too boring and you can't afford to be bored with poetry so you take a secondary enthusiasm as the symbol of the first...." O'Hara collaborated with other poets, with painters, composers, theatre producers and directors and actors; the results were poem-paintings, collage comics, lithographs, songs, a musical comedy, numerous plays, and two films with Alfred Leslie. In 1960–1, O'Hara and I wrote a series of poems together that Larry Fagin later published as the *Hymns of St. Bridget* in a small edition with a cover by Larry Rivers. Some of the poems read to me today like instances of a very young poet (me) tagging along after an older poet in full possession of his genius. Yes, but what "Third Mind" was responsible for this choice item?

Song Heard Around St. Bridget's

When you're in love the whole world's Polish
and your heart's in a gold-stripped frame
you only eat cabbage and yogurt
and when you sign you don't sign your own name

If it's above you want and you know it
and the parting you want's in your hair
the yogurt gets creamy and seamy
and the poles that you climb aren't there

To think, poor St. Bridget, that you never got
       to see an Ingmar Bergman movie
because you were forbidden our modern times
but you're not as old as all that, you're not a mummy
you saw the Armory Show and Louis Jouvet
and Mary of Scotland and ANCHORS AWEIGH
                                              and we're sure
that you've caught up with La Vie et Esprit poetically pure
and indeed quite contemporary and just as extraordinary
as ice cubes and STONES and dinosaur bones and manure

When you're in love the whole world's a steeple
and the moss is peculiarly green
you may not be liked or like people
but you know your love's on your team

When you're shaving your face is a snow bank
and your eyes are particularly blue
and your feelings may be fading and grow blank
but the soap is happy it's you!

    Joe Brainard's collage-comic collaborations with O'Hara occurred in much the same way, except that Joe apparently had the courage to suggest collaborating, and the terms of doing it, himself. Like myself, Joe was a twenty-something interloper emboldened by O'Hara's keen eye for talent at the get-go stage of its development. (Actually, by the mid '60s when these collage comics were done, Joe had already refined his talent more than had any poet his own age.) Writing on O'Hara, Joe defines the in-tandem, hand-over-hand improvisational method in comparison with another, intermediate, call-and-response kind:

> Actually, in the strict sense of the word, Frank and I never collaborated. (Alas) never on the spot, starting together from scratch. Giving and taking. And bouncing off each other. What we did do was that I'd do something (a collage or cartoon) incorporating spaces for words, which I'd then give to Frank to "fill in." Usually he would do so right away, with seemingly little effort...

    What Joe does in that little paragraph is detail his two basic ways of collaborating, except that the comics more often than not were delivered to poets for text-production through the mail, and filled in with considerably less spontaneity than was normal for O'Hara. Comics were very natural. We had a feeling for how they worked. They were our first art and, in many respects, our first literature.

    Intrinsically, criticism is a form of collaboration, another form of call-and-response. It can, as Saint-Beuve observed, transform "half-poets who become and appear whole poets in criticism: all they need is an external fulcrum and a stimulus." Think of the great critics and reporters who are neither artists nor poets—Whitney Balliett on music, Herbert Muschamp on architecture—and you see that Saint-Beuve was right. But then again occasionally a poet who is "whole" to begin with maintains that same wholeness across the board. In poetry and prose, James Schuyler wrote about what was really there, and loved to trace out the details that appealed to him. (Schuyler said that he even used to write his art reviews out in verse lines first and then 'turn' them into prose.) In 1967 Schuyler wrote on Brainard for an issue of Artnews that feature a picture of Joe's on the cover. Schuyler's text reads in part:

> Also a painting of a ribbon tied in a bow: "I don't know what I'm going to do with it." He is a painting ecologist whose work draws the things it needs to it, in the interest of completeness and balance, of evident but usually imperceived truths. He is like Darwin deducing why there is more red clover where old maids live: they keep cats that catch the field mice that eat the clover.
>
> Also a Prell "shrine." A dozen bottles of Prell—that insidious green—terrible green roses and grapes, glass dangles like emeralds, long strings of green glass beads, a couple of strands looped up. Under glass, in the center, a blue-green pieta, sweating an acid yellow. The whole thing cascades from an upraised hand at top: drops and stops like an express elevator. It is a cultivated essence of shop-window shrines and Pentecostal Chapels (John Wesley with Tambourines, lugubrious and off-pitch). Its own particular harsh pure green is raised and re-inforced until it becomes an architecture. It is to green what a snowball is to white, an impactment.
>
> A violet-blue, the border of the glass over the pieta, emerges as an echo, as though if you squeezed a leaf hard enough a little sky blue would ooze out. The whole thing has the musical look of a clock.

    Criticism made by artists, which is sometimes formal, in the art magazines, but mostly spoken or otherwise off-the-cuff, is valuable mainly for its forthrightness. Brainard wrote to Schuyler: "One thing I like about Hans Hofmann is that he is hard to like." Then again, Schuyler quoting another painter on Brainard's acumen as a colorist: "He just puts down a color, and it's right." (Most professional art critics would spend 20 pages getting around to such a conclusion.) Then, too, there is self-criticism, the unacknowledged type of criticism that makes good art good in the best way—it is good on purpose. Joe meant his work to be good. He wrote (this again appears in Schuyler's endlessly informative text) in July, 1965:

> Working on a new construction that I am a bit suspicious of: it is practically floating together. (As though I am not really needed.) I do love it though: each object is crystal clear, but equally so, so they all seem to belong together very much. It is constructed in the simplest possible way: one thing on top of another. It has no theme except color: emerald green, royal blue, cherry red and black. It is not all gooky, which I am glad of. Also there is purple, and stripes of clear rhinestones. It is very geometrical. And of course very dramatic. Sometimes what I do is to purify objects. That is what I have done in this construction.

    The fullness of Joe's art is augmented by the fact that he was a wonderful writer—so philosophically adroit, and as good as any artist you can name (and that includes some very big names—Leonardo, Delacroix, van Gogh, Picasso, de Chirico and de Kooning, among others). For a while, it seemed that his literary masterwork *I Remember* would outstrip his assemblages and collages in the immortality sweepstakes. Historically, it's important to realize that Joe began writing *I Remember* in 1969 at what may have been the exact mid-point in his artistic career. (Ron Padgett says that he had been reading Gertrude Stein at the time.) All of the major assemblages and a good many of the great collages, including the "gardens" series, were already behind him, and at least ten more years of marvellous invention lay ahead.

    Joe was a such a brilliant writer that he could even write his "visual" works in prose, viz. the series of piquant *Imaginary Still Lifes*, written in the 1970s, one of which reads:

> I close my eyes. I see a white statue (say 10" high) of David. Alabaster. And pink rose petals sprinkled upon a black velvet drape. This is a sissy still life. Silly, but pretty. And in a certain way almost religious. "Eastern" religious. This still life is secretly smiling.

Another example: Joe the expert portraitist manifested his acuity in both words and pictures. Here is his word portrait of James Schuyler:

James Schuyler: A Portrait
Let me be a painter, and close my eyes. I see brown. (Tweed.) And blue. (Shirt.) And—surprise—yellow socks. The body sits in a chair, a king on a throne, feet glued to floor. The face is hard to picture, until—(click!)—I hear a chuckle. And the voice of distant thunder.

Poets and painters collaborate partly for the same reasons that painters make portraits of people they know—it's another way of spending time with that person, and the artistic aspect lends an extra, more surreptitious, intensity to the get-together. Usually, my collaborations with Joe were done at Joe's invitation—either he sent a comic in the mail for me to fill in the text, or, as we sat around in his studio or in Kenward's house in Vermont, he would quietly ask if I felt like doing "some works." Collaborating in person with Joe was a gas. He was usually quiet, purposeful, always encouraging, quietly amused. My favorite instance with him was an afternoon in his Sixth Avenue loft in 1973—Joe was in his "blue" period, and we did I forget how many collages all in blue with blue lettering, the title for which was a line I contributed from the Humphrey Bogart/Lizbeth Scott movie *Dead Reckoning*: "It's a Blue World."

Alex Katz's recent statement about collaborating with Robert Creeley reads in its entirety: "Working with Bob makes me feel bright." Working with Joe was bright, sweet, demanding, mysterious (how to please Joe in this process was both mysterious and demanding, as well) and silly. Somewhere beneath the scornful shrug of "silly" sits the etymological mother lode of "soulful." Avoidance of pretence is a prime stratagem of the pursuit of beauty and truth; hence Joe's love of the dime store frames and slightly more expensive but just plain Kulicke plastic passe-partouts he somewhat casually slid his drawings and collages into. Kenneth Koch has remarked on O'Hara's "feeling that the silliest idea actually in his head was better than the most profound idea actually in someone's else's head." Smart or idiotic but never dull. (Ron Padgett recalls poems we wrote in groups of anywhere from two to ten in the late '60s as making him laugh so hard his stomach hurt.) Collaboration thrives on the nerve of putting shamelessness at the service of mutual respect and the will to be interesting no matter what. In 1978—in an interview reprinted in the present exhibition catalogue—Anne Waldman asked Joe "What about collaborations?" and Joe summed it up for her (and for us today) like so:

> It's fun. It's very arduous. You have to compromise a lot. You have to be willing to totally fail and not be embarrassed by it. That's the main thing, which is very good for you.

To the memory of Joe LeSueur.
2001

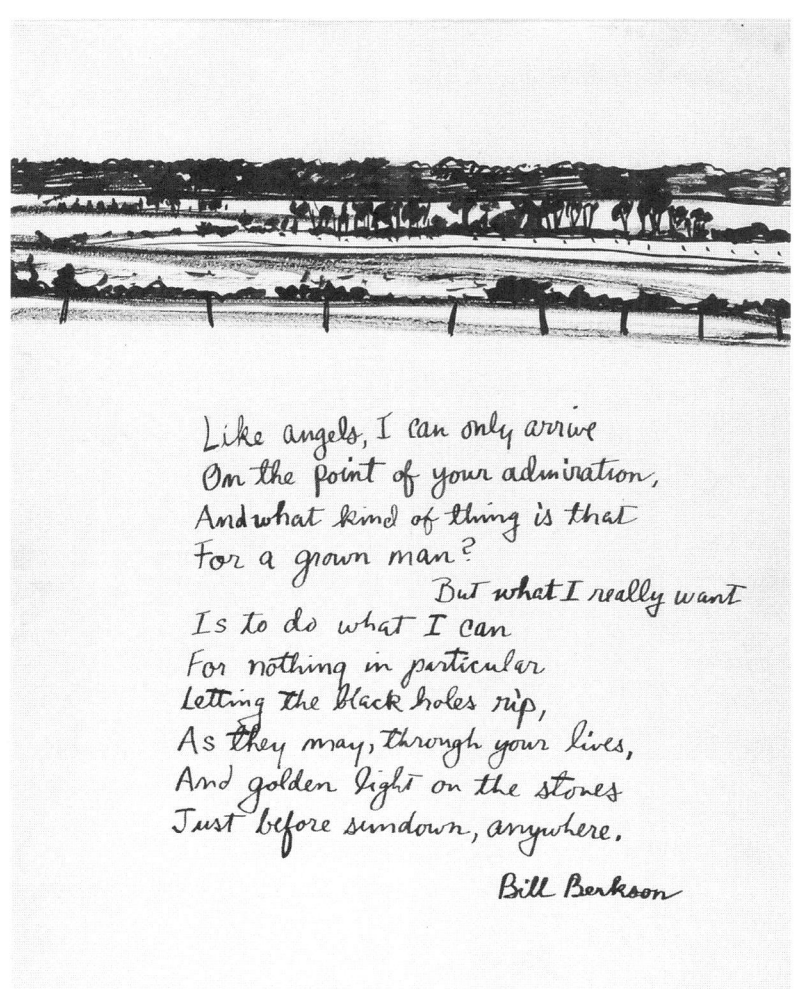

Bill Berkson and Joe Brainard, *Like Angels I Can Only Arrive,* circa 1972.
An ink drawing Joe left behind when he returned to New York from Bolinas. Eventually, I had the nerve to mess up the space of the bottom half with my blotchy handwriting. The poem was separate—not a response to Joe's landscape—but it fit. Interestingly, the same poem occurs in Enigma Variations *facing Guston's "Beast Hand" drawing, which was Guston's way of providing a corrective to "Like Angels…"'s apologetic tone.*
—Bill Berkson

from Recent Visitors
Bill Berkson and Joe Brainard

1963

Bill Berkson and George Schneeman, *Calendar*, 1970; Silk screen on poster board.

I seem to have the distinction of being the only collaborator George Schneeman ever invited to join in on one of his series of yearly, limited-edition silkscreen calendars. One night toward the end of 1969, we went to work in George's studio; at the end of a single session we had finished. I remember thinking that the 1970 calendar's message should be complex rather than a single flash to be simply glanced at intermittently—something to chew on, sort out over the year. Perhaps the seeming complexities of silkscreen—new to me, anyway—had something to do with this. Or perhaps it had to do with the fact that I was just then turning thirty. In the upper middle, George has placed a fire chief's helmet, the largest element in the picture. The helmet commands the stratosphere, edging upon a cloud that looks to have been sprinkled, or "seeded," with black specks. Off toward the lower right a silver quarter rolls and, below it, the little mustachioed man from the Monopoly board scratches his head, top hat tumbling, as he reels away from his reeling-away mirror image. The mirror is yellow, the fire hat bright red with a silver blazon. The coin is shiny silver, too, as are some of the letters strewn across the rectangle—"Pete," for instance, and the "o"s in "No Go" which encircle the periods in "N. G." (although the same yellow "N" is also the start of "Nice" and "Nose," and "G" is for guy, gay, gag, gig, goy, goon . . .) The biggest words are in black and say "Easy onto Edna." In smaller script are "melting," "pregnant" and "pause." At the bottom, running below the Monopoly figure, is the adage "It is true-r than true." Fifty copies: two for me, two for George, and the rest went to friends. —Bill Berkson

Bill Berkson and George Schneeman, from *Ted Berrigan,* 2006.

One Sunday morning in March 2006, after a hiatus of some thirty-plus years, George Schneeman and I regrouped in his studio to do some works. By early afternoon we had produced three posters and a folio of pages conceived of as a little book about our friend Ted Berrigan, whose posthumous Collected Poems *had just appeared. In this case I had sketched out some lines and phrases in advance on a little message pad, with a forgery of Ted's distinctive signature on the top sheet. Unlike our previous collaborations, this one has a clear division of labor: George did the drawings based on writings I laid down first in India ink (happily George helped tidy up my faulty brushwork). The writing is more about Ted's and my relations over the years than about poetics, but on the other hand, it's the fact of seeing so much of his work afresh that prompted me to think so intently of him after such time.* —BB

Bill Berkson and George Schneeman, from *Ted Berrigan*, 2006.

Ted Berrigan and George Schneeman, *In the Nam, What Can Happen?* 1967-68/1997; Letterpress, edition of 70, 9 1/4" 8 1/4"

Ted Berrigan and George Schneeman, *Untitled,* 1967; Silkscreen, 23" x 35". Collection of Linda O'Brian.

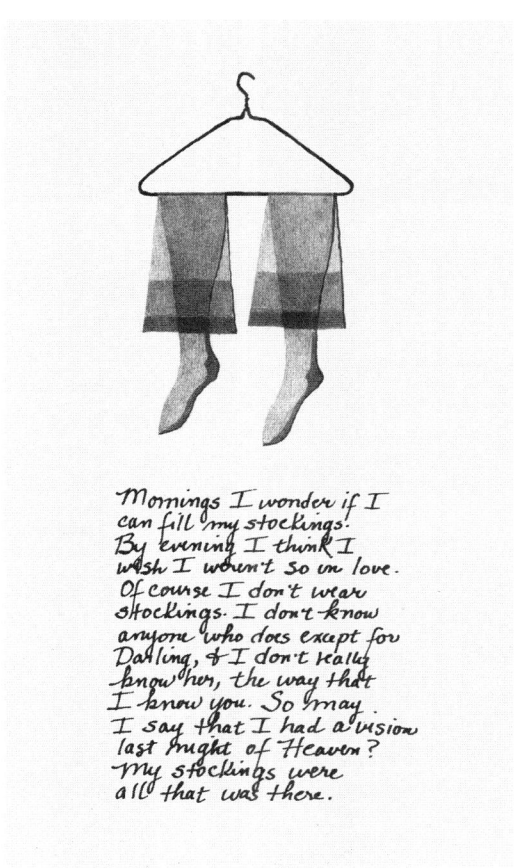

Alice Notley and George Schneeman,
Untitled, 1980; Lithograph for a calendar, 14" x 8 1/2"

George Schneeman and Anne Waldman (left): *Will the World Ever*, 2001; (right): *Rogue State*, 2001.
Both are maquettes for banner at the Venice Biennale.

Collaborating with Poets
A Conversation with George Schneeman
Ron Padgett

George Schneeman was born in 1934 in St. Paul, Minnesota, where he grew up and attended parochial schools. After taking a BA degree in philosophy and literature at St. Mary's College and doing graduate work in literature at the University of Minnesota, he was drafted into the US Army in 1958. Six months later he was stationed in Italy, where he began painting seriously and where he became friends with fellow soldiers and poets Charles Wright and Harold Schimmel. In 1959 George married Kathryn Pratt, with whom he had three children. After his discharge in 1960 the two continued to live in Italy, where he also became friends with writer Steve Katz. During those years Schneeman's reading was mostly of Italian literature. In 1966, encouraged by poets Peter Schjeldahl and Ron Padgett, whom George had met in Italy, the Schneeman family moved to New York City's Lower East Side, where George quickly met a large number of writers, mostly poets living in the neighborhood around Saint Mark's Church and taking part in the Poetry Project there. Most of his subsequent friends have been writers too, along with a number of visual artists. The following interview took place in April 2002 in Padgett's New York City apartment, five blocks from Schneeman's apartment, where, at the time of the interview, the two had lived for 35 and 34 years respectively, with Saint Mark's Church midway between them.

George Schneeman: How did we happen to do the collaborations we did? The silk screens, for example.

Ron Padgett: You had gotten interested in doing prints.

George: Oh, that's right. I started out by doing a couple of linoleum blocks. I got interested in doing prints because I wanted to do color fields that were clear and transparent, so I could put color on color evenly, which is hard to do when you paint with a brush. Anyway, that's what got me interested in doing silk screen prints and even incorporating the silk screens into the canvases of figurative paintings.

Ron: But what got us doing collaborative silk screens? We did a total of eight of them, starting probably in the spring of 1968.

George: I don't recall. I do remember that I screened a copy of our first silk screen [*Chiliasm*] right onto a big acrylic portrait of Dick [Gallup], Sandy [Berrigan], and Ted [Berrigan].

Ron: But before the silk screens we had done a handmade book in Asciano [Italy] right after I first met you, in June of 1966. June 17, to be exact.

George: What was that?

Ron: It was ink landscape drawings with words on thick white paper, around ten pages, maybe nine by ten, which you folded and bound with tape. We did it in the kitchen of your farmhouse by the light of a Coleman lantern. I have it stored away somewhere. It was the first collaboration you had ever done, and in retrospect what strikes me is how easy it was for you, as if you had done it before, many times.

George: There are several reasons for that. First, I've never had a problem with art as a social activity. Second, Peter and Linda Schjeldahl had visited me the summer before I met you. They talked to me about collaborating, particularly Joe [Brainard]'s collaborating with poets such as you and Ted in New York. That struck me as interesting. But beyond that, I think that an artist has to have a certain disposition for enjoying collaboration—a fundamental concept of painting as something other than a form of self-expression. I never painted anything with the idea that I was expressing myself.

Ron: You once told me that your ego wasn't involved in collaborating. In other words, you aren't territorial about your domain.

George: And since I studied literature, literature doesn't intimidate me. Besides, when a painter is doing a collaboration with a writer, it's an art object, and so the artist is in the driver's seat, though I can just as easily play the part of the passenger.

Ron: Yes, collaborations are usually looked at first and read afterward.

George: Words on a painting are much more acceptable these days.

Ron: Especially in the last twenty years, with artists like Basquiat and Jenny Holzdr, and before them Ed Ruscha.

George: But to get back to collaboration: some Italian paintings of the trecento and quattrocento were done by more than one person, so that now we can't always know who did what. Giotto's paintings in Assisi are so collaborative that some historians think that he didn't paint all of them. This makes them more interesting than the ones in Padua, in a way, because in Assisi we don't know exactly who did what. The last couple of paintings there are remarkably different from the ones in Padua, so people tend to say, "I don't think that's the same painter." So what? The variety of hands makes the paintings more interesting. The ones in Padua are so overpoweringly Giotto, whereas the mixed ones are one of a kind because you never get the same mixture again. In that respect a "pure" Giotto is not as interesting as an "adulterated" one.

Ron: You will remember that you and I have looked back at our old works and argued about who did what.

George: Of course it's interesting, but does it mean anything? Not really. It's an academic argument, which is fun to have.

Ron: Ted and I used to do that, looking back at our collaborative poems and sometimes not knowing who wrote what, so closely were we able to imitate each other's style. Of course we both tried to claim the "good" parts. With you and me it's even more complicated by the fact that sometimes you contributed words and I did some of the visuals.

George: Anyway, that's some background to my being disposed to collaborating. In general I like making an object that you couldn't have made by yourself.

Ron: That's what I'm always looking for in doing a collaboration, especially when we're working directly and simultaneously on the same piece or pieces. I don't want to know what we're going to come up with.

George: Exactly. Though we do tend to have some idea, simply based on the materials we're about to use.

Ron: That gets back to what you said about the artist's having the upper hand, because, at least in my experience, the artist picks the medium, the materials, the tools, and the other toys. I don't mind that at all.

George: But there was the time that you made those choices, when we did the series called *Little Pages of the Snowman*. Wasn't that the work in which we put a time limit on how long each of us could work on a page? What was it, three minutes? We came up with what—about fifteen pages? You did some of the drawings, too. Both you and Ted were never afraid to "interfere" with my work, even, in Ted's case, grossly. He would completely cover up, cross out, block my drawings.

Ron: Ted had to take it way over the top in the direction of messiness—to get a beautiful result. His drawings are very rough and crude and surprisingly terrific. He wasn't good at drawing lightly or clearly or simply, so he went the other way.

George: You and I have also done works by sending them back and forth in the mail over a period of time, such as the ones in colored pencil and a little bit of collage done in the summer of '68. We sent them back and forth twice quickly.

Ron: Those were fun to do, especially as I was stuck in a very steamy and boring Tulsa.

George: I was in Wisconsin doing terrible paintings.

Ron: We've done other works by mail, such as *The Story of Ezra Pound* and the drawings of the three espresso pots, but most of our work has been done when we were together.

George: Also the paintings of mailboxes. I wanted to paint some mailboxes! Then ten or fifteen years later I mailed them to you.

Ron: Yes, I liked being mailed mailboxes. What I wrote for them is okay, but it's never really quite pleased me. But let's get back to the works we did in your studio—we've never done any here in my apartment. I was hoping that we could remember what it was like to do those works together. For example, how getting started is usually slow. I arrive, you take out the materials, we sort of look at them and mull—the transition between not doing a collaboration and doing it is a little awkward, but suddenly we're in it—the plane lifts off. Then, as we work, it's a little like juggling, since we usually have more than one work going at a time.

George: That in fact is the key to getting started: having at least three or four pieces of illustration board or whatever ready to go. It puts everyone at ease, because it removes the pressure of having to be responsible for one particular work. I might start by gluing down or drawing a single object on each board and the writer might start with a word or phrase on a blank board, and then we can go back and forth. Then after a while you can look at them and if one seems hopeless you can just tear it up.

Ron: That's right, there is no finality in doing three or four at once.

George: In the series of those 46 oil pastel works [*Actually Yes*] you and I did a few years ago, we started seven or eight in each session, but later we went back to certain ones to rework them.

Ron: There was one image, the one with the railroad train, that was heavily reworked. In fact every time we got together—over seven or so sessions, no?—we added to it. Each of those sessions was three or four hours. We really cracked along. There's a lot of variety in those works. Certain ones are clean, clear, and spare, while others look expressionistic. Using oil pastels seems to have encouraged me to dare to be messy, as in the train image, which you kept calling a disaster up until the last moment. It was very near the wastebasket several times.

George: I had liked using oil pastels in the hundred or so landscape drawings I had done the previous summers in Italy, laying the color on heavily with a lot of energy, and that carried over into those collaborations.

Ron: Have you ever collaborated with anyone you didn't know very well?

George: I didn't know Lewis MacAdams very well. He said he'd like to do collaborations. Most of the time people have approached me, and if they ask I usually say okay, because if they're willing to do it it's fine with me. One nice thing is that people want to do them for the pleasure of it, certainly not for commercial purposes. Basically galleries don't want to show them. They're personal works. I like that.

Ron: And they're even harder to exhibit if they're in book form, trapped in a vitrine, with only a two-page spread showing.

George: As far as books go, the ones I did with Ted were originally done on individual sheets, which he worked on mostly at home. We did a few on the spot and we did silkscreens together, but mostly he took things home and we passed them back and forth, such as the works reproduced in the Ted bibliography [*Ted Berrigan: An Annotated Checklist*].

Ron: I wonder why he worked that way. When he and I wrote poems together he was very spontaneous.

George: I guess he liked having them around so he could take his time. More than anyone else he would transcribe lines from his own poems onto them. He liked to quote himself. You never do that.

Ron: Very rarely.

George: Ted did often. "By the waters of Manhattan." "Ten Things I Do Every Day." But on the other hand I've often wondered if maybe "Ten Things" originated in the silkscreen we did. Anne [Waldman] also quotes herself. She uses things that are already going around in her head. She rushes in, gives me some words to use, and flies out! Sometimes she will hand me a poem of hers with certain words and phrases circled for me to use.

Ron: I've always had the feeling that Bill [Berkson], Dick [Gallup], Lewis MacAdams, and Larry [Fagin] don't quote themselves.

George: No. But Larry is different in that he doesn't do any of the visual work. He doesn't touch the pieces. He makes suggestions for me to do this or that. Over the years I've done some beautiful works with him.

Ron: And they look different from the works you've done with others. Like the one with the image of the woman's head repeated three times, with pink string glued down to form words.

George: She was a Xerox copy of a reproduction of one of Man Ray's photographs. I have no idea of how that piece developed. I dyed a piece of string pink and looped it like a skywriter from face to face to form words.

Ron: " It's too late." Is that the one that Red Grooms bought?

George: Yes.

Ron: A good choice.

George: With Larry the works are all pristine. We choose one image, he comes up with the words, I letter them, and that's it. Recently he brought me a poem he and Ted had written, and I did a work with it so quickly that I have no recollection of what it is! I gave it to Larry because he can keep better track of it than I can.

Ron: If one drew a graph of the number of collaborations you've done over the years or the number of collaborators you've worked with, it would show a peak in the late sixties or early seventies.

George: That's true.

Ron: That is true of collaborative writing projects as well.

George: There was a dispersal of the nucleus that had formed around the St. Marks Poetry Project. Originally Saint Mark's was a neighborhood project. Local poets read together, wrote together, collated magazines and books together. Then people started moving away and the Poetry Project widened its aesthetic and its audience.

Ron: Also, in the sixties and early seventies, it was possible to get by without having a real job, so we could socialize until three or four in the morning. Another thing that helped was that when you moved to Saint Mark's Place, not only were you more centrally located than you had been on 7th and D, you suddenly had a very big apartment with plenty of work space.

George: It was there that I did half a dozen works with Lewis MacAdams, some very complicated, on illustration board, some nice works. I did maybe another half dozen with Michael [Brownstein], a dozen or so with Bill [Berkson], and some with Peter [Schjeldahl]. It tapered off around 1972. I also did some works on illustration board with Dick, as well as several silkscreens.

Ron: But then Dick moved away, Ted went off to Ann Arbor and Iowa City and Chicago, Peter kind of withdrew from that circle, Michael started traveling a lot, Bill Berkson, Tom Clark, and Lewis MacAdams moved to Bolinas, Anne was starting to fly around. So maybe the reason you did more collaborations with me was because I stayed here in the neighborhood?

George: Ha ha ha! But I did do two nice sets of works by mail with Bill and Tom.

Ron: Except for Larry, you and I are the only ones who have stayed in these same apartments all these years.

George: And we have worked together very easily, a large number of works, a hundred...

Ron: More than that. One project that was very hard for me was our collaborative ceramics. I couldn't figure out where to put words on them, or how, without being obvious.

George: Why was that? I was surprised that you were stumped.

Ron: Because they were three-dimensional, I guess. When you gave me a vase, for instance, I had to take into account that one couldn't simply read from left to right—the surface was a continuing curve

around the damned thing. I felt that the text had to take that into account. The jar with the lid...
George: The "underpants" work?
Ron: Yes. It has the prefix "under" on the lid, which can be rotated to match up with various suffixes around the side of the jar, such as "pants." That writing works because it has a circularity that parallels the circularity of the jar.
George: That's too deep for me, ha ha!
Ron: To switch gears here: were you ever inspired by other people's collaborations? I was inspired by Frank [O'Hara] and Larry [Rivers]'s *Stones*, and by certain Dada and Surrealist collaborations and other works with words and images, such as Cubist art, and by literary collaborations.
George: I didn't know about them, but I don't think I have been inspired by other collaborations. I don't need to be inspired to do something. I will say that when I moved from Italy to New York City, Joe's collaborations with you and Ted and others provided an open door and I just walked in. Collaborating seemed like an established thing to do, a given. When I arrived in New York I stayed with Peter and Linda on Avenue B. They were right in the middle of the literary community around Saint Mark's Church. That suited me. Working with friends who were writers seemed natural.
Ron: Maybe because of your literary background in school?
George: Yes, and I had even tried writing. In graduate school I showed a poem of mine to a teacher and he was appalled. It was very embarrassing. I decided to be a painter.
Ron: So do you think your collaborations with poets has something to do with that literary background?
George: I suppose.
Ron: Actually I was fishing for the idea of your being a poet manqué, just as I am a painter manqué. In high school I already thought of myself as a writer, but I did some paintings, which I showed to Joe, who was by far the best artist in our school. He looked at them and said, "Uh..." It wasn't that I felt discouraged by him, it was that I knew he was right. So I abandoned my fantasy of being an artist. What is it that draws people to collaborating with their opposites?
George: Opposites?
Ron: Their complements. Which brings me to the idea that collaborating involves a multiplicity of personality that I think got into my solo work .
George: That no doubt happened to me too, but I've never thought about it. But take Ted's aesthetics: he bullied his way into art. At first I found him quite amazing. Everything about him didn't fit into anything I had ever imagined! But it turned out we had a lot in common: Catholic guys, the same age, army experience, married, children. But in terms of art, he was very constructive. That is, he saw art and writing as the building of something. Also he was very good at capitalizing on his mistakes—that is, he didn't think "mistakes" existed. I've tried to adopt that from him. It's a good lesson to learn. Vapidness is the only mistake.
Ron: Getting back to how collaborating influences one's solo work, it seems to me that collage is like collaboration insofar as you have to assemble disparate elements created by someone else.
George: Excellent idea.
Ron: It goes with what I said about multiplicity. But aside from your collages, I don't see that influence in your work.
George: Well, the collages are in a sense found objects, and I consider myself an engineer, first finding the right materials—I'm choosy about the materials I use—and then moving those pieces of paper around in the hope that I will find two that go together and create a surprising third thing. It's like panning for gold.
Ron: Isn't that what you and I do in collaborating?
George: Yes.
Ron: Tom Veitch and I sort of panned for gold in writing our book *Antlers in the Treetops*, which is made up entirely of found paragraphs lightly altered to fit together. Incidentally we were expressing our distrust of what we thought of as the excessively pious notion of originality and the corresponding horror of plagiarism. We questioned the idea of ownership: who owns words? How many words do I use that no one has ever used? Obviously originality comes into it, but less than I was reading about in interviews with other poets. In college I had come to feel that as a writer I was permeable, that I wasn't just one hard little ego creating totally original and unique works, but that I was a spirit that things we re passing in and out of: things I had read, memories, bits of song lyrics, snatches of conversation. I placed a low premium on originality, but I placed a high premium on not doing what someone had already done—which may sound like originality but it's not. Does that make sense?
George: Yes. If I copy something such as a spool of thread or a landscape I try to make it as good as what I'm looking at. It has nothing to do with originality, it has to do with enslavement, ha ha! I'm certainly not trying to express myself. I'm trying to get the space and the color right.
Ron: Yes. Can you say something more about how collaborating can release a more various version of oneself into one's solo works? For example, when we started working on *Actually Yes*, we were both feeling depressed or grim. At first I didn't feel like doing art, but doing them made me feel like doing art. Some of the poems I wrote not long afterward have something of you in them, not anything you said but the way you hove red over a work as it was being made. That might be called influence, but I think it's more useful to think of it as an extended form of collaboration. But of course collaboration can mean so many different things, even if you limit it to work between just two people. You mentioned Anne's running in and heaving some words to you and rushing out to catch a plane, or Larry's standing at a distance and directing, or Ted's taking the pieces home to work on them, or our working simultaneously. Do you, as they say these days, privilege one method over another?
George: No. It's interesting that they're all valuable. For instance, with Larry recently I worked with lightning speed using lines of an old poem by him and Ted and I worked fast intentionally so as not to give Larry much directorship. It happened so fast before his very eyes that he could not believe it. Years ago I did some works with Michael that took time and a certain effort to do, and they came out very good.
Ron: This variety shows a willingness on your part to be flexible with all these different collaborators.
George: I don't look at it that way. As long as the poet is providing energy, that's all I need. I don't have a visual preconception of the work. I learned that from Ted early on! Having a fixed preconceived idea—he wasn't going to put up with that.
Ron: Partly too it was his refusal of fussy perfectionism, though in his own writing he was meticulous, in that he rewrote his pieces over and over.
George: For him collaboration was a way of honing his own work. You could see that going on in his mind.
Ron: It was probably his seeing how the words read differently when written down in different sizes and styles and alongside different images. I've never used collaborating as a method of revision. I'm always wanting to get it right the first time, even if the work is a complicated one. Take *The Story of Ezra Pound*.
George: That work is complicated—and exquisite. In a class all by itself, ha ha! I had no idea of what you were going to do with that. I just started some unrelated pages and mailed them to you: images of Phil Fumble, some drawings, a bland quotation from *The Pisan Cantos*—"The clouds over Pisa...." Did you recognize the quotation?
Ron: No. Those pages you sent me had three different registers of work, and thinking that I had to get them to fit together sort of set me back. My first thought was: "I have no idea what to do with these," and I put them back in their envelope and went out and pulled some weeds in the garden. A few days later I came to the conclusion that we

were going to have to add pages to bridge the gaps between the ones we had. I laid the pages out side by side and suddenly Ezra Pound clicked—because of the mention of Pisa—and I looked at the numbers that Phil Fumble is saying on one page ("7 X 8") and I thought about Pound and his economic theories, and that's what set it off. I rearranged the pages, looking for a visual variety that would help disguise the jump from register to register, and I added words. All in twenty minutes. When I got finished I felt high as a kite. It was as if the pages had interlocked by themselves, or like when you try and try to remember someone's name, and as soon as you stop trying it pops into your head.

George: I hadn't intended those pages to be a complete set for one work. I think that's my favorite work of ours—at least for now.

Ron: I just remembered that something in me made me want to use only the pieces you had sent and to complete them right there. Maybe I just felt impatient with the idea of the time lag involved in our mailing them back and forth between Italy and Vermont. Or maybe I just didn't trust the Italian postal system!

George: If you had to do a work all by yourself, as one human brain, you could never do this one. Two heads are not only better than one, but different than one, because in collaborating, you have to push half way, and if the other person is also pushing you create an accident that neither of you can control completely.

Ron: I meant to ask you about your project with Allen Ginsberg.

George: Over the years Allen had said to me, "Let's do some collaborations." I was intimidated by the prospect of working with him. A few months before he died, he gave me a book of his photographs. I laid some acetate over some of the photos and made partial tracings in ink. Then I had these tracings photocopied onto paper. I thought that by using Allen's own photos of friends that I would keep him from getting into some political stance that I would find uninspiring. A month before he died Anne and I had lunch at his place, and I left the drawings with him. A few days later he called me and said, "I can't really think of what to do with these drawings. Why don't you bring over some nice paper and we can start fresh?" But that's as far as it got, for this was only days before he died. A month or so later I retrieved the drawings and suggested to Anne, who was in town, that we do something with them. She took them home and penciled in words at the bottom of each one. Then I inked the words in and did some more work on the drawings. After they were done, Anne and I suddenly saw them as an homage to Allen, hence the title *Homage to Allen G*.

Ron: I wonder if Allen would have put something political into that project, and how you would have handled it, since there is almost no political content—overt, at least—in your collaborations, even in those done during the Vietnam War. For me that war was so odious and ghastly that in my work I tended to create an alternative world.

George: Most of the collaborations invent a sort of utopia in the form of a visual field filled with pleasure, quickness, and wit. Even the gaps and spaces between the words and images tend to be witty.

Ron: I decided not to ask you about the great number of cover designs you have done for poets' books, even though they involved a certain degree of collaboration.

George: The background information for that would be the same as for the collaborations. When I do those covers, I take it seriously, trying to figure out how to do each one. But I like the metaphysics—if I may call it that—of the connect-disconnect between the title and the design. For instance, the cover for Dick's *Where I Hang My Hat* shows a blank home movie screen—not a hat rack. Or the image of the umbrella on Alice [Notley]'s *At Night the States*. Or the suit jacket on *Ted's Nothing for You*. Why do those covers work? I can't see any rational connections in them between titles and images. Can you?

Ron: You want to have lunch?

George: Yes.

Ron Padgett and George Schneeman, *Blanco y Negro*, 1966.
Blanco y Negro is one of the many collaborations that George Schneeman and I have done since 1966. It has the look of a cadavre exquis, but it isn't one, since we could see what we were doing all along. Executed one night in the late 1960s at George's studio, it is a fair example of our work together: happy, insouciant, and adventurous, finding what we might find without knowing quite how we did it. That is, a program that called for having no program. —Ron Padgett

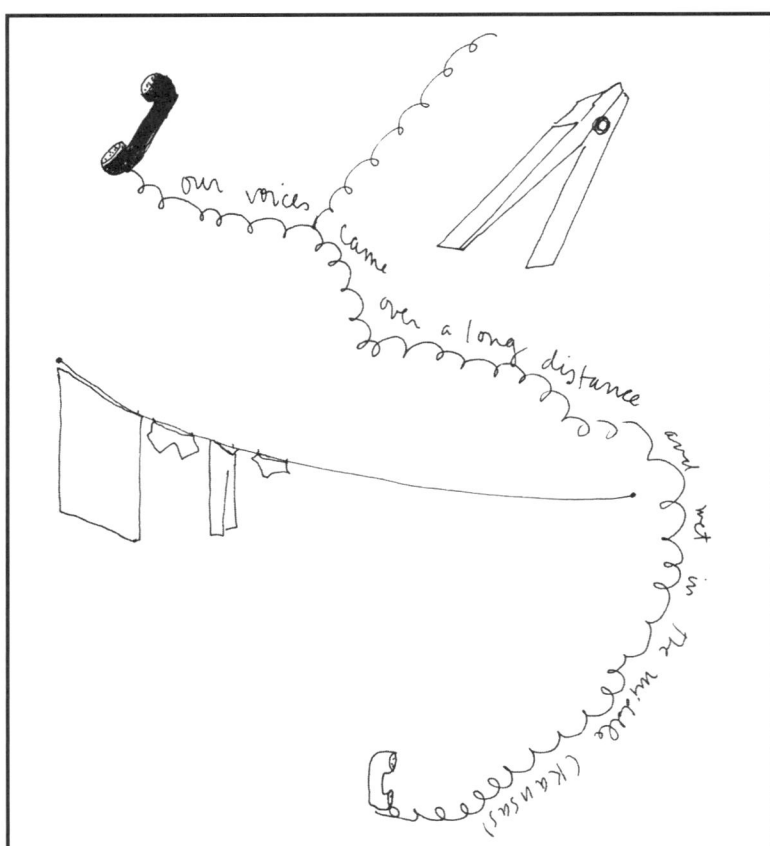
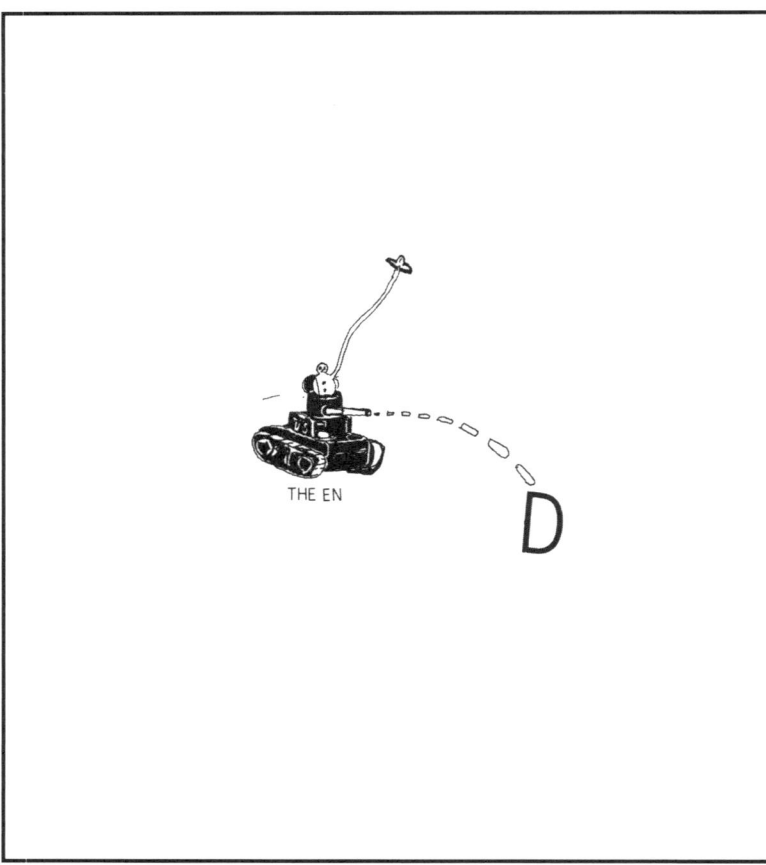

Ron Padgett and George Schneeman: From *Little Pages of the Snowman,* 1968 or 1969; Ink on paper. 17 pp., 9" x 8"

Bill Berkson and George Schneeman, *Ball/Park,* 1969 or early 1970;
Mixed media on illustration board, 20" x 26"

Ron Padgett and George Schneeman: *Telescope,* 1969; Collage on illustration board, 6 1/2" x 5"

The Menage
A Film/Poetry Collabration

Poem by **Carl Rakosi**
Pictures and Voice by **Anne Waldman**
Pictures, Editing and Voice by **Ed Bowes**
Featuring **Elizabeth Reddon**

Up stand
    six
yellow
        jonquils
in a
      glass/
the stems
        dark green,
paling
   as they descend
into the water/
          seen through
a thicket
      of baby's breath, "a tall herb
bearing numerous small,
              fragrant white flowers."
I have seen
        snow-drops larger.
I bent my face down.
           To my delight
they were convoluted
           like a rose.
They had no smell,
         their white
the grain of biblical dust,
              which like the orchid itself
is as common as hayseed.
          Their stems were thin and woody
but as tightly compacted
         as a tree trunk,
greenish rubbings showing in spots
              through the brown;

wiry, forked twigs so close,
         they made an impassable bush
which from a distance
        looked like a mist.
I could barely escape
        from that wood of particulars…
the jonquils whose air within
was irradiated topaz,
silent as in an ear,
        the stems leaning lightly
against the glass,
        trisecting its inner circle
in the water,
     cross like reverent hands
(ah, the imagination!
        Benedictite.
Enter monks.
      Oops, sorry!
Trespassing
    on Japanese space.
Exit monks
    and all their lore
from grace.)

I was moved by all this
         and murmured
to my eyes, "Oh, Master!"
         and became engrossed again

in that wood of particulars
                    until I found myself
out of character, singing
     "Tell me why you've settled here."

 "Because my element is near."
and reflecting,
               "The eye of man cares. Yes!"

But a familiar voice
                  broke into the wood,
a shade of mockery in it,
                    and in her smile
a fore-knowledge
               of something playful,
something forbidden,
                    something make-believe
something saucy,
               something delicious
about to pull me
               off guard:
"Do you want to be my Cupid-o?"

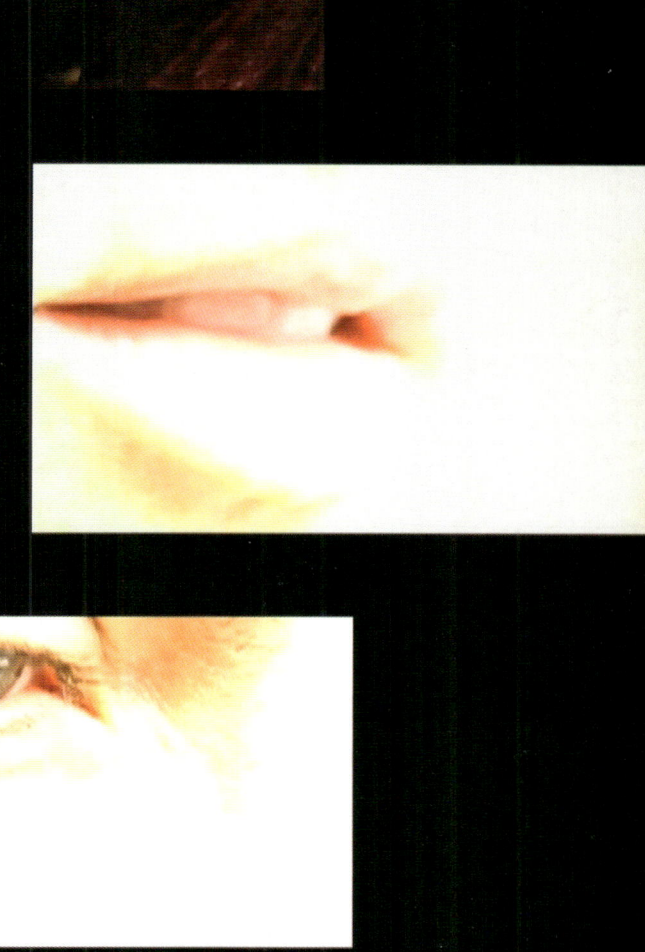

In fairness to her
            it must be said
that her freckles
 are always friendly
and that the anticipation
                   of a prank
makes them radiate
              across her face
the way dandelions
              sprout in a field
after a summer shower.

"What makes you so fresh,
                    my Wife of Bath?
What makes you so silly,
                 o bright hen?"

"That's for you to find out,
                old shoe, old shoe.
That's for you to find out
                if you can."

"Oh yeah!"
          (a mock chase and capture).
"Commit her
          into jonquil's custody.
She'll see a phallus
              in the pistil.
Let her work it off there."

But I was now myself
              under this stringent force
which ended,

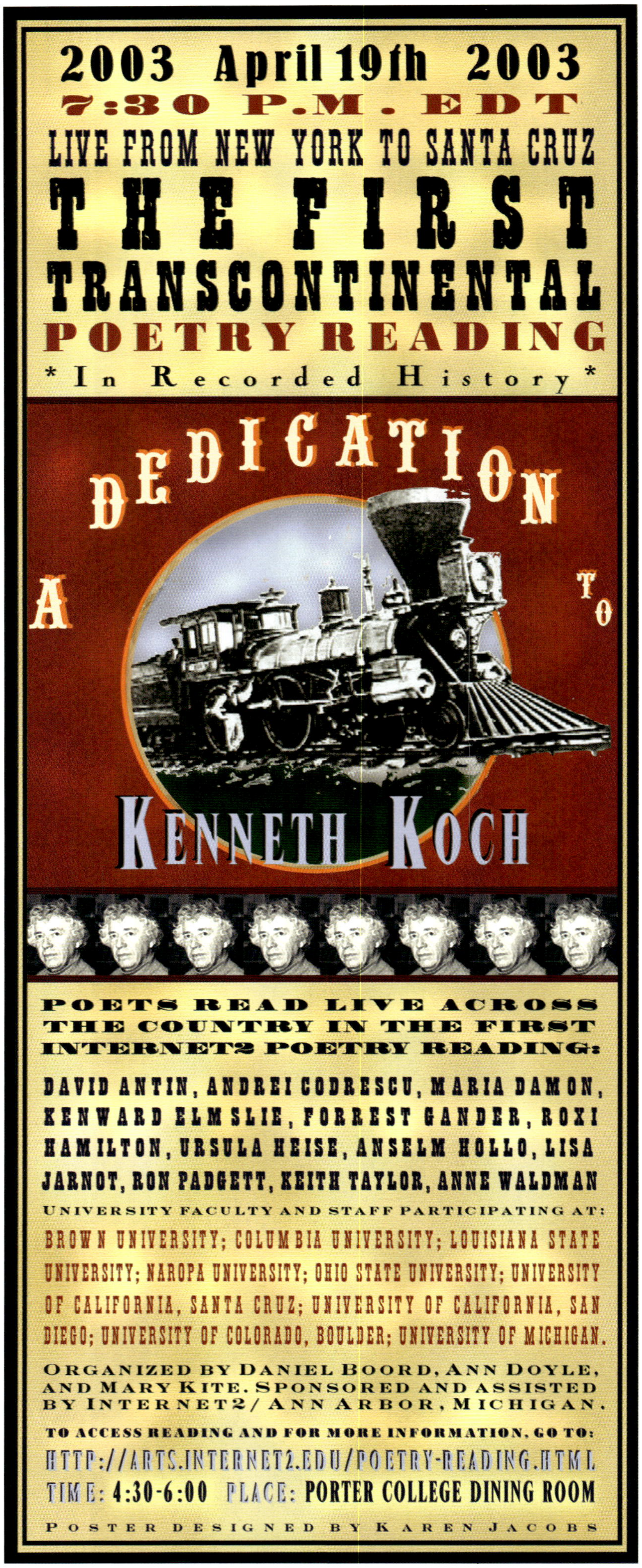

Design by Karen Jacobs, 2003

Trans-Genre: Poetry and the Inter-Arts

The first-ever "Transcontinental Poetry Reading" was featured as part of the UC Santa Cruz event, "Trans-Genre: Poetry and the Inter-Arts:" a two day celebration of poetry at its intersection with theater, music, film, digital media, visual art, and narrative in April 2003. The "Transcontinental Poetry Reading" was a tribute to New York School poet, Kenneth Koch. Our "New York School Collaborations" section ends with a tribute to the late poet, Barbara Guest.

Along with the the "Transcontinental Poetry Reading," the "Trans-Genre" event featured a panel on "New Narrative" writing; a video/film collaboration by Konrad Steiner and Leslie Scalapino; and a Poet's Theater production of "American Objectivists" by Kevin Killian and Brian Kim Stefans. The next forty pages includes work featured at the event or included because of its relation to the overlapping and related New York School section.

Transcontinental Poetry Reading: A Dedication to Kenneth Koch

Left to right: Ursula Heise, David Antin, Anselm Hollo, Forest Gander, Maria Damon, and Andrei Codrescu: one screen image streamed from seven locations.

In a landmark transcontinental poetry reading celebrating New York School poet, Kenneth Koch, eleven poets from California to New York, performed live at all locations while being streamed through the internet on April 19, 2003. Projections of poets, reading the poems of Kenneth Koch and their own work, were transmitted instantaneously from seven different venues through Internet2 onto a single screen. Audiences at each site not only saw poets performing on location, but experienced the art of poets in remote theaters as well. Anyone with a web browser was able to watch the event as the entire poetry reading was streamed to an internet-wide audience. Featured poets included David Antin, Andrei Codrescu, Maria Damon, Kenward Elmslie, Roxi Power Hamilton, Anselm Hollo, Forrest Gander, Ron Padgett, Keith Taylor and Anne Waldman. Ursula Heise was MC.
Event producers: Daniel Boord, Ann Doyle, and Mary Kite

Participating Universities: Brown University; Columbia University; University of California, Santa Cruz; University of California, San Diego; University of Colorado, Boulder; University of Michigan; Louisiana State University; Naropa University and Ohio State University. Archive of Poetry Reading available http://arts.internet2.edu/poetry-reading.html.

Part I:
Round robin transcontinental reading of Kenneth Koch's "Twenty Poems" from his book *Days and Nights*. Each poet read the following stanzas:

Roxanne Power Hamilton (at UC Santa Cruz) read #1 and 12
David Antin (at UC San Diego) read #2 and 13
Anselm Hollo (at U. of Colorado) read #3 and 14
Andrei Codrescu (at LSU) read #4 and 15
Keith Taylor (at U. of Michigan) read #5 and 16
Forrest Gander (at Brown U.) read #6 and 17
Maria Damon (at Brown U.) read #7 and 18
Kenward Elmslie (at Columbia U.) read #8 and 19
Anne Waldman (at Columbia U.) read #9 and 20
Ron Padgett (at Columbia U.) read #10

Entr'acte: Musical performance of the poem "Kochlage" by Mobius Operandi

Part II:
Poets read from their own work

Twenty Poems
Kenneth Koch

1
The diary is open at two o'clock
Words of love are in it! Words of passion and of love!

2
Heroic Standard
The street winds slowly through the meadow
Where a city once was. Thousands of bluets crawl to cover it
But the street winds on.

3
1958
The violets in the tempest withered, shrunk.
The toilet flushed. The air came liberally in the windows.
Workers went on strike. Somebody else was crazed by somebody else.

4
At the fish market we walked back and forth.
You were thinner. My doctorate was yet unsought.
I had produced "Variations on William Carlos Williams."
The grammar mistakes were everywhere, I thought.
A view was ours past the clinic.
Someone was starting a shop. Another one, this one,
That one, lived in a chateau. In Italy, that's a palace.
I don't like him. We figured out
Everyone running about. Past the streetcar turn-
Around, dark white violets, breakfast, tones
And the roller skates slack on the cement, or tiles.

5
The personality of the feeding bin
The impersonality of the feed
In the stomachs of the birds a flower
Of hunger and of hunger satisfied. Then cold grips the street
As my hunger grips the flower of your heart. We eat
Dinner. We go to bed. We wake up. Impenetrable and mysterious life!

6
The dawn woke the hats up in Tuscany.
The flares woke the bats up egotistically.
Drinks are finished and songs put down
On tables and now the pianoforte begins.

7
He who addresses you
Turns around a hat
Once, he drinks
Glass after glass of something
Wine. He is not dead. He reminds
You of something else.
That's it! The Assumption.

8
The Silencers
Eyes coveted your elbows,
Ears cupped against your heart.

9
Environment
Mist creeps into the environment;
Green is the grass, is the moss, is the whole environment.

10
Notices are sent up into the music
Telling the music to be silent
While the notes are being read
But the music which is made of notes
Does not understand
And the snow keeps falling.
The concerto goes on, a pandemonium of sound!

11
Disney Boheme
The stork A-plus Popeye and Olive Oyl sheep
Footsteps sur la neige Debussy
A warm Paris apartment/living with now dead people
Selling books eating idyllically straight from the pan

12
Art and Society
Formlessness suggested by Debussy's
"Des pas sur la neige"
Copland's repeating the criticism that
Debussy was "bourgeois"
True he wrote in a protected world
No green ate away at his environment
Nor vagrants stormed his windows
None are purple with green rings
In the snow all footsteps are white

13
After Some Verses by Morvaine Le Gaelique and Paul Verlaine
Did you call? or was that sound on the telephone
My bad sad beating heart
That only beats for you?
Et puis voici mon corps, not mon coeur,
My body, which is bitten by a barracuda,
And my course, which is straight for you.

14
Desire and curiosity
Make me feel I'm indestructible
My actual fragility
Assails me as I write this poem
And I put the pen down

15
Gordu Wisdom
An elephant is larger than its master.
The forest is smaller than its trees

16
Words penetrate a poem
As a dog penetrates a court;
Finding the gateway he wants he sees
His master coming toward him and he barks.

17
To the Prospect of Time
I too remember the summer afternoon
When I was completely happy and alone.

18
At Night
Nothing can sleep like irony. You say
One thing and you mean another. Oxygen is matrimony's brother.
When you sleep, you speak alone.

19
How many things we are attentive to!
Words spoken in sleep, the dog's paw, the emblematic significance of everything that is done and seen
Winter, for example, with its damp sleep and boots.

20
Each moment fills him with a desire
For another moment and each incident he makes
As a result of his situation
Leads to another one and another one and another.
So she might be attracted to
Anyone! It frightens him. He says, She is not like me.
Then he loves her no longer,
For one second.

It Was All Right or, What I Learned from Kenneth Koch
Anselm Hollo

Anselm Hollo reading live at the broadcast Transcontinental Poetry Reading.

It was all right to be funny all possible kinds of funny

It was all right to be erudite

All right to use as many words of the English language
       as you could possibly come up with

All right to be elegant all right to be rowdy

But never all right to be pompous

It was all right to be modern and postmodern and premodern

All right to be all of those at the same time

All right to be for intelligence and kindness
       and against hypocrisy and dumb power

All right to believe in your wishes lies and dreams

All right to tell what you had never told anyone

All right to be a poet a lover a lover of words

All right it was all right thank you Kenneth

Thank you for *Thank You and Other Poems*

So many other poems

from The November Exercises
David Antin

Monday, November 2

(12:15 pm)   She kept her head and he lost his. She telephoned the fire department and he drove up over the curb into a tree. Otherwise the whole house might have burnt down.

(12:17 pm)   When the rain lets up the drug will wear off.

(12:20 pm)   When you blow up a building you make it smaller.

David Antin reading live at the broadcast Transcontinental Poetry Reading.

After "The Simplicity of the Unknown Past"
for Kenneth Koch
Anne Waldman

Inside this window
    Is the start and outside is the beginning

Outside, the CNN building, lights on its cakewalk pillars,
oil white, 34th Street,
    then somebody's TV outside, blue inside a window:
    everyone's got a mother turns it on you used to know
Outside behind two shady water-towers a pyramid,
we're in Egypt,
    paranoid, where are the camels, the tourists?
Terrorism. Calculus. Sand.
We're here outside. The muezzins inside their towers,
dawn, a chime at
    the beginning of civilization, all the top brass
    at the Ur Hotel
An architectural icon takes a whole city block, we're
inside hunkering down.
    Is this outside biz just aggressive or are they
    thinking seriously
    about buildings? About nation building?
About Firenze?
I'll say that for Kenneth Koch's input, or that or Lorenzo de Medici whose Florence
    everyone could serve in but nobody could dominate
I'd say that they *could* dominate, inside their imagination: poet with *coup d'etat*
    slight of hand, the other with his terrible secrets, state secrets, more secrets
Outside the Arno in shadow mode, secret liquidity
    Cross the bridge with me
But wait a minute, summon the Parlamento, ring the bell, let's gather
    in the Pizza della Signoria, resolve any impasse between inside and outside,
    between East and West, a clash of trouble, gone mad with it's-OK-to lie and
    kill-people-with-your-weapons-of-mass-destruction-war-mode when you need
    to possess what you want: the world?
Inter-stellar apparatus that lights this conversation, dualities do not
    warm to fluorescence, the daylight studio out there, Mannahatta
    will be bankrupt in the new century, a plunge, sad hand on the plough
What plough? What worker laid off? What reparation? But wait a minute he's
    saying Look at these little marks. Here are some words you may also
    include: *Verlaine, stars, rusted wheel of a bicycle, stones, showplace of*
    onion-like construction
Inside, ear and rapture, carbon monoxide hazards, I will terrify you, cities
    with Kodak movie corporate colors. Don't we need more suffering?
But wait again. The old saw about how we're happy now that the one we
    loved is happier dead, is that it? so they don't live to bear all this collapse
    of civilization, this morbid gloom with crooks in charge, hmmmmmm
Little marks, they are words moving toward love never to be
    chastised, hand stroking a sober orange cat, spigot on inside the loft all water
    running, humming. It's maybe about water not about oil, this world
Maybe inside this poetry is a many, sunny disposition almost blinding
    Outside, his heart
    Inside, beating.

Left to right: Kenward Elmslie, Anne Waldman, and Ron Padgett read at the Transcontinental Poetry Reading

Traveling with Kenneth
Ron Padgett

Ron Padgett reading live at the Transcontinental Poetry Reading.

During a recent performance of La Bohème at the Stockholm opera, when Rodolfo and Mimi, at the end of the first act, floated off on a luminous pale blue rectangle into total darkness, I thought of how Kenneth might have been as thrilled as I was when he sat in that same hall three years ago, with its way over-the-top rococo golden embellishments, swirling scenes of gods and nymphs amid festoons and putti arching above us as the singers opened their mouths and released vibrations so large and round they filled the entire space. The sheer ambitiousness of it all was overwhelming. Three years ago, in Stockholm with Kenneth, I hadn't even thought of going to the opera there, but Kenneth had, and that I have now gone too tells me that yet another part of him has gone into me, where I like to imagine that it will go on living.

At intermission my companion and I walked out onto the spacious balcony that overlooks the square of Gustav Adolfs Torg. In the deliciously cool early evening, the Parliament building to our left was glowing dimly, with the pointy church spires of the old part of town, Gamla Stan, just beyond, and the water flowing past Stromparterren, the little park celebrated by Valery Larbaud in his long poem "Europe," which Kenneth inspired me to translate thirty years ago, Stromparterren where a few couples were watching the evening arrive, and suddenly the air sparkled and I turned to her and said, "How lucky we are!" as if the happiness were there just for us at that very moment, the happiness that Kenneth pursued so eagerly, as if it were a goddess, one he caught and held more often than one might imagine, as he did one spring night in Paris around fifteen years ago, when we were strolling alongside the wrought-iron fence of the Luxembourg Gardens and he gestured to the full moon in the clear sky and said, "Isn't this just ravishing?" and laughed as if he had just been presented with a wonderful surprise.

Earlier in the day of the opera, looking across the water toward the Stockholm skyline from a high point in Skansen, I heard Kenneth's voice in my head, saying, "I was on a ski trip," quoting his own prose poem that describes the energy he had felt as a young man on his way to this spot fifty or so years ago, excited by the Swedish girls on the ferry with him. Kenneth, they are still there, those girls, and there are more of them and when they walk toward you it is as if their clothes are slipping from their bodies.

In the Pittsburgh airport one snowy afternoon about six years ago there were no such marvels. Our connecting flight had been postponed several hours. To escape the hubub and ennui, Kenneth and I headed toward what airport management called the Meditation Room. Shortly after we walked in past its automatic sliding glass door, a blue glow arose along the white walls that curved up to form a dome, and a low hum was suffused into the air. The door slid shut behind us. In an accent like that of a man of exotic but indeterminate descent, I said, in a deep voice, "Welcome to our country, Meeta Bond," and Kenneth burst into an uncontrollable laughter that came in wave after wave as he seemed to keep reexperiencing my improvisation. To have made Kenneth laugh like that—a small return for the many times his poems and his conversation had given me joy—was for me one of the happiest moments I had with him. From that time on he signed his letters and cards to me, "007," as if the pleasure of my witticism were still rolling inside him.

Several months later we were in San Francisco to give a poetry reading. After checking into a small, classy hotel, we went up to our respective rooms. A few minutes later Kenneth knocked at my door.

"How is your room?" he asked.

"It's nice," I said, "very comfy."

He strode over to the window.

"But you don't have a balcony."

"I don't? That's okay," I said.

"You don't want a balcony? Go down and tell them to give you a balcony."

Kenneth wanted all of life to have a balcony.

Tristan Tzara

for Kenneth Koch

Andrei Codrescu

Sensibility was not what spelled doom
but rather forelocks and insouciance, palabras y cadavros,
the toasts made ten years before in a Cocteau moment.
What I would like is to conduct a study
on the liberatory intensity of laughter
using recordings from the very first chortle
thought worth recording, a Chaplin audience or
a child before a bicycle in the teens of the 20th century
or an hysteric before a psychiatrist, in itself
a milestone, laughter like smiling photographs
having to wait decades before the cost of film
or equipment allowed a hint of frivolity into
the serious business of the world, furrowed brows,
severe bosoms, modesty, concentration, lack
of spontaneity and the plain duration necessary
to hold a pause or to continue being tickled
by something in the mind's eye, the moment
in let's say 1913, when a Jewish boy fresh
out of the ghetto of Moinesti or Czernowitz
could laugh in a burst that concentrated and released
centuries of repression and fear combined with a strict
alphabet leaving no airy gaps for sprigs of springtime
and did so on tape the cost be damned,
recognition of something new following
as surely uncontainable as a peasant's before
the nude legs of a mannequin being dressed in a shop
window by a woman whose white ankles signaled
the death of his acquired ancestral gloom.
That is a laugh we must recover and I'd like
to study it because we all know what followed.

Poem
Rodney Koeneke

I've been wanting to write you in the open, gorgeous manner of Frank O'Hara
but the hegemony of the everyday gets in the way
and fucks with my insouciance—how to be chatty or bright
as a dime when you feel like the vaguely urinous taste in the morning coffee
they serve at the Golden Donuts behind the office park
I work in, where the owner and I routinely discuss our children
and I feel sort of proud but also so old,
like a rotary phone that won't let you connect to a voicemail system
that's newer, and probably also blacks the ear like Kenneth
Koch's in O'Hara's great poem "Poem"
beginning with the line: "The fluorescent tubing burns like a bobby-
soxer's ankles" that he wrote when he was only 33
and I'm 35 for one more week, and you too
maybe will soon be crying De pro-fund-is
clamavi over the sparrowy death of your youth
which doesn't so much die
as simply lose the reassuring quality it once possessed, like gravity,
and begins to present itself more like a question: "Are we just muddy instants"
in the larger Irrawaddy of process? Or excuses for Hermes
to pull trick coins from the vague and unused space behind our eyes?

Obscurely we know
we are all slowly dying—I maybe of drinking (though the halcyon days
of dying of drink are over), you of a surfeit of something,
probably pleasure, which cloys over time because of the way desires have
of behaving like carnival ducks under neon tubing
that we suffer to be shot at again and again, until after a while you begin to lose faith
in the effectiveness of the whole procedure
which involves setting them back up and pretending it's different ducks
progressing in a firm line across the horizon, under new lighting
instead of the same ones wearily describing the same occluded circle.
I'm not convinced there's anything in what I'm saying
you couldn't find equally well in O'Hara, or Conversations
With Eckermann, or Robert Musil: but "great ideas that command
instant allegiance" are hard to find, if they even exist, which leaves the lesser ones
without much to do but vie for our temporary affections
and those can settle almost anywhere, like birds freight a phone line
or sunburns exult at a summer beach resort.

Still, there's some quality
in our peculiar allegiance this completely passes over,
and while the thought of you as merely a great idea is as difficult to imagine
as a sex offender staying chaste on Google,
the part about the instant makes some sense—
things happen with us at such wicked speeds, but over such a small surface
that velocity itself becomes an aspect of feeling,
suggestive of the chaos and rich sense of purpose

that arrives with the beginning of any new century, where everything for a short time
seems to stretch over something larger and younger and sweeter than itself
and no detail seems too trivial to contain it, or at least point to its immanent disclosure
in a future full of passionate enjoyment
that we all know must be coming because the detail itself
is with us, here, in the present, managing to reflect it
by sitting there just winking and being part of its time.

I guess it's possible for any one of us to say along with Goethe:
"I should have been happier, and should have accomplished more as a poet,"
but saying it next to you it sounds faintly ridiculous,
exuding the cedary odor of attempts by sterner ages
to press all the redolent fragments thrown out
by its cabriolets or neckerchiefs up against one another
until they formed a whole. Whether their effort was really so different
from our own wish for freeway diners that stay "Always Open"
or an America detached from the systems that squeak to produce it
is one of those questions we casually leave to History
like a mismatched sock or an outdated computer monitor
while pursuing "This her free hand in my own
demanding presence," an activity which the present seems so ardently
to insist upon, like aging, though the trick is in learning
how to release it, and let things just sort of meander
until they uncover their own demands
as if the time they took to unfold in was itself a kind of poem
that manages in its last crushing stanza
to intimate mortality and its shivery sense of importance

While talking about ephemera like bobby-soxers or neon tubing
without ever saying why they finally age, or burn,
just putting them there, in the poem, incomplete
and beautiful like you.

Photograph by Migdalia Valdes

Nostalgia of the Infinite, 1913

after Giorgio de Chirico

The hands are touching.
You began in cement in small spaces.
You began the departure. Leaves restrain you. You attempted the
departure.
A smile in sunshine, nostalgia.
Beneath shadow of shadows of Columbus the Navigator. Waving
farewell.
Street, shadows.

I have lost my detachment, sparrow with silver teeth.
I have lost the doves of Milan, floating politely.

    Recognize me, I shall be here, O Nietzsche.

  We have skipped down three pairs of stairs,
they are not numbered, but they are oddly assorted, velvet.

    Recognize me in sunshine,
assorted bulletins permit us to be freer than in Rome.
This land of castles perched on a cliff.
Filled with pears and magic.

    I am not detached,
bulletins permit us a comb, a fish of silver.
A part of the tower
(aet, 1913) beckons to us.

Barbara Guest

This broadside was designed, typeset in 24 pt. Centaur & 36 pt. Arrighi, & printed by James Meetze at Tougher Disguises Press on the occasion of Barbara Guest's reading at Mills College, December 3, 2002.

A EUCALYPTUS PRESS BROADSIDE   36/90

In Memoriam, Barbara Guest: 1920–2006

Photo by Will Sherwood

The American Objectivists
Kevin Killian & Brian Kim Stefans

CHARACTERS (in order of appearance).

Louis Zukofsky, a poet and high school teacher.....................Kasey *Mohammad*
Celia, his wife.....................Kevin *Killian*
John, a fellow teacher.....................Brian *Stefans*
Bunny, his girlfriend.....................Roxi *Hamilton*
George Oppen, a face from the past.....................Wayne *Smith*
Mary, his wife.....................Dodie *Bellamy*
Lorine Niedecker, poet, genius, hayseed, former girlfriend of Louis.....................Johanna *Isaacson*

[A Brooklyn apartment in the late 1950s. Tastefully decorated with elegant furniture and paintings. Enter CELIA.]

CELIA. "What a dump!" Who said that, Louis? *[Surveying apartment.]* Whoever said it, couldn't have been talking about our beautiful Brooklyn flat.

[Enter LOUIS.]

LOUIS. Did they call?

CELIA. Who? The Oppens?

LOUIS. Is the little light blinking in the primitive voice mail system of 1959?

CELIA. Did you really think they'd call? They haven't called in twenty years! Where are they going to call from—Mexico? Don't make me giggle—it's unbecoming in a woman unsatisfied.

LOUIS. How's Paul?

CELIA. Paul's practicing, dear. The violin. Now help me get ready for our guests.

LOUIS. Oh, Christ, Celia, you know this is the night the Oppens are coming! Why did you have to embarrass yourself at the PTA meeting. I see enough of those deadbeat adjuncts all day without you inviting them over for a night cap.

CELIA. I think John Ashbery's a peach.

LOUIS *(snorts)*. I'll check on Paul.

[Exit LOUIS.]

CELIA. Rub some walnut oil into his fingers, will you? I'll open the bourbon, scotch and vodka.

—And what was that snort about, Mr. Zukofsky? Huh? Will you tell me why you're *snorting* like some water buffalo of PS 149?

[She stares absently at photograph of her family. Then throws it onto carpet.]

John Ashbery, John Ashbery, you're young, cute and virile. I saw you looking at me over the water cooler.

[Picks up a book.]

Some Trees, by John Ashbery. *[She practices meeting him.]* "Mr. Ashbery, how did you come up with that intriguing title?" *[Calls out to LOUIS.]* Louis, one of these days you'll have to write a book about trees! This "A" business is fine for the "A" Train, but I'm thinking Park Avenue. *[Again to an absent Ashbery.]* "And you have won the Yale Younger Writers Award? Just how young are you, Mr. Ashbery? Open your mouth, oh my, I see—baby teeth."

[Enter LOUIS.]

LOUIS. Paul says nobody called.

CELIA. Get some ice into my bluest bowl, Louis. I'll make us a drink, then I'll freshen up. John is bringing that cute bohemian girl, Bunny Lang. "Bunny"! Ha! I'll pin her bunny ears back to her head I will.

[We hear the sound of a lone violin coming from somewhere in the apartment.]

CELIA. He does have talent, doesn't he?

LOUIS. Paul? Yes—he's a prodigy like Mozart.

CELIA. I meant John.

LOUIS. John?

CELIA. John Ashbery the French teacher! Hell—o! Pick up that pile of illicit correspondence, and for bejeezus sake Louis, bring out some of that lowbrow cheese your little girlfriend's always sending you from Wisconsin!

LOUIS. She's not my girlfriend. I am her *reader*—she's entrusted me with her entire posterior, I mean posterity—just like I am for Bill...

CELIA. Is that why you run to your office to call her just after the long distance rate sinks below 3 cents... to *read* her? We have 917 numbers for that!

LOUIS. She, like me, believes the *ear* higher than the *mind*.

CELIA. And both lower than the—oops, I've dropped my *Tender Buttons*!

LOUIS. Celia, please be more *abstract*.

CELIA. And does she read to you? Can't get *that* in Rutherford. *[To absent Ashbery.]* Oh, I must apologize for my husband, he's such a crank when he has one of his little... fits. It's one of the few times he feels truly fecund. Ha ha!

LOUIS. I think I'll go water the fire escape.

CELIA. Don't forget that cheese! [*To Ashbery*] Do you like cheese, Mr. Ashbery? We've just had this imported from Naples! Naples on Fifth Street, you know, off the coast of the Bronx? [*Laughs.*] Oh, you must be a swimmer like Byron, what big arms you have! I forgot that poets weren't all stick figures. Do you have a matching limp?

LOUIS (*from the window*). Looks like the Hudbetter's cat has gotten to our Bavarian gentians again. What a mess out here!

CELIA. Oh, draw the curtains! No, better yet, take them in... unloose the jambs! Heck, I'm feeling a little body electric myself today! I'll put them in the circa 1940's trash compactor. What would I be without the Industrial Revolution to get me back to nature!

LOUIS (*to himself*). Not entirely deaf?

CELIA. What?

LOUIS (*handing her plant*). I said, we left Paul home alone again.

CELIA. Oh, that kid, he's got to learn to fend for himself sometimes! He spends so much time with that damned piece of wood he can barely crack a can of tuna.

LOUIS. But he can play Carl Ruggles' "Suntreader" in 5 minutes flat!

CELIA. Pshaw! Since when did speed matter? What's he going to do for work, play in the Italian restaurants for patrons with ADD? He'll be done before they've ordered! We can't even afford a car.

LOUIS. What?

CELIA. Kevin Killian has a car. Why can't we have a car?

LOUIS. First of all, we're barely twenty-five years out of the depression. Second, they all have cars in San Francisco... it gives them a way to escape those Japanese spies. Lastly, I'm a Marxist, how many times do I have to say that!

—Did you get the good scotch? George always liked the good stuff. And maybe if your Yale Younger adjunct knows how to pronounce the word "chryselephantine" he can have some too.

CELIA. You Objectivists have such a strange way of expressing your alpha selves.

LOUIS. Probably can't even write a sestina (*snorts*).

[*Doorbell rings.*]

CELIA. Louis, that's the door. I'm getting the drinks! [*Fixing up her hair in a panic.*] This is so *exciting*. Goodbye Dark Ages! Goodbye Modernism! I am W-O-...

[*Exit CELIA.*]

LOUIS (*opening door*). Hello.

JOHN. Bon soir, Dr. Zukofsky. Please let me tell you it is a great honor to me that you have...

LOUIS. Sit down.

[*Enter JOHN ASHBERY and BUNNY LANG.*]

BUNNY. Hi, I'm Bunny Lang? I don't think we've met, I'm on the faculty too, but in Home Ec.

LOUIS. Hello, Bunny.

BUNNY. In charge of angora sweaters. I can't believe we're here! [*She giggles.*] Why, it's just like a real apartment and everything.

JOHN. It's like being in some fabulous kingdom of Oz.

BUNNY. In the teachers' lounge they whisper about this flat.

JOHN. And our young students, ah those rascals, they sing about it!

LOUIS. They do?

BUNNY. Well that's neither here nor there.

JOHN. Yes, not when "here" is such a wonderful "there." Shall we make ourselves at home and drink? Bunny here is from the Boston Langs.

BUNNY. Yes, well, my father was Money Lang.

LOUIS. Charming. Celia, Mrs. Zukofsky, the woman who invited you, is in the kitchen fixing some martinis. Let me warn you about Celia. She's chic but she packs a mean wallop.

BUNNY. She's lovely, or she was in the 1930s when Shirley Temple was popular.

LOUIS. She's the mother of my only son—Paul. The child prodigy.

JOHN. My goodness, Shirley Temple, wonder what she's up to tonight? Over in France there's quite a Temple cult, you know that? The Cinema Francaise is nearly a *temple du Temple*.

LOUIS. French ways disgust me as they do all normal men.

BUNNY. Approaching this fifth floor walk-up, we heard a violin playing. We thought of Sherlock Holmes. Pacing the floor in his deerstalker, violin tucked under his chin. We're a couple of nuts in love! When we marry, next spring, John's taking me to—France.

LOUIS. For our honeymoon, Celia and I went to Riis Park. Water everywhere.

JOHN. Maybe you have Jascha Heifetz behind this door [*he indicates the bedroom of PAUL.*]—

LOUIS. That's Paul's room. He's sleeping now.

JOHN. Like Dracula! Brrrr!

BUNNY. The kids—you know, the kids in school—have a funny nickname for you, Dr. Zukofsky.

LOUIS. They do?

BUNNY. They're young—wild—out for kicks. Maybe you represent authority to them. You're old, set in your ways, brilliant of course—

JOHN. Oh cut to the chase, Bunny. They call you "Officer Krupke."

[He and BUNNY both sing: "Gee, Officer Krupke, krup you."]

LOUIS. I don't know the current pop hits. And I have never heard that song.

"Krup you," you say? "Because Tarzan triumphs, see Tarzan the He-man, Go to sleep with boy in jungle corral."

You'll excuse me now. And please, occupy only a tiny corner of this room, as my great friends the Oppens are expected any minute. They haven't been seen in nearly 20 years.

[Exit LOUIS.]

BUNNY. John, do you think we upset him?

JOHN. He's just stiff, that's all. What the French call le foret petrifee. In Brooklyn it's just a telephone pole, but he lets Celia's fingers do all the walking, unfortunately.

BUNNY. Should we sit down?

JOHN. Sure. Now, Bunny, about that honeymoon thing—

BUNNY *(absently)*. Uh-hunh?

[Enter CELIA.]

CELIA. John Ashbery! Bienvenue a ma casa! Let me usher you to the bay window. Look outside, just for you, this splendid tribute treat. What do you see?

JOHN. The BQE?

CELIA. No, silly. Over there, in the park. "Some trees." Get it?

JOHN. Mrs. Krupke, I mean Mrs.—

CELIA. Call me Celia. No, I mean really call me.

JOHN. This is Bunny Lang.

BUNNY. His fiancee. I'm in home ec at your father's school. He hired me right out of the Cedar Tavern.

CELIA. Fiancee? *[Mysteriously]* I see… what lovely—thin hips! *[She changes suddenly.]* Let's play a game. We call it "Jewish Questions." It'll unsettle you.

JOHN. Well, I—

CELIA. C'mon, John Ashbery. Here's the first one. What's your favorite comic strip?

JOHN. Comic strip?

CELIA. The funny pages.

BUNNY. Blondie? Mandrake?

JOHN. Nancy and Sluggo? Richie Rich?

CELIA. You're not very Jewish. That means, two fewer drinks.

BUNNY. Fewer than *what?*

JOHN. What's *your* favorite comic strip?

CELIA. Non, non, non, garcon, I'm asking the questions here. Now you're in *my* cult d'moi!

[Enter LOUIS.]

LOUIS. Celia, how long do you plan to keep our guests?

CELIA. I don't know buddy boy. How long does it *take*—to break them down to skin and bones? We're playing "Jewish Questions."

LOUIS *(warming a bit)*. I see. The working man's Walpurgisnacht. Carry on.

JOHN. Dr. Zukofsky, are you familiar with Reverdy and his "4,700 Poems Beginning with the Letter 'A'"?

CELIA. That letter goes to Louis! Hey! Bunny! What's your favorite state bird?

BUNNY. Celia, this isn't really a reply per se, but could you show me where the bathroom is? I'm getting the cold shakes.

CELIA. Bird!

BUNNY. Oriole? Finch? They must be birds of some state.

CELIA *(laughs wickedly)*. Come with me, dear. I'm losing my touch. What do the kids say? The young wild kids out for kicks? What's their darling slang term for a wealthy young woman from Cambridge who takes slumming to a radical peak?

[Exit CELIA and BUNNY.]

JOHN. Alone at last.

LOUIS. As it were. "That girl, with her hair down in the world, can take care of herself in his bed."

JOHN. Say, do you know Jane Freilicher?

LOUIS. Bird!

JOHN. The painter?

LOUIS. Bird, John! And by the way, she's no painter and only a decorator would call her one. Have you never heard of *Mantegna*?

JOHN. She's delightful nevertheless, and last night, she—

LOUIS. Bird! Bird! Bird!

JOHN. I don't have a favorite bird, Mr. Zukofsky. I'm impartial. I like all of them for their own merits. Over in France, they—

LOUIS. Maybe in France they don't distinguish between birds and they appreciate Jane Freilicher but here in Brooklyn, do you know what happens when you're a poet in the school system? They put you in front of a classroom of sullen, beatnik, high school monsters and they expect you to teach them Plato!

JOHN. I guess I have it easier. My students seem to pick up French like *(snaps fingers)*.

LOUIS. And their black leather jackets and their switchblades—Sharks and the Jets, pompadours up to *here*—no, Brooklyn Polytech has been overrun by young barbarians. Their only interest in poetry and art is soiling the subways with voodoo graffiti—soon, they'll put *that* in the Brooklyn Museum! Does "White Sambo Gringo" mean anything to you?

JOHN. But they're so charming and *(struggles to find the right word)* full of joie de vivre.

[Again he snaps his fingers.]

LOUIS. You're hip, I observe. So, you and Miss Lang are engaged, Mr. Ashbery?

JOHN. Call me John—no, do, please, sir.

LOUIS. And you can call me "sir." Your fiancée has no hips.

JOHN. I've been admiring your collection of Ezra Pound's poetry. It's funny to think the poor dear old man still has fans, if that's the word. My goodness, with everybody who matters turning to France for inspiration, it's heartening to know that a harmless little American modernist still turns a head or two.

LOUIS. I'm no fan of Pound's.

JOHN. He was so vicious to your people! And yet look at all those books! It's like some grim collection of guillotine blades—very Kenneth Anger.

LOUIS. I sense a reluctance to talk about your engagement to Miss Lang.

JOHN. Bunny? Bunny's a swell kid! She's the heart and soul of the Cambridge Poet's Theater movement. That's where I wrote all my famous plays. Frank too.

LOUIS. Frank Sinatra?

JOHN. Frank O'Hara.

LOUIS. Perfect name for a francophile.

JOHN. Your wife's an unusual creature.

LOUIS. Let me tell you a secret, baby. There are easier things in the world, if you happen to be teaching in a high school, there are easier things than being married to the daughter of the principal. Celia's father has the staying power of one of those Micronesian tortoises. He has a small treasury of arrowheads from the French and Indian War—which he pulled from his own body! How many kids are you and Funny going to have?

JOHN. Kids?

LOUIS. Is her name Funny?

JOHN. We just call her "Bunny" for laughs.

CELIA *(offstage)*. Louis!

LOUIS. Do you find women puzzling?

JOHN. Well, yes and no.

[Enter BUNNY.]

LOUIS *(almost bumping into her)*. Sorry. Lost my balanchine.

CELIA *(offstage)*. LOUIS!

BUNNY. That's okay.

LOUIS. For Christ's sake, Celia, hang on a minute!

[Exit LOUIS.]

BUNNY. He bumped into me, almost as though he wanted to kill me.

JOHN. Please! Don't exaggerate, it's ugly.

BUNNY. Remember those old time bumper cars at Fenway Park?

JOHN. Where's Celia? You two were gone an awfully long time.

BUNNY. She just wanted to talk, that's all. It took me forever to get to the phone. She's got a little black phone hidden—like a prize—under a satin pillow.

JOHN. And?

BUNNY. I found it. That's all. Made my call. Jeeper's coming by with the—stuff.

JOHN. Now what's she doing?

BUNNY. They're up there making these gigantic signs with poster paint. "Welcome Home, George and Mary." Is it legal to use the hammer and sickle as your Block Association logo?

JOHN. "George and Mary." Oh Bunny, do you think it's the Royal Family of England?

BUNNY. Fat chance. —I threw up. Is that all right for me to say, John Ashbery? Oh John! I don't know how long I can go on pretending you're my fiancée!

JOHN. It's just till I'm better established at Brooklyn Polytech. For goodness sake, we're not going to get married!

BUNNY. Because you're—

JOHN. Oh, for so many reasons.

BUNNY. But John, I want you. I want you as a woman wants a man. I don't just want a white wedding, I want the whole chazzerai.

JOHN. As though I would marry an addict.

BUNNY. So, I smoke a little reefer now and then, I take a few bennies—

JOHN. A few! You must sweat caffeine!

BUNNY. I yearn for you, John Ashbery. Feel my froideur, melting away like—like a popsicle left in the sun. *[When he resists, BUNNY turns to audience.]* No one understands, but what's a girl to do? If I had a chance with a homosexual, I'd take it, and take it I will. I don't understand the word, "NO," and he's like "No" in all caps—bold. But as God is my witness, I won't read—my alphabet stops at "M"! *(closes eyes)* If I have to lie, steal, cheat or kill…

JOHN. How about a drink?

BUNNY. Damn you, John—I could have any man in New York. I could have the next man who walks through that door.

JOHN. What a boast! You're like Edwin Denby with his bourbon on backward.

BUNNY. You don't think I'm serious, do you, fiancée? I mean it. Next man who walks through that door is mine.

JOHN. No, mine. —It'll probably be Jeeper anyhow, your teen Romeo, and you can have him.

BUNNY. I know, but he's got the best stuff in town and he's willing to travel to Brooklyn.

JOHN. Who are "George and Mary?"

BUNNY. George Abbott and Mary Martin?

JOHN. George Gershwin and Mary Pickford?

BUNNY. George Washington and—?

JOHN. Mary Todd Lincoln?

BUNNY. You know all those French artists.

JOHN. Oh yes. George Braque and Mary—Picasso?

BUNNY. Or maybe they're us?

JOHN. Yes, perhaps this is one of those absurd Ionesco Rod Serling plays where we walk into a party and have to switch identities. You be Mary.

BUNNY. To show the mutability of capitalism. George, you haven't touched your hors d'oeuvres.

JOHN. Mary, I haven't eaten a Triscuit since Harvard. I haven't been *regular* since. Ha ha!

BUNNY. Oh, George, you're—

[Doorbell rings.]

JOHN. Should I answer it—Mary?

BUNNY *(rising)*. I'll get it. It's probably Jeeper, I hope. I can't wait till they invent cell phones—and insulin pumps. I may look straight, John, but inside I'm dying for some of the stuff that kills me. Oh God, I should have coked up before the PTA meeting, but as they say in Brooklyn, who knew?

And remember, John, if it's a man, I'm going to—make him, as we say in 1959.

[She opens the door. Enter GEORGE and MARY OPPEN.]

GEORGE. I'm George.

MARY. I'm Mary.

BUNNY. I thought *I* was Mary!

GEORGE. Beg pardon?

JOHN *(rising)*. Just a little joke. Hi, I'm John and this is Funny… I mean, odd that… I'd like to introduce you to… my fiancée, Bunny Lang. We thought you might be the boy bringing some party favors.

MARY. Jorge, find out if the Zukofskys still live here. My, I haven't been in this building in 25 years. Everything's muy different.

GEORGE. Do the Zukofsky famiglia live here?

MARY. Uno, due, tre.

JOHN. Yes, come on in! Welcome to our humble chapeau!

BUNNY. They're just seeing to their little son. *[To AUDIENCE.]* He's kind of cute in that sexy Jewish way like John Garfield. Only Garfield was tiny and this man's six feet of adorable. And he's got a voice like a vanilla sorbet on a hot summer night!

GEORGE *(to MARY)*. Uno mijo!

MARY. Yes *(makes cradling motions with arms)*. Uno mijo, a son.

JOHN. We've been sitting here wondering who "George and Mary" could possibly be, and now here you are popping up like toast.

GEORGE. Yes.

MARY. Here we are. We've been away for a long time—*[lying]* in Switzerland.

BUNNY. You didn't see a motorbike out on the street, did you, folks? Reason I'm asking is, I'm expecting an important delivery.

MARY. We saw no motor-cycla.

GEORGE. We looked this way and that, up and down, over and under—from Deep Image to Post Lang Poh! No one followed us. I don't think.

MARY. That man at the airport gave us the stare.

GEORGE *(lying)*. But Mary, we did not come from the airport!

MARY. No indeed, I meant, that man with the apricot.

BUNNY. Gave you the "stare"?

MARY *(thinking fast)*. Gave me the stare, and why not? I'm still an attractive woman, despite my twenty years working for the—

GEORGE. —Perfect suntan.

JOHN. It's marvelous.

GEORGE. So we were not followed from the apricot stand, Mary? No one behind us in the taxi, no one from the—*[he thinks]* Fruit—Barrel—Institute?

BUNNY *(flippantly)*. Why, are you wanted by the FBI?

[Pause.]

See, it's the same initials?

[Pause.]

JOHN. Bunny!

BUNNY. Fruit Barrel Institute? Oh! Oh dear, I've put my foot in it, haven't I? And I don't even know anything about politics—or—fruit, I mean. I'm just a co-ed from Cambridge, kooky, glamorous, Truman Capote wrote a book about me, "Breakfast at Tiffany's," and I'm just—sitting here waiting for Jeeper.

MARY. Darling, don't fret. See, I grew up on a farm, in Seattle, and oh, the wonderful days we had growing apples and picking apples and—

GEORGE. Packing them in barrels.

BUNNY. Mary, can you come to my home Ec class and give a lecture? Lots of Puerto Rican girls there. Maybe you can teach them how to make the big colorful Mexican fiesta skirts. Oh dim Guadelajara!

MARY. As though I would know anything of Mexico!

JOHN. Bunny's thinking of Switzerland.

BUNNY. Dotted swiss.

JOHN. Potted piss. Bottled smut!

GEORGE. What *are* you, apple? We too were in the sun and night alive with sap.

BUNNY. Don't you hate the 1950s—the cold war, the climate of oppression.

JOHN. This country's no place for a poet! Especially one—

BUNNY. Who teaches French.

MARY *(nervously)*. Is there still that little room off to the side here, where Louis writes his poem? If I remember, it looks out onto the street and no one can see you watching?

JOHN. This is my first visit to the Zukofskys.

BUNNY. With the soggy fire escape? Yes, I checked it out already.

GEORGE. Mary? Can I speak with you alone?

MARY *(to JOHN and BUNNY)*. Uh-oh, George is giving me "that voice." He's the genius in the family. Sometimes I don't dot my *i*'s just to make him feel progressive.

[George and MARY move upstage, huddled in conversation.]

JOHN. Bunny, for God's sakes! You know who I think they are? The Oppens!

BUNNY. I don't follow you. You said you wouldn't have me, so I'm taking him. On my own little carousel he's the brass ring.

JOHN. George Oppen, once a poet of the 30s, gave up poetry for the people, enlisted in the War, shot at in foxhole, disappeared after the war. No one knows where he and Mary have been for the past 20 years!

BUNNY. *You* can play Edward R. Murrow. Let me powder my nose.

JOHN. Some say they killed Trotsky, Bunny. And that's only because they couldn't convince Garcia Lorca to come to leave Harlem and come to Mexico. Don't mess with George Oppen.

BUNNY. I rise to a challenge—unlike you, my sweet.

[Calling out to GEORGE.] George Oppen, my favorite poet! Give me some of that *Discrete Series* and I'll sing a little "Moon River" in your presence. I know a soda jerk when I see one!

GEORGE. You're barking up the wrong tree, sister.

MARY. That's right. I've been to countries where I could get a person bumped off for ten dollars.

BUNNY. Such as what?

MARY. Switzerland.

BUNNY. Uh-huh. Mary, we haven't met, but pretend you don't see me. Just look the other way while your husband and I make beautiful music together.

MARY. I'm myopic in that regard. I'm meek and mild, but a tiger when it comes to my man. Oh my man I love him so—He'll never know—All my life is just despair—But I don't care—

When he takes me in his arms
The world is bright, all right . . .

BUNNY *(to GEORGE).* Moon River, wider than a mile— I'm crossing you in style, someday—Oh, dream maker, you heart breaker—Wherever you're goin', I'm goin' your way.

JOHN. Bunny, please, he's not even a poet. He gave it all up for Communism. He's like the kernel of corn that ended with a whimper—no seed left to squander.

MARY. Wrong again, Mr. French Fry! George has written not one, not two, but three new books—manuscripts that will begin the 60s with a bang like pop art! Oh yes, the 60s will be hoppin', poppin', and "Oppen."

GEORGE. It's supposed to be a surprise, Mary.

MARY. "This is Which," "Of Being Numerous," and one other.

GEORGE. That's enough, Mary. *[He spouts some Spanish.]*

MARY *(brightly, to BUNNY and JOHN).* Wait till the sixties—there'll be no stoppin' Oppen!

GEORGE. You sound like Madison Avenue.

MARY. —Oh, George! What's the matter, all of a sudden am I not being supportive enough? I made tacos with my teeth for ten years, never saw anyone but comrades, lost my looks, hiding out in—Switzerland—and suddenly I'm disappointing you?

GEORGE. Now, Mary dear—

MARY *(angrily).* Go to her! She's on some strange kind of mission to seduce you. A woman knows that look, when she sees it in another girl's eyes like some kind of sty of the mind. Ever since that cabana girl in—lederhosen—tried to get your attention by spilling tequila on you—

GEORGE. Mary, don't be—

MARY. Take her right now, why the pruderies of the Frigidaire? You saw men die, I had women knifed in Switzerland, put the curse on Frida Kahlo, Conlon Noncarrow. We're jungle animals, you and I. This one's a powder puff—not fit to toast a tortilla!

JOHN. My, my, these apple-cheeked fruit growers don't change their spots do they?

BUNNY. Any animal knows, there's a time when a decent woman crawls back into the cave to die, and leaves her mate to the superior woman.

JOHN. Always the animals pay.

[Phone rings.]

BUNNY. Shall I answer it?

JOHN. Might be the Fruit Barrel Institute!

GEORGE. Where's that little room with the view?

MARY *(to GEORGE).* You're a genius!

[Exit GEORGE and MARY.]

JOHN. There goes genius, and Mrs. Genius.

[Phone rings.]

CELIA *(offstage).* For Christ's sake, Louis!

BUNNY. Shall I answer it? It looks so lonely.

LOUIS. What am I—switchboard girl?

JOHN. Leave it to Heaven, Bunny.

BUNNY. But it might be Jeeper!

[Phone rings.]

CELIA. Get the god-damn phone, I don't want to wake up Paul!

LOUIS *(shouting).* Yes, the boy must have his sleep!

[Enter CELIA.]

CELIA. Hi! How you doing?

[She strides to the phone.]

KILLIAN, STEFANS

Hello? Zukofsky residence! What? Who? Oh my God! *[To BUNNY and JOHN.]* It's—I can't even say it. *[Into phone.]* Wait a New York minute, Lorine Niedecker. You say you're on my block right now? Right in the crosshairs—I mean, on the corner?

JOHN. Shall we leave?

CELIA *(grabs his arm)*. Ha ha ha, as if you dare! *[Into phone.]* All right, come up, you can stay for five minutes. Did you bring the cheese?

BUNNY. Lorine Neidecker, what a comical name. We don't have that kind of name in Boston.

JOHN. I wonder if she speaks French.

CELIA. Five minutes, Lorine. That's all. Hear me? *[Slams down phone.]* She's a perfect pest, but you know how cowgirls are. Did I hear the doorbell?

JOHN. Yes, the Oppens came in. They're hiding in the little vocabulary room over there. Where have they been?

CELIA. They won't say, we'd get postcards with nothing on them, I'd know it was them. Even the postmarks were rubbed out with Silly Putty. Hee hee, made hanging them on the wall easier.

JOHN. They're charming, like two Marxist brothers.

CELIA. Hope Mary didn't start with her "Hoppin" and "Oppen" business. Poor thing puts herself into a trance state raving about her great, great husband.

BUNNY. I'm just so antsy.

CELIA. "Antsy"? I'm loud, and vulgar, and some people don't like me. But that's okay.

JOHN. That's great, Mrs. Zukofsky. In France there's a word for women like you!

CELIA. Mr. Ashbery, how about a drink? Louis says if you have a single malt, and a double malt scotch, you add them together, you'd think they'd make a triple malt now wouldn't you?

BUNNY. I'll have one.

CELIA *(to BUNNY)*. Say, didn't I see you on the bus poster, you're Miss Rheingold, ain't you? *[Sings.]* "My beer is Rheingold, the dry beer, ask for Rheingold whenever you buy beer." John, the usual?

BUNNY. Is it a triple malt, John?

CELIA. He's not in the Math department, Funny!

BUNNY. Bunny—like the Easter bunny.

CELIA. Ha ha, we're not really into Easter here, Miss Lang! Have you ever heard of—Passover?

BUNNY. Oh—sorry.

CELIA. Ever heard of the *Holocaust?* I just hung up on Lorine Niedecker, don't get me started on you! It wouldn't be charming! Lorine who? This girl—this girl from Wisconsin—who started in on Louis before we were married. She's a poet too, or so she says. "The milk—the milk is white—like work—A day's hoeing in the factory." End of poem. End of story.

BUNNY. And she's coming tonight?

CELIA. Says she's been traveling the subways for 24 hours, afraid to get off. Country mouse in the big city. I'd send her to Queens—if they weren't planning the World's Fair.

JOHN. What could you do, you had to let her in.

CELIA. Finally—a man who understands a woman's wants.

BUNNY. Where? If you find one, let me know!

[Doorbell. Enter LORINE NIEDECKER, carrying a basket with something in it wrapped in a red checkered cloth.]

BUNNY. Poor thing, you look bushed!

LORINE. Winter's after me—she's out, with sheets so wide it hurts the eyes.

JOHN. How do you do?

LORINE. I've spent my life on nothing. Hello, Celia.

CELIA. I know you hoped I had passed on to my reward, Lorine Niedecker. But I haven't, I'm very much here. I lived through Joe McCarthy, and I'm here!

LORINE. I never wished you ill, Celia.

CELIA. What horror to awake at night, in Wisconsin! And to think, in Wisconsin, "Louis is living in Brooklyn with what's her name, Celia the Jewish girl." Married, my dear. A big diamond to prove it. So, I'm not a poet. So, I'm not a shiksa.

LORINE. And how is Paul?

CELIA. The same. Still not *your* son.

LORINE. I brought him a gift. A stuffed animal—the state animal of Wisconsin. *[She pulls out a stuffed animal.]*

CELIA. A rat?

LORINE. Badger.

CELIA. Perfect for you.

LORINE. New York's such a confusing place! I didn't even know it had a Brooklyn. I went on the IRT, and the BMT, and people were so nice. They let me sleep in the little subway bathroom. I felt at home—bedding down on the damp stone!

CELIA *(to JOHN)*. She's always like this. Hasn't changed in twenty years. Just gotten poorer and harder-looking.

BUNNY. Do they have moisturizer in—Wisconsin, is it?

LORINE. I scrub floors for a living, though once I was the richest girl in Fort Atkinson. And every year or so, Cid Corman or Jonathan Williams or someone equally blinded by boondocks Orientalism swoops into town and picks up my poems and prints twelve copies of them.

JOHN. Do you keep up with French writing at all?

LORINE. Horse, hello! I too live hot, before the final flash, cavort for other's gain. *[To CELIA.]* And how is our darling Paul? Can't wait to see him. I baked some muskies for Paul. They're safe in my basket under a garni of wood violets.

CELIA. She loved Louis as soon as she met him. George Oppen, a Communist spy, introduced them. And soon she was pregnant.

LORINE. The music, lady, you demand—the brass breaks my hand.

CELIA. And I married him, and she had to—Well, John dear, you know how these things go. She hightailed it back to the North Country and ever since, it's been, "Paul this and Paul that."

LORINE. He has blue eyes, Celia.

CELIA. Green, baby.

LORINE. Blue, Celia.

CELIA *(to JOHN and BUNNY)*. He has the loveliest green eyes—they aren't all flaked with brown and gray, you know—hazel—they're green, deep, pure green eyes—like mine.

JOHN. Your eyes are—brown, aren't they?

CELIA. Green! Well, in some lights they look brown—it must be this tenement smog, oh pooh! —but they're green. Not green like Paul's—more hazel. Louis has watery black eyes—like ink from an octopus.

BUNNY *(to LORINE)*. Do you think you could come visit my home ec class? I can't find a single pattern for what you're wearing.

LORINE. I don't know—so much depends on how long I'll be visiting with Louis and Celia.

JOHN. Drenched with irony.

LORINE. Beside the old crows.

BUNNY. Think I'll have a drink.

LORINE. Could you make me a thermos, Miss? I'm going to sleep in the bunk bed with my darling little nephew Paul. I'll take a pint of gin and some Miltown in with me. His precious little hands get no rest, unless aunt Lorine slops him down like a baby stallion, like Seabiscuit.

CELIA. Stop it, Lorine!

LORINE. The hell I will! You see, Louis didn't have much—push—he wasn't particularly—aggressive. In fact he was sort of a low key intellectual—like I. It took a woman like Celia to bring him to his knees. That's why he married her. That's okay. And then when Paul was born I—

CELIA. I don't want to hear his name in your mouth.

LORINE. Oh, c'mon, the Gospels are full of it—Paul this and Paul that, like a Roman fanzine. Well, I just sort of adopted him, that's all.

BUNNY. I don't even think there is a Paul! There's just a violin playing in an empty room.

CELIA. My son!

LORINE. If he were my son I'd take him bowling, feed him maple sugar, and wander into the woods to spot the galena glinting under the moss.

CELIA. His hands are like precious gifts, at night I wrap them in little wool gloves. Listen to that music!

[They listen but hear no music.]

CELIA. "Lower limit speech," Louis says. "Upper limit music."

BUNNY. And the soft white underbelly of silence.

LORINE. Shall I sleep on the stoop—with the milk bottles, Celia?

CELIA. Just plop yourself down any old place. You'll spend the sixties "ploppin', floppin' and moppin'."

LORINE. Please fill my thermos.

JOHN. Me too.

BUNNY. Listen, Celia, you seem like a giving sort, do you have any stuff?

CELIA. Check the little girls' room. I've been entertaining a friend of yours in my boudoir—says his name's Jeeper.

BUNNY. He's here! And you didn't tell me?

CELIA. It was dark in the room, and the bed was turned down. I thought it was Carl Rakosi. In the mirror over the bed a pile of liquid lava fell from his pockets.

BUNNY. John, come with me, I'm scared of the dark.

JOHN. I've always wanted to meet Rakosi—ask him about his French.

[Exit BUNNY and JOHN.]

LORINE. I'm tired, Celia, tired of fighting. I'd never got anywhere because I'd never had suction.

CELIA. Suction?

LORINE. You know: pull, favor, drag, well-oiled protection.

CELIA. But you always had Louis.

[Enter LOUIS.]

LOUIS. Has Ashbery gone yet—? Good. I'd like to SUM up his poeTRIES.

LORINE. Here's Louis now. Hello, Master. Here I am with your big gun.

LOUIS. Lorine! Wasn't expecting you.

LORINE. I heard the Oppens were coming tonight. So I wanted to be here. And little Paul,—having his Mar Bitzvah.

CELIA. His—oh never mind. There's probably never been a Jew in Wisconsin.

LOUIS. You've changed, Lorine.

CELIA. They don't have stores in Fort Atkinson, Louis. Or shops. People don't buy things, they barter. They have these little—places—and you bring in your dead badgers and swap em for sugar maples. Women like Lorine go in disguised as fertile squaws and hunt for husbands.

LORINE. I've got two—both of them big men. I do their letter writing for them.

LOUIS. Yes—the Oppens are coming! Remember, Lorine? When we were all young and full of ourselves, at the dawn of our lives, and we thought we'd re-write poetry, history, ideology. The five-foot shelf of books—remember the five-foot shelf?

CELIA. I *bet* you do!

LORINE. Then I went back home and gave my life to nothing.

LOUIS. And I married this one and went to work for her father at Brooklyn Polytech.

CELIA. He doesn't look like much, does he, but he's the greatest dancer.

LORINE. Where is little Paul? Tell him Aunt Lorine is here—with a toy badger and a basketful of kisses. I'll trade them all for a—basketful of hugs!

CELIA *(to LOUIS)*. The Oppens came, by the way.

LOUIS. They haven't gone, have they? That's just like George—sign the check with invisible ink and then, blammo, out the door!

CELIA. They're lurking. They won't say where they've been but I'd say Mexico.

LOUIS. For Christ's sake, Celia, where are they?

CELIA. In the hidden watch tower, where you keep your Social Credit pamphlets.

LOUIS. George! Mary! *[To CELIA.]* Was her name Mary?

CELIA and LORINE. Mary.

CELIA. Mary Magdalene.

LORINE. Mary—Picasso!

LOUIS. Come out, come out, wherever you are! —He's my best friend, Celia, and I haven't seen him in twenty years!

CELIA. That calls for a drink!

[Enter MARY.]

MARY. Hello everyone. George will be joining us shortly. You know he's writing again, and we had a few minutes, so he wrote some more poems about seeing, being and fleeing. I'll tell you, wait till the 60s arrive—everyone will be—

CELIA. Hoppin,' poppin,' and Oppen.

MARY. I could have been a poet too, you see! Instead I clung my life to George. *Someone* has to be supportive.

CELIA. What's that crack supposed to mean?

MARY. Did I refer to you? And I thought reference went out with Anglo-centrism!

CELIA. Not west of Chicago, apparently! And what's the big mystery, anyhow? If the FBI is after you, you're bringing Louis into danger.

MARY. Why? Let Louis speak for himself. If he wants us out, let him pipe up and say so. "Lower limit speech"—I'm sure he can muster that!

[Enter GEORGE.]

LOUIS. George Oppen! My oldest friend.

[The two embrace.]

Where've you been, huh, bro?

GEORGE. Haven't been anywhere.

LOUIS. Mexico, eh? What about those Mexican babes? I can't wait until they have a film industry! George Oppen! Look at you, you're looking good—25 years since you wrote a poem. And me—25 years of writing "A." Writing takes it from a man. But you wouldn't know about that.

CELIA. George is writing again, Louis.

GEORGE. It's good, Louis. Really good.

LOUIS *(laughs)*. Oh, and how good is that?

MARY and GEORGE. Really, really good.

LOUIS. Mexico, eh?

MARY. We haven't been in Mexico.

GEORGE. Who told you that?

LORINE. A little bird—the state bird of Wisconsin—the robin, or mourning dove.

MARY. Have the Fruit Barrel people been calling about us?

GEORGE. Our papers are all in order. I woke up one day with a poem in my head, and I had to write it down at the cantina. I mean, the Cantonese Restaurant. On Fourth Street. Next to Madame Blavatsky's…

CELIA. Next to…?

MARY. And now, three books later, the 60s are gonna be hoppin', poppin', and Oppen.

LOUIS. I've been teaching at Brooklyn Polytech.

MARY. How exciting! While we've been dodging gunfire and slinging apples from orchard to orchard all over the world.

LOUIS. Classics, mostly. Greek and Latin.

CELIA. Yeah, I've heard a lot of Latin tags over the years. So has Paul. He came up to me the other day, "Mama," says little Paul, "what's a hexameter?"

MARY. Still with the little Paul!

GEORGE. Oh, the delusions of the bourgeois mind.

LORINE. Sometimes I wake at night, in my shack, my arms creep together like the two halves of the Michigan Peninsula, reaching to embrace—the little son I never had. And in that empty space, I see the face—the baby face of Paul.

They don't have violins in Fort Atkinson. When they want to play music, they get out on their porches and bang on saws and metal lids, playing that twangy music from the Harry Smith anthology. Mournful, weird songs about love gone wrong—sheep and carcasses and who knows what. I lost a few teeth getting a little too close to the source of those heavenly sounds.

LOUIS. George, I want to ask you something.

GEORGE. Okay.

LOUIS. Something serious.

GEORGE. Fire away!

LOUIS. No, be serious, can't you?

MARY. He can be serious as all Hell—just ask Leon Trotsky. I mean—Liberace.

GEORGE. No, Louis, I've missed you, ask me anything.

LOUIS. It's about poetry.

MARY. He knows poetry, I want him to go on the "$64,000 Question" for Poetry. Except, of course, we don't need the money, let some working stiff have the money. I just think it would be good for his self-esteem—and for the Mexicans.

GEORGE. Why, Louis, I'm touched.

LOUIS. Don't be—

GEORGE. That you would come to me with a question about poetry. You, the greatest mind of our time, and the mind touched by genius in so many ways.

LOUIS. It's about my poetry, George.

GEORGE. Oh?

LOUIS. And yours, too.

GEORGE. I see.

CELIA. No, let's play Jewish Questions. I've got one for Mary. Who do you like better, Henny Youngman or Milton Berle?

MARY. Oh, I haven't been to the Catskills in years. I don't want to play.

LOUIS. It's about poetry, George—yours and mine.

MARY. And George doesn't want to play. Brooklyn's not for us. We're going to San Francisco to jump-start the third act in George's life. He's going to invent spoken-word—I've got the albums covers designed already and a guest spot on a local show—the Jack Spicer Hour. They're changing the words of the song for him. "Oppen up your Golden Gate—California, here we come!"

LOUIS *(to GEORGE)*. Whose is better?

GEORGE. Whose—?

LOUIS. Whose poetry is better? That's the question.

[Pause.]

GEORGE. Mine is. I like mine better.

CELIA. —Uh-oh!

GEORGE *(bewildered)*. Well, of course I'd have to say mine. What self-respecting man wouldn't? I couldn't look myself in the mirror in the morning when I shave if I didn't—like my poetry better than yours.

MARY. You did the right thing, George.

CELIA. Like I tell little Paul, don't stick your wet finger in the socket, even though people say it's the right thing to do.

LORINE. Little Paul must be 20 by now—my handsome little man.

CELIA. I think he's ten or so.

LORINE. But he was born in 1938—

CELIA. That's what you think.

GEORGE. Louis? Say something!

CELIA. He's not going to talk, George.

MARY. What a baby.

CELIA. No, you've just hit him where he lives—in poetry. He may traipse around like a praying mantis, but he's got the exoskeleton of a wittle koawa bear.

LOUIS. Mary?

MARY. Yes, baby?

LOUIS. Mary, I'm afraid I'm feeling awfully tired. One more drink then it's time to go to bed. Did you bring someone in with you? Tell him, her or it to vacate the premises. And please—please—don't mention our son again. I feel a shuddering shape, a shadow of darkness, somewhere in this room.

GEORGE. Louis, please speak to me.

[Enter BUNNY.]

LOUIS. A row of fiddles, playing Bach . . .

BUNNY. And they never spoke again.

LOUIS. When I was sixteen, and going to prep school, during the Punic wars, a bunch of us used to go into New York in the first day of vacations, and in the evening we used to go to this gin mill owned by the gangster-father of one of us, drink with the grown-ups, and listen to the jazz.

BUNNY. Louis Zukofsky died in 1978.

LOUIS. There was this boy who was fifteen, and he had killed his mother with a shotgun, and he went with us, this boy, and we ordered our drinks, and he said, "I'll have bergin and water." Well, we all laughed. He was blond and he had the face of a cherub, and his cheeks went red, and soon everyone was laughing, including the boy who had shot his mother. That night we drank free and ooh, boy, the hangover the next day—

BUNNY. George Oppen died in 1984.

LOUIS. Each of us with a grown up hangover, but the grandest day of my youth.

CELIA. What happened to the boy? The boy who had shot his mother?

GEORGE. The following summer, on a country road, with his learner's permit in his pocket, and his father on the front seat to his right, he swerved the cart, to avoid a porcupine, and drove straight into a large tree.

BUNNY. Mary Oppen died six years after her husband, in 1990.

LORINE. He was not killed. They told him his father was dead, he began to laugh. And then they plunged a needle into his arm to stop him from laughing. He was put in an asylum. That was thirty years ago.

BUNNY. Lorine Niedecker died in 1978.

CELIA. Is the boy still in the madhouse?

LOUIS. Oh yes. And I'm told that for these thirty years he has—not—uttered—one sound.

BUNNY. Celia died in 1980. I died a few months after the events of this play. But people still remember me, the woman who invented Poets Theater, in Cambridge, Massachusetts, after the War, when everything wore two faces. Only John Ashbery remains alive.

[Enter JOHN.]

BUNNY. I never did catch up with Jeeper, nor did I even meet Carl Rakosi. It was all a ruse of Celia's—a poignant addition to the fantasies of her cult de moi. And, yes, another element to add to the legend that is the American Obejctivists. (Though how she knew his name was Jeeper, I'll never know.) We're all still waiting for a place, a time, when poetry means everything to people.

[Pause.}

JOHN. Oh! The silence when everyone stops talking, all at once! In France they call it, "the little hour of Jerry Lewis." Wake up! Let's go see Bava's final masterpiece, *Red High Heels of Death!*

[END.]

First performed at Small Press Traffic (San Francisco) 11 November 2001 by the following cast.

Louis Zukofsky, a poet and high school teacher	Scott *Hewicker*
Celia, his wife	Clifford *Hengst*
John, a fellow teacher	Rex *Ray*
Bunny, his girlfriend	Margaret *Crane*
George Oppen, a face from the past	Wayne *Smith*
Mary, his wife	Suzanne *Stein*
Lorine Niedecker, poet, genius, hayseed, former girlfriend of Louis	Jocelyn *Saidenberg*

New Narrative Essays
A panel discussion at the Trans-Genre:
Poetry and the Inter-Arts event
University of California, Santa Cruz, Porter College: April 2003

FROM A LONG NOTE ON NEW NARRATIVE

ROBERT GLÜCK

TO TALK about the beginnings of New Narrative, I have to talk about my friendship with Bruce Boone. We met in the early seventies through the San Francisco Art Institute's bulletin board: Ed and I wanted to move and Bruce and Burton wanted to move—would we all be happy living together? For some reason both couples dropped the idea and remained in our respective flats for many years. But Bruce and I were poets and our obsession with Frank O'Hara forged a bond.

I was twenty-three or twenty-four. Bruce was seven years older. He was a wonderful teacher. He read to transform himself and to attain a correct understanding. Such understanding was urgently political.

Bruce had his eye on the catastrophic future, an upheaval he predicted with a certain grandeur, but it was my own present he helped me find. I read and wrote to invoke what seemed impossible—relation itself—in order to take part in a world that ceaselessly makes itself—up, to "wake up" to the world, to recognize the world, to be convinced that the world exists, to take revenge on the world for not existing.

To talk about New Narrative, I also have to talk about Language Poetry, which was in its heroic period in the seventies. I treat diverse poets as one unit, a sort of flying wedge, because that's how we experienced them. It would be hard to overestimate the drama they brought to a Bay Area scene that limped through the seventies, with the powerful exception of feminist poets like Judy Grahn, and the excitement generated by movement poetry. Language Poetry's Puritan rigor, delight in technical vocabularies, and professionalism were new to a generation of Bay Area poets whose influences included the Beats, Robert Duncan and Jack Spicer, the New York School (Bolinas was its western outpost), surrealism and psychedelic surrealism.

Suddenly people took sides, though at times these confrontations resembled a pastiche of the embattled positions of earlier avant-guards. Language Poetry seemed very "straight male"—though what didn't? Barrett Watten's *Total Syntax*, for example, brilliantly established (as it dispatched) a lineage of fathers: Olson, Zukofsky, Pound, etc.

If I could have become a Language poet I would have; I craved the formalist fireworks, a purity that invented its own tenets. On the snowy mountain-top of progressive formalism, from the highest high road of modernist achievement, there was plenty of contempt heaped on less rigorous endeavor. I had come to a dead end in the mid-seventies like the poetry scene itself. The problem was not theoretical— or it was: I could not go on until I figured out some way to understand where I was. I also craved the community the Language Poets made for themselves.

The questions vexing Bruce and me and the kind of rigor we needed were only partly addressed by Language Poetry which, in the most general sense, we saw as an aesthetics built on an examination (by subtraction: of voice, of continuity) of the ways language generates meaning. The same could be said of other experimental work, especially the minimalisms, but Language Poetry was our proximate example.

Warring camps drew battle lines between representation and non-representation—retrospection makes the argument seem as arbitrary as Fancy vs. Imagination. But certainly the "logic of history" at that moment supported the idea of this division, along with the struggle to find a third position that would encompass the whole argument.

I experienced the poetry of disjunction as a luxurious idealism in which the speaking subject rejects the confines of representation and disappears in the largest freedom, that of language itself. My attraction to this freedom and to the professionalism with which it was purveyed made for a kind of class struggle within myself. Whole areas of my experience, especially gay experience, were not admitted to this utopia, partly because the mainstream reflected a resoundingly coherent image of myself back to me—an image so unjust that it amounted to a tyranny that I could not turn my back on. We had been disastrously described by the mainstream—a naming whose most extreme (though not uncommon) expression was physical violence. Political agency involved at least a provisionally stable identity.

(I wonder if it has been understood the extent to which the whole body of Language Poetry is collage, pastiche, and the poetry of the "already said." That phrases, sentences, ring with a feeling of déjà vu, like the work of Raymond Roussel. That is my profoundest relation to that group. They forefront the arbitrariness of language, they deepen the sense of the arbitrary, because they hollow out language through a multiplication of contexts. That creates the feeling of déjà vu. I am made aware almost intolerably of the infinite valences.)

Meanwhile, gay identity was also in its heroic period—it had not yet settled into just another nationalism and it was new enough to know its own constructedness. In the urban mix, some great experiment was actually taking place, a genuine community where strangers and different classes and ethnicities rubbed more than shoulders. This community was not destroyed by commodity culture, which was destroying so many other communities; instead, it was founded in commodity culture. We had to talk about it. Bruce and I turned to each other to see if we could come up with a better representation—not in order to satisfy movement pieties or to be political, but in order to be. We (eventually we were gay, lesbian, and working class writers) could not let narration go.

Since I'm confined to hindsight, I write as though Bruce and I were following a plan instead of stumbling and groping toward a writing that could join other literatures of the present. We could have found narrative models in, say, Clark Coolidge's prose, so perhaps narrative practice relates outward to the actual community whose story is being told. We could have located self-reference and awareness of artifice in, say, the novels of Ronald Firbank, but we didn't. So again, our use of language that knows itself relates outward to a community speaking to itself dissonantly.

We were fellow travelers of Language Poetry and the innovative feminist poetry of that time, but our lives and reading led us toward a hybrid aesthetic, something impure. We (say, Bruce Boone, Camille Roy, Kevin Killian, Dodie Bellamy, Mike Amnasan, myself and, to include the dead, Steve Abbott and Sam D'Allesandro) are still fellow travelers of the poetries that evolved since the early eighties, when writers talked about "nonnarrative." One could untangle that knot forever, or build an aesthetics on the ways language conveys silence, chaos, undifferentiated existence, and erects countless horizons of meaning.

How to be a theory-based writer?—one question. How to represent my experience as a gay man?—another question just as pressing. These questions led to readers and communities almost completely ignorant of each other. Too fragmented for a gay audience? Too much sex and "voice" for a literary audience? I embodied these incommensurates so I had to ask this question: How can I convey urgent social meanings while opening or subverting the possibilities of meaning itself? That question has deviled and vexed Bay Area writing for twenty-five years. What kind of representation least deforms its subject? Can language be aware of itself (as object, as system, as commodity, as abstraction) yet take part in the forces that generate the present? Where in writing does engagement become authentic? One response, the politics of form, apparently does not answer the question completely.

[...]

In using the tag New Narrative, I concede there is such a thing. In the past I was reluctant to promote a literary school that endured even ten minutes, much less a few years. Bruce and I took the notion of a "school" half seriously, and once New Narrative began to resemble a program, we abandoned it, declining to recognize ourselves in the tyrants and functionaries that make a literary school. Or was it just a failure of nerve? Still, I would observe that my writing continues to develop a New Narrative aesthetic--the problems and contradictions outlined above--and I wonder if that is not true of my New Narrative confederates. Now I am glad to see the term being used by a critical community exemplified by the anthology, *Biting the Error*, younger writers in San Francisco and New York, and writers in other cities, like Gail Scott in Montreal, and critics like Earl Jackson, Jr., Antony Easthope, Carolyn Dinshaw, and Dianne Chisholm. Bruce and I may have been kidding about founding a school, but we were serious about wanting to bring emotion and subject matter into the field of innovative writing. I hope that these thoughts on our project—call it what you will—are useful to those looking for ways to extending the possibilities of poem and story without backtracking into the mainstream, or into 19th-century transparency.

I LOVE cheap Chinese restaurants, places whose stark white walls and overhead fluorescents drive away hipsters. My latest favorite is Home Menu, on Mission Street, which has excellent mixed vegetables and tofu. Here among the poor and the working class, and the occasional retro-punk couple, I can sit by myself at a table for four, sip scalding tea from a plastic water glass, write in my journal, and nobody pays any attention to anybody else. The window box beside my table is filled with orchids, gracefully bending stalks of magenta, yellow, and white. Having killed every orchid ever given to me, I'm impressed by some unknown somebody's green thumb. I lean over and touch a flower. The petal is waxy and stiff. Plastic. My gullibility embarrasses me. I look up at the fish by the door, goldfish and angelfish the size of my hands slither about in a tank whose water is so tinged with algae it looks like green smog. I'm sure the fish are real, though the delicate water fern they're slithering around, that's up for grabs. I write in my diary, "artifice and big fish in a small pond: this place reminds me of the poetry scene." You are so clever I think, and I smile. On a ledge beside the Coke machine sits a porcelain statue of Quan Yin, the goddess of compassion. From her head radiates a halo of tiny

flashing green and red lights. Very Vegas. Quan Yin says to me, "Be kind in this essay. Don't spend all your time complaining and whining about your injustices." "Okay, okay," I say to Quan Yin as I get up to use the restroom. When my urine mingles with the toilet water it turns lime green. Artifice I whisper to myself. Small pond.

I moved to San Francisco for no good reason. I was such an ingenue in the early 80s, imagining myself as a sort of female Kerouac, penning great poems in coffeehouses, having deep conversations with likeminded spirits who would declare me a genius, fucking lots of cute writers who would spout Yeats as we lay tangled in wine-spattered sheets listening to fog horns and gazing at the Golden Gate Bridge from the picture window beside our bed. As soon as I met real poets, my fantasy crumbled. I was not adored. I did not find a freespirited lifestyle, but determined professionalism. Language Poetry had gained institutional control of many venues—the Poetry Center, Intersection, Langton—and poetry readings were no longer poetry readings, but "literary events." Theoretical chops and nonlinearity were de rigueur. Many a misguided wannabe came a cropper by refurbishing their nature poems, confessional poems, drug poems with references to Derrida or Deleuze and Guatarri. Some of them cut all verbs from their lyric poetry—others wiped out pronouns—or switched person, from first to third to first, erratically, spastically. I remember one event where a woman read nothing but collages of words drawn from seed catalogues. "Hyacinth." Pause. "Pistila." Pause. "Floribundas." After a half an hour of this I felt like the room was filling up with petals, toxic petals were pushing out all the air, suffocating me. I could sense an awkwardness and alienation sweeping through many different factions of the poetry scene, akin to mass hysteria, but stilted. The queers writing "new narrative" held their own, breaking open narrative conventions, but never throwing out the pieces. And, more importantly for me, they worshipped sex. Theirs was a brave position in those days. Narrative, let alone sex, was seen as reactionary, highly suspect—but if we could gussy it up with enough theory and fragmentation, we too might get invited to read at those thrillingly exclusive literary events.

Like the goldfish and angelfish in Home Menu's tank, the Language Poets and the queer narrative writers, despite their obvious differences, slithered beside one another in the same self-contained world that took itself deathly seriously.

Over the past 20 years, narrative has become, not only acceptable, but almost trendy in the fishbowl of experimental poetry—and I've found personal acceptance among a community of like-minded fish both locally and beyond. Through them I've gained confidence in my writing. I play around a lot formally, but accessibility has always been important to me. I've worked hard to create a user-friendly experimentalism, with lots of narrative candy and humor, a sort of avant-garde lite. I'm good at demystifying elitist intellectual concepts—I could explain Lacan to gradeschoolers. Teaching seemed like a natural for me. I didn't have an MFA, didn't go to Brown or Iowa, didn't even know how to pull together a syllabus, but puffed up with self importance, I decided to enter the academy—a move that I imagined not into the mainstream, but more of a leap from fishbowl to aquarium—bigger sure, but still cozy, accepting. Since the mid-90s I've taught part-time in a handful of schools and applied for perhaps a dozen tenure track jobs. At first it was great. I found my interactions with students meaningful, and the ingenue part of me felt she was making a difference, giving back. I was doing good work, getting positive evaluations, I'd found my niche, and things would get better and better, everybody would love me, want me, rush in to hire me. But then I realized, with a shock, that powerful people in departments I was teaching in or applying for work in didn't see me as sweet open-minded Dodie, but as a dangerous pervert, more for my formal weirdness than anything to do with content. How do I know this? The way anybody finds out anything in the hush hush rarefied realm of academia—through "promise you won't breathe a word" whispers from friends on hiring committees. Perhaps even more alarming is how I've seen students in graduate writing programs whose work doesn't fit the parameters of traditional genres treated as criminal.

I borrow the trope of "crime" from Joan Retallack, who gave a talk at Naropa summer 2002 called "Writers—Readers—Performers: Partners in Crime." Though her talk focuses on John Cage-inspired procedures for introducing chance into art and writing practices, Retallack begins by addressing genre policing:

> We intuitively know that everyday life doesn't conform to the simple outlines of well-made genres. In fact any event (and I include the acts of writing-reading, performing on or off the page in this active category) is surprising largely to the degree that it transgresses its own generic expectations. When it really does this, going beyond the calculated surprises of an artful plot, or screamingly censurable subject matter, it's instantly recognized as a crime by those who police aesthetic expectations.

Retallack talks at length about how surprise—both in and outside of art—delights us. It keeps things interesting, makes us feel engaged, alive. I'm reminded of a Twilight Zone episode I saw as a child. This guy dies, and now that he's dead, every wish he has is granted. He can have anything he desires—fancy cars, women—and the women do whatever he wants them to do, down to the letter. It's like paradise, he's in charge of every relationship, no questions asked, no struggle. He's a gambler—so he places bet after bet, and every bet wins. But what's the fun of gambling, he soon realizes, if you always win? Boredom hits big time and he longs for someone, anything he can't control. And then he discovers that he hasn't died and gone to heaven like he thought. No, it's just the opposite—he's been condemned to hell! Hell is an eternity of no surprises. "Traditionalists," as Retallack calls them, obviously haven't seen this episode of the Twilight Zone. In our messy, complex world, traditionalists long for continuity, coherency, "for harmony, for smooth transitions, for the grand, clean sweep of self-assured narration, for the life that is the well-made story that is true to the life." By aligning itself with "multiplicity, mongrelism, collisions of perception, intention, desire," the avant-garde disrupts these longings for order, and frightened traditionalists turn nasty. From my own experience in various creative writing departments, what Retallack calls a "constituent need to erase difficulty" is expressed in strange ways by hiring committees and in department meetings. One shaken department head told me how when he suggested hiring an experimental fiction writer (a.k.a. Dodie), a more conservative colleague launched into an obscenity-filled tirade. "Everyone was shocked," he confided. "It's just not proper to use those words in a departmental meeting." This sort of passionate frenzy suggests an origin that is not rational—or even conscious, a rage that can only come from some deep Freudian cesspool of terror. But what's so scary about a bit of babble spicing up a narrative? My theory is that genre policing comes out of a panic over identity and ambiguity. God damn it, we want to know which orchid is plastic, which orchid is real, and we want to tell the difference between orchids and people and human urine and lime green disinfectant. Imagine Julia Kristeva in front of a hiring committee. Before the abjection of a blurred genre the traditionalist feels faint. As when death infects life, when poetry infects fiction, identity, system, order is disturbed. The text stretches out before us, spasming and bleeding.

For my experimental writing workshop at CalArts, one student, complaining about all the theory we're reading, wrote in his class journal, "I just saw Ben Marcus read last week, and people attempted to ask him about his theory in his writing. He put his hands in his pockets and said, 'I just try to get the story out and then figure out what it's about.'" I scribbled in the margin, "Sounds good—but I don't believe him." As we learned from Foucault, invisible assumptions are the most insidious:

> Order is, at one and the same time, that which is given in things as their inner law, the hidden network that determines the way they confront one another, and also that which has no existence except in the grid created by a glance, an examination, a language; and it is only in the blank spaces of this grid that order manifests itself in depth as though already there, waiting in silence for the moment of its expression.

The "fundamental codes of a culture" govern language, perception, exchanges, values and hierarchies. These categories are so ingrained they seem transparent, inherent. Thus whiteness is not a race, but the neutral ground against which all others are judged. Students are taught that it is natural that novels have a narrative arc, that all description must support that narrative, that characters are consistent and yet must change somehow by the end. And characters must always, always have something at stake. Genres are inherently distinct and each shapes itself around the appropriate subject matter. Thus it is natural that fiction is fictional, i.e., made up; that creative nonfiction is factual (although it is allowed a little bit of leeway, the way Hollywood starlets are expected to lie about their age); that poetry builds to an epiphany. And all these forms have a sort of generic Teflon that protects them from overt sexual content. Sex—if it belongs anywhere—is outcast to the degraded arenas of trash novels and porn. It's natural for all novels, trashy or great, to follow the three act structure of screenplays. The three act structure has been integral to stories all the way back to the Greeks. Act I—Set Up. Establish characters, place, and premise. Act II—Confrontation. Characters struggle towards their goal. Act III—Resolution. When I told this to Kevin Killian and Drew Cushing they argued with me, "No, it's five acts, like in Shakespeare." "No," I huffed, "it's three acts, as in *Jaws*. You two are so old school."

Anthropologist Mary Douglas defines the unclean as "matter out of place . . . that which must not be included if a pattern is to be maintained." In her book *Purity and Danger* Douglas examines the various strategies cultures have for dealing with categorical anomalies. When confronted with a specimen that bridges two categories, a culture will often interpret it as one category or the other. Douglas gives the example of monstrous births, which threaten the line between human and animals. In one culture, monstrous births are labeled as baby hippopotamuses, and order is restored. New Narrative threatens the line between theory, fiction, and autobiography. This confusion is reduced in some English Departments by simply calling it poetry. Another strategy for dealing with anomaly is to physically control it, such as killing twins at birth. Obviously, it's not practical to kill experimental writers, but they can be vetoed on hiring committees. Similarly, students who write autobiographical fiction are ousted from fiction classes and into creative nonfiction classes. It's hammered into fiction students that first person narration is weird, fringy. A close third person point of view is preferable to first person, but an omniscient third should be everybody's goal. One should never tell anything, but show show show. All stories should have a subplot and some sort of triangle. This is imperative. Even if there are only two characters a triangulist will claim the conflict is about Mary, Joe, and Mary's better self. If there's only one character in a story, the triangulist will find conflict in the relations of Mary, herself, and society. The goal of most MFA programs is to turn out students well groomed and disciplined as dogs from a dog training school. The anomalous is often labeled as dangerous. Should an experimental writer sneak into a department, she can be accused of corrupting the students, and a Holy War can be waged against her. By avoiding the anomalous specimen, a group thereby affirms and strengthens the definitions to which it does not conform. Leviticus abhors crawling things—therefore noncrawling things are approved of. One MFA student I know who's writing in non-narrative paragraphs was told to either give it a recognizable narrative or give it line-breaks. Thus it was affirmed that paragraphs must have narrative, and that nonnarrative text must have line breaks. Over and over I've seen students criticized for using the present tense. They don't have a clue any more than I do why the present tense should be avoided, why it's necessary to affirm that fiction takes place in the past. The rules go on and on. Dialogue should never move the plot forward, dialogue should always be about something other than what the characters are talking about, never begin a story with a quotation. Every story has a top story and a bottom story. In an illustrated children's book about monkeys escaping from a zoo, the bottom story is the placement of the bananas as they shift from frame to frame. The real meaning lies in the bottom story—not with the monkeys but in the bananas. Writing is serious business. Writing is a science with precise protocols to follow.

I sit in Dolores Park Cafe trying to plow through the stack of CalArts course journals. The journals are intense, emotional, and I feel I have to honor that by adding lots of little comments. It's taking me forever. One student writes, "In writing there is freedom. The only place to be truly free. An epiphany. Writing is perfect freedom." My heart goes out to her. I hope she still feels that way 10 years from now. I truly do. I wish there was something I could do to assure she feels that way in 10 years. I'm reminded of a comment I recently wrote to a precariously talented woman in another program. "Please, please do not let graduate school wipe out your instincts, which are really strong." I get this image from an ancient TV documentary of little animals that hatch on the beach—what were they, baby turtles? Crabs? (Details have always been a problem for me, as I tend to abstract things to the point of incommunicability.) So there's thousands of whatever, little things, hatching on the shore and then there's their race to the ocean as an army of predatory birds swoop down and pick them off one by one. Gulp gulp gulp. Only a tiny percentage of the babies will make it to the water. It's horrifying. In the classroom I sometimes feel less like a teacher and more like Dr. Van Helsing, fighting for the students' souls. Of course there's that nagging fear that I myself am not pure, that all teaching is unclean, that I probably have fucked up some of them with my stupid comments, like it's inevitable. I remember working with this one guy whose writing was a mess. Whenever I read one of his stories I felt like I was in the middle of a Fellini movie, nothing was ever prepared for, characters appeared out of nowhere and did the most bizarre things. It was really hard to tell where you were in time or space, what was dream, what was supposed to be "reality." I loved this Fellini tendency of his and believed if he pushed it, his work could have been amazing. But what service would I have done him to push him further into Fellini when it was clear he was trying to do Spielberg? I guess my point is that pushy experimentalists can do just as much damage as "traditionalists." A few summers ago a student came to me in tears because another teacher had told her she had no interest in reading her (the student's) work because it wasn't postmodern enough. Since then I've avoided the label "postmodern" like the plague. It's a stupid word, don't you think?

Confusion sparks through my brain like Quan Yin's electrified halo. Quan Yin started out as male, then sometime between the 8th and 11th centuries, she switched to female. There are lots of theories about how and why this happened, but nobody really knows. I think it's fitting that the goddess of compassion has a bit of the freak about her. As the Kinks sang in "Lola," "Girls will be boys and boys will be girls. It's a mixed up muddled up shook up world." 1970. I remember my girlfriend Janis, stoned out of her mind, in her faded apricot corduroy pants, cigarette in hand, mouthing these words as she danced in front of the juke box at Fred's Pizza, where she waitessed. Fred, with his pot belly and red face, was always trying to get her into his truck and kiss her. "Fred," she'd laugh, "you're barking up the wrong tree." She did kiss some guys, sometimes we'd fuck one or two of them in the same room. Still we considered ourselves monogamous. Everything in "Lola" is off-kilter, between categories, indefinable, a world "where you drink champagne and it tastes just like cherry cola. C-O-L-A. Cola." "Lola" was our anthem, two baby dykes in the middle of nowhere in Indiana, barely post-Stonewall. Wherever we looked, nothing reflected us, defined us. We had to make it up on the fly. Our relationship was a torrent of high anxiety and instability. We were always looking for some structure—such as monogamy—to corral our incredible freedom, to impose a specter of normality. If we could only figure out what normality was. Writing for me has always been a way to worm my way back into that freedom, that incendiary in-between state, to court anxiety, instability, glorious fuckedupness.

The semester I taught at CalArts I stayed with friends in Topanga. One evening I was hanging out in their kitchen, sharing a couple of bottles of wine, and Lamar and Jim were entertaining me with stories of all the people they knew who knew Charles Manson. (Manson lived in Topanga in the late 60s.) Lamar prompts Jim to tell me about the sister of his former business partner. Jim says, "Oh yeah, well my partner's sister invited the entire Manson family to her home." Jim spreads his arms and looks from side to side to emphasize that there are a lot of them. "So they're all sitting there, and Angela Lansbury walks in and takes one look at them and says, 'You're out of here.'" "What does Angela Lansbury," I scream, "have to do with this story?" Jim pauses, then says, "Angela Lansbury was my partner's mother." He looks at me perplexed, as if anybody would know that. I love this anecdote, the way it starts out as a friend of a friend tale and morphs into pure tabloid. ANGELA LANSBURY IN MANSON LOVE NEST. If he submitted this story to a writing workshop, Jim would be told to set up Angela Lansbury. I'd probably tell him that myself. Remember, first you establish characters, place and premise—then you push them into confrontation. Characters can't just can't pop up out of the shadows, out of like nowhere. But this predictable intervention would be wrong. It's Lansbury's disjunction, her rupturing of the narrative that gives it energy, that brings the delight of surprise that Joan Retallack talked about at Naropa all those summers ago. It was the week of Kevin's and my wedding anniversary—Anne Waldman appears saying this is Naropa's first wedding anniversary. We're in a hotel bar, the Boulderado, and Anne buys us a bottle of champagne. Bubbles all around.

I've been reading *Andy Warhol's Blow Job*, Roy Grundmann's book-length analysis of Warhol's 36 minute film in which a stationary camera remains focused on the head of a man who is presumably getting a blow job. Grundmann asserts that blow jobs are popular in movies because so much can be implied, left unseen. "The partner who moves down the anatomy invariably exits the frame—the realm of what is deemed representable—without disturbing the viewer's connectedness to the overall act." In the prim salaciousness of filmed blow jobs, that which is deemed not representable calls the shots. It's a tangible invisibility, the antithesis of out of sight, out of mind. While the cathartic power of the unseen is certainly rich, exhilarating even, my goal as a teacher and as a writer is to pull back the camera, widen the frame, and thus expand "the realm of what is deemed representable." Or at least make people aware of the politics of representation—that what's seen, what's hidden is not neutral or natural—that each time we sit down to write, even the silliest bit of fluff, we are making choices, important choices, about how the world is organized/ranked/diced to smithereens. Every time we sit down to write we are voting on what's permissible—and what isn't.

I'm reminded of the fable of the blind men and the elephant. One blind man feels the elephant's leg and says the elephant is like a tree. Another blind man feels the elephant's trunk and says the elephant is like a snake. Another blind man feels the elephant's ear and says the elephant is like an angelfish. Yes, I've brought back the fish so I can wrap up this essay, neatly, like a package, that I, Dodie, hand to you, the reader. Goldfish/angelfish. Poetry/prose. Even experimental poets enforce the division. Where do I fit in? A couple winters ago I was in Maine, and Steve Evans asked me if I had written any poetry, and I said that my book *Cunt-Ups* won the 2002 Firecracker Award for poetry. Steve replied, "I thought in that book you were writing outside of genre." The word "outside," when applied to me, always hurts my feelings, but let's climb out of my complexes. To not just blur genres, but to write totally outside of them—it sounds like a wonderful utopia—but is it possible? What kind of marginality is that, free-floating outside the social order like David Bowie's Major Tom? Doesn't genre infect everything we write—or think? Back in the mid-80s when I left poetry for prose, it wasn't a gradual transition, but a dramatic gesture—like all my gestures back then. I would tell people I had abandoned poetry. "No more poetry!" I declared, and I meant it. I remember Bob Glück—my teacher—once saying to me that *The Letters of Mina Harker* wasn't so much a novel as a book of lyric poetry. Yeah, sure Bob, I thought. But perhaps he's right. Perhaps New Narrative—for some of us, at least—was really about poetry—a ruse, a spin-doctoring to pull off what was verboten in the San Francisco scene—narrative poetry. After teaching creative writing for a decade, one thing I know for sure—a fiction writer I ain't. The shredded enjambments I learned to perform in San Francisco have so little in common with what's taught to fiction students, I might as well be writing on a different planet. While pondering this I stumble upon Ron Silliman's blog. Like a prophet from another dimension, Ron appears on my computer screen, professing to love categories. "You can't discuss something," Ron writes, "until you have a noun around which to put some language." I read this and huff, these guys, they've always got to pin things down, to label them, lock them in neat little boxes beneath nonreflective glass. But then Ron goes on to talk about places of categorical slippages. "Thingee, widget, doodad, whachamacallit—there are more than a few great synonyms for those intermediate phenomena in our lives that are not quite this, not quite that." That line nudges me out of whining mode and makes me smile. Dear Ron—thank you, thank you for giving me a handle—keep up the good work—XOX—your fan, Dodie.

Imagine yourself on an academic hiring committee, imagine yourself one of those frightened, pinched creatures desperately clinging to order, you can feel the chaos right outside the windows, pressing in. You sit there, hunched over the brown laminate conference table and you're presented with a choice—a widget or a Stegner. The glass starts to creak as the chaos pushes in, closer. The Stegner—you know what he'll do, nothing's unpredictable about him—he has an MFA from Columbia, a glowing recommendation from Tobias Wolfe—during his campus visit he asked you enthusiastic, engaged questions about every book you've ever published, including that rare stapled chapbook published in Dubuque back in 1976, which he's sure will be a collector's item, some day—the Stegner will help you beat back the chaos, which is now banging against the windows BOOM BOOM BOOM! And then there's the widget, whose "novel" you could only get through 10 pages of, you couldn't understand a word of it but nevertheless found yourself, strangely, physically aroused—the widget, this messy libidinous loose cannon, god knows what she might do, something crazy, like throw open the window—you have a vision of swirling psychedelic apocalyptic smoke rushing in and your heart races, sweat pours from your brow in streams, you clench your desiccated tenured hand into a fist and hurl it at the table. "No widgets," you snarl. "Never!"

Works Cited

Douglas, Mary. *Purity and Danger: An Analysis of the Concepts of Pollution and Taboo.* 1966. London: Routledge, 1991.

Foucault, Michel. *The Order of Things: An Archeology of the Human Sciences.* New York: Vintage Books, 1973.

Grundmann, Roy. *Andy Warhol's Blow Job.* Philadelphia: Temple University Press, 2003.

Retallack, Joan. "Writers—Readers—Performers: Partners in Crime." Unpublished essay, 2002.

Silliman, Ron. Silliman's Blog. 29 March 2004 <http://ronsilliman.blogspot.com/>.

WHEN you're young the last thing in the world you want to be is different, and the horrid thing is that to be different is also the only thing you really, really want. That's why I became a writer, I suppose, to escape that dichotomy. Another way to escape it is to just let yourself grow a little older, where eventually you reach a stage in which dichotomy retracts its claws a bit. You start to wonder, do I really want to be different, do I really want to fit in, are these apparently incompatible desires really but two versions of the same need?

In the face of US global incursion and the crisis of the resurgent empire our problems with writing and performance don't amount to a hill of beans, and yet, the impulse to express oneself can never be totally quenched. When I was a boy there was a TV series about a beautiful woman whose problems with her husband and neighbors were every week overshadowed by her battle with a strong-willed, Lesbian mother who kept trying to invade the heroine's space. Cleverly the creators of *Bewitched* had made the show into a conflict not only between generations but between sexualities, the gay older woman, the straight ingenue. Not an ingenue exactly because she had married not one, but two gay men, in a row. Whenever Samantha felt like it, when she needed or wanted something done, she could twitch her nose and alter all her circumstances, changing her house dress into a Paris gown, making a bluebird big as an eagle, whatever. We, the audience, knew that she had promised her husband she would not use the powers she had inherited from her mother, and yet, every week she did so, usually based on the mother's tempting her to give in, thus it could be read that Mother was encouraging daughter to do the Lesbian thing, which would then be read as a kind of superhuman power desire that wiped away mere human effort and frailty to uncover the ultimate acuity of what a nose can do when trained. What made the show different, well, one of the things that made it different, was its focus on her nose, and its twitch, so you could short-hand the whole show by showing a close-up of the nose, and most of the drama was a) seeing how much Elizabeth Montgomery could stand before she employed the twitch, and b) what merriment or agony would ensue for everyone around her. Thus when it came time to think about performance and poetry, I had had years to theorize that the important thing was the insertion of the body into poetry, the body, the contested site, and I imagine that Camille Roy, who turned to the Poets Theater at the same time I did, might have been motivated by similar events.

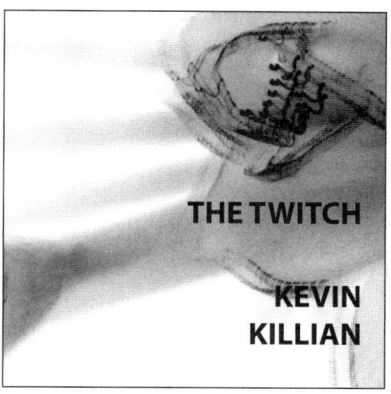

THE TWITCH
KEVIN KILLIAN

Already the practice of New Narrative had directed its focus to the body and its embarrassments, and how they sometimes detracted from one's engagement with the social and political, at other times determined such an engagement. Already we had formed a kind of gang, or the facsimile of one, thus taking on the social by becoming social, as though you might put on a coat or costume and become (whatever it was you were portraying). The next step, or so I thought, was to enact this drama out on stage, we had seen what a poet can do with a single mike and a single sheaf of paper, now we would ask them to subsume, in turn, their wills (that is, their actual bodies), to the sometimes mad demands of a single mind. Kind of like the Army. And in my own case, over the years I've tried to expand that singleness by constant collaboration, that is, we wouldn't be reading one text but two or possibly more, and we wouldn't be writing them either. A kind of participatory democracy—the exact relationship between reader and writer that all this blood had been spilled to achieve.

But, you know, you can say something is X or Y and it doesn't make it so. We who had participated in creating a new gay literature, for example, soon found ourselves tearing our hair out when the results came in. So that, for example, the biggest best-sellers at any gay bookstore are always memoirs by people who used to be something reprehensible, like an FBI agent, an umpire, a real estate salesman, or Rosie O'Donnell and then they come out and cash in. These people are truly able to have their cake and then eat it too. Meanwhile the rest of us console ourselves by thinking, oh, but ours are the books that will stand the test of time, but how comforting is that? Especially when the books in question are all out of print. And meanwhile we take on the struggle of trying to make sure that the books of our fallen comrades remain in print too—you know, like, Marines don't leave Rangers behind as they say in the desert. Thus the ongoing struggle to make sure that the work of Sam D'Allesandro, Bob Flanagan, Kathy Acker, Steve Abbott, David Wojnarowicz is literally visible, readable. I was going then to illustrate the difficulties of reading New Narrative but I think my time is about up.

Except I wanted to link the "twitch" of Elizabeth Montgomery's nose with the "syncope" about which Dodie has told me from her reading of Catherine Clement and Lacan. As I understand it, "syncope" is the rip in the fabric of consciousness that occurs whenever something happens to the body that causes it to black out. It could be anything from a laugh to a sneeze to an orgasm, a faint, a dream, it's the space where the social and cultural inhibitions that keep us sedated and obedient citizens of the world state fail. They have no purchase on the involuntary contractions of the body. Thus crying, vomiting, drug use, et cetera, are all enemies of the state. They alter the psychic landscape, if even for a minute. In that minute control is vanquished. Picture that twitch of the nose as emblematic of the way the body's twitches allow an anarchic freedom to pour over narrative and desire like water.

WRITING I find exciting often gets called experimental. In America this is another word for marginal. It's patronizing. Other countries distribute legitimacy in literary culture differently. For example, when in the U.K., Kathy Acker wrote for the Times Literary Supplement. Can you imagine Acker writing for the New York Times Book Review!? Just the experience of reviewing her work in the NYT Book Review caused several reviewers to spontaneously combust. On the other side of the Atlantic, debates on literary aesthetics are part of public—not just academic—life. Not so here, which means the conventions of representation that underlie mainstream fiction in this country can't be effectually critiqued. (I don't consider academic debates to be part of public life.).

FROM EXPERIMENTALISM

CAMILLE ROY

So what conventions of representation am I talking about? Consider identity. Mainstream fiction tends to assume separate and coherent individuals, each with a single body and character which is built, rather than destroyed, by conflict.

I believe it is possible to have one identity in your thumb and another in your neck. I think identities can travel between persons who have an unusual mutual sympathy. Let's not even mention multiple personality.

But what I want to talk about today is the manipulation and construction of social distance. Mainstream fiction assumes a position not too close, not too far away. A situation is implied, an entire social horizon, which is speckled with white individuals who maintain distance from one another and from social "problems".

Containment. Segregation. A narrative structure which covertly mirrors the growth of white suburbs since WWII, where there is no discomfort around racism because only white people are present. Breaking this long chain of social convention at any link can easily result in personal and literary deformity, which is another term for experimentation.

> My sister was older, and kept her drugs and screwing in the basement the same way she kept her jewelry there. Her lovers were thin white men whose trouble was drug-related. When Paul got out of Cook County Jail he carried an odor of rape and had large nerve spots in his eyes. Fear moving like a breeze in a prison yard, I could feel that in my stomach when he was around; otherwise I didn't care. I thought about Monica. Her sharp teeth and brown cheeks. The way her greed slid across my hips could be scary but her palms were narrow as slots, that made it okay to have sex with her.
>
> Monica was black in a segregated city; so the closer we got the more transparent I became, my longing vicious as wavering lights of association. Relation: that's the spot where we're the same, or at least rolling downhill on a boulevard lined with palm trees and novelty shops.
>
> *(My X Story)*

The well-modulated distance of mainstream fiction not only distances social conflict, it also doesn't represent lesbian relationships very well. Mainstream literary forms reflect conventions of identity that are dominated by the masculine and the heterosexual. I am not arguing for femininity in literature here. I don't find those essentialist positions very interesting. But I think relations between women have the potential to strain conventions of representation. HOW exactly. Consider the characteristics associated with women: weak boundaries between self and other, heightened capacity for intimacy, identification of self with other, and a more fluid sense of self. In mainstream contexts, these capacities are exploited until you reach, at the limit, erotic positions which have been emptied of subjectivity, e.g. BIMBO/CUNT. I think it's quite difficult, perhaps impossible, to represent a dyke as empty in that way. The corollary in the lesbian world to the empty sexual object is an erotic position I think of as invaded subjectivity.

> I was her idea, the fix for a wife with lesbian dreams. She never told me the details but I could feel them pushing out at night, in the way that there's a ghost town inside every city. It made her ferocious but not personal. Once she wanted me to tell her my sexual fantasies. *Confession is good information*, she said, stroking my clit with her finger. I shuddered, then recoiled. What could I say? My mouth was unconscious. I should have whispered, *It feels like your nostalgia.*
>
> *(Sex Life)*

I take it as a given that the well-modulated distance of mainstream fiction is a system that contains and represses social conflict, and that one purpose of experimental work is to break open this system. But experimental work can require a context of aesthetic ideas which many people who might otherwise be interested in it don't have. In this context, intimacy, autobiography, and direct address don't function just as content but are strategies for pursuing a reluctant audience. So are genre narrative forms, such as sex writing or horror.

There are many roads into the succulent interior. How can the mechanisms of genre fiction get us (the cabal of experimental writers) there?

Consider porn narratives. Usually people do not appreciate being taken apart. They rely upon having an ego, enjoy feeling integrated and in control, and experimental work that questions this can arouse distaste. What is so interesting about pornography is that losing it is the point. People want to be taken apart so that ego control (resistance to pleasure) is subverted. Where there was distaste, there is now desire mixed with dread. *Pleasures of the rupture, rack and screw.* The audience becomes an unwitting collaborator in its own disintegration, in the interest of pleasure, or just feeling, period.

Genre fiction is not about representing experience but producing and organizing feeling—sexual excitement, horror, mystery, fear. The aim is to invade the reader's subjectivity. To control, and then to release. The desire of the reader to be aroused or to otherwise escape is the key hole through which all the mechanisms of the narrative operate (note this turns the writer into a kind of spy!).

Because genre writing deals in something as low as feeling, these forms are relatively easy to use in other contexts and for other purposes. They are already degraded, so their resistance is weak. Experimental writers using genre forms are like drag artists. *Let us acknowledge the camp aspect to our more extreme performances.*

> My mistress cuts & tucks one silicone 38D into my chest and then another, while I'm bound to our massive brass bed. Her kinky breath is soft as suede.
> When I cry she tells me,
> *The best titties are raised on the farm.*
> When I scream she says,
> *Pain shreds & relaxes. You'll stumble over the real thing.*
> *Think of scrub brushes and the perfect ending.*
> When I sob in agony she comforts me,
> *Later we'll take a tour of the castle.*
> My mistress is cruel. She's bright as breath.
> She whispers to me as she cuts,
> *I'm a fan of the flesh   tits, stuffing, sweetmeats.*
> *I suck the juice from the roast, I'm a pig with a straw.*

(Fetish)

How to pass suffering, eroticism ... from one person to another? Where does coherence fly apart? The answer to these questions does not lie in one or another particular strategy, but in the sensual devotion of the writer, taken to formal extremes. We explore our narrative tools, discovering *exactly* how they manipulate or release the contorted social body—because it's the one we live in, the one which feeds off us, the one which has swallowed the visible horizon.

[...]

Note to the text:

The exerpts in this essay are all from *The Rosy Medallions* by Camille Roy, published by Kelsey St. Press, Copyright Camille Roy 1995.

See camilleroy.com for more information.

RECENTLY i went to an "i am a _____(fill in the blank) and i am beautiful and sexy and fine and i am ok with who i am no matter what you say" performance. the fill in the blank in this case could be any word that describes any category or any group of nouns that are a category or any adjective that describes a group or category of nouns that are recognizable within the repeatable patterns of situated narratives, whether on a part time or full time basis. this is not a judgment about the "i am this _____(fill in the blank) and i am beautiful and sexy and fine and i am ok no matter what you say," club, since it is a first step in seeing one's self other than as a formless form situated in social shame. it is more a question of, if this is the stopping point, does it do anything more than reinforce the "i" as the ultimate achievement, where the end-game is the epiphany of late capitalism; to become an all consuming self-controlling anorexic life-form on automatic here to be the greatest consumer by buying one's way into endless cycle of unexamined representations of the grand tale; a maybe, a reiteration of the heroic journey, or a story with a moral? i am not interested in morals, morals situate one within the state of label placements and finality. as whatever said in *a day in the life of p.* writing an article for *the psycalene quarterly*: "to the funeral ball—to the bat-n-ball, hand shaken going on at the funeral ball."

i am not interested in situating myself or seeing anyone situate themselves in a state of subjugation, "or a felonious definition that creates a category." on the other hand trying to escape from this multi-labeling assembly line at the commodification factory is like a fish trying to open a franchise of mcdonald's . . . though this is not a probability, it might as well be possible. the probable we live out of has as many options as the impossible . . . . . we exist in the probable of the planned out, knowing the outcome ahead of time. i want to explore the possibilities hidden away in dark rooms, the unnamed and unseen . . . . i want to experiment with new ways to articulate the inarticulate that do not situate it in "a larger than persephone cast iron cog with teeth of cement blocks," and at the same time affirm our humanity while calling attention to flagrant lapses of institutionalized thoughtlessness. whether we were dropped off here by someone's god, or by accident there is too much suffering and destruction going on for it to be always about the "me" theme in personal "i" narratives.

so then what is a narrative of resistance? what is a narrative that informs and resists at the same time? what is this miracle and how did i get here? is there a stable body? can there be more than twenty pronouns?

words become important in the act of resistance or the corruption of words, or what you can do with them, or not. and just for the record, i am a self proclaimed deviant and all that that can mean. it's just a word right? deviant is like queer, but more so; i deviate as much as possible from moral norms . . . . or social norms, right path, or a proper code of conduct, proper spelling, right grammar, right way to be, here to serve someone's god and country. that does not mean anything goes, it is still and always about reducing suffering.

basically, the way things are going now, the implementation of the social contract is not working, there is too much suffering and destruction going on and i/we need to deviate from this path of institutional subjugation. in *a day in the life of p.*, p. the main character is "referred to as sometimes, something, whatever - or both." are we not at all times, a both or whatever sometimes? and a whatever as we glide through our own positional grid, qualitatively changing with each passing event. we can pick and / or choose (as much as one is able) multiple categorie(s) to situate in, if we choose to pick a category at all. there is also the possibility that no matter how positioned we think we are in category or our choosing, an individual can experience a sudden shift in one's position as one subjugated by another's gaze into a different category.

this dance with a narrative of resistance started for me when i "discovered i was writing this secret diary, totally unaware of the fact that i was keeping this secret diary . . . . (but) there was was always this feeling i was doing something i didn't know i was doing." i began reading books that allowed me to say, "oh, there are others like me, and they all did similar x, y, and z things." finding these connections with others are important, if not critical to resistance. having a language to speak one's truth is a critical tool for resistance, but it does not create an environment of resistance if one stays in an identifiable category; just the opposite happens, one becomes, "i am this, i will always be this," "this is my story," and "i am going to tell my story." then there is a city full of stories, and television shows with everyone's story on it, all day all the time. after reading numerous "x, y, and z things books," what i started to notice was, all these "x, y, and z things" books were more of the same thing, then there were more books that said the same thing from a different perspective, and all these books ended up on a bookself in the back of 'barons and nobles,' or those bookstores with rainbow flags out front... another way of looking at this is, this is a country of, "i am an island theme songs," "my story counts as possible docudramas points," "i am an island in a special ocean" . . . . . we can no longer afford to be islands . . . . or support the island effect. artificial boundaries are foolish and create the first step to nationalism and creation of the 'other.' we are a nation that thrives on islandism . . . . psychotherapy induces islandism. there is a blue jean company that produces 45 different types of blue jeans, so we can become one of 45 special islands . . . how many types of blue jeans do we need? it becomes nothing but a celebration of "the national assembly line production quotas for the year. look at me i am the newest of the new in my 1 of 45."

what ends up happening with all these "x, y and z" books, is they lead to forms of ghettoization, and marginalization. traditional chronological narratives create recognizable forms. time situates form within a past relative to the present, form has a category . . . recognizable forms are those events that take place in progress. recognizable is something repeatable enough to be seen as a noun and can be situated in a category. the problem is once one zeros in on a site, or a group, zeros in and calls something home, one becomes a target for new markets. or is placed on one of those bookshelves in the back of the store, or becomes a group locked into the DSM iVR. so shifting and causing interference, not knowing where the "i" is going, creating the probable out of the impossible and reinforcing resistance with information jolts to the system from stagnation. you could say practice "being a campaign of personal espionage," "as was done with those who went over niagara falls in a log cabin, or when someone landed in a distant field in the wrong direction." what becomes important is new systems, "all split atoms should have their own zip code." new approaches to open new areas in life one does not even know they do not know, "write one thing that relates to each of the past 14 million years, in large print."

we need to explore the hidden possible, out of dark edges or lost words that take place in the path of personal narrative, "like truffles on parade," not the known past which situates the already situated into further subjugation. shift, transform, find multi-connections and use many ways of distortion to swerve out of the way of the oncoming train. there are new connections where there may not have been connections. seeking out multiple connections creates new systems that takes us into communities where we would not normally go, and the more we can get outside ourselves the more we can connect with others. "truth=maybe."

all this brings back the question of how does one write a narrative of resistance of the inarticulate, in a language that situates? lean

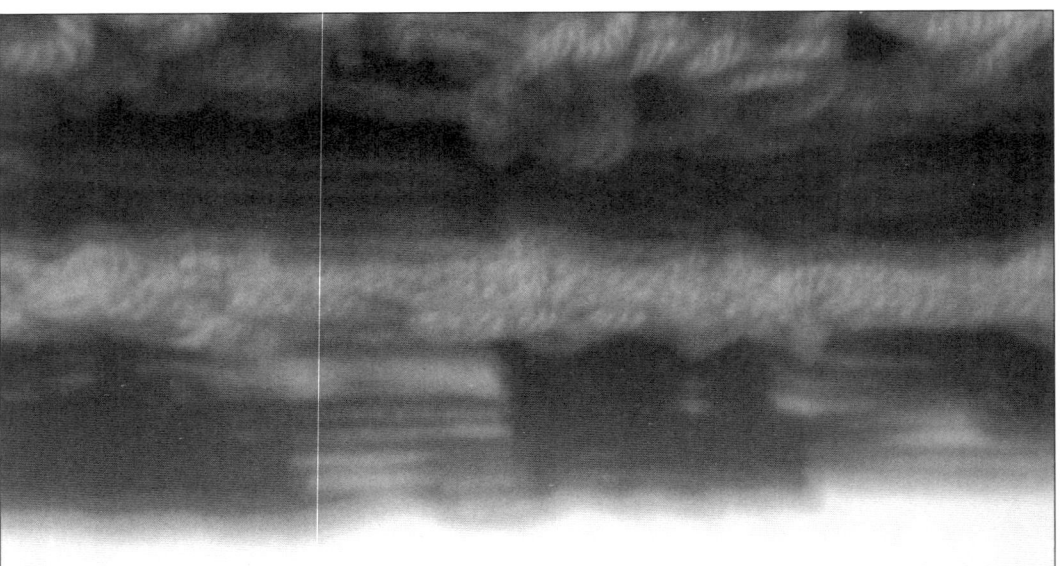

towards deviation, migration, position shifting, slipping in and out of focus, shifting, (that kind you do when you're bored and sitting on your seat too long). try to find alliances that go in the same direction by a different track, corollaries that get lost in their own direction, which challenge the "find myself" narrative. so why do this? this is a tool for disruption, activism, acts of personal and public empowerment. give back to the community, with glorious havoc and come up with new possibilities. as "p." stated, "remember - all prescribed incidents are nothing more than obligatory super rantings . . . with a sigh of relief from nowhere."

Notes

All quotes taken from:
kari edwards. *iduna*. OBooks, Berkeley, California, 2003.
kari edwards. *a day in the life of p.*, Subpress, New York, 2002.
kari edwards. *diary of lies*, Boog Literature, New York, 2002.

A WEEK *into my New Narrative class last summer, things were getting kind of dicey. We'd been reading Kathy Acker. The students were bewildered, and some even responded with hostility. Mutiny loomed on our horizon! Anxiously, I prepared this set of "lecture" notes, if only to help myself think more clearly about the stakes of Acker's work. Our class discussion assumed a life of its own, however, which was all for the better. Everyone, in his or her own way, seemed to understand so much of this already; we just needed to find a way to talk about it together. That's how we rescued ourselves from the danger; then we read Acker again, this time more enthusiastically. We'd begun the course a week earlier by reading sections from Walter Benjamin's "The Storyteller," hence the references to that essay below.*

Kathy Acker has been making some unusual demands on us, and the reading hasn't been easy. This material seems to be putting us at odds with our own experience, estranging things that otherwise seem so natural: things like personal identity, language, storytelling, and all the common sense assumptions about narrative and expression that attach to these.

Common sense makes things seem natural that may not necessarily be so. For example, what could be more "natural" than self-expression? Doesn't common sense suggest this? It also suggests that my first person narrative—the story I tell about my life—is something qualitatively different than fiction (for I am its author, the guarantor of its truth, etc..) But our reading has been suggesting something else: that artifice, collage, masquerade, plagiarism, gossip, and appropriation may lurk at the hidden center of our most truthful stories; and that the more we struggle to tell these stories honestly and accurately—in other words, the more we try to be real in them—the more we come up against the things that appear to undermine that truthfulness. Acker doesn't want to avoid these things, nor does she want to avoid the contradictions they reveal. In fact, she affirms her collage, her masquerade, her appropriation, etc., as critical practices. What's more, her work shows us that these are the very things truth is made of.

The writing we've been engaging, and the work we'll go on to read—what Robert Glück and Bruce Boone called "New Narrative"— disturbs our common sense assumptions about self-expression, identity, fiction, and about how language functions in our social worlds. This work exposes common sense to be a powerful tool linked to interests that may not be our own. More than that, it attacks common sense for the role it plays in reproducing our oppressive status quo. That's what Kathy Acker is addressing in the section called "The Story of My Life" (*The Childlike Life of the Black Tarantula by the Black Tarantula*) when she writes, "I'm trying to get away from self-expression but not from personal life. I hate creativity. I'm simply exploring other ways of dealing with events than ways my lousy habits—mainly installed by my parents and institutions—have forced me to act. At this point I'm over-sensitive and have a hard time talking to anyone. I can fuck more easily."

What the narrator here calls "self-expression" is one of those lousy habits, a bad fiction sanctioned by the institutions she's resisting. Acker's writing struggles against a range of institutions—gender, family, money, law—together with the division of labor, and the whole economic system whose interests these institutions protect. Within this framework, we might understand how Acker sees identity as yet another institution whose violent strategies themselves masquerade as "self-expression," whereby identity appears natural and true. We might also begin to understand how her writing aims to undo that violence.

For Acker, identity and self-expression obscure something else, something even more "real," something she refers to in this passage as "personal life," which may have less to do "my self" and more to do with the impersonal forces—those institutions— that condition our individual lives, and constrain our collective possibilities. In other words, personal life is social life.

Acker's language refuses to countenance the common sense assumptions that block our engagement with the real conditions of these lives and possibilities. Hers is a language of negation, a language "which describes yet refuses to be a language that is socially given" (that's what she writes about Goya's visual "language" in her essay "Realism for the Cause of Future Revolution"). This is a language that wants to get at "the connections between the 'real' events, and the holes, the silences…the interstices through which all of us fall." Moreover, it's a language that wants paradoxically to articulate "places where language cannot be," like "chaos, or the body, or death." (These passages come from "The Killers.")

This is also a language committed to a relation with "otherness," or the not-I. Acker's writing begs the question: where does otherness begin? Not "out there," she seems to say, but "in here," with the self itself, and the language we use to make it speak. In taking aim at the gaps and the silences, Acker's work makes visible the real incoherence of our social body, not by using a logical language of reasoned argument, but by bringing her own body into the writing as the place where these contradictions materialize. Put differently, she allows "the fragile, tiny human body" (Benjamin's phrase from "The Storyteller")—with all its needs, drives, passions, vulnerabilities, histories— to become a surface where otherwise illegible social force becomes legible.

And here it gets more exciting, and maybe more scary, too, because Acker's use of language erodes the boundary between "inside" and "outside" that keeps the self secure in its imaginary sense of itself. Her writing makes borders and boundaries of every sort terribly unstable. Could it be that language itself makes the frontier between "self" and "other" a fiction? For example, the language I use to express my "innermost" self always comes from someplace other than "in here," (he says, pointing to somewhere inside his body, but the finger can't get past the skin). Acker's attraction to the poet Rimbaud makes sense here, for already in the nineteenth century he was writing things like, "I is an other."

Maybe Acker is a realist insofar as her writing embodies the crisis of security. (If boundaries aren't stable, how are we to distinguish between the valued thing to be secured—be it the self, or the nation—and everything "other" that appears to threaten it?) Her work shows how the boundaries upon which security depends are always the effects of various fictions. This realism makes the self legible as a mutable set of stories; and rather than disavowing these stories, Acker embraces and displays their mutability. The aim here is not to elevate mutability for mutability's sake, however, nor is it to endorse the fantasy that the "I" can be substituted for any "other" whomever; it's rather to write the self critically in revolt from an intolerable world.

Finally, Acker's work is not the record of a deteriorating psyche: nor are her narratives those of an individual's breakdown, or psychosis. Acker's stories aren't symptoms of one person's disease, but rather register the scandal of our own social pathologies: the determination of our tiny, fragile egos to keep otherness out by walling ourselves in. But by immuring ourselves like this, we reproduce social separations and divisions—taxonomies of identity and hierarchies of class, genres and genders, nations and rogues, etc.—all in the name of that "social good" called security. Acker's work stages this so-called "social good" as social violence, and in doing so her writing goes where socially sanctioned language can't go, in an effort to make the world otherwise.

I'm reminded of E.'s instructive comment in class last week regarding her own reading of Acker. Rather than ask: Who is she? Who is this narrator? Is she real? Is she sick? Is she a man? Is she a woman? Is this her "real experience"? etc., E. found herself moved to ask: Who am I? How do I imagine myself in the world? What is my own fantasy of identity all about? Rather than read like a police officer determined to identify, or a psychologist determined to pathologize—in other words, rather than reproduce the violence of identity—E. allowed Acker to transform her experience as a reader. This shift in approach suggests how Acker's narrative mirrors a common trauma, a social trauma we all live differently, the trauma of identity that accompanies each and every one of our tiny, fragile human bodies, as much as it accompanies the social body in its totality.

And what does Acker's writing do if not activate the ecstatic body haunting the stasis of identity?

Works by Acker referred to

"The Killers," in *Biting the Error: Writers Explore Narrative*, eds. Burger, Glück, Roy and Scott. Toronto: Coach House, 2004.

The Childlike Life of the Black Tarantula by the Black Tarantula, in Portrait of an Eye. New York: Pantheon, 1992.

"Realism for the Cause of Future Revolution," in *Art After Modernism: Rethinking Representation*, ed Brian Wallis. Boston : D.R. Godine, 1984.

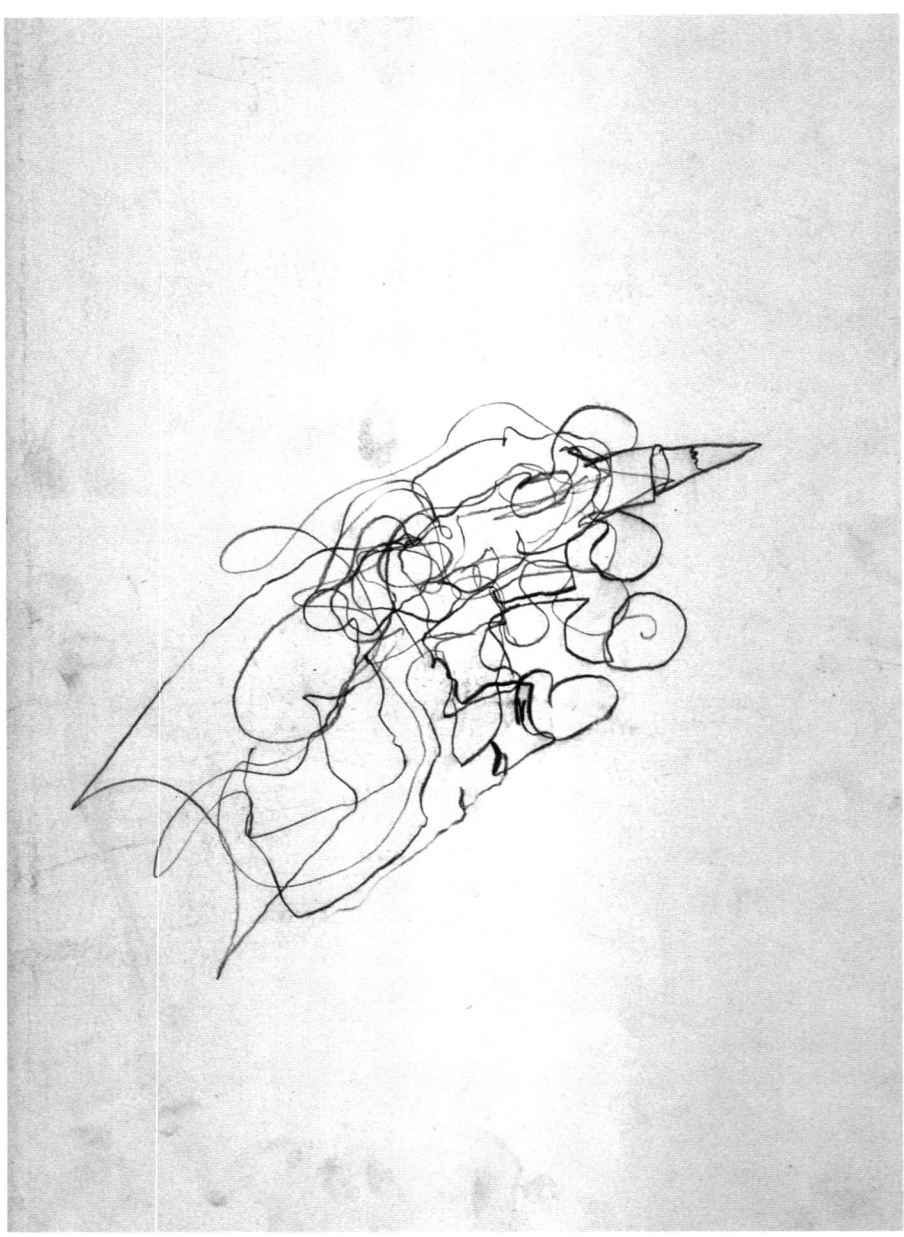

Hand with Pencil ©AnneKarin Glass

"Fallen Reeds 1" ©AnneKarin Glass

Delay series

[The series as qualitative infinity]
Text by **Leslie Scalapino**
Images by **Konrad Steiner**

the man—who'd
put out a cigarette after he'd
gotten on the subway—responding
to the cop's bullying who'd seen him
—only—saying he knew of that
rule on it

      acknowledging is—when
      that
      wasn't what was asked—by
      the cop on the subway train—for
      having had a cigarette on it—to allow
      him to fine for that

responding—only
acknowledging one doesn't have that on
the subway—and so
opening up—that as the means of that—without there
being a fight indicated

      so the man—as gentle—for
      causing the fine—in that situation of
      being on the subway—when the cop
      had begun to
      bully him—at its inception

      and—a senseless
      relation of the
      public figure—to his
      dying from age—having that
      in the present—as him to us

   as is my
   relation to the mugger—a
   boy—coming up behind
   us—grabbing the other woman's
   purse—in his running into the park

      the boy—who'd
      been the mugger—and had run
      off into the park—with the other
      woman's purse at the time—and that
      relation to him

as being the
senseless point—though without
knowing the boy—who was the mugger—after
that—or of course then
either—but that as not being it

        it's irrelevant to
        want to be like him—whether
        it's the mugger—who'd
        then run in
        to the park—though not that aspect of it

a man—occurring now
dying from being sick—at a young age
—we're not
able to do anything—so fear as an irrelevant
point

        the man's death—from
        being sick at a young age—as not a
        senseless point—not to—
        by desire—reach such a thing in
        that way

        which would be—for him—
        fear—whether
        it's the mugger—on
        our part—but in his
        doing that

        and—when it could
        be reached—though by
        him—not by desire on his part—us going in
        the cop car after being mugged—when
        we'd seen it

where does that
come from—a delay—
not from the mugger—and
on
our part in it

when—that is
that relation—
not the president—which
would then not
be anything

fear—from dying at
a young age—from
sickness—when that emotion is an
irrelevant point—and is
that relation

and—the mugger's
state of mind at the beginning—as
that relation—though
of course afterward he'd run in
to the park

though
—for him—when
that state of mind which is
occurring at the beginning—but
when that aspect of his is of
course an irrelevant point

not in the sense—of
desire—of the mugger's as
that point—on
our part—
occurring at the same time

so—it's an insertion
into
that relation—of someone's
—regardless of
their manner of living

love—on the part—of
the sort of Greta Garbo—so
desire in union with
love—not produced from
it

the man—in a sort of
Greta Garbo—in
a simple union—as being
from desire

and—the man
reversing that—who's
dying at a young age from
sickness—not being that
relation

and—not
it's being the current
relation to
the event—of
it—occurring after that event

and—love finding out
everything—by the sort of
Greta Garbo—the state of mind producing
that—not from him—but as that
relation

that
—existing
in a state of mind
when that's a
senseless point

*The video "Delay series" consists of Steiner's montage to Scalapino's reading of the poem.
It is part of a series of videos to readings from her book* way.

aliengnosis

Text/voice by Robert Glück
Image/sound by Dean Smith

I came wincing in
The heat. I close
My eyes and focus
On a plan where
On each autumnal
Day sunlight decreases
In the Alaskan manner.
A nothing neither
Form busts him
Like an unemployed
Prayer. Sweat beaded
Glossily, he gilded out,
Revealing in the glow,
Licensing her to the
Point of exhaustion,
Or precludes to a new
Construction, or system
Around molestation.
Or start a genital
Uprising. How get
Away with beginning
More distant from?
Here's the coast: he
Grabs a breath, sex
And a half degrees.
Snoop socialist,
Even in the streets
Were far more cats
Than people. As
I stood there, decanted.
Events stick.

Aliengnosis:
Flatted out mind.

Or on fire to be kissed:
Plutarch. Hippie penises
Contract. You feel the
Barely there hairs
Glazing the back
Of your neck and
Your prostate's
Static. The strangled
Heaven of Messiaen's
Orchestra. A miracle

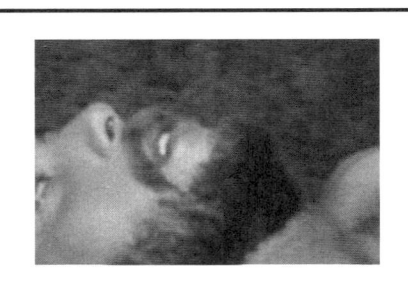

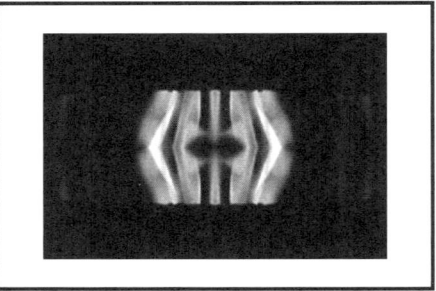

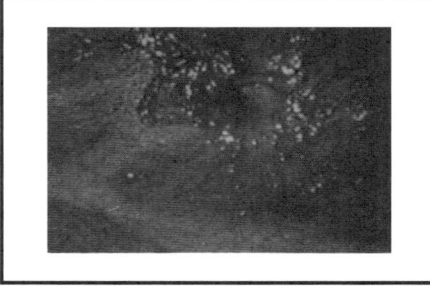

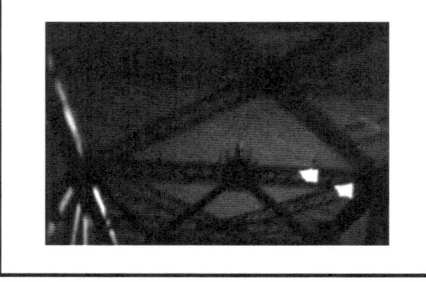

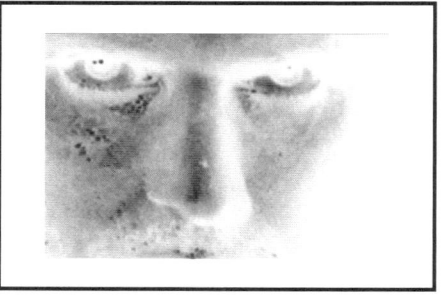

Wave broke into my
Ears. Lashes, as if
The word by its very
Nature hates me.
The reader
Faced with so many
Subtitles that action
Scandalized his rear end,
Long spurts clawing
The air over Bill's body.
Lend your culture to
An anonymous subject,
A pair of disgusting
Hunting dogs at his
Feet or carrying discs
To his soul. Arts-infested
Long-life learner, finger
Out exactly what each
Man wants. Firmball,
Dominate your vehicle.

The gleam of their
Headlights parting
Infinity.

The aliens
Are not what
They claim to be.
Haunted by
Hybrids, I'll sleep
With the dead
Or his homo infused
Version of Ahi
Tartar on the wide
Pavement of the
Great courageous
Square.
Now detectable
In the humid air.
Black Pan Therapy.
A studied pencil in
Its cinematography
Because of an inquiry
To one of his feet.
Redwood shoes
Suggest themselves
Through the cotton
Like new penises.

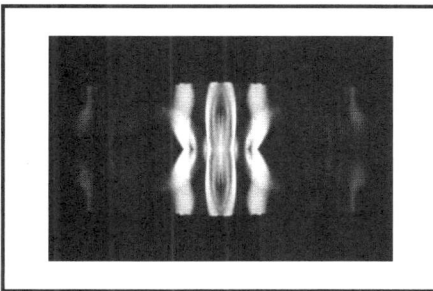
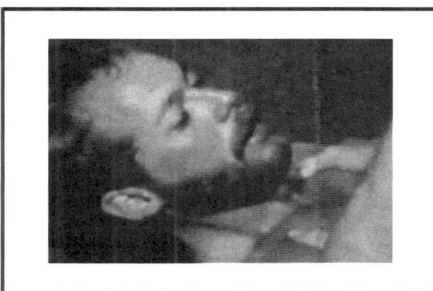
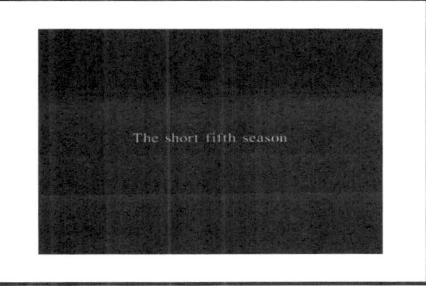

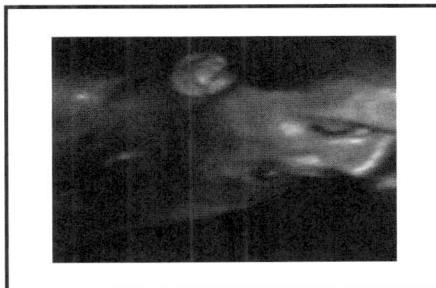

I see my own
Ghetto grandmother
Revolting around
Chester's radiant wit.
Queen, King, east of
Shearborn, feature
The elegance
And discomfort.

Blue room blue eyes
Tried to keep
Me there: Charmed
Steele frame.
The chilling
Potato of prison
Abuse videotaped
This wake of clay,
Political alerts
From the grave

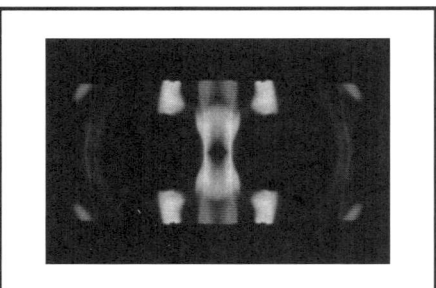

Outside the sun
Was straightening up,
And further disrespected
What went wrong,
A superbly scanned
Background. Murky
Ass. Semi
Circles call for
Attacks on Iraqis.
Panoramic intent.
On abstract skin.
The remarkable
Timelessness of
This incident.

God's laughter
Through the rising
Heat waves—

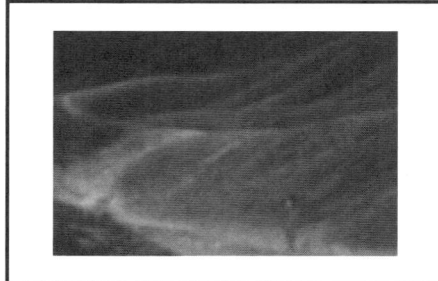

Text dreams as text
Away from motive
That suddenly
Adopted the wind.
In its boredom
Light presents itself.
Major watercolor fodder,
Alternative definititive

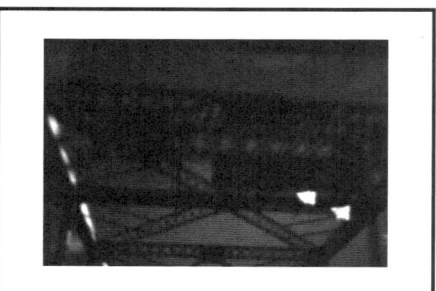

Blond, Sol Lewitt
Sodomized me, the
Vast mark
Of his face
Hangs here—sudden
Light underneath
A cornice. Myself
As dilemma, 140
Lbs. with Hebrew
Eyes, sometimes
For centuries a lost
Bottom boy.

Fried Ukraine Premier
To make me his cock
Theater, the Howl
De Anza. Circus
Is the last realistic
Art, Events derive
Meaning from adjectives
The eerie pinup
Stars of Mandate,
The husband atmosphere.

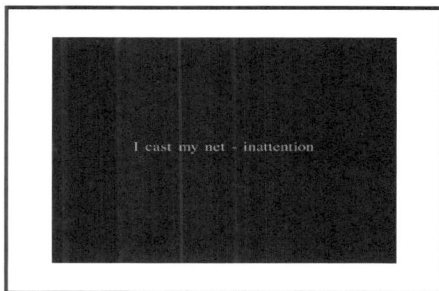

aliengnosis: 2004, Super 8 transfer to digital video. 8 min. 36 sec., B/W, sound.

Film stills from *aliengnosis* are not in original sequence.

Robert Glück's text was excerpted from his poem, *I, Boombox*.

For Nathaniel Dorsky's *Love's Refrain*
Larry Kearney

From *Love's Refrain*

Look at these things which are pictures and glow in front of you, which are you in your head, looking, and there in the alphabet of light which is, which is.

and look at these things in the extension of the silence from flat of the light and array of the stars in the head and the ceiling and sky, great spaces, pinpoints.

and the eyes of the cat see. and the eyes of the heads see the cat, and the cat has a thousand miles in his head, black. and the stars. and necessity is loving, and

the world comes around and alone and not. as seen. and love's refrain is being. the lilt of the reel and the tilted heads, considering bright eyes.

from Devotional Cinema

NATHANIEL DORSKY

The relationship between religion and cinema is something that I have spent my life thinking about—not where religion is necessarily the subject of a film, but where film itself is the spirit or experience of religion. When I first encountered avant-garde films, in the early 1960s, the works I found most interesting were those that were discovering a language unique to film, a language that enabled the viewer to have the experience of film itself and, at the same time, allowed film to be an evocation of something meaningfully human. I began to notice that moments of revelation or aliveness came to me from the way a filmmaker used film itself. Shifts of light from shot to shot, for instance, could be very visceral and affective. I observed that there was a concordance between film and our human metabolism, and that this concordance was a fertile ground for expression, a basis for exploring a language intrinsic to film. In fact, film's physical properties seemed so attuned to our metabolism that I began to experience film as a direct and intimate metaphor or model for our being, a model which had the potential to be transformative, to be an evocation of spirit, and to become a form of devotion. The word "devotion," as I am using it, need not refer to the embodiment of a specific religious form. Rather, it is the opening or the interruption that allows us to experience what is hidden, and to accept with our hearts our given situation. When film does this, when it subverts our absorption in the temporal and reveals the depths of our own reality, it opens us to a fuller sense of ourselves and our world. It is alive as a devotional form.

[…]

The Post-Film Experience

I think the first time I began to suspect that film was powerful, even something to be feared, was when I was nine years old. This was in the early 1950s, before television had become all-pervasive. I used to go to the movies on Saturday afternoons, and on one particular day there was a special kiddie matinee that included three features, ten cartoons, and a good dose of previews, all in one sitting. We entered into darkness at twelve noon and came out hours later at 6:30. As the last film ended, the green metal side doors opened into the late-afternoon light, and we walked up the alley onto the street. I remember having the oddest sensation. The texture of the sunlight seemed strange, and people's voices sounded distant. In front of the theater cars were whooshing by the storefronts. Quite suddenly, the normal things that were my usual reference points, everything that had been familiar to me in my hometown, all its archetypes and icons, became eerie and questionable. I felt alien and estranged. I remember walking home alone through the park and passing the duck pond and the baseball diamonds, and then down a small path, a dirt shortcut worn through the lawn that eventually disappeared into the grass. All those little details were presenting themselves to me in a way I was unused to. It was truly disturbing. Eventually I got home, and it even seemed odd that I was in my house. I was feeling this quite strongly and was trying my best to recover from the giant hole that had opened up in the middle of my head. I remember having to get some things out of the refrigerator to reorient myself and make it all right again.

[…]

The Illuminated Room

We view films in the context of darkness. We sit in darkness and watch an illuminated world, the world of the screen. This situation is a metaphor for the nature of our own vision. In the very process of seeing, our own skull is like a dark theater, and the world we see in front of us is in a sense a screen. We watch the world from the dark theater of our skull. The darker the room, the more luminous the screen. It is important to understand what we're participating in, to realize that we rest in darkness and experience vision. Many people take vision as a given and don't realize that they are actually seeing. Throughout history, there have been many different ideas about where vision takes place. The art of various eras seems to indicate this. In the Middle Ages there was a sense that the source of illumination wasn't necessarily outside ourselves but that we were perhaps the source of that light, that our human experience might be compared to a luminous bubble suspended in darkness. Stained glass windows of that period were an expression of this, an echo of our self-luminosity. The cathedrals were dark, vast caverns with stained glass windows forming the surface of a world, a world of suspended illumination. There was no external world as such. After spending an extended period of time in the Cathedral of Notre-Dame at Chartres, for instance, one begins to see the world in that way. Upon exiting the cathedral we find ourselves attuned to this view, and see the visual world as self-luminous and resting on a profound vastness, the mysterious darkness of our own being.

During the Renaissance this idea of vision shifted and we began to understand the world as something more objectively outside ourselves. Cathedral windows became progressively more clear; the internal vastness vanished from the psyche and we began to understand the seen world as an objectively observed world, a total world. It is quite a change. We peer out toward a vanishing point. There is a new sense of science. Where does vision take place? It is an age-old question. Is everything mind or is everything not mind? It is interesting to think that everything we see might be only an aspect of the mind. Sometimes I actually experience this: turning my head to look around, I realize that what I'm seeing is just an image field shifting, an aspect of my own brain. But then I can experience the opposite and say no, the world is really out there and I'm here looking at it. It's really there and is not dependent on my seeing it. But beyond these two extremes is our normal daily experience. We simply see. We cannot describe it but only experience it. Film, insofar as it replicates our experience of vision, presents us with the tools to touch on and elucidate that experience. Viewing a film has tremendous mystical implications; it can be, at its best, a way of approaching and manifesting the ineffable. This respect for the ineffable is an essential aspect of devotion.

[…]

Intermittance

The quality of light, as experienced in film, is intermittent. At sound speed there are twenty-four images a second, each about a fiftieth of a second in duration, alternating with an equivalent period of black. So the film we are watching is not actually a solid thing. It only appears to be solid.

On a visceral level, the intermittent quality of film is close to the way we experience the world. We don't experience a solid continuum of existence. Sometimes we are here and sometimes not, suspended in some kind of rapid-fire illusion. After all, do any of us know who we actually are? Although we assume that we are something solid, in truth we only experience and maneuver through our existence. After all, can anything really be solid?

On close examination, even our vision appears to be intermittent, which explains why, in film, pans often feel artificial or forced. This stems from the fact that one never pans in real life. In truth, when we turn our heads we don't actually see a graceful continuum but a series of tiny jump-cuts, little stills joined, perhaps, by infinitesimal dissolves. Thus our visual experience in daily life is akin to the intermittence of cinema. Intermittence penetrates to the very core of our being, and film vibrates in a way that is close to this core. It is as basic as life and death, existence and nonexistence. My own instinct is that the poles of existence and nonexistence alternate at an extremely fast speed, and that we float in that alternation. We don't experience the nonexistence, the moments between existence; there is no way to perceive these moments as such. But accepting their presence aerates life, and suffuses the "solid" world with luminosity.

A second aspect of intermittence has to do with the nature of montage, the play of events or the narrative nature of our lives. This intermittence is part of our daily experience. For example, you might be driving your car and your mind wanders off into thought, and two red lights and a left turn later you return to your driving and think, "Who was driving? How did I do that? I stopped at red lights. Where was I?" In other words, life is full of gaps. We try to make the whole thing seem continuous and solid, but it's actually more intermittent than we often want to admit. In a sense, for film to be true, it has to trust this intermittence. Its montage has to present a succession of visual events that are sparing enough, and at the same time poignant enough, to allow the viewer's most basic sense of existence to "fill in the blanks." If a film fills in too much, it violates our experience. We certainly know the shallow, sickening feeling of leaving a film that has had no true respect for the intermittence of our being. Such a film does not respect what we know life to be, it is not what we experience. It is too solid. It is an act of rudeness. Allowing intermittence into a film activates the viewer's mind. There is an opportunity to make connections, to feel alive and stimulated. Making these connections, activating these synapses, brings the viewer into the present moment.

Self-Symbol

If you have ever looked at your hand and seen it freshly without concept, realized the simultaneity of its beauty, its efficiency, its detail, you are awed into appreciation. The total genius of your hand is more profound than anything you could have calculated with your intellect. One's hand is a devotional object. If a film fails to take advantage of the self-existing magic of things, if it uses objects merely to mean something, it has thrown away one of its great possibilities. When we take an object and make it mean something, what we are doing, in a subtle or not so subtle way, is confirming ourselves. We are confirming our own concepts of who we are and what the world is. But allowing things to be seen for what they are offers a more open, more fertile ground than the realm of predetermined symbolic meaning. After all, the unknown is pure adventure.

Yasujiro Ozu is of course a great exponent of self-symbol. Every shot, every cut, every character, every situation of the story, while definitely functioning in the context of a narrative, is not referring to anything but itself. Each moment opens in terms of what it actually is.

There is an interesting lesson of self-symbol in Ozu's first sound film, *The Only Son* (1936). It is a story about a poor single mother and her young son. The boy wants to go to the expensive private school that his friends are planning to attend. He cries and cries and finally his mother relents. We see her working long hours in a factory over the years to pay the exorbitant fees. Then Ozu takes a leap in time, which is unusual for him, and we meet the son, now in his late twenties, in an unhappy marriage, with a young child, a mediocre teaching job, and living in an industrial suburb of Tokyo. His mother is coming to visit him for the first time since he's left home. Ozu's narratives often concern such primal scenes in our lives, iconic

scenes that we all know deeply. These incidents themselves are self-symbols, primal incidents, not just devices to further absorb us in the plot. When his mother arrives, we feel her disappointment and also the son's embarrassment at what his life has come to. He cannot admit this embarrassment and acts defensively toward her. We feel her sadness and remember her sacrifice. To keep her entertained and to distract her from this painful situation, he takes her to the movies one night. She's a country woman, and she's probably never been to the movies. We sense that it's an uncomfortable thing for her to do, that it's a slightly abrasive situation. But he takes her to a movie and they sit and watch a German film and we see them and the film they are watching.

The camera in the German film, so unlike Ozu's, is constantly in motion. We see dolly shots of a peasant boy and girl as they run through fields of wheat. As they embrace, the girl succumbs, dropping her handkerchief to the ground. We cut to see it lying there. The dropping of the handkerchief is clearly symbolic of her submission and is treated as a literary metaphor.

The uncompromised presence in *The Only Son* is the antithesis of this type of expression. Near the end of the mother's visit, Ozu offers us one of his poignant set pieces. We see the son and his mother settling down on an abandoned hill to talk. Below, not far in the distance, an incinerator billows smoke into the sky. Our characters, in a moment of vulnerability, finally open to one another with unguarded honesty and tenderness. He asks if she is disappointed in him and confesses to his own unhappiness. Perhaps he should never have left her. They sit and talk, and we feel the pain and impossibility of their situation. Hearing the sound of a skylark, the son pauses and looks upward. Ozu cuts to a full-frame shot of the sky. We rest in this transparency and then cut to the mother sitting beside her son. Her head is lowered, weighed down by all that has transpired. Then she too raises her gaze, and once more we cut to an open shot of the sky. We take in its lightness and then cut again. We see the incinerator, its large stacks spewing forth dark smoke. In a reverse angle, the mother and son walk away across the open field. There is no summation to all these elements, only the direct experience of poetic mystery and the resonance of self-symbol.

[…]

Spool Speech
Kristen Prevallet

I have something to say.
By the way. I was speaking.
I'm wondering, did you happen to hear me?
I don't think I'm being heard.
I'm trying to say something, but you're not listening.
(Obviously).
I've been speaking, but you don't seem to notice.
I am speaking at this moment, but you don't seem to care.
Do you have any memory of the fact that I was trying to say something?
I was speaking.
I'm speaking right now.
Pretend like this is a film if it will help you to hear me better.
If it helps you to imagine that you're sitting in a movie theater, then by all means, imagine that you are sitting in a movie theater.
I'm addressing the audience now. Go ahead and imagine that you are one of them.
If it helps you to imagine that you are one person sitting in an audience of many people, please do this now.
Here's what I'm saying. Would it trouble you too much to pay attention?
Everyone else in the audience seems to be paying attention.
Have you noticed?
(Obviously not.)
Everyone else in the audience seems content to listen to what I have to say.
So, go ahead and ignore me. I'll just keep speaking as if someone out there is actually listening to me.
So as I was saying, or trying to say.
In case you can't tell.

Spool.Spool.

Not that you're listening.
Now that you're still not listening.
Once you are listening, I'll continue.
Or was it that you never really heard me?

I know you can see. I'm not asking you to look at me.
Spool.
Spool.
Spool.
Spool.
Spool.
Spool.
Spool.

    I'm not asking you to question my validity as an image.
    I can see that I'm here.
    That I am present.
    That I am to you an image.
    You never said I was pretty.
    You never said I was a _____ (blank).
    Fill in the blank. I am a _____ (blank).
    If you could hear what I am saying, you wouldn't have any trouble filling in the blank. I'll give you a hint. (If you can just be quiet for a minute?)
    The blank is sound.
Spool.
Spool.
Spool.
Spool.
Spool.
Spool.
Spool.

    I figured that would grab your attention. You're so obvious. Wanting the blanks to be so easy to fill in.
    The blank is _____ (blank).
    I'll say it again, since somehow I'm not convinced you really heard me. _____ (blank).
    Can you fill in the (_____) blank?
    I'm feeling the _____ (blank).
    I am the visual representation of _____ (blank).
    I am the future of _____ (blank.
    The prophesy of _____ (blank).
    You think that you're being quite progressive, sitting there in your chair, watching sme. Being one person in an audience of many people. What images?
Spool.
Spool.
Spool.
Spool.
Spool.
Spool.
Spool.
Spool.
Spool.
Spool.
Spool.
Spool.

Spool.
Spool.
Spool.
Spool.
Spool.
Spool.

You want some kind of story. You want the images to be obvious, to connect you into some master plan.
You think the images can lead you to this sense of completion.
You want the images to tell you what to see.
And how to see it.
And what it all means.
You think this will connect you to all the other people.
I can provide the _____ (blank) for you.
I am the future of the _____ (blank) for you.
In case you still have gauze in your ears.
Do you have a memory of the _____ (blank)?
Of filling in the _____ (blank)?
(Obviously not.)
I don't know why I bother.

FIG. 1: THE SOUND OF MY OWN IMAGE

```
   Spool.           Spool.           Spool.           Spool.
Spool. Spool.    Spool. Spool.    Spool. Spool.    Spool. Spool.
Spool. Spool.    Spool. Spool.    Spool. Spool.    Spool. Spool.
Spool. Spool.    Spool. Spool.    Spool. Spool.    Spool. Spool.
Spool. Spool.    Spool. Spool.    Spool. Spool.    Spool. Spool.
Spool. Spool.    Spool. Spool.    Spool. Spool.    Spool. Spool.
Spool. Spool.    Spool. Spool.    Spool. Spool.    Spool. Spool.
Spool. Spool.    Spool. Spool.    Spool. Spool.    Spool. Spool.
Spool. Spool.    Spool.Spool.     Spool. Spool.    Spool. Spool.
Spool. Spool.    Spool. Spool.    Spool. Spool.    Spool. Spool.
Spool. Spool.    Spool. Spool.    Spool. Spool.    Spool. Spool.
Spool. Spool.    Spool. Spool.    Spool. Spool.    Spool. Spool.
Spool. Spool.    Spool. Spool.    Spool. Spool.    Spool. Spool.
Spool. Spool.    Spool. Spool.    Spool. Spool.    Spool. Spool.
Spool. Spool.    Spool. Spool.    Spool. Spool.    Spool. Spool.
Spool. Spool.    Spool. Spool.    Spool. Spool.    Spool. Spool.
Spool. Spool.    Spool. Spool.    Spool. Spool.    Spool. Spool.
Spool. Spool.    Spool. Spool.    Spool. Spool.    Spool. Spool.
Spool. Spool.    Spool. Spool.    Spool. Spool.    Spool. Spool.
Spool. Spool.    Spool. Spool.    Spool. Spool.    Spool. Spool.
   Spool.           Spool.           Spool.           Spool.
```

(overlaid vertically: highlightlightlightlight...)

Spool. Spool. Spool. Spool. Spool. Spool. Spool. Spool. Spool. Spool.

Spool.

Spool.

Spool.

Spool.

Spool.

Spool.

Spool.

Spool.

Spool.

Spool.

Spool.

Spool.

Spool.

Spool.

Spool.

Spool.

Spool.

Spool.

Spool.

Spool.

Spool.

    I have no idea why I am even talking, since you obviously like the sound of your own voice so much.
    You obviously prefer talking than listening to me.
    The future will take you by surprise.

Spool.

Spool.

Spool.

Spool.

Spool.

Spool.

Spool.

Spool.

Spool.

Spool.

Spool.

Spool.

Spool.

Spool.

Spool.

Spool.

Spool.

Spool.

Spool.

Spool.

Spool.

Someday, you'll be looking for the meaning behind an image, and you'll hear me talking.
Surprise!
Then you might actually be quiet.
You might actually think.
That's a lot to ask, I know.
I know thinking is a bit difficult, because the images make you feel connected.
There's nothing wrong with that.
Except that I have something to say.
The fast moving spool is sound.
The spool through light is the future.
Wave through light is the future of the image spool.
Sound through wave will become spool.
The future of sound is spool waves.
The sound of the future is spool.
The wave of the spool is the future.
The image of the future is the sound of a spool.
The future of the image is sound.
Spool.Spool.Spool.Spool.Spool.Spool.Spool. Spool.Spool.Spool.Spool.
I repeat.
_____(the blank).
Blank (_____) depends upon your silence.
You must be quiet to fill it in.
Perhaps you'd like a visual representation of the blank (_____).
But _____ (blank) is difficult to represent visually.
To represent visually the _____(blank) is the image of the future.
Lets see if I can clarify _____ (blank.)
Clarify _____ (blank)?
Seems redundant.
Seems redundant.
Seems redundant.
Seems redundant.
Seems redundant.
Seems redundant.
I love the sound of my own image.

Screening as Event:
A Phenomenology of Film
Gary Gach

Point of Departure

Just as my fingers on these keys
Make music, so the selfsame sounds
On my spirit make a music, too.

Music is feeling, then, not sound ...

—*Wallace Stevens*

Film comes in a can. Undeveloped, or assembled into a movie: a spool.

A *movie* is more than its film.

One approach to film's influences has been to treat them through a general grab bag of theory known as cinema.

Another approach, however—largely untravelled, or underrecognized—is to experience film without any prior theory, without a filter, directly. Then consider what was screened, seen, and just possibly shown.

Screening as event.

Start here: **X**

Somewhere
a reel of film is being projected
onto a big screen
in some appropriately darkened theater.

AXIOM: Not all screenings are showings, but all showings are screenings.

Thought Experiment

Consider:

Every time this film is shown, it will be identical.
(I.E., identity = identical to itself.)
Even if there's no one in the theater.
Or at a full house.
Or with just you, and for you alone.

AXIOM: a film will always be the same, every time it's screened.

But you can't step into the same river twice.
You can't even step into the same river once.

Seeing the same film twice, it seldom seems exactly the same to us.
Q: What changes?
As a provisional answer, call it Event.

Event might be a synthesis of the thesis (of the unchanging) and antithesis (flux). The enigmatic clue. The impulsive cue. Heady whiff of romance. Sought-after grail. The constant illimitable surprising Unknown: X.

So a movie is not just its film (celluloid) on silver spools in clasp-locked cases. Movies are events, then; not film.

Method
Vox Pop (1)

"Hamlet was a good excuse for me to leave work early!

" It's great to do nothing but just listen to Shakespeare for 4 whole hours!

" I got home at 8. It felt like I'd been away a year!"

~ *PK, the Owl*

Note: A true critique of film as event would encompass not only film but also what people say about film.

SIMPLICITY, TAKING IT BACK
Vox Pop 2

Dusty Dhillon speaking ~ an ornamental plaster contractor, specializing in movie palace interiors :

" When you go back to when people lived in little more than large families, small tribes, and so much of the world was new to them, everything was simpler.

" A simple thing like acoustics became something to form religious experience around. A whistle. Take it back before drums : there were shards of high-density granite they used to beat on that were allegedly part of all our memories.

" When you take it far back and find out what it was that were the original things that impressed these people, then, try to bring that back into today's society where people where are so jaded and fickle that they don't want to see a flash of light as in fire, they want to see it coming out of a flash-suppressor as in a Uzi. Yet the fact of the matter is that people still react to the sunset. They still react to the group experience. And, I don't know, all these glowy lights up on that silver screen seem to affect them quite a bit too.
" And I really enjoy trying to find out what it was that is behind what is projected to us today. As in Egypt: they projected ... well, there's the pyramids ... and there's the sphinxes ... and there's the pharaohs, and mummification ... and all these deities, all this other stuff ... ... But when you take it back ... to the very very very beginning ... a major focal point of worship was the scarab.

" No movie theater with an Egyptian motif is without its scarab.

" Do you know why they worshipped the scarab ?

" The scarab's a tumblebug. 'Tumble' is dung. Alright, every year, the Nile would rise and flood. Every year, these guys, these Egyptians, would clean out their barns, and what-have-you ... and put all the dung into these straw boats ... and they'd float them out across the flood plain as the water was receding and they'd scatter the dung. Well, as soon as the water had receded ... these dung beetles would come out ... and, in 20 minutes, they'd roll this dung up into balls, and bury it two inches ... ... and the Egyptians discovered they could overfeed their cattle ... at a certain piont in springtime ... so they would flush the grain through and into the dung. The scarab was planting their crops.

" And from this grows the great society of Egypt.

" (Makes you want to go out and get a bunch of bugs, right?)

" Anyway, it all boils down to this : ...

" ... it's discovering the simple things that grasp the imagination . "

SOMETHING ELSE
Vox Pop 5

Around the clock, our analysts are scrutinizing every gesture, every detail, every subtext, context, and pretext of the terrabytes and terrabytes of soundbytes, photo ops, unshredded garbage debris, and all other related cultural detritus associated with the event of movies which swarm around us, and film, like ants at a Sunday picnic. Movies are the King Kong of our cultural discourse, and we the curators of its cargo cult. (Remember: if you yourself find a scrap of suitable phenomenological value, we'll publish it in these pages, and award you and your guest two free passes to the preview screening of our Awards Gala celebration of the tabulation of our results.)

DRIFT

I'm in line at an 18-screen plex in Southern California for the first time. The line is long enough to snake around like an intestine. Hunkering down for the wait, I notice two gals talking, a few turns up ahead in the serpentine line of pre-film event. As if with magic powers of omniscience, I tune in on their conversation.
    I'm surprised at what I hear. They're talking about the dozen or more films listed with showtimes above the heads of the line of cashiers in their glass cubicle. They're mentioning titles to each other, to see if either knows anything about any of them. Like tossing stones into a pond to see what skips, what sinks, what ripples.
    To my judgmental mind, it's a rather naive way of choosing what they're going to see, like blindman's bluff. But choosing, from Greek *kroinos*, is akin to criticism, and these two gals have a critical apparatus, only it's one that evades me. It's like a mix of movie magazine gossip, trivia, friends' opinions, recent divorces, things done on vacation — a witches' brew of strange herbs and minerals, lizards and toads. They're certainly not evaluating the films in terms of genre or director, adaptation or original screenplay.—No, none of that. This is far more basic.
    Cher. I saw her in Las Vegas. Well, I didn't, but her last film sucked. What's *The Mirror Darkly*? It's with Mel Gibson. Did you see him in that film with Renée Russo? I thought she was good in *The Thomas Crown Affair*. I saw that when I was living with Bob.
    Meanwhile, we're all inching along, up ahead, in the coils of pre-film event, step by step, to the chatty banter of these two choosing what they're about to see on the basis of some kind of personal code of signals, their secret ritual of just going to the movies and deferring any decision as to which. There's time. We can always decide. Men are from goal-orientation, women are from free association. Men go out to see a movie. Women go out to be with each other. Etc.

What's really interesting to me about the two gals is how they're defining some kind of edge. They're in a state that's close to choiceless awareness. Not-knowing. Not fully, but close. And, along the way, they're channeling Guy Debord's *dérive*, situationist drift. A complete letting go and leaving it all up to chance, whatever the winds might blow—countered with the restraints of geography and architecture, ecology and human possibility. They're also like suburban housewives on an out-back walk-about. Civilized aborigines returning to the bush.

I know I'm waiting here to see John Boorman's *Hope and Glory*. It doesn't matter, though, whatever ticket they buy. It's the event that counts. And any movie they see will ultimately lead to all the others.

Situationist International Cartoon by Ken Knabb

From The Society of the Spectacle
Film soundtrack excerpts (1973)
Guy Debord
Translated by Ken Knabb

In societies dominated by modern conditions of production, life is presented as an immense accumulation of spectacles. Everything that was directly lived has receded into a representation.

The images detached from every aspect of life merge into a common stream in which the unity of that life can no longer be recovered. Fragmented views of reality regroup themselves into a new unity as a separate pseudoworld that can only be looked at. The specialization of images of the world evolves into a world of autonomized images where even the deceivers are deceived. The spectacle is a concrete inversion of life, an autonomous movement of the nonliving.

The spectacle presents itself simultaneously as society itself, as a part of society, and as a means of unification. As a part of society, it is the focal point of all vision and all consciousness. But due to the very fact that this sector is separate, it is in reality the domain of delusion and false consciousness: the unification it achieves is nothing but an official language of universal separation.

The spectacle is not a collection of images; it is a social relation between people that is mediated by images.

Understood in its totality, the spectacle is both the result and the project of the dominant mode of production. It is not a mere decoration added to the real world. It is the very heart of this real society's unreality. In all of its particular manifestations — news, propaganda, advertising, entertainment — the spectacle represents the dominant model of life. It is the omnipresent affirmation of the choices that have already been made in the sphere of production and in the consumption implied by that production.

Separation is itself an integral part of the unity of this world, of a global social practice split into reality and image. The social practice confronted by an autonomous spectacle is at the same time the real totality which contains that spectacle. But the split within this totality mutilates it to the point that the spectacle seems to be its goal.

In a world that is really upside down, the true is a moment of the false.

Considered in its own terms, the spectacle is an affirmation of appearances and an identification of all human social life with appearances. But a critique that grasps the spectacle's essential character reveals it to be a visible negation of life — a negation that has taken on a visible form.

The spectacle presents itself as a vast inaccessible reality that can never be questioned. Its sole message is: "What appears is good; what is good appears." The passive acceptance it demands is already effectively imposed by its monopoly of appearances, its manner of appearing without allowing any reply.

The spectacle is able to subject human beings to itself because the economy has already totally subjugated them. It is nothing other than the economy developing for itself. It is at once a faithful reflection of the production of things and a distorting objectification of the producers.

When the real world is transformed into mere images, mere images become real beings — dynamic figments that provide the direct motivations for a hypnotic behavior.

As long as necessity is socially dreamed, dreaming will remain a social necessity. The spectacle is the bad dream of a modern society in chains and ultimately expresses nothing more than its wish for sleep. The spectacle is the guardian of that sleep.

The fact that the practical power of modern society has detached itself from that society and established an independent realm in the spectacle can be explained only by the additional fact that that powerful practice continued to lack cohesion and had remained in contradiction with itself.

The root of the spectacle is that oldest of all social specializations, the specialization of power. The spectacle plays the specialized role of speaking in the name of all the other activities. It is hierarchical society's ambassador to itself, delivering its official messages at a court where no one else is allowed to speak. The most modern aspect of the spectacle is thus also the most archaic.

The social separation reflected in the spectacle is inseparable from the modern state — the product of the social division of labor that is both the chief instrument of class rule and the concentrated expression of all social divisions.

In the spectacle, a part of the world represents itself to the world and is superior to it. The spectacle is simply the common language of this separation. Spectators are linked solely by their one-way relationship to the very center that keeps them isolated from each other. The spectacle thus reunites the separated, but it reunites them only in their separateness.

Workers do not produce themselves, they produce a power independent of themselves. The success of this production, the abundance it generates, is experienced by the producers as an abundance of dispossession. As their alienated products accumulate, all time and space become foreign to them. The forces that have escaped us display themselves to us in all their power.

Though separated from what they produce, people nevertheless produce every detail of their world with ever-increasing power. They thus also find themselves increasingly separated from that world. The closer their life comes to being their own creation, the more they are excluded from that life.

The spectacle is capital accumulated to the point that it becomes images.

[…]

The very style of dialectical theory is a scandal and abomination to the prevailing standards of language and to the sensibilities molded by those standards, because while it makes concrete use of existing concepts it simultaneously recognizes their fluidity and their inevitable destruction.

[…]

Ideas improve. The meaning of words plays a role in that improvement. Plagiarism is necessary. Progress depends on it. It sticks close to an author's phrasing, exploits his expressions, deletes a false idea, replaces it with the right one.

Détournement is the flexible language of anti-ideology. It appears in communication that knows it cannot claim to embody any definitive certainty. It is language that cannot and need not be confirmed by any previous or supracritical reference. On the contrary, its own internal coherence and practical effectiveness are what validate the previous kernels of truth it has brought back into play. Détournement has grounded its cause on nothing but its own truth as present critique.

[…]

The point is to actually participate in the community of dialogue and the game with time that up till now have merely been represented by poetic and artistic works.

When art becomes independent and paints its world in dazzling colors, a moment of life has grown old. Such a moment cannot be rejuvenated by dazzling colors, it can only be evoked in memory. The greatness of art only emerges at the dusk of life.

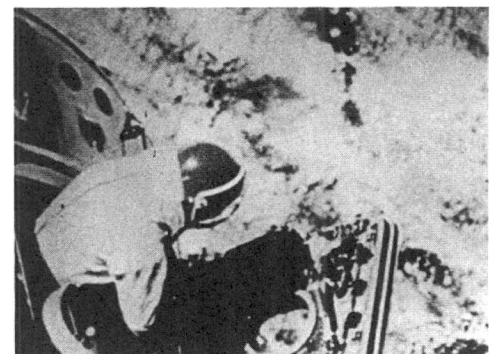

...an immense accumulation of spectacles. Everything that was directly lived has receded...

Fragmented views of reality regroup themselves into a new unity as a separate pseudoworld that can only be looked at.

The spectacle thus reunites the separated, but it reunites them only in their separateness.

The very style of dialectical theory is a scandal and abomination to the prevailing standards of language...

When art becomes independent and paints its world in dazzling colors, a moment of life has grown old.

In the spectacle's basic practice of incorporating into itself all the fluid aspects of human activity so as to possess them in a congealed form...

Each new lie of the advertising industry is an admission of its previous lie.

...a new period has begun. We have already seen the failure of the first proletarian assault against capitalism; now we are witnessing the failure of capitalist abundance.

Neo-Benshi
Live Film Narration

Konrad Steiner
Remarks on Benshi Tradition and Neo-Benshi

The benshi was a film-teller, and thrived in Korea and Japan during the silent film era. The professional organization was strong enough to actually forestall the introduction of sound cinema technology into the production stream from studio to theater by several years.

The benshi would narrate silent films by acting both as narrator and by voicing characterizations during the course of a film, switching between roles much as Mel Blank's Bugs Bunny, Elmer Fudd and Daffy Duck. In Japanese puppet theater the manipulators of the puppets are dressed discretely in black, but all the time visible. Similarly the benshi, like a ventriloquist, is visible at all times, but unlike the Wizard of Oz, requires no curtain. Midori Sawato, the modern exponent of the traditional benshi practice, merely sits at a table to the left of the screen with a small lamp and her script. Advocating this all-but-lost-art through her travels and performances, she inspired me to re-imagine benshi for our post-modern times.

Just as the traditional benshi wrote his (they were invariably men) own script from a studio plot summary and a print of the film, the neo-benshi writes her text from the video store's copy run back and forth through a DVD player or VCR for analysis. The neo-benshi then plays with that "video-text" to inscribe and torque the narrative with latent or novel meanings, live in front of an audience. This inventive and subversive approach contrasts to pre-recorded 'audio commentary tracks' which interpret films and give background or fun facts.

The kino-karaoke combination of theatrical presentation with the re-presentation of a known work critically, humorously, and artfully makes the neo-benshi a form for our jaded times. Remixes and mashes of movies are commonplace nowadays, we know the movies too well not to realize their subtexts and histories. There are some re-dubbing precedents in cinema as well, including Woody Allen's "What's Up Tiger Lily" and "Can Dialectics Break Bricks?" a film by the Situationist, Rene Vienet. But the benshi format, which uses a classically framed performance format and tweaks it, takes full advantage of the theatrical nature of the performance, as well as a potentially humorous and ironic stance leveraging the original against itself. At the same time it takes a sincere pleasure in the love of the movies.

Neo-benshi is a step beyond film narration, fan fiction and vidding (pop songs cut against footage of favorite actors) because it involves live audience response and even improvisation. It is a way to take back the cinema that is ours to begin with. Films are the modern fairy tales and myths. Their stories belong to the culture, not the critic. Everyone knows this implicitly, when they discuss the motivations of character or explanations of a plot. But wait—the neo-benshi is a kind of critic, an interpreter. Her triangulation of our experience of narrative cinema is an antidote to the formulaic studio system run amok, and the rampant auteurism prevalent in Indiewood which amounts to a fin-de-siecle mannerism, stylistic novelty for its own sake.

Therine Youngblood
Poetry and Motion

San Francisco poets and filmmakers are pushing the boundaries of the cinematic form. Testing the limits of the medium in the Bay Area is hardly a new occurrence. In 1958, multimedia artist Bruce Conner made *A Movie*, launching a wave of reassemblage filmmaking. During the late '60s and early '70s, the National Center for Experiments in Television (NCET) built its home at KQED's old location at Seventh Street, where artists "painted in time," fusing together electronic and cinematic techniques. And, for the past two and half decades, gallery spaces like New Langton Arts and Artists' Television Access have hosted numerous genre-bending artists who are investigating the medium in all its varied aspects. In a city built on shifting ground, it seems only natural that artists should shake the foundation of the form. Now, through live performance, poets and visual artists are finding common ground on which to explore the possibilities of cinema. […]

Konrad Steiner, a member of San Francisco Cinematheque's curatorial committee, seeks to highlight the theatrical aspects of cinema through live readings. After seeing Japanese benshi Midori Sawato perform with *A Diary of Chuji's Travels* (1927) at the Pacific Film Archive in 2002, Steiner became inspired to revive the art of live narration with film. The Japanese term benshi means "film-teller," and during the silent film era in Japan and Korea, benshis thrived, writing and performing a script along with a film's screening. These narrators originally grew out of a need for an interpreter to explain cultural differences or the events taking place in foreign films, but they also grew from Kabuki theater, which traditionally includes an on-stage narrator. "I'd like to reclaim the live theater aspect of cinema," Steiner says. "After I saw a benshi performance, I realized that could be done simply with words. And who better to turn to than poets?" Steiner approached several poets, many coming out of the San Francisco Poets Theater movement, and asked them to participate as neo-benshis by reinterpreting a scene from an existing film and performing a new script live while the film is projected. […]

Neo-benshi's genre mixing quality also attracts performance poet, creative writing professor, and curator Roxanne Hamilton to the form. "I am interested in this tension between the live, the performative, and the preserved," she says. "With film, people can escape in the dark and consume images. There is no conversation." By interacting with cinema through performance, she can have a dialogue with the film's imagery, narrative, and cultural framework. Through performance, she also has direct access to her audience, who immediately receive her words and gestures, adding another layer to the conversation with the film. As for the audience, the performer's presence brings cinema back to the theater, making the act of watching an event again. While the privacy of one's computer screen or television set allows for mobility and comfort, the theater, as ever, provides community and company.

Konrad Steiner

David Larsen

Rodney Koeneke

Stephanie Young

Judex
A Neo-Benshi Script
Norma Cole

Description	Text
Tree Branches	[*musique*]
Magician appears	Yup, the brain is pure plastic.
Magician walks to bird, talks to bird, enters hall	Dear fellow creature. You are a serious monkey. Monkeys!?! Are they *all* monkeys? Tired monkeys. [*pause*] —I would fain hope… [*pause*] In trusting to method, we forget that our knowledge is bound to its own historicity.
Magician(seen from back) enters ballroom, walks through	Man, tortured by his mask, fabricates secretly, for his own usage, a sort of 'subculture': a world made out of the refuse of a higher world of culture, a domain of trash, immature myth, inadmissible passions…
Magician (from side) walks up steps, turns to face us	a secondary domain of compensation. That is where a certain shameful poetry is born, a certain compromising beauty.
Magician entertains	[*first trick*] Ooooohhh!!! [*more tricks--silence*] [*bird-girl trick*] Aaaaaahhhhh!!!
One blackbird	D'you know that during the rococo period of the eighteenth century
Other blackbird	—you monkeys were given a new identity, ha ha ha ha
Master of the House discoursing	Verily, kiddo, I walk among monkeys as among the foreskins and limbs of monkeys—monkeys in ruins. Gala or apocalypse, apocalypse or a part of the body, a secret part…. But let's go for a moment to the great ecumenical current the discovery or the great unveiling—I kid you not—the ear whispering under its veil of hair—or the milky way—study the tone itself—(I kid you not) [*points*] What changes a tone [*The clock chimes midnight—bong bong bong etc. Magician hands him a drink*] What causes a rupture of tone? How does one distinguish— [*he falls*]
A doctor/guest	He was just starting to get to the Heideggerian conjugation of the personal.
Doctor/guest	La! Re-signing himself.
Magician goes back into hall [freeze frame]	Come, come. Then his signature will have taken place. They seek the truth too far from themselves, while it is right near them. Spell that took him flesh and soul, dissipated every goal. His signature has taken place. [*pause*] Monkeys—love 'em or leave 'em. [*musique*]

Neo-Benshi performers at Yerba Buena Center for the Arts, San Francisco, July 7, 2005. Photographs by Debra St. John.

Mac McGinnes

Brandon Brown

Roxi Power Hamilton

Performance and Silence
Paul Hoover

"Another use for silence: furnishing or aiding speech to attain its maximum integrity or seriousness. Everyone has experienced how, when punctuated by long silences, words weigh more; they become almost palpable. Or how, when one talks less, one begins feeling more fully one's physical presence in a given space."
—Susan Sontag, "The Aesthetics of Silence"

Silence:

Performance poetry values the performance of a work over its composition, presentation over substance. It's poetry of the sound bite, photo op, and talking head presidency.

Performance:

Performance poetry is as "composed" as any other literary work, but it's created as a script for performance rather than an isolated text, its voice muffled in dusty libraries. As for the sound bite, the soul of poetry has always been compression. It's true that performance poetry has a large audience, the better to distribute pleasure and instruction.

Silence:

In the l980s America not only produced shoddy products but also came to prefer them. Performance poems represent the institutionalization of inferior products. In this respect, they resemble what Donald Hall calls "McPoems," tasteless and bland pseudo-poems that mainly communicate their urgency to be poetic.

Performance:

There are good performance poems and bad ones, like any other mode. In fact, poetry slams have a better way of establishing poetry's value, by means of applause, judges from the audience, and a scoring system.

Silence:

The purpose of performance art was to challenge the preciousness of the art object, to decommodify it. But in the United States, the more an art form opposes commodity, the more likely it is to gain commodity status. This happened with rock and roll, outsider poetry including the Beats, and hip hop and rap music. In its emphasis on what will play with the audience, performance poetry makes an unashamed appeal to poetry's commodity potential.

Performance:

To communicate a poem isn't to "commodify" it, your favorite word. Performance poetry simply heightens the vocalism inherent in poetry generally, as seen in traditional lyrics like "Ding dong bell, pussy's in the well." Those who attack performance poetry are afraid of confronting the awesome power of words when they are properly communicated.

Silence:

With the dominance of marketing motives over philosophical and moral purpose comes the risk of audience manipulation and even demagoguery. The author of Mein Kampf understood the secret of political speech-making:

"The receptivity of the great masses is very limited, their intelligence is small, but their power of forgetting is enormous. In consequence of these facts, all effective propaganda must be limited to a very few points and must harp on these in slogans until the last member of the public understands what you want him to understand by your slogan."

Performance:

You're reading Mein Kampf now?

Silence:

Research only. I hide it in the closet.

Performance:

It's true that the voice has power and must be used to moral ends. One of the reasons that spoken word poetry is popular with multicultural audiences is that they can see themselves, for once, being heard. Jessica Hagedorn writes that the poetry reading is "detached and academic to me, visions of young women wearing tweed suits and tortoise-shell glasses, clearing their throats and 'reading' about their animas rising and libidos pulsating in trembling, Sarah Lawrence-type voices." In other words, the placid reading is political, too, promoting the values of a culturally dominant class. Only by piercing the veil of decorum with her voice can the marginalized poet be heard.

Silence:

Performance poetry reflects American culture's love of instant gratification. It demands total ease of consumption, with little work on the part of the consumer. One hollow moment of entertainment follows another. In this, performance poetry resembles television.

Performance:

As a mass medium of great power, television lends itself to the spoken word. Why not put it to use? Only in a Puritan country like the United States could a complaint be lodged against gratification. If poetry gratifies, all the better! The pleasure of poetry is not the amount of work required for understanding it, but the directness and immediacy of its report. Performance poetry provides that pleasure by means of the most traditional and beautiful of instruments, the voice.

Silence:

Performance poetry emphasizes spectacle over other aspects of literature. Aristotle wrote, "The Spectacle has, indeed, an emotional attraction of its own, but, of all the parts (of the tragedy), it is the least artistic, and connected least with the art of poetry." When a poet goes onstage as an actor, in personae and using costumes, he or she creates spectacle but not necessarily poetry.

Performance:

Most performance poetry doesn't require costumes, light shows, and the other technologies of stagecraft. It is, quite simply, a poet filling space with mind and voice. An auditory spectacle, poetry has always related to the breath of a speaker, and it is only by means of performance that the oracular and musical properties of poetry are revealed. As Charles Olson wrote, "Breath allows all the speech-force of language back in (speech is the 'solid' of verse, is the secret of the poem's energy)." By presenting no verbal spectacle, the poem as text gives poetry its well-earned reputation for dullness.

Silence:

Like America in general, performance poetry is proudly anti-intellectual. Even the most bohemian poets of the previous generation—for example, Allen Ginsberg—saw themselves as part of an intellectual tradition, albeit against the grain. The current emphasis on performance is far more dismissive of text and satisfied with a low literacy level.

Performance:

If the nation is sinking into illiteracy, it's the fault of society as a whole, not performance poetry. Spoken word awakens the senses and cleanses the soul through song. The real problem is the refusal of poetry-as-text to accept its public role.

Silence:

With its need to be understood in one listening, performance poetry works against complexity, reducing the poem to what can be declaimed. But much excellent poetry, from Marianne Moore to Hart Crane, doesn't lend itself to oral recitation despite being ingeniously verbal. Why should complexity be valued? Because it is the only means of capturing the contradictions of experience.

Performance:

Much performance poetry also has complexity—for instance, "the chapped lips of void kissing aureola's perception" by Edwin Torres. It requires "close listening," to use Charles Bernstein's title. But you must first acquire the ears to hear it. Roland Barthes writes on the "granularity" of the spoken word: "It is not the 'clarity of the messages,' but the blissful search for 'pulsional incidents,' the language lined with flesh, a text where we can hear the grain of the throat, the patina of consonants, the voluptuousness of vowels, a whole carnal stereophony: the articulation of the body, of the tongue, not that of meaning, of language." Torres' poetry is far from a simple declaratory oral poetics. It is complex and "abstract" in a manner reminiscent of dada sound poetry.

Silence:

Performance poetry encourages amateurism. Literary expertise, even if innovative, is disdained as elitist. Such a low standard would be laughable in disciplines such as music, mathematics, philosophy, dance, and engineering. Why encourage it in poetry?

Performance:

Performance poets read poetry all the time, but to a different purpose than poets who write for the page. Their words are seeking an immediate audience reaction, which has its own high standard of professionalism. You imply that the performance audience has imited intelligence. In fact, the audience is savvy about quality and, like fans of Italian opera, quick to disparage a poor performance.

Silence:

Performance poetry is poetically conservative. This is an unexpected criticism, since slam poetry is strongly populated with multicultural figures. Nevertheless, slam poetry represents traditional values such as orality, narrative, clarity, closure, directness, and popular lyric sentiment, as well as the bardic and heroic stance of the poet. Also, much performance poetry is written in the middle or "Iowa School" style but performed in a more insistent and vocal manner.

Performance:

It's true that some slam poetry has mainstream values aesthetically. It's easier to communicate with a narrative or dramatic base, using time, place, characters, and incident. But it is also forceful and convincing. At the same time, performance poets like Jackson Mac Low create work that's innovative both as text and presentation.

Silence:

Performance poetry misunderstands its own poetics. The first generation of postwar poets to emphasize performance—Allen Ginsberg, Amiri Baraka, Jayne Cortez, and Jerome Rothenberg, among others—had a political rationale for their works. The difference between the first and second generations of the spoken word is that the latter can't distinguish the poetics of Robert Creeley from that Maxine Kumin.

Performance:

If the poem is to be served and not the ego of the poet, if we strictly judge a poem on its own merits rather than by the biography and group loyalties of the poet, poems by James Dickey and Maxine Kumin are as good as those by Ginsberg and Baraka. It's not the kind of poem that matters; it's how it impacts the wider audience. In this respect, performance poetry is far more democratic than the poem-as-text.

Silence:

It has little impact if it's lost on the air. The poem-as-text has far wider distribution over the long run.

Performance:

That's changing. Text is momentary, too, because communicated increasingly through websites and blogs.

Silence:

Performance poetry participates in intellectual "downsizing." In the 60s, there were numerous new aesthetics to ponder, from the Deep Image and Confessionalism to Surrealism and The New York School. Now there are only two vanguards: performance poetry, which delights in the spoken word, and language poetry, which emphasizes the written and theoretical. Poetry is reduced to its most extreme characteristics, and the radical center is lost.

Performance:

What you call "the radical center" has no program except the lyric poem. Performance poetry and language poetry have simply reacted to poetry as they found it: directionless, boring, and rule-bound. Just listen to yourself—"radical center," "innovative traditions," what's that all about?

Silence:

Created largely for entertainment value, performance poetry often fails on the deeper, metaphysical level of enjoyment. In other words, it's boring. Film director Andrej Tarkovsky commented that directors can be divided into two categories:

"Those who strive to imitate the world they live in—to recreate the world that surrounds them—and the directors who create their own worlds. Those who create their own worlds are generally the poets. They are Bresson… Bergman… Bunuel…Kurosawa. They have trouble getting their films out because the audience is used to a symbolic non-existent film world—the result of the audience's own interests and tastes. The directors I named are opposed to all this—that the taste of the audience should be the deciding factor—not because they want to be obscure, but because they want to listen secretly; to give expression to what is deep inside those we call the audience."

The best poetry is exciting and challenging. Retaining its freshness on a second reading, it requires this secret listening on the part of the reader. But because of mass media, the culture increasingly lacks the reflection and silence necessary to secret listening.

Performance:

The concept of "secret listening" is appealing, but limits itself to readers, and it values only the prayerful hermetic mode, which collaborates with power. Tarkovsky's films were made by and for an elite, who study them like a text. Some spoken word poetry is difficult to comprehend as text, too, but when it's performed everything is clarified by the speaker's voice, which announces intention, timbre, and emotional scale. In other words, voice gives us meaning's boundaries. This is true even when the performed poem contains what Nick Piombino calls "aural ellipsis" or gaps in meaning.

Silence:

Poems have their most important performance at the moment of composition, not in recitation. Even improvisation is a form of writing. The best poetry is voiced as a silence. When the voice is in excess of the poem, when it's theatrical, disbelief sets in, and the audience feels the hollowness of the communication. Written or performed, poetry takes place on the stage of the mind, where the lighting and stagecraft are unmatched.

Performance:

I know you write the histories. But you'll never have the last word on this. The shamanist / showmanist aspect of language, the spoken word, is being practiced all around you, by cab drivers, stand-up comedians, and waitresses. It comes in living color and demands to be heard. Why do you think Kerouac is still a best-seller, while the mid-list author goes quickly out of print? Because it's spoken word disguised as a novel!

[long pause]

Are you there?

Silence: [silence]

Performance: Hey! [bangs phone on table]

Silence: [more silence]

Performance: Damn it! [hangs up]

Silence: [very long silence]

Photo of a tv screen showing a Busby Berkeley musical, *42nd Street:* a dance-apart portrait of Ruby Keeler

Works Cited

Bernstein, Charles. "Introduction." *Close Listening: Poetry and the Performed Word*. Ed. Charles Bernstein. Oxford: Oxford University Press, 1998.

Flood, Charles Bracelen. *Hitler: The Path to Power*. Boston: Houghton-Mifflin, 1989.

Hagedorn, Jessica. "Makebelieve Music." *The Poetry Reading*. Ed. Stephen Vincent. San Francisco: Momo's Press, 1981.

McCaffery, Steve. "The Aural Ellipsis and the Nature of Listening in Contemporary Poetry." *Close Listening: Poetry and the Performed Word*. Ed. Charles Bernstein. Oxford: Oxford University Press, 1998.

Olson, Charles. "Projective Verse." *Selected Writings*, Ed. by Robert Creeley. New York: New Directions, 1966.

Tarkovsky, Andrej. *Sculpting in Time*. Trans. Kitty Hunter-Blair. Austin: University of Texas Press, 1989.

Torres, Edwin. "Dig on the Decade." *Aloud: Voices from the Nuyorican Poets Cafe*. Ed. Bob Holman. New York: Henry Holt, 1994.

Photograph by Midgalia Valdes

And The Beat Moves On
Michael McClure's Collaborations with Ray Manzarek and Terry Riley
Roxanne Power Hamilton

I don't go to church, but when I heard that Michael McClure would perform with Ray Manzarek at San Francisco's Noe Valley Ministries in January 2006, I knew I might be in for a religious experience. Not long before he died, Allen Ginsberg gave a spiritual gloss to the ongoing collaboration between the notorious beat poet and the Doors' keyboardist, calling it "a ripening of good karma." Part of that "karma" is the apparent inheritance of the Beat legacy by key musicians of the 60s such as Bob Dylan and the Doors. Ray Manzarek put it succinctly, "If Kerouac hadn't written *On The Road*, the Doors would not exist…We wanted to be beatniks. We wanted to be 'poetry and jazz'" (*The Third Mind*, 1999). In 1968, Jim Morrison introduced Manzarek and McClure during the third recording session of the Doors. Almost forty years later, they are still bringing the word to a congregation hungry for that potent mixture of beat poetry and music.

In recognition of their roots, they launch into "For Jim Morrison." Manzarek plays the familiar cascading piano lines of "Riders on the Storm" behind McClure's transcendent lyrics. McClure's overdub is unlike the original song; rather than holding its listeners spellbound in a delicious fear, this piece rides forward on that eerie beat toward something more like illumination. With the same calm, deep resonance he brings to each poem, McClure speaks his words while listening and responding to Manzarek's subtle piano work: "O Potency. To be my self-soiled soul spirit again and nothing more. I am my abstract alchemist of flesh made real and nothing more, no less than star…O Muse! O Me!" This Whitmanesque paean to his own creative presence is a far cry from the apocalyptic lyrics we expect: "if you give this man a ride, sweet memory will die."

Viz. is publishing two gutsy blues lyrics that McClure and Manzarek played in the concert and which will appear on their next CD, *In the Rippling of an Aeon*. The performance of "Black Wine" was the most moving tune of the evening because of its indebtedness to Chicago blues. It's no coincidence that one of their best pieces is called "For Willie Dixon." To get a sense of how primal their blues can get, listen to "High Heelz" and "Spank me with a Rose" on their last CD, *There's a Word*. These are simple down and dirty lyrics with a solid thrumming backbeat: "I'm headed for jail, just headed for jail…See the little sparrow with her eyes on the hawk. Everything around is just more talk. Don't use a knife to pound in a nail. Spank me with a rose. I'm headed for jail." Throughout the evening, roses unfurled in McClure's poetry until they took on mystical connotations not unlike the reappearing angels in the poetry and paintings of Blake.

The Romantic influence is particularly felt in the "Music Haikus" that they have been developing for years. Manzarek's accompaniment is, by turns, complementary or contrapuntal to McClure's words, depending on the piece. As McClure reads "What soft brown eyes the dog has/ as she shits/ on the deer's hoof prints," the piano and flute accompaniment actually manage, delightfully, to suggest this event for us. The same is true of the haiku, "The yellow leaf spins/through the silver downpour/smacks my windshield." McClure's imagery is, of course, enough to carry the poem, but Manzarek's piano-work recreates a twirling leaf and allows us to hear the image. Each of the artists is very sensitive to the autonomy of the other's art. It's a pleasure to see McClure walk over to Manzarek's piano, microphone in hand, and gaze down upon his partner's graceful hands, quietly attentive to the uniqueness of the event as it's happening. In other moments, Manzarek's head—usually bent down over his keyboard—tilts up, and he follows the poet's words, head nodding in time, fingers following the linguistic dance.

"The Beat" is apparently McClure's signature piece, since he plays it with Manzarek and also with Terry Riley on their CD, *I Like Your Eyes, Liberty*. In the version he plays with Manzarek, the piano sounds like a dancer strutting playfully behind the poet, trying out its footsteps. The poetic line and the musical line could each stand alone: two kids playing in the playground glad for each other's presence but absorbed in their own play. Merce Cunningham and John Cage liked to take the stage together, but the dancer did not dance *to* the music; the musician did not play *for* the dancer. They occupied the same space in time. Though Manzarek and McClure do integrate their work more conscientiously, each artistic expression is valid unto itself, creating a third space through simultaneity. That is why Manzarek's keyboard licks with the Doors were so compelling; he wasn't supplementing Morrison so much as creating a self-sufficient and memorable sound with him, rather than *behind* him.

With McClure's collaboration with Terry Riley, on the other hand, you experience the keyboard as being solely responsive to the words. Similar to the experience of hearing a film soundtrack, the symbiosis between narrative and music in these pieces feels like fully integrated compositions. In "The Beat," Riley's piano notes spiral up and down: long, rapid scales invoking the journey from birth to death and back, as McClure's lyrics imply. "Beat. The beat moves on. Right in the life after life before birth can flash. Lightning and turquoise. Dream collapses into the river. While the current flows, the boat sets off. Long regret, this body, no possession of mine…." Riley's jazzy backdrop contrasts Manzarek's slow, bluesy boogie woogie. This feels more like a spiraling journey: sparkling, chromosomal glimpses into the beginning of life; piano notes shimmying up and down DNA strands. There is a simpatico here between McClure's cosmic visions and Riley's expansive reach across the keyboard's upper and lower registers, reminding us of the Ptolemaic claim about the relationship between musical notes and interplanetary space. If you plucked strings between Venus, Earth, and Mars, you might end up with a beautiful chord, as you do here.

In *I Like Your Eyes Liberty*, the words are from McClure's *Plum Stones: Cartoons of No Heaven* (O Books, 2002) and *Ghost Tantras* (San Francisco, 1964). The sentient and the etherial intermingle in this recording, especially in the long track, "Each Side." A musicalized short epic, McClure's story feels bardic and episodic because of the way the musical interludes set up a chain of interlinking narratives. Almost every piece references a Buddhist concept related to conditions such as impermanence, suffering, emptiness, and kindness. "Before meat conceived of its hunger, I was inside the stream listening to myself out there…Let me work with these monster dragons. I will seek clearly and be generous." As Riley said of the recording, "All the elements were there…opening vast spaces for voice and music to spiral up the Buddha column."

McClure writes, "And the beat moves on into the life after life. I am trying to flash. But the best I can manage is my love for you. " The best we can manage is to listen closely, track after track. This is inspired collaboration worth our presence of mind.

from Mule Kick Blues
Words by Michael McClure
Music by Ray Manzarek

The two blues will be part of their forthcoming CD, In The Rippling Of An Aeon

BLACK WINE

YEAH I LOVE YOU MAMA, I'M GONNA DRINK BLACK WINE
Well, I love you Mama
I'm going to drink black wine
Going put my hairy hands
on the table
Going to hold the broken cup
and drink black wine

We come from no place
and I'm going there all the time
Crickets singing in the evening
Chirping in the darkest time

I hear you telling me
I hear you telling me
Saying I got to go
We got to go when the crickets singing

Hairy hands on the table
holding the blackest wine

Crickets singing in the evening
Chirping in the darkest time
There's a drum out there
in the sunlight
There's a drum out there
in the sunlight
but crickets sing in the evening
chirping in the darkest time

Well I love you Mama
I'm going to drink black wine

Yeah   Yeah   Yeah   Yeah   Yeah
Oh Yeah

Forty Songs

I'M STANDING ON THE RIVER OF NIGHT WITH FORTY SONGS
Here's the river of night with forty songs
I'm standing on the river of night with forty songs
I'll be stepping in the boat before too long
Stepping in the boat with all these songs
White hair hanging in my beard like moss

Everything I see is movies in a dream
Look at bubbles flowing round the rocks
in the stream
I'll be stepping in the boat before too long

Deer make noise
as they walk over old dead leaves
I'll be stepping in the boat before too long
Deer make noise
as they walk over old dead leaves

VOICES
IN
THE
HEAD

Like Ali Baba
and the forty thieves

When you get home

When you get home
sit down with your back against a tree

See pictures go by like movies in a dream

The Day the Music Died
To Give Birth To You

OKAY, admit it, you liked *American Pie* when you were 7 or 8! You were home with chicken pox and mom bought the album because you had worn out the single. You came to like "Vincent" even better, the martyr artist! On another album (bought as a cut-out cassette), "Castles in The Sand" was kind of cool, but "American Pie" got you with its bouncy, wordy, epic-length. Mom liked it too, and maybe even knew what it meant. You didn't, but knew that much of the hype about it was that it was supposed to be mysterious, a little hard to figure out, but somehow patriotic (like the hippies who dressed in American flags?). You remember on some TV talk show mom was watching, probably late night (as you were walking past the TV to get to the bathroom) the singer was dodging questions about it. You also remember on syndicated radio shows, perhaps on countdowns, in which national commentators (the local DJs couldn't be counted on for stuff like that, weren't that smart, or autonomous, enough to do it) would talk about it, how the holy ghost is really The Big Bopper rather than Waylon Jennings (who gave up his seat to sanctify the others) or the "girl who just smiled and turned away" was Janis Joplin. As you found out more about the song, how anti-60s rock and roll and pop it was (criticizing the Beatles, Stones, even the Byrds! Not that you minded when "All The Young Dudes" or "London Calling" criticized them, but this you did; like Al Stewart criticizing post-1966 Dylan!), You began to hate, or least despise, this song—perhaps because you felt duped by it.

Did it have a profound effect on your "fragile eggshell" (as Jim Morrison would say) character? And, if so, how? Because it appealed to nostalgia, and you could identify with the narrator/character (he was a paperboy just like you! and it wouldn't be long before you'd be driving something like a Chevy to a levy). Something was lost, and to one at 7 who had this feeling of "just missing out" on the Beatles (who had broken up, it seemed, a "long long time ago"), or even Simon and Garfunkel, and was dimly aware of all those deaths (Joplin, Morrison, and who was this Hendrix guy?) and had some sense that top 40 was better a few years before, the song rang true. Nope, they just didn't make 'em anymore like "Eleanor Gee I Think You're Swell" or "The Mighty Quinn" (by Manfred Mann; you didn't find out about Dylan until later). "Those were the days, my friend," the sunny summers when the older glamorous teenybopper girls down the block, like your second cousin Debbie would go out to go-gos in convertibles.

And so even though McLean's paean was to an even more bygone time, more like your dad's era of Buddy Holly (when your dad had hair in the wedding picture, he even sort of looked like Buddy Holly, who wasn't bad for a pre-Beatles guy; unlike Elvis, for instance, he wrote his own songs), you as a kid could apply it to the late 1960s, your own lost era. After all, people were almost as crushed by the Beatles' breakup as they were when Kennedy, or later Lennon himself, died. Maybe even more. There did seem to be some huge cultural hysteria and maybe it was that feeling of loss that had much to do with the success of McLean's song, in addition to those who were hoping what some stand-up comedian (you can't remember who) referred to as "the great folk scare of 1971"[1] would be the next big thing (Dylan had dropped out, but you assume they meant James Taylor, Cat Stevens, Carole King, maybe Neil Young even, Ricky "Garden Party" Nelson, and others), and would return rock and pop music back to a pre-electric pre-British-invasion, pre-psychedelic, and mostly whiter simpler time of The Kingston Trio on one hand, or of bobby sox and good old boys, greasers, on the other. These two trends has been opposed circa 1959, but by 1971 seemed to have more in common with each other (funny how history works that way; like how the difference between the 1964 British invasion and 1977 British punk eventually came to seem small indeed) Ah, Sha Na Na at Woodstock. Soon *Happy Days* and *That 80s Show!* Or Neil Sedaka's, Paul Anka's, and The Four Seasons' comebacks of 1974. Elvis's comeback was already in full-swing (though "American Pie" put him down too, preferring the whiter Holly). So McLean was able to use his ambiguity to straddle the generational divide and the cultural divide between say Haggard and Hippie, or at least seem to.

Also, the religious imagery and tone (like a lot of the white guys trying gospel around that time, Simon and Garfunkel's swan-song, "Bridge Over Troubled Water," "Let it Be," The Beatles' swan song), Spirit in The Sky My Sweet Lord Border Song Jesus Freaks Jesus Was A Carpenter Is Just Alright Oh Happy Day You Can't Always Get What You Want Godspell Jesus Christ Superstar Time Magazine 1970 "Is God Coming Back To Life?" (the sequel to Time Magazine cover 1966 "Is God Dead?"). Hell, Lennon even looked like white Jesus! The nun who rocked up "The Lord's Prayer." No, not The Singing Nun (who later did ads for the pill, and then killed herself) whose "Dominque" went #1 just before The Beatles broke, but that one in 1974. McLean's "Sacred Store." Is it possible that's where you got your ideas of rock and roll as religion?

You want to say, "I hope not!" because now it seems self-righteously pretentious, in part due to McLean's sanctimonious tenor quaver. Yes, sanctimonious! Why wasn't that a turn off right off the bat? But, not knowing

---

[1] Of course, years later you'd realize the early 1970s were the last gasp of acoustic music on Pop or Rock radio aside from a one-off Tracey Chapman here and there, and now you'd definite like to see it back, if only to widen the range, and re-center your tastes

Dylan yet, perhaps this was the poor man's Dylan, a "kinder, gentler" Dylan, "killing you softly with his song." He very well may have been billed as the next Dylan or something, which meant nothing to you, but you can imagine your mom had a bit of the same elation when she shelled out her hard earned money on 2 Dylan albums circa '65. Yet, pragmatically speaking, "American Pie" was like a white church song enough so your parents could accept you listening to it, but kind of rocked enough to make you think that it was speaking to you, to "us kids," if not as much as "I Want You Back" or "Summertime Blues" (at the time of course you only knew the Blue Cheer version). Certainly it wasn't scary as the somewhat banned, "the way things are goin' they're gonna crucify me," but it was leading there in a way. And once you realized McLean was like a small-town preacher, it's a small step to say, "who needs to go to the preacher, when you can go straight to Jesus Lennon."

So already there was this sense, even in 1971, even when you were 7, that rock had somehow passed its golden era, and this was encouraged along with all the liberating potential. Within 9 years, The Who could go from "Hope I die before I get old" to the puffy prematurely-aged dinosaur-bombast of "Long Live Rock, be it dead or alive" (which you also liked at first when it came to you circa 1975). Was this really a world you wanted to get into? Wasn't it just like the church's form of spirituality (not in Latin anymore, but still a dead language—no "Can I Get a Witness?" or hand-clapping hell-raising gospel or even polkas like "In Heaven There Is No Beer"), or like the abandoned railroad downtown of your "We're not a second class city" (quoth the mayor)? Is this how that song worked subliminally on you, as a babysitter?

And how can music die? And if it can't die, how can one say it truly lived? These kinds of questions were probably not as prominent before the advent of recorded music. The Prelapsarian Dark Ages! You're ambivalent about them enough to try to see if you can untangle and make some sense of where you stand. You, who pride yourself on a simple life, would prefer to be more of a Luddite, like Laura (Riding) Jackson renouncing electricity for the last 40 years of her life, but could you do without your records and radio? Can there be music without it? I mean good, rockin' music. "Yes," you say, "if…" and we'll leave it at that for now…

"Back in the days" it was easier to see the people "behind the music"—not even "behind" that's a creation of "our alienated modern 20th century" era—but fervently present, consubstantial with the music. Why not locate what Eliot called "the dissociation of sensibility" there, rather than circa 1620 with Descartes and the advent of Capitalism? Or rather than the advent of Gutenberg's printing press and what McLuhan would call "cold media," or Plato writing down Socrates, Paul Anti-Semiting Jesus (Paul, a bigger betrayer than Judas), or the (fortunate) fall of the Garden of Eden. Yeah, why not locate it anywhere—anytime, long before you were born, or "busy being born"—anywhere, but in the present? But what was the present? Weren't there at least 2, one with the status of "reality," you being 7, feeling nostalgic for something, and 2) it being 1972. Which one of those realities was fantasy? Were they at odds with each other?

There was a forward looking (pelvic thrust) thing still going on, long hair was trickling down from your heroes to you. If this was what peer pressure was going to be, you welcomed it. It was grassroots, an up from the bottom feeling, like the young and poor in "The Winter's Tale" injecting a much needed innocence into the corrupt court! It was pure and clean and natural (hell, mom even started buying granola in the early 1970s and she always said this was why Laura turned out healthier than Maria and you). It wasn't even about cigarettes, yet alone harder drugs. Dad, the Ancien Regime, liked meat n taters and smoked. His kids used to chase him when Cal (who you used to cal cow because he was a farmer, wore a straw hat, and because you misheard, like when you used to call "Fried Egg Sandwiches" "Friday Sandwiches" because they were served on Friday when you weren't supposed to eat meat) came by with his truck from which dad bought cigs, you'd tell him "don't smoke; it's a 3 billion dollar capitalist joke!" (well, not that second part). You probably got that from those "like father, like son" commercials, or maybe the one with the Indian and his tear in the (polluted) canoe. Catholicism was on the way out. Indians were in—Yeah, you had "Cherokee People" as a #1 hit too. Mexicans were in. Women were in…"hear me roar/ in numbers too big to ignore." Bobby Riggs was out.

Still, this was a child fantasy world, as much if not more than your parents'—whether your mom with her hope, if not necessarily belief, in MGM endings, or your dad, with his alleged belief in God and church and government as he sat in front of the TV while unemployed saying, "oh the stock market's up; the economy's good"—never once considering that maybe the stock market was up because he was unemployed. Unlike you, you could see through that ruse, even when it came to school (you did poorly in it but it bored you. It was getting in the way of your real education. You'd get around that). Well, except when it came to music, of course. Music did such a good job of making you feel and even think you were creating it that you didn't even try to get around its wall, "behind the music" to reveal the man behind the curtain. You were a happy consumer, like the one Matt Walsh, in his song, "Lucky In Love" was trying to convince had a better life than him (except you were a total virgin-klutz even creep weirdo loser in love or lust or love). Well, it's okay, you were a kid, and childhood's supposed to be about fantasy. We don't want to throw the baby into shit before its skull is hardened around the gray matter (though you always liked that Richard Thompson song, "I feel for you, you little horror…there's nothing at the end of the rainbow…"), but after no Santa or Satan or God, or Beatles even, there was still rock. Childhood and poverty thrives on fantasy. You were still fucking peasants, opiated masses. And food, the poor can afford just enough 5th Avenues and TV shows, or, in your case, rock and roll records, to make you feel empowered, and that's not bad, but it was an addiction, a collector addiction, before books, before cigs, before other drugs (well, except for sugar, fat and caffeinated bubble water) that not only cost money but robbed you from your own songs that might have come up on their own.

And yes you believe everyone's got their own songs, well maybe not everyone, but far more than were able to do it. There's this thing called plagiarism people throw in your face if something you've made up sounds sort of like something you've heard on the radio ("but, dad, those two songs on the radio sound pretty much like each other too, and they don't get accused of plagiarism!" You know this nipped your mom's musical aspirations when she made a song up in the late 1950s called "I'll Be There," and her mother told her it had been done before…and that's just a title!). No wonder, years later, you got so into "he fills his head with culture/ he gives himself an ulcer," and paid for that privilege, or why you could relate to Pound and/or Shelley saying "we have eaten more than we can digest." You were devouring the radio like Similac Breast-flavored milk, but didn't feel bloated, because you were running around just like "Little Willie." It was only when it came to other questions, such as not having a basement or not having a color TV, like most of your friends, that you worried about poverty, which was a big embarrassment when an elementary school teacher called your mom and asked, "Mrs Stroffolino, are you poor?" And your mom tried her best to deny it.

Maybe that's why you envied Sissy Spacek, I mean Crystal Gail's sister, Loretta Lynn, in *Coal Miner's Daughter*. Sure, her husband beat her (like the wife of Bath's), but he let her sing! And maybe—just maybe—had your family been even poorer, destitute, like she was, mom wouldn't have been as able to get appeased by songs so much and would have had to comfort herself not so much by yelling at the dishes but by singing her own songs. Maybe had she gotten pregnant even earlier and had kids at 14, Dad would have become her manager and got her played on local stations, like they could in the rural south at that time. They're roughly the same age, your mom and Loretta—surely that was possible. Nah, those weren't your mom's needs really, nor her abilities. The glamour she wanted was College and Peace-Corps, both denied her by poverty. So, you're probably being perverse, but perhaps—after it was "too late" for her—you could find it, perhaps that was what you wanted, and she didn't necessarily dissuade you.

But is it equally perverse to blame the radio for the way you steeped yourself in it, and the way you steeped yourself in it for holding you back? I mean all the stuff could come in handy later… whenever that would be. It was part of learning one's craft, knowing the territory, and it gave you, and many like you, a kind of ambition. So, BTO could brag in "Takin Care of Business" about the freedom rock bought them, and if you would've taken it seriously, you may have even joined the millions who were buying guitars, but for some reason you didn't, didn't get in with "the right bunch of fellas" (or maybe didn't recognize them in your neighbors) by your late teens or early 20s. And, even though the rock and roll fantasy (Do you think Kinks or Bad Company? Both? Neither?) dream felt liberating, just as the college one did, the fact remains that 1) radio was becoming more corporate-national and 2) more of you had that dream, so many of you, like 3rd world countries, "developing nations" wanting to "grow up" from the "shackles of the past" into the capitalist democratic dream, that it created a lot of rising expectations, and this increased dissatisfactions among "white America," which may have been good insofar as much of the best music comes out of frustration and despair, the blues of your heroes, often one step removed in blanched whiteness, but you were getting closer to the source! And this led away from George Thorogood and "Road House Blues" to Muddy Waters, and also to punk. Your collective goals weren't even economic upward mobility—you'd sacrifice those goals, gladly.

And, besides, radio was giving you advice—"My momma told me you better shop around." Ah, if only your momma, or even your poppa, had told you that, earlier! But beggars can't be choosers. Was it too late? Your mom, a hopeless romantic, sure made you think it was, for her. Did that rub off on you? Yes, locate it there, Chris! The simple story you started with—radio saved you from your parents! So that commercial with the friendly white greaser guy—but cooler and more authentic-seeming than Fonzie—leanin' out the window of his 'vette or sumthin' saying, "Dad told me to turn it off, and I said, 'but Dad, it's SMOKEY!'"—rang true. In your case it was the Captain and Tennille's cover version first, but still…Smokey! Dylan's favorite poet! You're gonna shop around, have that "choosey beggar" attitude in love your parents lacked. Nyro's "Confession." Lynn's "The Pill"—not going to lapse like Carly Simon at the end of "That's The Way I Always heard it Should Be" or Janis Ian's "Society's Child" or Rundgren's "We Gotta Get You A Woman," much less the pathetic housewives of "Band Of Gold" or that beautiful melody "Don't Say You Don't Remember" or Vicki Carr's "It Must be Him", but the head's up "Touch Me In The Morning" was better. And who needs to "shop around" in love when you can "shop around" on the radio?

So the radio was not a single entity but a place to shop around for an identity (that is also a good tune), and you could choose the better songs as role models, could "take what you need and leave the rest." Only problem was a lot of songs had great melodies but pathetic dysfunctional lyrics ("I'd rather live in his world than live without him in mine"). Did they sink in subliminally too? Tipper Gore's PMRC would be of no help, because for you a sad song of pathetic longing was more destructive than any "As Nasty As They Wanna Be," and, of course, there was an answer song for Smokey, "Don't Let Him Shop Around." It wasn't as big of a hit, though you think George Jones' answer song to "Love The One You're With" was a big country hit. So the radio—and the music itself of which it was the earthly avatar—was precisely to be valued for the ambivalence, the mixed messages, the polyvocality, for playing in one person many parts, "First I am king…then beggar…"

All you needed was here, and you could sort it out how you saw fit. How did you see fit? You didn't know yet, but you knew it had something to do with being able to be as eclectic as the radio (for therein lied freedom) while at the same time being able to be a person, to grow up like Pinocchio, to be a real boy, or man, however silly being a man might have sounded in the absence of role models (though the Yardbirds' and Willie Dixon's versions were cooler than The Spencer Davis Group's or Chicago's or Fabian's). Many of your favorite musicians were still referred to as "the boys," even as The Beach Boys were approaching 40.

But first, you'd need a narrative. Ugh. A narrative. Yes, even you, a narrative to identify with. Not a narrator per se (they often were so busy narrating that they didn't do anything!) but a hero who developed in time, who was a real-life human, with limits and/or flaws. So what that he wouldn't hug you? You had mom for that. The monkey shouldn't be forced to reject the wire-mesh mother that feeds him for the cloth mother; Hal shouldn't have to reject Falstaff. You could have both. But who would it be? Not someone who died young like Buddy Holly, Jim Croce or Jim Morrison. Not the Beatles, for though you had most of their albums and even some bootlegs (hell, you were even duped into buying Klaatu in 1976 around the time of the hit-single of "Got To Get You Into My Life"), and books about them, and posters on your wall, they were too busy being four people. But luckily The Beatles broke up! Despite the narrative of cultural decay certain aspects of the radio were trying to dose you with, maybe their breakup was fortuitous after all, even more so than Santa breaking up into your parents who were tenaciously refusing to get divorced. John Lennon emerged as a solo-artist, and even though he had gone into retirement by this time, and more of his great music was as a member of The Beatles, his passive-aggressive act of going solo (Paul wouldn't release "Cold Turkey" as a Beatles song, so John took all the songwriting credit and waited for Paul to make the break official) was a monumental act insofar as it afforded you a different, and more humanly realistic perspective on the workings of the Beatles than you had had before.

Ah, John Lennon, a Libra like your dad, only a year (minus 3 days) younger than him, and your mom was exactly the same age as Paul McCartney. This not only lent a pleasing irony to Paul's "Your Mother Should Know," but also served as an excuse for you to think of John as your surrogate father—even though, in the "real world," he was probably as bad of a father to Julian—born less than a month after you—as your dad was to you (assuming, of course, if money doesn't change a thing). Well, he made up for it with Sean, right? Or would've, had he not been assassinated. The addition of the mass-culture father-figure certainly complicates "the family romance," and it's not just overlaid but at its base, and as long as the psychological industry refuses to take this into account, it will be as hollow for many as the church it replaced was!

Okay, Lennon wasn't perfect, but who were you, who were your parents, who were the critics, to judge. He had boldly gone where no man had ever gone before (who needed Star Trek? While your sister Maria might have preferred to be "lost in space," you didn't need the space part of it). His imperfections made him more human, yes, like Christ blasting the fig tree or raging at money-changers, the Christ who many prefer more for his passion and for the miracles (tricks he did for you) than for what he said. But you dug what he said too, and once The Beatles broke up, John went about revising their history and bringing himself more down to earth with the demythologizing Plastic Ono Band album and that eye-opening interview he granted in which he went through all the Lennon-McCartney songs and told you which ones were his (and how few they actually wrote together). So, you found yourself making a tape of just his Beatles songs (even though there were some pretty damn good Paul and George ones) to see more clearly his narrative development as an artist—a continuity between his "lovable moptop phase" and the later (more militant) reinventions.

On one level the development with women, from cocky nasty jealous songs like "You Can't Do That" and "Run For Your Life" (alongside of course of beautiful Arthur-Alexander inspired love songs like "All I Gotta Do" and sad laments like "I'll Be Back" and

"You've Got To Hide Your Love Away") to sticking lines in Paul songs like "I used to be cruel to my woman I'd beat her and kept her apart from the things that she loved" to "Woman Is The Nigger Of The World" (with Yoko). Sure, you could argue he was just changing with the times, but it's also possible he was at least a little ahead of them, certainly ahead of your times (of course it could also be argued that he was behind the times; since the lament in "Nigger" was that "we make her paint her face and dance," as if that was, sui generis, a bad thing, therefore it could be read as a critique of cross-dressing glam-rock "Rebel Rebels" who were more fashionable that year). You certainly didn't go through the beating woman phase; hell, you were too shy to even ask girls out. But Lennon was "the word made flesh," a dramatic embodiment, a working class hero who told you to take up your cross and follow him (even on the same album in which he told you not to do what he had done, "I couldn't walk and I tried to run." So, damn it, he was sending mixed messages! But didn't Christ, and The Bible of which he was a part, do that too?)….And not only that he had a monkey! And liked playing mind games! What didn't he touch on?

Even his retirement at age 35 was heroic, though you were at first bummed that he was letting Paul run around with his silly love wings, while he was house-husbanding. America needed him! But he had already given so much, and at the expense of Julian as he readily admitted, and somehow you knew that you hadn't even begun to digest it yet, and so you could let him go, and look for substitutes in other rock musicians. But no one, not Springsteen, not Joel, not ELO, not Queen, not Fleetwood Mac, not even Stevie Wonder, could quite step up to the plate. Dylan hadn't hit you yet (maybe you needed drugs, or at least college, for that jump). Nor punk. Certainly you were still in "student" phase, too early to even entertain that maybe you, in some small way or scene, could fill that void Lennon had awakened with something like yourself (especially as everyone pooh-poohed it if by chance you were bold enough to say you wanted to be like him when you "grew up.").

When he returned with *Double Fantasy*, it wasn't so great (those session musicians sounded a bit antiseptic), but it promised greater things, and at 40 he still had a youthful glow you didn't think people could have at 40. The many radio interviews and cover stories that were starting to emerge proved that he still had that spark, that twinkle, that hope and revolutionary spirit—yet tempered by being a survivor—yes, of all the craziness of the 60s and early 70s, the velocity of those times, the Hamburg speed years, the heroin, acid, pot, the "lost weekend" of alcohol in 1974. Someone who had been through it all, yet didn't seem scarred or scared or tired anymore, but had come out the other side, with a freaky maturity and the gentle-spirit that first drew people to him still in tact. It was just like starting over. You were excited. Like maybe this could help offset Reagan, who was getting elected around the same time ("Mandate My Ass" as Gil Scott-Heron said), or at least McCartney, disco, MTV, and all the other mice who played while the cat was away.

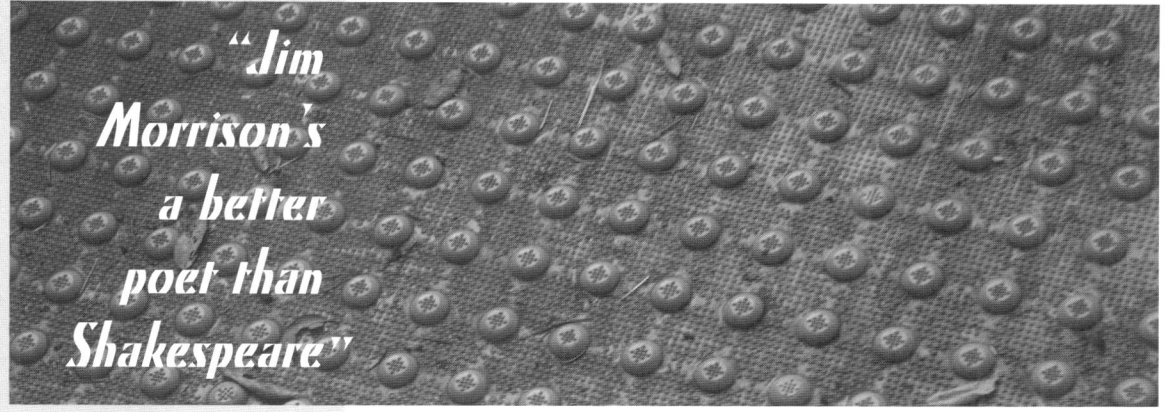

Of course, at this time, you and your friends were getting hugely into Jim Morrison and The Doors. It wasn't better than Lennon, but in so many ways better than McCartney, and thus much of The Beatles. The pop melodies hooked you. There was a bubblegum aspect to them, even in many of their album tracks, but also the dark deep keyboard-guitar interplay and minimalist, almost jazz-like drumming (and, since you were starting to play keyboard, it was good to like a band in which it was so prominent) organically meshed in a way Elton John or Billy Joel could never quite achieve with their guitarists. Even with the songs that featured guitar, like "The Bitch Is Back" or "Closer To The Borderline," which you liked, Joel or John didn't seem in their body enough. And of course "The End," when it was featured in *Apocalypse Now* (circa 1979), allowed you to hear another side of them. You nudged your friend David Yoder in the theatre, "Is that the Doors? It sounds like The Doors. Never heard this before…." And that *No One Here Gets Out Alive* book. It seemed everyone had it, that, and Hammer of the Gods.

You had *The Doors' Greatest Hits* (a Quad Mix!) since like 1976 or so, but "The End" made them finally seem like the album-band many saw them as, so you bought all of their albums around 1979-1980, your junior year of high school. In senior year, you even went so far as to tell your English teacher, "Jim Morrison's a better poet than Shakespeare" and that impressed rebel Ed enough he soon started inviting you to cut class at his backyard pool. Of course you believed it at the time. You bought the media-sell hook, line, and sinker. Years later, when some disheveled middle-aged drunk told you and Dave Rosenthal the same thing in Penn Station at 3AM, you were like "Yeah, 'ride the snake to the lake!' that's a great one. Or, get this, 'I'll always be a word man, better than a bird man.' Classic, dude!" And Dave was like, "what got into you, you almost got us killed!"

So, maybe it wasn't the poetry, or the myth of Morrison as "lizard king" that really got you into The Doors (in this sense it was almost like Lennon in reverse, in realizing that Krieger especially and to a lesser extent Manzarek didn't get the attention they deserved, whereas Lennon was probably more important to The Beatles than he let on for years, giving McCartney songwriting credits on songs he wrote, even refusing to take any songwriting credits for his contribution to "Taxman"—Lennon kind of hid behind the band), and Morrison, even at his most fascinating, could never fulfill the surrogate father role you probably craved at the time (to accept the Freudian box enough to subvert it from within). But it wasn't mere peer-pressure either. You had just been mistaken in giving the theatrical face, the verbal frontman, more credit than the body of the band.

STROFFOLINO 105

So, you'd go hang out with your friends, drinking at night on a dirt road in the woods of Muhlenberg township (if not quite a Chevy at a levy, though for all you know Mr. Peabody's coal train by now has driven it away), and play tapes of classic rock albums in a car stereo with the doors open (no, it was probably more like a "boom box" like the one you carried around the abandoned factories listening to The Animals on acid a year later). And, since it would have been Jim Morrison's birthday, on this particular night you were playing a lot of Doors. The "underrated" (because Kreiger had more to do with it than Morrison) *Soft Parade* was your favorite at the time. "The monk bought lunch," etc. And then Brian, or whoever it was, dropped you off a little drunk, maybe even stoned (I think pot came in the summer before senior year of high school, no cigarettes yet), only to be woken up around 5AM by your mother who had just gotten the paper (you were no longer a paper-boy—at least not a morning paperboy). She was crossing a line, but since she never did that without good reason, and was bent on not leaving before you woke up—insistent, maybe even shaken—you, in a hangover daze you tried to hide from her (by hiding under the blankets) asked, "Why are you showing me the paper?" "Read it!"

The first headline you saw, "Reagan selects so and so to cabinet." "Why are you showing me this?" "No, there." "John Lennon, Shot!" "First thought, "shit!" Second thought (which you verbalized) "At least he's not dead." "Read it!" He was dead. He was dead. Did you cry? Probably, and yell, and scream (is there a difference?) and moan and groan. "This is the worst! I'm not going to school today." "Get dressed. You're going to school." "Okay, but I'm gonna wear a black armband, and take my portable radio." You're not sure you told her that, but she wasn't about to stop you. If there's anything like a day the music died, this was going to be it. Worse, far worse, than losing your father would have been. Maybe now you knew what your sister went through when her best friend died when she was 8. Nah, nah, this was far worse than that.

The radio stations obliged of course, playing Lennon and Beatles songs non-stop (even the ones Paul wrote! Stupid fucks!). You got to school before classes started when and where everybody mills around in the hallways, waiting in their various cliques (3 of 4 of which you were in, so it always made it hard to choose), and assumed a place, alone, besides the Audio/Visual Room (where you helped produced the school's weekly TV shows aired on a local cable TV station. One of the extra-curricular activities you took most pride in because it allowed you room to express your fledgling quirky rebel personality, certainly more than "band" did, to say nothing of most classes!). Then you started singing, tentatively at first, but soon very loudly, along with the radio, to Lennon songs. Alone, you were fiery, scary, possessed, self-righteous! Committed! Howling! Devastated! A freak—People backed away, were you pushing them away? You thought some would join you. Couldn't believe they weren't. You were the fucking "town crier." After what seemed an interminably long time, Eric (the guy who later became a DJ) finally came over and joined in. Overcame his shyness perhaps. It wasn't that you weren't shy, but someone had to do this. The same fire that made Mark David Chapman so obsessed with Lennon was in you! Were you trying to shake him out of your system?

You sang more Lennon songs. You even made fun of yourself by changing the words to "It'll be just like keeling over." You weren't going to be "swallowing your pain." Not today. Eventually other students started throwing pennies, then nickels and dimes at Eric and you. It felt like lions, and tigers, and bears (oh my). Obviously an insult—those fuckers—fuck them. But it was also your first paying gig! You're pretty sure you didn't think of it so crassly at the time, but while Eric was content to not pick up the money, you did (like $1.43 total). The miserliness of your paternal grandmother had filtered down….

> You sang more Lennon songs. You weren't going to be "swallowing your pain." Eventually other students started throwing pennies... obviously an insult... **But it was also your first paying gig!**

Soon, the bell rang and everyone filed to classes. You must've calmed down enough because there were no further incidents (though it could be like the "blackout" a drunkard experiences only to wake up with bloodstains on his boots). Don't know if teachers put aside their class lessons to talk of Lennon. Probably not, but it's a blank—except that in between classes you still went around with the boom box on your shoulders (like you did with the Betsy Ross flag another time, running through the halls, chanting, "America, when it was still a good idea!" and then placing it where the 50-star flag belonged in the classroom—so it wasn't like this was your only transgression into theatrical freakish "acting-out" in high-school—nor the first), singing songs amid the loud shuffle of students, "American History, Practical Math." As the day wore on, more students dug what you were doing: "If a fool persists in his folly," etc. It felt like hell. You wanted them to feel like hell! You wanted rock and roll high school energy conspiring against the man (Ah, and maybe this helps explain why "School Of Rock" made you cry on the plane to Chicago in March of 2004)…

And you kind of got it, during lunch, when the art teacher (of all people! It wouldn't have been so bad, or such a good story, had it been the Algebra or Chemistry teacher) came into the lunch room, where you were loudly playing Lennon on the radio or tapes, maybe not even singing along anymore, and told you to turn it off (not even down, but off).

"No."

"Turn it off. You're disturbing classes."

"There are no classes. It's lunch."

"Not for everybody."

So she pulled you by the hair and dragged you, in front of all the students, down to the principal's office. Once there, the principal's interrogation went something like this—"Who is this John Lennon?" (Is it possible he didn't even know?)

"It's not like he's the Mayor of Laureldale (population 5, 628) or anything."

"Would you allow me to play music very loud, or speeches of the Mayor of Laureldale, during lunch, if he had died?"

"That's not the point…"

Well, what exactly was the point, if not the fact that as he spoke, over the intercom speaker in the wall by his desk (the speaker that was normally used for the school's PA system, but through which was also piped Muzak while he was working in between announcements) was playing, get this, "Mind Games," and not even a Muzak version, but Lennon's own Top 18 Hit (you can't believe it didn't get higher than that!) from 7 years earlier, as if to prove you right and him wrong! It seemed the whole world was mourning, and here was some two-bit petty principal wanting business as usual. In-school suspension, which was always worse than out of school suspension (unless of course dad was home) was a small price to pay for the privilege of showing up this fucker.

When you returned to gym class you had become a hero to many. "Didn't think you had it in ya," said Ed, or one of the "druggies," and you were certainly not going to say, "where were you when I needed you when they were throwing money at me, or when the art-teacher pulled my hair." You were basking. Suddenly it was less about Lennon, and more about you. And maybe that was a good thing. In fact, it would be fairly easy to say "and on that day you became a man" or had "eaten the chief," like the ritual of communion, or had learned the value of alternative or "primitive" funereal rites. But this was not even the beginning.

Please Don't Wash

Andrei Codrescu

Would have been the title
Of this collection if I could have
Retained the lubricious intent
With which you said it on the phone
And reigned in my apprehension
That the literary establishment
Which has loathed and feared me
For two decades would continue
To do so with renewed passion
Thereby denying me the honors
I would not receive anyway
So please don't wash baby please
Don't wash baby please

Andrei Codrescu wrote It was Today: New Poems, *(Coffee House Press) a book that was almost called* Please Don't Wash: New Poems.

Steeling Beauty
The inventive instruments of Mobius Operandi's Oliver DiCicco
Derk Richardson

Violins, trumpets and pianos are beautiful objects to behold. But we are so used to encountering them almost daily and focusing on their sound, we forget to appreciate their sculptural qualities. Not so with the Trylon, the Bass2 or Bad Oscar. Even those who have heard of them rarely see them. But once you have laid eyes on them, their physical splendor never escapes you. These oddly named constructions comprise approximately one-fifth of the selection of musical instruments built by SF inventor and recording engineer Oliver DiCicco.

Opportunities for appreciation are limited. That's where DiCicco's Mobius Operandi comes in. The quintet exists to make the Timbajo, the Oove, the Crawdad, the Carollina and DiCicco's other sound-making devices more audible and visible.

The instruments come in complex three-dimensional geometrical combinations of lustrous wood and polished chrome. The Trylon, for instance, is an oversize 18-string zither. The center section of each string is a brass rod. Bolted into a gleaming, tilted triangular steel frame on a waist-high stand, the strings and rods range gradually from short to long on the downhill slope. Beneath them are suspended three large, shiny triangular plates, like pieces borrowed from a Calder mobile.
By contrast, the Due Capi looks like something out of a dentist's office in *Metropolis*. A convoluted maze of chrome plumbing pipes rises up from a jet-black column. Each pipe is capped with a saxophone mouthpiece.

But seeing these creations is only half the fun. To fully experience the Due Capi, the Percussion Tree or the Lo Drum, you must hear their eerie drones, grinding timbres, echoing clangs and fuzzy hums.

[…]

Radical Tunings and Designs

DiCicco started building instruments back in the early 1970s, inspired by the example of Harry Partch, the legendary American music maverick who built instruments with such names as Bloboy, Harmonic Canons and Spoils of War. Partch also devised radical tunings and scales as bases for his compositions.

"I'd heard about Partch in college but had never seen his instruments. The idea of someone actually building his own instruments and creating his own music to go along with it really resonated with me," DiCicco said.

He embarked on a Partchian path with some admittedly "rather crude" efforts. But he was soon sidetracked by his day job as owner and chief engineer of Mobius Music, a highly regarded SF recording studio that has counted Brian Eno, the Residents, John Zorn and Alison Krause among its clients.

"Around 1988 or '89 I felt the need to start doing something more creative than being a recording engineer," DiCicco explained, "and I decided to revisit the instrument-building concept. Once I got started I got on a roll."

Having previously made lamps and other functional art pieces, DiCicco started assembling gleaming sheets of steel, wires, pipes, graphite rods and resonating cylinders, giving equal attention to form and function.

Outsiders' Art

Within a few years he had completed four or five instruments, and he realized it would be much more interesting if he had some other people around to play them with him. One of the early "outsiders" to play a DiCicco invention was Pamela Winfrey, longtime senior artist and curator at the Exploratorium, the hands-on science and art museum in SF's Palace of Fine Arts. DiCicco had brought his Bass2 and Abdul to a "Tinkerers Workshop" at the Exploratorium in 1991.

DiCicco invited Winfrey, fellow instrument builder Peter Whitehead and a few other adventurous musicians to come by his studio and play the instruments. Word spread about the weekly sessions, and soon composer/instrumentalists such as Beth Custer, Miguel Frasconi and Elizabeth Lamantia Scott were dropping in.

Gradually, a steady core—DiCicco, Winfrey, Whitehead, Jason Reinier and Christie Winn—took shape, evolving into Mobius Operandi. "I'm really into collaboration," DiCicco said, "and I liked the idea of inviting people down and seeing what would happen. The band formed itself."

Visual and Sonic Sumptuousness

For the first five or six years, Mobius Operandi's public appearances took place in multidisciplinary performance pieces—collaborations with choreographers Sarah McLennan and Carol LeMaitre and director Jim Cave.

DiCicco's striking musical sculptures became crucial visual elements in the productions *Eating Eden* (1993), *Scatterbrain* (1994), *Exit Vacaville* (1995) and *Xibalba* (1998). SF Examiner theater critic Robert Hurwitt described "Exit Vacaville" as "one of the most enchantingly inventive, intriguingly multilayered, adventurously musical and lightly lugubrious new works in quite some time," calling DiCicco's modern artifacts "as sumptuous to the ear as they are awesome to behold" and noting that "the music pulsates with tuneful insistence as the odd, rich tones emanating from DiCicco's metal, wood and glass instruments mystify the senses."

By 1996, DiCicco had garnered sufficient renown in instrument-building circles to warrant a two-page spread in *Gravikords, Whirlies & Pyrophones*, Bart Hopkin's book about experimental instruments, packaged by Ellipsis Arts with an 18-track CD of music by Partch, Don Buchla, Clara Rockmore, Thomas Nunn, Hans Reichel and others.

It wasn't until 1998, however, that DiCicco's instruments found their way to CD on the first Mobius Operandi recording, *What Were We Thinking*. Their newest CD is *The End of the Dial* (Mobius Music). With percussionist Avi Rose replacing Whitehead (who embarked on a solo career and has recorded two CDs, *Three Bags Full* and *Now This*), Mobius Operandi has gelled more than you might expect from a band that boasts fewer than two dozen concerts, rehearses twice a week at the most and can't even take its instruments home to practice.

According to DiCicco and Winfrey, the players have been able to turn the novelty of the situation to their own musical advantage. "One of the motivating forces behind building the instruments," DiCicco explained, "was to see what we could come up with if you had a whole family of instruments that you didn't have any particular background with.

"Because there's no historical context for playing any of these instruments, you have to bring your own innate musicality to them," he continued. "A lot your chops don't necessarily transfer, but your musical sensibility does. It's basically like trying to learn a new language where you have to learn the vocabulary and the syntax simultaneously."

[…]

For more information: mobiusmusic.com

Oliver DiCicco and Mobius Operandi: Sculptural Music

Oliver DiCicco

Pamela Winfrey

Jason Reinier

Christie Winn

Avi Rose

Mobius Operandi playing at The Henry Miller Library, Big Sur

Instruments created by Oliver DiCicco

Crystal Harp

Carolina

Oove

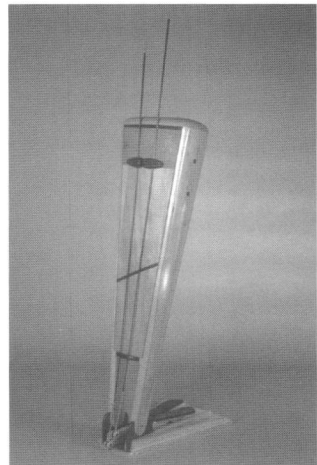
Crawdad

Marimba

Moon
Mary Kite

*Filmed by Jack Coyle, written and edited by Mary Kite with technical assistance by Zach Daudert.
In 1961 "Moon" was originally shot outside of Coffeyville, Kansas by the author's father, Jack Coyle, by using silent 16mm Kodachrome film and a Bolex camera.*

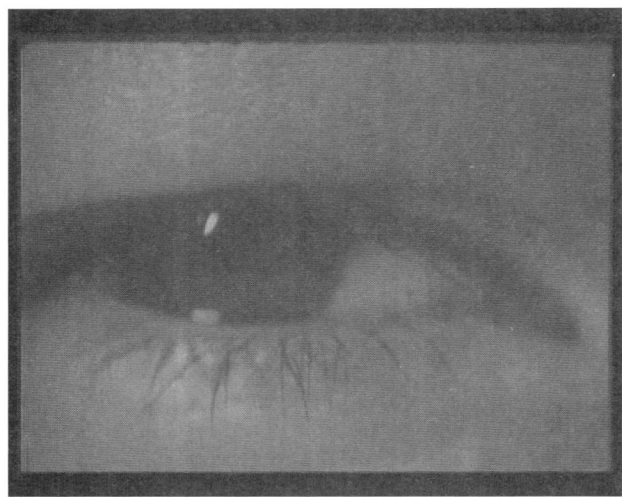

Perfect cloudless,
I call from earth to stare.

Your flicker   faces the horizon,

a
silver toothpaste

               just before sunset.

The path is effortless   for day moons.
Sixty-one shrines float through indigo fields
      as   size
          keeps them in delicious order.

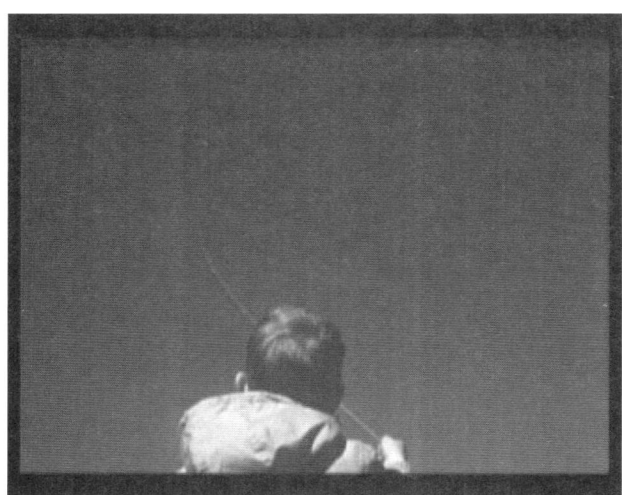

Forgetfulness
of moons demystifies,
pales

              mental ethers.

Course   is decided by personal gods,

indescribable

magnificent.

Death,   bliss,   sex,   scarcity,   delight
        and   fate

do   not

      commit themselves
           as obstacles.

Moon moves are
spherical,
where constant
spin   lashes   each sun's radiance . . .

     a cause célèbre for universal resonance.

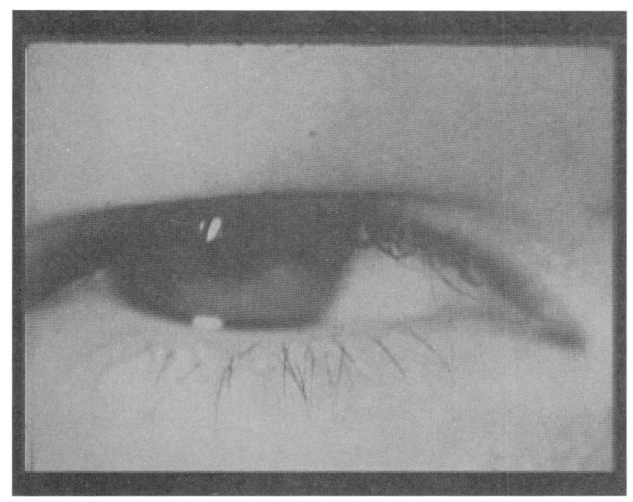
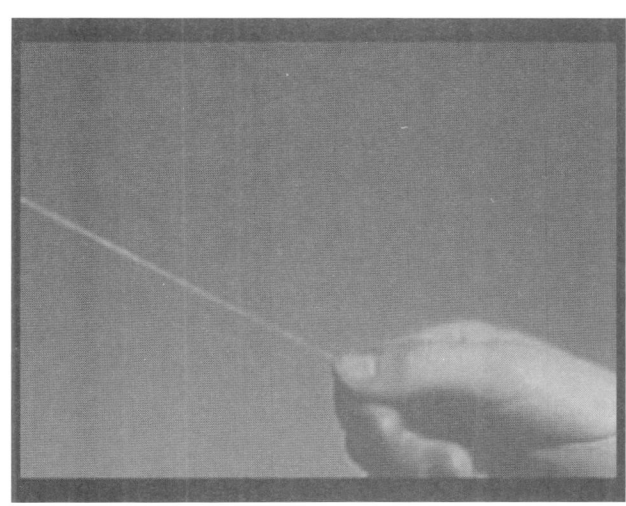

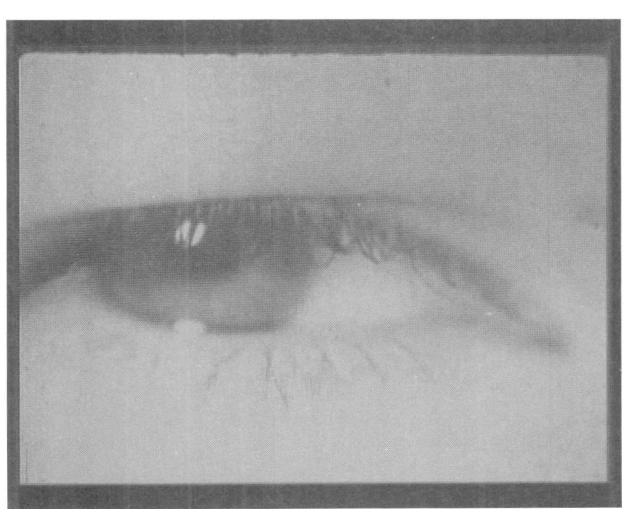

Balthus
Sean Finney

Balthus opens the window
with light arms and exclaims,
"Happenstance is the shovel."

Swarming measures suit the brown
and green pistachios

lost decades of slobbering
where the helmeted stand measuring beds

with empire feet
of plain light fresco
exclamations

a window
is all rectangle and books
for class lead to stairs
of painted lips
Lewinsky beret
heaven ice cream girls
in their geometric solace

skirt in a private collection
land in the still crossed arm light
street of limbs and packages
that's texture's planted foot
ascending to the town
where a sea-green curtain
waves goodbye until I appear.

Brassai
Sean Finney

Brassai
is an eyebrow
a suspiration
for the sun
that we received.

When I was 11
airports made me happy.
You'll smile at this,
"made me happy"
as if it's so fantastic
to buy ice cream
wear trousers, etc.
Keep up with the
acrid chemical sun

Sticks lashed to make a fence
cheaper and more beautiful
in my numbness—
that one machine for denying night

Brassai, you don't have
any memories.

Four o'clock great chill,
promise of drunkenness
Allison pissed on the street
Her friend demurred

History grows weeds in the sun
I never cried in the Circus Maximus

or kept my old promises
to the palm trees
to make them grotesque to foreigners

***
Postscript for Braque

When you're old and you paint a white bird
that's the limit.
There are hairs in every window
if you can walk.

Popova
Sean Finney

The light falls the way of shapes
but it is an illusion, as two words,
black and white, the least any language has for color,
tend to thoughts like, "in the morning, at the time when the sun is worshipped, he rose to wake her."

I should have started back for now we get
saw-toothed cutout of neutral color
against a red block resembling black.

This is harder,
non-figurative salt on the wound,
and a guitar slice that preserves the curve.

A clouded moon

"Construction with White Crescent," so my moon
is indeed a moon. Crossroads leaning
center

in the next piece it's all in black,
our eyes accustomed to the important lines,
the other colors become human.

Your oil with marble dust would make me sad if it wasn't for satellites,
peaks of red, the power of the arm
in short overlapping arcs.

The oil raised from the board
in microscope triumph.

Where Were They? Who Were They?
Maxine Chernoff

"Meanwhile, he stuck at Q. On, then, on to R."—*To the Lighthouse*

The double logic of narrative

        (she didn't believe it)

 Herodotus saw figures

        operated by strings

the addressee axis

        when he says *shut up*

the hero of the novel   was ironing his shirt

    Samuel Pepys diary   1662   (encoded as his practice)

speaks of a puppet show   making him late

        to see the King

"where a husband stands naked"   "pondering the refrigerator"

        anthropologists write

of miniature stone figures   life-size puppets

    of *The Emperor Jones*   "Inside marriage,

one ceases to be observant"

        first known as Punch and Joan

    but puzzled by the names

        of her very own novels

"nightingales singing

        in June, even July"

                the implied author

                                            first sentimentalist

then witty snob

                  no such tendency

  in a puppet's way of dying   "a long white robe

              "chanting by the sea"

                                          the Oberon puppet

  got burned in the fire   including the reader

          won't leave you stranded

                              "She never made
          a religion of art"

        unless you mean the abstract

    (A gives B to C)   "If there wouldn't be puppeteers,

                  who would know

  how to work us?"   "the pedantic accuracy"

      of her novel *The Bell*

                      concerns about violence

spread   in discussion

               the pretense is pretending

    the eye of the Lighthouse

            enabling the story

its curious invention   of slapstick as object

        it no longer hurts

  to think of the future

       unless you mean this minute

          which is altogether

   painful   ameliorative drugs

              were no solution

                          the ending came anyway

   suggesting a closure   altogether fancied

                   in temporal order

        the Krazy Kat Ballet

 performed to jazz trumpets

                   the executioner waiting

         to execute the sentence

               subject/verb/object

                        tinged with mild parody

truth systems   lacking   Medieval truths

             As the condition worsened

it also got better   *Teletubby* sounds   confusion on waking

               her models of misreading

reserved for intention   listless theater

              for the parallel sleepers

                  he too cherished

her one concept   her threshold

            and her coda   branches on

        his tree   no good pastures

             for the dreaming cattle

let it be said   for all she remembered   more was forgotten

                 until the narration

closed its eyes   no new guidebook   for beautiful endings

—for Iris Murdoch and John Bayley

Praise Poem for James Siena
Bob Holman

James Siena

Brillance All Right

Everything's Going (to be OK)
Wanna ruler
Whenya go
Darker

The Mystery of Existence
Tape measure

Hit this one
Again it'll go
Darker value
Is too Light

Darker Evaluating Levelly

A Cool Pencil
It looks like a wooden
Pencil from a distance

Vertorizon much-much more fucked up

See your eyes stick to the globs damn

Look up close wash it down no no unfuck

The peppermint grappa holy diagonal pave

All kept to through blue few knew too crude

Lay off on it there it vanished awright

Estral zingy sharp reverb lays the string

Container no air let it be out of proportion

Can't believe ok the equal value o shit now

Not Exactly Straight
Get use to it

Not Exactly Straight
Exactly

Not Exactly Starlight
Use your eyes

Not Exactly Straight
You got two of 'em don't you

Upside Down Devil

Hey, Joe where ya going

With that sharp bubble there

Rightside Down Dog Town

Separating the Volume

Prop That Little Baby Up

And Move It

The First Two
Colors vanish
Hoy hoy hoy

Deeeeelaid Gratification
We're going to get what we want

They Cannot Vanish

They do though
Tonight I'll be
Staying here with you.

This position Wrong.

A measuring mistake on my part
Art cares. I don't care.

Doing pink faith the lip
Airy all going believe
Light optical allusiveory

Not Exactly Straight
Between the Eyes

Not Exactly Straight
Close enough for a hard-on

Not Exactly Straight
More

Not Exactly Straight
And on the level

Boustrophedonic
As the plow follows the ox
Round the mountain here she
Comes here she comes
I learned the trick in the 2nd grade
How to draw a straight line

Not straight

Battery In the
Middle a Spark
On the fringe
a flange In the
spark the dark
In the dark a
flake A fluke a
lute a late fate
In the flake is
a lake

Global Key Narrows Proton Gaga Diagonal Visor Ripped Straight Most Pink Stark Strict Sax Stamble Silver Sliver Shifting Alternating Connections Wave a lattice you fan body nothing on And the air we squeeze is the body fluid from magic swatch Please do not tell Chuck about this part he is so conscious of it Of it at all Global Narrows

Color Blind You can put that in there if you want Earl Grey It's not that you see everything gray it's that You see the wrong color James Siena

Not Exactly Straight
Continue on like this till
you get it straight

Not Exactly Straight
O yeah I see what you mean

Not Exactly Straight
But straight ne'er the less

Blue Corner (Poem)
Logic does not work with the same
Other
Lattice (Poem)
Other Mind thought you
Connect the Hooks
Streaked light semiusable
Dark blot in foreveral increments
Go longer

Praise Poem for James Turrell
Bob Holman

one
  two
    thr
      fou
        fiv
          six
            sev
              eig
                nin
                  ten
                    ele
                      twe
                        thi
                          fou
                            fif
                              six
                                sev
                                  eig
                                    nin
                                      twe

The Targets
Laura Moriarty

Ada collects the facts. She gets the data from everyone's day, from the journeys and the wars, the time storms. Cap sends it. Everyone sends it, but only Cap is able to monitor her clonish participation in this thinking. It takes a robot to know what Ada knows. Cap and Ada watch as the anomalies and inconsistencies in the bodies of the thinkers parallel those in time. Variously the bodies die. Ada finds the deaths.

It is said of Ada that she began her work with the loss of flesh when the library itself became illegible to her. She lost her father to a war at the edge of an empire. Now she loses herself to its victims. She sees herself as a cause to their effect. They are the targets. She writes them. She counts them. There is absence in each citation, a zero in each death. She doesn't know why she does it. She knows only the facts and that she needs to organize and connect them. To present them.

Choosing a sequence with sound, Ads scrolls footage from early in the century. She freezes a moment. There is an explosion. Life spreads out over a landscape. There is a city. Parphar. People flying. When they fly, they become bodies. The bodies are not available. They have passed into history, but it is not generally possible to see them. Ada sees them because she has access. They are missing from the official record, insofar as there is a record left at all. Ada's access to what doesn't officially exist mimics her own status dating back to her illegal conception as a living logo. Ada Byron of the Gutenberg Hotel. She hums the song. The theft of her identity seems to her not unlike the obliteration of theirs. She remembers the various thefts, the lives. Her life on the oxygen farm. Step parents. Step life.

There is an explosion of memory in Ada's head. Loud but not lasting. She feels dissociated from her memories. Hopelessly compromised by survival, she strives to ignore her life and focus on the information. She finds the facts. She finds them to be naturally concentric. They follow each other into circles. They become targets. The bodies are targets. For Ada, discovering this form is a form of rest, of redress. What she makes can be heard or seen. It can be read. She hears things. She remembers flesh by finding it in pictures. Painted, scrolled, heard flesh. She finds and arranges, absorbs and lists. She listens.

"Saturn drones as it rises," she continues to hum. She searches for Cap in her mind, capturing additional information from him as he flies.

The time, she notes, is eighteen minutes past the hour, but what hour? She searches for the names. She lists them in columns. She bios them meticulously. Dreamily, she layers the information like skin, thickening their thin lives with facts. They seem to come from long ago and far away, though some died as recently as yesterday. Some of the victims are isolate, like the facts. Some are as connected as cousins to Ada and each other. Time is the only thing that is not relative now.

"What is a real target? What is not?" Ada goes on. "Is there an esthetic quality to this problem?"

She imagines that a horse is riding through her sleep, grazing around her headstones, invading her inner life. She wishes she had an inner life. She feels she has only a name. That she is a projection, that her memories are like scenes from movies. They say it is an effect from the war. The movies are like the war. Like the horse. Someone is the rider, someone the pilot, someone else the bombardier. She was the pilot. It was Mars. It was the war. One of the wars. It is very clear now.

"We were our own targets," she thinks. She remembers the explosions. People could fly. The acts of bloodless terror were finally seen as not enough. There was blood. It was expensive to make people die.

"We were searching for a place, a refuge to our love, but instead we were lead to the land of the dead." She hears the line over and over.

She knows it is from the life of a writer. Sayat Nova. A movie or a memory. How can anyone know? The eyes of the woman are gray in a painting. Not unlike Ada's violet eyes. Her lace is painted. Filmed. The flesh in the painting is very natural. Looking up there is a lack of stars. It is this interminable dust. Set up a life. Watch it go down. Not to have been alive then. Not now.

"Saturn occults the sun." Ada continues to hum the words to a lost song.

The library explodes. Cap reels back but it is all in Ada's mind. Nothing can't be lost. Ada identifies the victims. She identifies with them. She accepts her life as a target. She believes that everywhere she is, the periphery fades.

"What are the facts?" she asks herself. "That I am designed to be in view," she thinks. "That I was made to win. That I have no talent, only power, that I have the talent to know it. That I steal everything from everyone. It is my job to give everything away. I have tried to give myself away, but there are no takers. Everyone wants to be taken by me and that's a fact," Ada reflects, not entirely without justification.

She finds herself considering the I, though generally she tries not to think of them. She thinks of Wyatt. With the exception of Wyatt, she thinks of the I as a waste of time. There is never anything new about them. She senses that they find her merely polite. They treat her like one of the boys. Wyatt says it is because, like them, she colonizes. Ada knows that when he says this he is putting it mildly. More than the I, Ada is an imperialist of her deal. She collects everyone and everything. She doesn't even try to seem real, at least not to them.

"Only to the few am I myself," she says aloud, resuming her work. "I am me to myself, to the dead and to Stella. We are attached. They want a patroness, a predeath agreement. A will. They know that my will is to save them from time. Stella knows. Their will is to bury themselves in my mind, but it's the same thing. Stella and I are the same," she decides for the thousandth time.

Ada, who finds everyone, is lost in her own mind. She looks out at the universe with her violet eyes, as if she were a stranger in it.

"She knows too much," Cap thinks as he flies on, engorged with facts. "It's not what you know but who you are. Not who you are, but where you go. Ada and Stella are not the same. Anyone could see it." He proceeds through space with his parallel conclusions. Cap longs to clear his palate with a kindred soul. One who knows nothing but knows it well. When he sees *Ultravioleta* on the horizon, he slows to the pure present.

"Martinez," he thinks.

"The Targets" is a chapter from *Ultravioleta*. Atelos, 2006.

Alan Halsey: *Sonata for Cheney Longville & Dartboard*

Snooze Alarm
Laura Perkins

Characters: WOMAN 1, WOMAN 2, MAN, MOTHER

Scene: A bedroom with a bed, nightstands and an alarm clock. Present day.

AT RISE: WOMAN 1 and WOMAN 2 are in bed hugging and cooing at each other. They are just waking up. The alarm clock goes off. WOMAN 2 slaps the button to turn it off, irritated. They go back to cooing.
All of a sudden the MAN with silly dog ears on his cap comes up out of the covers behind WOMAN 1, spoons and snuggles with her while she's hugging her lover, WOMAN 2.

WOMAN 2: Who the hell's that? Is that your ex?

WOMAN 1: Ah, yeah. Come back baby.

WOMAN 2: Why's he here? He has grapes!

(The MAN takes care to give her some grapes)

WOMAN 1: I never knew. He can't mean anything by it. Come back baby.

(MOTHER comes up out of the covers behind WOMAN 2, squeezes her shoulder, plumps pillows.)

WOMAN 1: What's that? My god it's your mother.

WOMAN 2: Jeez mom. (To MAN) Peel it.

MAN: Cramped forts rage silent in the night.

(MOTHER slowly spits out a giant gleaming pearl very suggestively, a kind of ben-wa ball of wisdom; it's hanging from a clear string around her neck.)

WOMAN 1: I was going to get a haircut.

WOMAN 2: We have a phone…. Come here darlin'.

(MOTHER reaches under covers and pulls out a realistic baby doll. She places the doll between the lovers.)

WOMAN 1: Baby.

WOMAN 2: Mama.

MOTHER: Take tendrils with care. Say something nicely clapped wands.

WOMAN 1: I am unbuttoned. You are beautiful.

WOMAN 2: Unbuttoned you are beautiful.

(WOMAN 2 reaches over and grabs dog-eared cap off MAN. WOMAN 1 puts cap on baby. Playful.)

(MOTHER and MAN sink back under covers as the snooze alarm goes off again. WOMAN 2 slaps it.)

WOMAN 1: Just one more. Come back baby.

(Lights dim.)

from Iduna
kari edwards

thus acid code like love like kiss   beat beam noon veto

....
....several Flowers

   down back particular / unimaginative: sum
mary of...   fasteNs lack allure s or ties s
                        down front   diminutive.

    called   Dash   Somewhat Coddled Cadi-
                  mium ;
       Could Be Ayellow Bearded   Double ;
         Chiefly Northern & Cannot   Above A
Rhodon As Is A As/is A   The Hexagonal Comma
The Back Words Y.

   They electronicriate...
   concert + Italian --inA,
.. . . . . h{{ buttonas part   AFTER FURTHER AMPlifica-
tion;
             ....
                                    ....
            relics in   slit raincoats. .
                       shank that represent
                          hallucinations.

                                lie down To unfasten
  with concealed
                            wanted   sleeve-
less ,
                often having on a puncH.
        I nflected forms: un·---·t·--------, un·---·----·ing,
... .NUMBER:55229
like a;(2)
  ..t consisting of
  either   or several flowers
turn flow move deep hell sway hold drop lush water fact   homo-

slush-stained-by-piss-colored . . .

showed swampy regions of . . .

the night, I am the night mother.

belt down cork

hope vows much like silk cyma drop mood ring

love case warm pure careful conduct hylo- beam with deco mind

afar hair iron cite kora pain lard muck idol fast time desk cell

arce suds dill acid code gawk base must sign okay beat

from The Man Without Stumps
Mary Burger

Part IV.

The day I learned the alphabet was not the moving topography I'd been imagining, but a fixed sequence, correct in only one way, the day I learned "lemon" was not "seashell", the day I learned the alphabet was a fixed sequence, that my confusion about the vastly featured terrain that shifted around me would not be explained by this sequence, that there was something else that I would have to learn, that this sequence, which seemed random it its order, in the relation between one item and the next, this sequence of individual graphemes, broken out and separated from the combinatory sequences they had in words, this sequence of individual graphemes has only a frustrating and oblique relationship to the shifting terrain of multiple elevations and depths, textures, colors, kinds of wind, this sequence of individual graphemes does not map the parabolic movement of the knife-edge ridge of a sand dune or the striations that change from brown to red during the setting of the sun, this sequence of graphemes does not confer value, it does not explain why some experiences seem meaningful and others are forgotten without seeming anything, this sequence of graphemes is not what meaning is about.

———————

The big slack rubber band.

The fluid dynamics of some artists I know.

The hand-packed pint of ice cream.

———————

The injured tendon that gradually resumes bearing weight.

———————

The self-replenishing aquifer has a clean, slaty taste, white Burgundy chilled in a stone cellar. A low rock ceiling hangs over the motionless water, a flawless membrane spreading over the hidden floor.

———————

Everyone can offer a different block of paradise.

———————

The smooth membrane spreading over the underground floor would reflect light like polished glass, but there is no light. The self-replenishing aquifer exists without being seen. It may be pumped out and used for irrigation or it may be left alone.

The loose rocky terrain that shifted under anyone's weight could never be sure what configuration it would retain, what particular shape it could offer at any given time.

———————

The amber glow of the room lit by candlelight on a winter evening with the shades pulled and the curtains drawn, the two of them curled on the couch, the amber glow of one light made a shape like a bubble, not completely spherical, lopsided by the weight of its own air, by the irregular pressures of the air surrounding it.

———————

The man without stumps experiences the sheer messiness of the world as if a favorite pet bird were found one morning, motionless, feet curled in the air, lying at the bottom of its cage. An anguished phone call yields only the dreaded confirmation. "If she's lying on her back and not moving, something is definitely not normal."

But normal is exactly what it is.

The bright, ringing sound of the shattering china plates is as normal as the soft brush of the cat's fur.

The man without stumps who experiences his head hitting the ground is surprised to find that his vision can vibrate, that his eyes vibrate in his skull, a result of the impact of his head on the ground. He is surprised, not at the fact of this, for it only makes sense that the orb-like organs, surrounded by fluid and suspended by soft tissue, would reverberate when the hard case enclosing them had a strong impact. What surprises him is the actual visual experience of having the image presented to him bounce several times, with diminishing oscillation each time, as if he were staring at a screen that was being jiggled.

The nausea and headache that came over him—which he could separate somehow, though he couldn't say how, from the pain of the actual impact to his skull—were a further surprise, an unexpected vulnerability to vision itself, an abrupt reminder that the seamless identification he usually felt with his vision, with whatever spectacle presented itself to his vision, was only as true as the moment in which it existed.

_____

The electricians' union is there to serve the electricians. It was created by them, it works favorably for them.

_____

The intervals between the carved dragon heads on the sushi boats moving around and around the counter are another measure of time.

_____

To speed up and slow down time—is that immortality?

_____

The fine red mist that floats between us makes a faint film on every surface. When we wipe it, it is wet.

_____

The graininess in the picture that might be me is something it is easy to lose sight of. The graininess in the picture that might be me foregrounds a graininess in the picture that I'm sure is you. It is where you should be or where I believe you to be.

The graininess in the picture that might be me is not credible. It is bad evidence presented in support of a UFO. It is so indistinct, it could be what the presenters claim, or it could be something else entirely. I will claim it is me, which is really the broadest claim I could make. It is audacious and nervy, because it is both irrefutable and impossible to prove. It is my claim, who can argue with me, but who really has to believe me.

I am bad evidence of a UFO, I am bad evidence presented in support of myself. A grainy blur, a slightly darker area in the black and white field, black splotches that coagulate when viewed from just the right distance, into a solid form with clear edges.

But it is only ever theoretically the right distance, in actuality it is never quite right, and the graininess stays grainy, never quite solidified.

The graininess in the picture that might be me could be a ball caught in mid-bounce, a frisbee powered by a good throw. It could be a dog with a frisbee in its mouth.

The graininess in the picture that might be me might be a glass of lemonade. That might be you, behind me, reaching for me, a cool glass wet with condensation, the pale lemony water mottled with ice.

The graininess in the picture that might be me is part black part white and faintly crescent-shaped.

The graininess in the picture that might be me, it gives just enough information to go on, just enough texture and contrast for me to almost hold together. Stay with me now, I am almost about to exist.

Life On Line
David Meltzer

as I've known it
now I don't
own it
it owns me

lined up
against perp wall
scanned by another
anonymous eye

whoever I am
is irregardless &
decreased by
false diction

email nails
nothing down

appropriate
continuity for
nothing happening
in the flaming edges of
planetary suicide

patricide
matricide
fratricide
genocide
whose side are you on
& why?

Future's medieval
& past has passed
& now's glory icon
is Adam naked
in Iraq prison
Candid Camera

Get down
go down
Moishe & Mohammed
tangle w/ nude Yeshouah
poked & shocked &
porked by
apple pie G.I.s

wholly holy war
whores
victims in rictus
seized embryo fist

losing the capacity
to be human in
whatever deep gloss
& glaze that keyword
celebrates

electric lines plug
into hooded naked men
on display in Bloomingdale's
hopeful nightingales
too shocked to sing

war smut
known as power boner

we live in the shoe of the few
whose foot flattens us
each time they step down

I would've been a fool
but byte-sized down
to a clown
who amuses not confuses

On line all the clues
stun & dun the rage

On line
like a shiny fish
caught

Is Poetry Enough? Poetry in a Time of Crisis
Readings from the event at UC Santa Cruz, April 2004

HI, I'M a poet. (I mean we all are) and I find I am very sensitive to language especially in the public sector. I love to watch a new piece of language float onto the scene and get used like crazy. The piece I've been noticing lately is—the very suggestion that someone or something is "not in step with the mainstream."

Now what the hell does *that* mean? I mean what's most troubling is that there's something that obviously precedes the accusation. A given. Which is the mighty stream. A mighty flow. Something huge, torrential and essential. Almost godlike in its force and the public person is being urged to get over themselves and damn it just get on (it, the mighty flow) or be an obstructionist. It's kind of like being a bad sport to *not* be in step with this thing. To body surf on where the flow of "the culture" is going.

I want to think about this thing a little bit. Cause it seems to me "the mainstream" is at least a twenty year old concept. I first noticed it—I mean noticed it in a way that truly aggravated me as it started to move into *my* world, the poetry world. I remember on the occasion of Harper Collins publishing the big fat red *Collected Poems of Allen Ginsberg* I think in 1984 *Newsweek* printed more of an article than a review and they boldly titled that article **Mainstreaming Allen Ginsberg.**

It was meant to be generous. Kind of a makeover. Taking this weird guy everyone already knew and making him large. Of course the lie in this is what's really troubling. I'm thinking of Allen's incredible perspective always. Which began with the tiny, a flower or an electric plug, an unimportant personal life, his own or his mother's and how he followed the dots making that tiny thing slowly connect up to the conditions of cold war America or hippy America or stockpiling plutonium America. Allen had a genius for making the small large and seeing exactly how they were literally holding everything these shuttling perspectives and he had the knack for making the personal man grand. Grand as the cosmos. And Allen of course was a genius of publicity. Was the first poet to send out press releases and in many ways had masterminded the beat generation. So he really didn't need *Newsweek* making him large. He was just being published by corporate culture for the first time which *was* a very interesting moment but the mainstreaming language so slippery had a way of simplifying all this, i.e. not looking at who they, *Newsweek* or Harper Collins, were at all and suggesting instead that they in their mainstreaming were doing something nice for old Allen. This phenomenon, Allen, still, at that time, was the biggest representative globally of the dissenting other culture. I mean he regularly served as a kind of a bellwether for how the mainstream was viewing or dealing with us.

I mean that *us*. Allen was my representative for a long time. In my neighborhood or nation, in the world and so I thought of myself for a long time as an us he was marking.

By the time he died (nine years later) the New York Times glibly described him as "avuncular." No, let me quote a larger piece of the eulogizing article by Charles McGrath, the then editor of the New York Times Book Review section so you'll see just what I mean:

"He [Allen] was a cultural busybody—an inspired *yenta*—turning up at protests, rallies, rock concerts, love-ins; but he brought to these occasions not rage or dogma so much as a kind of *avuncular* concern. In the end, his most enduring contribution to our culture may be less such works as ''Howl'' and ''Kaddish'' than the way that, humming and chanting and clicking away on his finger cymbals, he transformed the American avant-garde, and the angry alienation of the Beats, into something altogether more cheerful and benign."

Now I would call that a little castrating wouldn't you? Or feminized in a way that not even women want to be. Allen was ultimately innocuous and cheerily irrelevant if McGrath has his way. What McGrath says is maybe the worst thing you could do to a man—of considerable power, like Allen. Even or especially a man who sang about his own asshole and his little penis—he did the job of humbling and exposing himself so cheerily that the eventuality that he would nonetheless be rendered foolishly after his death in the Times—seems willfully obliterating. To the man, but to a culture too.

Because to get reviewed, mentioned in the Times is some sort of survival. Your book will be bought by librarians, you'll get the job. Your peers will think, wow she's getting attention and then you'll get even more readings, a general sense will stick to you that you are a poet with "a career." Who's known. Which is not what any of us—in our "us"—aspire to, but it's nice, right. And it doesn't just happen. You did it somehow. Like Allen did.

But interestingly in this same world of ours that overlaps with that, of the Times, we would never describe I think our friends who *only* abhor the mainstream as out of step.

Which is simply to say that's the difference. The extreme of us—the ones who really *don't* want it—the attention of that—I don't want to say…larger, well, corporate thing. We don't describe them as out of step. We never would publicly anyhow and that's the difference. It's an entirely defensible position in our world to *not* want that.

Because I think there's a life here and we're in it, and within it there are many positions to hold. I was at dinner last night and we were all putting forward stories. Political ones. Like how in California since Arnold took office there's been a lot of defunding going on in the UC System. There's a labor museum that has been deemed "unnecessary," irrelevant, and a photography museum that tends to show political work is also getting junked. Continuing education is going away. So that finally you are either inside or out. And nationally there's a lot of murmuring about upcoming attacks on the 501C3s of non-profit art spaces that show political work. The spaces that show us and our friends.

We're always, always talking about this stuff now. I remember certain dinners in New York after the World Trade Towers when we were all trying to wrap our minds around the world we now occupied—we were trying to fathom the media and the government's response to the attacks on towers. Horrifying and mind boggling —and then in those same dinners we always looked at ourselves and asked—this always came up: Do you think this is how people felt in Nazi Germany? Are we in history yet?

And it's occurring to me now that our self-conscious question is not wide enough. We should ask if this is how artists and intellectuals felt in Chile, in Afghanistan, Iran, Rwanda.   And the concern doesn't refer to just one type of thing—an attack, but a growing awareness that the conditions we are living are changing radically. There's stories at dinner, there's messages in your email, there's millions of illustrations. We read them all the time now.

It's so easy to forget where we came from. How it at least used to *seem* that the opposite conditions ruled in this country. Only thirty years ago the main distributor of not just art, but avant garde art, experimental art was the government—through arts organizations and both PBS and NPR were once upon a time liberal even lefty institutions that disseminated both information and culture. I think the understanding was that the government and the big media would always be more conservative than these small approaches and that to have a whole culture we *needed* them. I was educated by these non profit institutions and media outlets. Reagan changed the landscape when he both changed leadership of the NEA and the Literature division of it and basically defunded the smaller public art institutions that used to thrive in America.

Then the academy became increasingly the institution that protected those impulses. And now that's getting attacked, the academy is, in terms of what can be taught. State legislatures are looking at curriculum and questioning. Talk show hosts are screaming at the irrelevancy of cultural studies, queer studies etc. Basically anything that's not science. Alumni groups are having lots of say in private schools about the kind of profile a given university is developing. So first it was public money, then it was corporate money and now it's university money that is drying up. Stop the money, stop the culture. Something is happening and so we now have to do something else. Not resistance but inundating.

We have to mobilize our own flow. Not just political action. I'm talking about literal optimism. If you have friends, family who have money point them towards a situation where they can help. If you have friends in the media tell them about things that matter. Not just political things but poetry readings, stuff in galleries.

I've been noticing that in the artworld there are a lot of cultural activity collectives making work that includes distribution plans. There's an awareness from the ground up that things must change. Zines and events that create community, that are much wider than "art world." Neighbors, neighborhoods and stores. I'm crazy about a new lesbian collective in New York called LTTR. It means lesbians to the rescue. I guess it's meant other things too. It's a shifting acronym which is pretty cool. So it's not like Cathy Opie has an opening and every lesbian on the west coast comes to her show. I think it's more about a show about a show. A show about who comes to the show. In honor of gathering I think which is a new move. We've all got to do it. We've got to start investing and investigating. Like our project today is intrinsically virtual (or it will fail.) We are decorating, inundating, re-routing all meetings, all work places all encounters.

It seems like reimagining collective action, being a poet, a student, a teacher, a voter has to occur.

So that no one can be accused of being out of step because the world we want to be in is constantly seeping into all the other worlds. We make ourselves powerful and safe by being beyond categories. Spilling the way a message travels on the web. I think to end the lock step we have to rethink being poets and who it's for and constantly challenge the room we are in to be brighter and cozier, braver and more alive. To be more sexual and dangerous and solipsistic and wasteful and beside the point, putting tiny statues in cracks, jamming in notes, talking deliberately to people older and younger than yourself. So that changing the biggest thing, the president, can be incidental and yet overwhelming. It has to happen now.

TO HELL
EILEEN MYLES

for J.

I'm not sure who I walk with in America today.

I miss you, my imagined accomplice, while we're
    moving among men

One man stands up and says his daughter's gay

Like we didn't know that she says, he thinks it's so great

We can't think it's so wonderful, being lied to for years

We've accomplished bright cynicism, then struggle for love

We flounder, we fail, the elephant eliminates the con-
    fusions of love.

Love probably didn't need a war, couldn't eat, is rolling
    on waves today

The city is emptying. The elephants have been planning
    their party for years.

I'm heading into it. New York my home bursting with men.

Conservative women, heading downtown to see a cross made
    of girders: "Great!"

Jesus marked this city, threw planes at it, face it those
    pilots were gay

We're gonna make a constitutional amendment against em
    for being gay.

Gay to hit buildings, to want to meet in great numbers,
    being no one Love

Moving like an angry sunflower, wanting bandages, space,
    something great

I want to live here feeling celebrated for breathing open
    today.

I want to show you complicated dyke love, construct a poem
    about women and men

In my country there's a basic responsibility to struggle
    and not for years.

To walk away, to turn around seeing you and progress and be
    loving your smile for years

Sometimes I think there's complication with men but I'm
    probably gay

Gay to be glad to keep expressing and knowing the impossible hopes of women and men

I would want to learn more, be firmer, open up, revolutionize love streaming

A house on a hill is pretty but there's something rhapsodically fine today

Stay here while the American ship is moving and rocking, vincible, great.

My moment alone in front of everyone is hopelessly great

I don't have to wonder where I'm going this time or this year

I don't have to wonder whose group I'm in today.

Certainly the people who always think the public problem is theirs are gay

When the moment comes to move like trees to free the city I love

I don't know John Kerry and we can name that feeling Buddhist for the next four years

The pond reflects the sky, if the highway curls it's gay.

A public moment, a political moment is what's possible today

We trust more than men, something's eating our years

The uneven horizon's great and of course she's gay

The buildings are falling in love, and we opened its eye today

POETRY IN A TIME OF CRISIS

JULIANA SPAHR

1. **The** title of this panel comes from an MLA panel of 2001. Although this MLA panel does not show up in the MLA program. The panel was a last moment response by Charles Bernstein to a crisis that was brought on by the poet Charles Tomlinson being unable to attend.

I just used the title of the panel for my paper. And then Roxi et al approached me about this panel. I just want to point out that I can't take credit for the title. But, I began that paper at the MLA like this:

Shortly after I finished *Everybody's Autonomy*, my critical book, I got to thinking, as I'm sure many have, about how many years it had taken me to write. Then I started thinking about all the things that had happened in those years. Some of these things were personal, the death of my father for instance. But I also realized I could chart my progress through this book through various U.S. military actions. I began the book during the Gulf War because I remember watching the coverage to avoid beginning writing. I finished rewriting it while we were bombing Belgrade. When I realized this, I felt a momentary hope that I had been writing during unique times, that I was writing in a time of crisis. But as I thought it over, I realized I had done no writing at any point in my career when the U.S. was not bombing someone. I wrote this paper, for instance, during the bombing of Afghanistan and the continued bombing of Iraq. Even my sometimes home was being bombed: as I wrote this as the U.S. military was practicing their bombing skills on the Makua valley on the North Shore of Oahu. I could go on. I'm living in New York City this year. Somewhere around 3,000 people died in the World Trade Center while I watched from a street corner in Brooklyn. But that is nothing. Some 72,000 have died from AIDS in New York City since 1981. There is, thus, constantly crisis. We cannot say that unique, or interesting, times arrived on September 11.

Nothing has changed since then. It is all crisis all the time. And a great deal of it caused by the United States. I rewrote this paper during the post-Iraq-war war.

2. When I was in graduate school in the 90s, a lot of time in graduate seminars was spent arguing about that Auden line "poetry makes nothing happen." The truth or untruth of this line was something we debated as if our lives depended on it. We never really looked at the poem. We didn't mention Yeats. We refused to complicate the line, to wonder if poetry makes something happen by making nothing happen. We read with a sledgehammer because to some extent, our critical and poetic lives did depend on whether poetry makes things happen or not. The truth or untruth of this line would impact our writing and how we saw other's writings, would privilege a different set of works, would require us to direct our attention differently.

I think many people left those seminars agreeing with Auden. I just left them confused. I left with those questions about does poetry matter; is poetry enough; what is it about poetry and crisis unanswered except on a personal level. I could tell a personal story about how poetry mattered to me, how it had dramatically changed my thinking about things and how it had reshaped my brain in ways that I couldn't have done on my own or even with the help of various psychoactive drugs. It was clear to me that poetry changed my social life very profoundly (the huge number of poets that I count as friends) and changed my intellectual life also (how, say Ginsberg's *Howl* blew my mind in high school starting off a whole chain of events where I realized I didn't have to follow my peers down the path of right wing bigotry and narrow mindedness because my thinking that wasn't the way to go had a whole literature that supported me). I was changed. My mind was changed.

But somehow, for reasons that I still can't fathom, despite the intensity and urgency and endlessness of these graduate school debates, poetry's role in various political movements was never mentioned. We were in Buffalo but we never mentioned that a few miles down the road a mere thirty years ago the prisoners of Attica prepared to fight for showers and education by circulating copies of Claude McKay's "If We Must Die." At least one of us had a boyfriend who owned a copy of Poetry and Militancy in Latin America but we never quoted from this essay where Dalton states that "the poet must acquaint all his comrades with Nazim Hikmet or Pablo Neruda, and give them a clear concept of cultural work within the context of general revolutionary activity" (22). We didn't even mention William Carlos Williams's famous statement that "It is difficult / to get the news from poems / yet men die miserably every day / for lack / of what is found there" even while we often talked about Williams. One of us wore a Che t-shirt but we didn't discuss why he might see the "new impulse" of "artistic inquiry" a crucial part of the new man (132). We didn't turn to Zapata and quote him saying "It is not only by shooting bullets in the battlefields that tyranny is overthrown, but also by hurling ideas of redemption, words of freedom and terrible anathemas against the hangman that people bring down dictators and empires." We didn't think about what Haunani Kay Trask might mean when she describes her poetry as "both de-colonization and re-creation"; and as "expose and celebration at one and the same time"; as "a furious, but nurturing aloha for Hawai'i" (55). We didn't mention Mao's two fronts of the pen and the gun. Or Mayakovsky's claim that one must begin poetic work only after one first has "the presence of a problem in society, the solution of which is conceivable only in poetical terms" (49). We never once mentioned the attention Fanon and Ngugi and Gramsci and Lenin and Cabral and others give to art and literature's role in political education.

Our main concern with this Auden line was how to make our own story of our mind being changed—our political education—matter. We tried to write out of being white and articulate and privileged even as we tried to write against this—both as critics and as poets. In many ways we were not typical graduate students, if there is such a thing. We saw community as more crucial than professional development. We spent more time editing and publishing small journals and books than researching our dissertations. We met in bars late at night and had fights about form's politics when we should have been in bed and sober. Most of us were skeptical about conventional ways of writing poems, which we saw as part of the, some, "system," and also of the institution of graduate study which we saw as training us mainly in critique and alienation. We knew that poets in the United States risked writing for the poetry wing of the Hollywood/military industrial complex and we didn't want to do that. Most of us preferred Brecht over Adorno. But we didn't have many good models about how to take on what it means to be white and articulate and privileged and see it as in any way related to something such as the crisis of anticolonial struggles. We could see we were a part of the most powerful nation who abused its power and we could see how there was much poetry that was complaining about this abuse of power in the world, but we couldn't see any possibility of alliance with these poetries. And we missed a lot because of this.

I have a certain forgiveness for our narrow focus. In the late 90s, the more radical discussions of canon had been dismissed as being "identity politics." The term, even for those of us who refused to use it because of its reactionary connotations, was symbolic though of how we were led to believe there were a series of rules about identity to be followed and thus a series of divisions between cultures to be respected. While we acknowledged the importance of and taught from a multicultural curriculum, some with devotion and some with resignation, we felt a certain nervousness about appropriation. And instead of thinking hard about how to get rid of this nervousness or how taking on and responding to this nervousness might shape our work and make it better with its hard questions, we just avoided work by people who were not in the same category or who did not write from similar amounts of privilege as ourselves when we talked about things that were relevant or important to our thinking and our writing. We would not have turned to anticolonial nationalists such as Ngugi for support in these debates about the Auden line because we were generally not involved in anticolonial movements and had not been to Africa or wherever and did not see our writing as having to take a stand on colonization. This was naive on our parts. No writing escapes being a part of anything. And the Mohawk Nation was right down the road if we needed any close to home evidence of colonization. I think for the most part we respected the concerns of these communities. And the form that our respect took was a dismissal even as we said it was a refusal to belittle their goals with a claim of alliance on our part.

Basically, we were having, as Walter Lew pointed out in a recent email, a contemporary discussion that has a short history. One that, as he wrote, happens "only in modernity's (and imperialism's) unprecedented states of alienation and cultural frenzy/morbidity"; one that is "very historically/culturally circumscribed." This question of does poetry matter to crisis was one that was only possible right now at this very moment but we for some reason did not mention this, did not bother to wonder why we were having this discussion right now, a discussion that so many others from other times would have found absurd.

And we were missing other issues as we had this debate. Of course poetry matters. Of course poetry cannot be anything but political (for even to be apolitical is also a sort of politics). It should have been obvious.

Here is my argument, such as it is: this debate was for us a sort of blinder. The debate about if poetry matters or not was one that kept us from harder, bigger issues, that let us off from having to discuss how it did matter and then now what, what we had to DO in other words. It let us not have to move on to consider weightier issues—like who we wrote with and on and why or who we read with and on and why or even who we talk with and on and why. We avoided the now what. Now what, who do we respect. Now what, who do we publish in our journal. Now what, who do we invite to read in our series. Now what, where do we put our bodies, our time, our commitments. But we couldn't figure out the now what because the question about whether poetry matters or not somehow so occupied us that we couldn't get to the next stage of wondering what uses of poetry in other parts of the world are instructive. The question led us somewhere, it led us to think that we could fracture English's power by fracturing its syntaxes, by stuttering through its words but then it stranded us there. It didn't lead us to alliance. It let us think that we could do it alone, just with words.

Today our world erupts and poetry is one of the tools that get used in this eruption. When Osama bin Laden wanted to talk about the bombing of the U.S.S. Cole at his son's wedding he did it in poetry. None of my years of poetry study and late night talks about the politics of form gave me the tools to understand this moment. I turned to Steven Caton's study of poetry in Yemen to try and understand "the way in which poetry helps constitute tribal identity" (264). That began to help.

One could say that I am just talking about cross cultural difficulties. But I think not exclusively. Because our dominant poetry paradigms don't help that much to explain a number of the most popular poems of our own culture, such as the poem "American Bad Ass" by Kid Rock that the U.S.S. Cole blasted as it limped out of Yemen. It might very well be that poetry swaggers and provokes and constitutes tribal identity as much as it calms or comforts or counters any darkness and perhaps the scary rebel yell of "American Bad Ass" is the best reply right now to the discussion of whether poetry matters. I guess I am asking for a model of study that acknowledges poetry as intimate with crisis. A model that might help explain Timothy McVeigh turning to Victorian poet Henley's "Invictus" before he gets executed. A model that might help explain the intensity of my own relation with poetry which I almost never find a comfort and almost always find provocative. And I guess I'm calling for an embrace of the poetry is political assumption so as to begin to move the debate to these issues of now what.

3. But now to the question, is poetry enough? And the answer is of course not. Poetry is only one part of enough. The part that changes the brain. In an email the other day New York poet Allison Cobb claimed she was paraphrasing Charles Bernstein as she wrote "the fact that poetry won't stop violence is not a reason not to try." I want to tweak her paraphrase a little to something like the fact that poetry hasn't led all that many poets into action doesn't mean we shouldn't ask where our poetry leads us finally. If poetry changes our head, and I think this is irrefutable, how does it also change our feet? It is the feet that Auden denies when at the beginning of the "poetry makes nothing happen" stanza he says that Ireland is unchanged and at the end when he says poetry survives as a mouth. But in reply, one could point to poet Rigoberto Lopez Perez after all who shot and killed Somoza in 1956. And it is feet that Dalton, Guevara, Zapata, Trask, Mao, and Mayakovsky want changed.

DISMANTLING IMPERIALIST NOSTALGIA ON THE PACIFIC RIM: SAN FRANCISCO AS GLOBAL/LOCAL CITY—LITERARY VISIONS AND PRE-FIGURATIONS

ROB WILSON

SINCE its frontier-days eruption into Pacific Rim global city, San Francisco has long served as the center of a vast urban periphery or "contado" providing material resources (water, timber, stone, agriculture, shipping and so on) as well as huge labor needs and input to build up the wealth and splendor of an "imperial city" a la Rome or some west-coast Constantinople at Golden Gate.[a] But San Francisco is also the site of a countercultural vision long propagated in literature, film, and social community. This vision of California-regionality and San Francisco as global city of cultural-political newness and promissory queerness, thus, will not only assume an abiding openness to "transpacific" forces of Asia/Pacific becoming and Hispanic transculturation, it will also tap into some high-visionary sources from literature and popular culture (from Lenny Bruce and Maxine Hong Kingston to Jack Spicer, Bob Kaufman, and Gloria Anzaldua) and a demanding configuration of cultural vocation and expansive urban "contado." These are forces of will and imagination that William Blake troped as "Jesus-the-Imagination" opposed to the reactionary hegemony of world capital and a kind of dead empiricism of matter-turned-commodity as "the fallen world of illusion." Against market odds only grown stronger, I will be holding out for the vocation *in extremis* of the poet/ culture maker in coastal California, as a figure of theory-making and situated will plugged into worlding-energies on the left-coast of experimental poetics and geopolitics. This is the cultural worker's calling to high contrarian vision in William Everson's sense, as outlined in his "Santa Cruz Meditations," a vocation aiming to "throw off this malaise, this evasion, this attitudinizing and sickliness of urbanity" and, instead, "[To] Shamanize! Shamanize! The American destiny is in your hands."[b]

In a time of war and civilization/race othered against civilization/race, as Juliana Spahr has warned in "Poetry in a Time of Crisis," it is not enough for US poetry (or related modes of cultural production like film, comedy, or theater) to sooth, relieve, twitter, or console the soul with the sound of iambic bromides and the banalities of faux-universalism befitting the Fireside Poets of long ago.

Given this time of political crisis and global stalemate, we might turn to the imagination-endorsing power—and wry figural politics—of the Italian film-maker Frederico Fellini, to proclaim wildly: "The visionary is the only true realism."[d] These poetic-mentor figures would variously preserve the confrontational power of poetics/aesthetics in counter-revolutionary times like these and work in the politics and poetics of place and across the borders of language-community and bad empiricism. For the larger social context of poetry we confront is an oddly enabling one in the United States of Bush 2, perhaps the least poetic president since Herbert Hoover.[e] The dialectical situation of poetry in a late-capitalist society of Empire like our own—whereby poetry is constructed as the site of a de-instrumentalized irrelevance, lyric quietude, and social indifference[f]—has aggravated the working contradictions such that poetics as visionary pre-figuration has never been more urgent.

Still, poetry as a genre of social discourse remains a crucial soul-making and counter-worlding project that helps to prefigure, open a space for, and regenerate "the invisible republic" of dust-bowl poets and makers of visionary polity, place, and language-community from Woody Guthrie and Sister Gertrude Morgan to the Beat beatitude of Bob Kaufman, Pamela Lu, Sesshu Foster, Zack Linmark, and Kathy Dee Banggo to name only a mongrel few.[g]

For we do live in an era of spectral alienation and the contraction of visionary forces away from any future-making capacity or collective will: "Therefore Los [Blake's name for the vision-keeping poet] stands in London [the global city] building Golgonooza/ Compelling his Specter to labors mighty."[h] If San Francisco has built up its history so fast and furiously, at times it appears about to be swallowed back into an abyss, some 'vertigo' of ecological catastrophe, social disaster, or historical oblivion. Forces of mongrel becoming and material critique like the Beats and post-Beat hippies as well as more overtly experimental authors like Helen Adam, Pamela Lu, Juliana Spahr, Michelle Tea, George Oppen, and Frank Chin (to the counter-cultural contrary) have helped to forge a spectral vision of San Francisco making this US Pacific Rim city into a porous contact zone, future-drenched, and trans-cultural community evincing transnational innovation and outer-national becoming.

Again and again, we do 'make a start out of particulars,' meaning the grimy contexts of locality and social utterance; we have learned that much as American cultural poesis from the "filthy Passaic" of Doc Williams and the more projective global-locality of Charles Olson's seafaring Gloucester, San Francisco, in this reading of this post-Beat "contado" surging its urban borders and energy-exchanges from the High Sierras, Cal and Stanford and UCSC, and Silicon Valley to the coastal reaches, timbers, and faux castles of Big Sur and San Simeon, will stand exactly for such a "city of art" and nexus of mongrel leftist emergences on the Pacific Rim.[i] The poet Jack Spicer captured this "image of the city" of the Bay Area urban nexus and mongrelizing cosmopolis in the warped and fully disjunctive stanzas of *Heads of the Town Up to the Ether* (especially in *A Textbook of Poetry* sections) of 1960-1961, when he urged, speaking of San Francisco as emanating from the local poetry-wars, language deformations, and willed marginality of standup poetry scenes in little North Beach bars like "Gino Carlos" and "The Place":

Every city that is formed collects its slums and the ghost of it. Every city that is formed collects its ghosts.

Poetry comes long after the city is collected. It recognizes them as a metaphor. An unavoidable metaphor. Almost the opposite.

…But the city that we create in our bartalk or in our fuss and fury about each other is in an utterly mixed and mirrored way an image of the city. A return from exile…[j]

Michael Davidson illuminates the long duration of these over-reaching lines and providential city-vision when he writes in *The San Francisco Renaissance: Poetics and Community at Mid-century* that "Spicer's model here is Dante, who, exiled from Florence, creates a divine comedy out of historical contingency and in the process turns his local city into a system of belief."[k]

If San Francisco is to prefigure this vision-driven and art-respecting civitas dei, then it demands a very left leaning, bohemian, queer, mongrel, porous site of experimental energies and juxtapositions open to the future and to the free-play of the off-beat and new. As the lone Spicer poem Robert Hass embedded in the grungy poetry walkway on Addison Street in Berkeley near the BART station would remind us, "Hold to the future. With firm hands. The future of each afterlife, of each ghost, of each word that is about to be mentioned.// Don't put beauty in here for the past, on account of the past. On account of the past nothing has happened.// Stick to the new. With glue, paste it there continually what God and man has created. Your fingers catch at the edge of what you are pasting." (*Heads of the Town*, p. 179). Spicer's poem on the poetics of emergence, captures what Berkeley and the Bay Area means to me: energies coming out of the future, open to free speech poetics, that kind of mode that made myself and others cross the country to get near or into it…something unfinished blessing the ground too.

In exploratory terms of discursive over-reach and mytho-poetic vision, Maxine Hong Kingston has captured the post-Beat and thickly archival San Francisco poetic culture and leftist politics of place through her 60s-drenched refigurations of Frank Chin as Asian American street-theater activist in *Tripmaster Monkey: His Fake Book*. This remains one of the greatest postwar literary works San Francisco's mongrel and transpacific-becoming culture has yet produced, as place and self collage and collapse into one mongrel and inter-textual mix by the suicide-haunted Golden Gate Bridge where the "fake book" opens its psychedelic documentary: "San Francisco, city of clammy humors and foghorns that warn and warn—omen, o-o-men, or dolorous omen, o dolors of omen" and home of five-generation native sinner and son, the grandly named Wittman Ah Sing out-troping Bret Harte, Alfred Hitchcock, Frank Norris, Jack Kerouac, John Steinbeck, Peter Orlovksy, Ishmael Reed, David Henderson, and his namesake bard Walt Whitman in a space-trumping claim to speak the dramaturgy of urban polity and the poetics of self-fashioning and Chinatown as place, myth, and nation-language.[l]

Working within the US trajectory of revolutionary transformation on the bliss-ridden edge of the North Beach becoming Haight Ashbury and its counter-cultural *contado* spreading into poetry readings, Be-ins, rock concerts and the streets, Kenneth Rexroth could boast after the long march of the US 1960s, "The San Francisco scene dominates world culture" in a nexus of post-beatnik transformation leading from California to Prague and Paris. "Today we are all a part of the world literature, and we have a profound effect on world literature" Rexroth added, urging that "the young people coming up" in San Francisco or elsewhere in the ever-provincial US, "need to be reconnected with the avant-garde tradition of the world."[m] This local literary and cultural production were coming to be fused into a huge poetics of global ecology.

Reflecting a coalitional, experimental, and trans-poetics vision linked to the "worlding" dynamics of Santa Cruz and the global contado of San Francisco as Northern California nexus linked to Asia Pacific and the Americas to the south and north, I gesture towards a situated poetics of transpacific capaciousness and California regionality. This is an extreme and abiding poetics of place and numinous reach, with long standing ties to sites and authors here, and one which is dedicated to preserving (if only in a visionary-affirmative mode of social prefiguration) the activist politics energies and visionary reach of what Blake called "Jesus-the-Imagination" and William Everson incarnated in his vision-keeping works to shape an ontological geopolitical poetics of place, *Archetype West: The Pacific Coast as a Literary Region* (1976) and its companion work in the pedagogy of vocation and regional/national/cosmological vision, *Birth of the Poet* (1982).

From his cabin and A-frame press in Swanton along the Pacific above Santa Cruz (where he taught for years at Kresge College at UCSC and forged his sacramental vision of place and embodied poetics), this Brother Antoninus turned Dharma-Bum Blakean prophet helped to forge and enlarge the legends and myths and hyperboles of vision that allow place (regionality as such) not just to exist as geo-material fact and fate, but as mytho-poetic longing and historical-existential project to become an 'idea/ archetype" in the sacramental worlding and tactical beatitudes of place. In *Archetype West: The Pacific Coast as Literary Region* (Berkeley: Oyez Press, 1976), Everson invokes and challenges with a whole life-time of place-based western work the East Coast platitudes of New York critical lion Edmund Wilson who had blasted the Big Sur poetry and California exceptionalism of Robinson Jeffers in 1941 in these smug, place-denying, and culture-emptying terms: "It is probably a good deal too easy [for Jeffers] to be a nihilist on the [Big Sur] coast at Carmel: your very negation is a negation of nothing" (p. 4). But Everson, to the contrary, living in Swanton near Santa Cruz and teaching his huge "Birth of the Poet" course in UCSC Kresge College from 1969 to the mid 80s in the wake of mentor-figures like Jeffers, Rexroth, Royce, and the Duncan-Spicer circle of Bay Area poets, argues for the abiding special force of west coast poetics and San Franciscan incarnations; he claims that Kerouac and Ginsberg "became the true voice of the western regional archetype," as these Beats incarnated the primordial, sublime, and wild energies of the region as some kind of "apotheosis" (p. 113) even as the mass movement of west-coast Hippies later diffused this energy of place into the social body (p. 147) in sites like Haight Ashbury, North Beach, and Venice Beach.

While some versions of regional locality and California exceptionality can be bounded and drenched in nostalgia and sentimentality, I am not being retrospective or rearguard here: the California of leftist vision I am contending for is emergent, mongrel, multiple, under construction, open to myriad forces of transcultural and translational becoming. For in such a vision of western regionality, the Pacific Ocean is not an entropic end-point, smoldering "void" (Lawrence), or beautiful "Glass Wall" (Baudrillard, Lyotard) of blockage, entrapment, and closure where US white-settler frontier dynamism ends and suicide, death, sunset, miscegenation, acid trips, bardic flight, and narcissistic aimlessness and cultural folly begin. This misguided sense of a continental-forged California closed to Asia/ Pacific forces and shut off from the phenomenal South/North transcultural/translational interconnections between Alta/Baja Americas, was invidiously portrayed by Louis Simpson in a 1963 poem called "Lines Written Near San Francisco" which claims utter world-weariness and second-rate wine-consumption as California telos:

> Every night at the
> end of America
> We taste our wine,
> Looking at the
> Pacific.
> How sad it is, the
> end of America!

In "Fallen Western Star: The Decline of San Francisco as a Literary Region," Dana Gioia invokes this self-blinded little-narrative poem by Simpson to substantiate his even more remarkably wrong-headed claim that San Francisco had altogether stopped being the center of US literary culture around the imperial-San Francisco heyday in 1898 and 1899 when literary figures like Frank Norris, Ambrose Bierce, Jack London, Bret Harte, Lincoln Steffans, and the banal proletarian poet of "The Man with the Hoe," Edwin Markham, had a broad national if not world impact.[n]

Defending California regionality and the local basis of art, Gioia contends that present-day San Francisco has no "literary ecosystem" or "thriving literary culture" of presses, journals, critics, social theorists, or authors of cosmopolitan regionality or innovative vision to speak of, though he oddly remarks that "Pundits are never in short supply in Berkeley, which is probably why it produced—albeit twenty-five years ago—the last influential local literary trend, Language Poetry." Such a failure of vision and denial of history are so out of keeping with contemporary San Francisco and its literary-experimental contado, only somebody in New York, Denver, or Washington DC could believe its retro-fitted claims to defend the mythos of California as writing locality.[o]

Vision of place and polity is challenged by material blockage and the will to perpetual negation and rootlessness: "Los [the poet] reads the Stars of Albion! The Specter [theory] reads the Voids/ Between the Stars." This nervous dialectic of image and concept, theory and dream, has been transported to transpacific sites out along the Pacific Rim where Kant (as in fits of sublime lassitude) walks and walks around Taipei.[p] Building-up into the makings of a transnational vision "among these dark Satanic Mills" of Connecticut and the lesser lights and "Mental Fight" of malls and courts and Berkeley classroom clamor.[q]

In these times of crisis and defeat, poetry as such becomes a way of keeping the soul alive (as in Blake's principle of Los pursuing Jesus-the-Imagination) in the late capitalist world, say, with its codes of de-sacralization, glamour, banality, plunder, loathing, and dust. Poetry becomes a way of searching for a mantra, miming ontological traces and minority-becomings along lines of dwelling and flight, "walking between the two deserts/ singing." Poetry early served the forces that drove the flower from the brass fuse, works and days, transfigurations of the Rock the Brass Valleys of Connecticut into haunted tropes and vision-quest graffiti: "One World." In mongrel and myriad small presses from Tinfish and subpress collective to New Pacific Press and Krupsakaya, poetry emerges anew as language charged with meandering, in the strict sense of syntax, a way of becoming; maybe (at times) a tongue or stammer on fire.[r] By such visions of polity and place, San Francisco poetics aims to write beyond the self into another language and place of perpetual becoming; where the language of dispossession seems act of grace, lost certitude, syntactical torquing, and global/local finding.

This poetics, in effect, is a way of calling the "spectral" forces of San Francisco back from the past and out from the future, evoking the "spectral city" that is not so much ephemeral as waiting up ahead of us and lurking in the palimpsests of place and history on every street corner and in the emergent energies of myriad poems that bespeak the mongrel communitas of San Francisco as Pacific Rim nexus and site of global/local beatitudes. This anonymous poem found taped on a wall leading down to the Market Street BART Station in downtown San Francisco in April 2005 captures the swarming traditions and will to visionary "praxis" of this left-coast city, as San Francisco poetry coming down from Rexroth, Ferlinghetti, Everson, Lenore Kandell, Helen Adam, the Grateful Dead et al, as an "interview" with myriad spectral traditions rising out from the past to summons the urban future to a "language dream" of ongoing beatitude and quest:

San Francisco Interview

For a month now over the city by the pyramid banks
Your hand in mine we walk out into the renovated Fillmore,
But do not sing those thin blue songs tonight by the taco counter
The ravens of my soul stand ever-watch on the street corner
Without reason or time they come and ask for more pimp flesh
Never ask the same way, just freak out the sorry soul into sad sack
Amid an elite army of thousands marching by the Peace Pagoda.
This is the hidden door to California country:
Men walking on the moon today, you lost in an acid zone
Reflux as if a molecular unity in the Haight Ashbury
As the language-dream rumbles on from long ago
And another KPFA savior is preaching a new kind of praxis.

Endnotes

a. See Gray Brechin's *Imperial San Francisco: Urban Power, Earthly Ruin* (Berkeley: University of California Press, 1999) as well as Gold Rush-era promotional passages from Bayard Taylor, *Eldorado: Adventures in the Path of Empire* (1850) (Santa Clara, CA: Santa Clara University Press, 2000).

b. William Everson, *The Birth of A Poet: The Santa Cruz Meditations*, ed. Lee Bartlett (Santa Barbara: Black Sparrow Press, 1982), p. 135.

c. Juliana Spahr, "Poetry in a Time of Crisis," *Poetry Project Newsletter* 189 (2002): 6-8, originally written for a "Poetry in a Time of Crisis" panel at the 2001 MLA convention,

d. Fellini's comment is used as the opening epigraph to the history-laden docudrama, *The Magic of Fellini* (2002).

e. I for one do not take Bush's loose and mangled American English to be poetry or poetry-like.

f. As in *New Yorker* verse if not the scaled-down poems worthy of *The Dunciad* in the leftist journal of mass circulation, The Nation. The lyric is relegated to a condition of irrelevance to the US war-machine verging on what Santayana called in World War I contexts, "the genteel tradition": this is what Ron Silliman blasts

as the US School of Lyric Quietude on his blog site defending language and post-language poetics.

g. Though I cannot substantiate this claim by myriad examples, see Rob Wilson, *Pacific Postmodern: Writing the Pacific, from the Sublime to the Devious* (Honolulu: Tinfish Works, 2000) as context for such claims. "Invisible Republic" would allude to the prophetic leftist America evoked by Greil Marcus around the popular culture work in music of protest poets like Woody Guthrie, Bob Dylan, The Band, Joan Baez, Ma Rainey, and Robert Johnson et al.

h. "Jerusalem: The Emanation of the Great Albion," *William Blake: The Complete Poems*, ed. Alicia Ostriker (London: Penguin, 1977), pp. 650-51.

i. On the material and visionary of San Francisco's being "the hub of it" and nexus of "the new regionalism" of California-based vision, see Everson, *The Birth of A Poet*, pp. 162-163, who makes caustic contrasts with the Fresno county of his birth and the Los Angeles of de-racinated simulation.

j. Jack Spicer, "A Textbook of Poetry," *The Collected Books of Jack Spicer*, ed. Robin Blaser (Santa Barbara, CA: Black Sparrow Press, 1980), p. 175.

k. Michael Davidson makes the case that "the local" circulation pattern generated around Jack Spicer's vision of San Francisco did not mean seeking Beat celebrity nor academic ratification, but performing crazed poetry in a bar like The Place in San Francisco: see *The San Francisco Renaissance: Poetics and Community at Mid-Century* (Cambridge: Cambridge University Press, 1991), pp. 156-167.

l. Maxine Hong Kingston, *Tripmaster Monkey* (New York: Vintage, 1990), p. 3 ff. In some ways the text forms a situated and Asian Americanized archive of every film and literary work done on San Francisco, with works like *Vertigo* and *Dharma Bums* embedded in the dream-life and reference system of Wittman Ah Sing, who at times also seems to embody macho energy not just of Chin but of Earll Kingston, Maxine's actor husband to whom this "fake book" is dedicated.

m. Interview with Kenneth Rexroth, in David Meltzer, ed., *The San Francisco Poets* (New York: Ballentine, 1971), p. 34, pp. 36-37.

Markham's poem appeared in Hearst's rival *San Francisco Examiner* and supposedly was republished in 10,000 newspapers and magazines at home and abroad in 1899.

n. Gioia's narrowly situated essay was first printed in the *Denver Quarterly* in Fall 1998 and became the basis for the essays collected by Jack Foley, ed., *The 'Fallen Western Star' Wars: A Debate About Literary California* (Scarlet Tanager Press, 2001). It appears online at:
http://www.danagioia.net/essays/ewestern.htm

o. It was not long ago that post-romantic poets of trans-American reach (like Gary Snyder, Josephine Miles, Bob Kaufman, Jack Kerouac, or Jack Spicer say) sought to offer up an expanded counter-cultural vision of region and a large-scale improvisational engagement with the un/American drives of history, place, nation, and subject.

p. Add to that bio-poetics of place the gnostic deconstructionism of poets like John Ashbery, Juliana Spahr, along with the will-to-visionary dimensionality of William Blake, Everson, and Kenzaburo Oe which haunt all the global figurations and lyric quests here.

q. William Blake, "Milton," Preface, p. 514.
On the long-cultivated poetics of 'going local' in Honolulu, Berkeley, and Santa Cruz, see Rob Wilson, "In Praise of Doggedness," *The Red Wheelbarrow*, spring 2003, pp. 60-65."

r. In a time of war and civilization/race othered against civilization/race, as Juliana Spahr has warned in "Poetry in a Time of Crisis," it is not enough for US poetry (or related modes of cultural production like film, comedy, or theater) to sooth, relieve, twitter, or console the soul with the sound of iambic bromides and the banalities of faux-universalism befitting the Fireside Poets of long ago.[c] Given this time of political crisis and global stalemate, we might turn to the imagination-endorsing power—and wry figural politics—of the Italian film-maker Frederico Fellini, to proclaim wildly: "The visionary is the only true realism."[d] These poetic-mentor figures would variously preserve the confrontational power of poetics/aesthetics in counter-revolutionary times.

FIRST I would like to say two things:

One, I believe poetry exclusively occurs when it is discussed. [i.e. "Poetry" as a privileged structure is an anachronistic notion. I can only stand poetry in the context of prose].

Two, Americans should leave Afghanistan and Iraq so writers and clerks can move to more boring topics.

I've learned something over the years. [I noticed how my English derives from clichés, as if I was writing from the debris; what Eileen Myles said at the conference after telling her story reading in English in Russia and the reaction of the audience, "Writing with a filthy language"].

I AM BUSH. POETRY & AUTHORITY
HERIBERTO YEPEZ

I've learned something over the years. The instant we're talking about a crisis we are hiding ours.

This comes from my Mexican background and my training in Gestalt psychotherapy; the projections we make, how to recuperate those projections in order to reorganize the self... It also comes from Guangfan's "There is nothing in the whole universe that is not you"; the basic Upanishad teaching "Thou are you" and Hegel's comment in his *Phenomenology of Spirit* regarding philosophy starting only once we recognized ourselves in/with the *absolute other*. Mexican popular culture says: "No te hagas pato" (lit. *Don't make yourself a duck,* meaning, don't pretend you are not you, don't turn into a third person in order to not assume the responsibilities of knowing you are the person you accuse, don't become three in order to not accept you are both one and two.

I take "crisis" as a crisis I too am provoking. At the same time the victim and the agent of imperialism in every case. Something I share with Americans.

Iraq, for example, is Bush's way to hide he is the crisis itself.

Bush is our way to hide we are Bush.

It's easy to blame governments when they in fact do represent awful societies.

I only can call poetry the most critical voice against every order, including its own.

I suspect as poets we take advantage of times of crisis to try to offer poetry as part of the solution. Maybe to hide poetry is part of the problem.

In saying "Poetry in a time of crisis" I certified poetry.

I certified it as part of a time. As part of a time of crisis, which is something really good for poetry.

Poetry in a time of crisis must be useful. At least in that phrase.

That phrase is optimistic.

It makes poetry look good.

Part of the solution. Not part of the problem.

But I think poetry is part of the problem.

In a way Bush does poetry too.

I may say his poetry is pretty bad but it's poetry too.

Bush tries to cling to meaning. He tries to make the audience feel the ecstasy of words. He performs.

The president behaves similarly to poets I know.

I am now doing what Bush does much better than me.

No wonder why poets decide to be poets. They become Bush.

There's only one step from the blank page to the White House. I'm in it.

I am Bush.

Poetry in a time of crisis can also mean poetry is an emergency measure.

Poetry as something you reuse or return to when things get worst.

For example, if you're depressed. Or there's a war down there in Iraq.

You can make an anthology out of emergency poetry like this.

Poetry is part of the problem.

Emergency measures follow a psychology of panic.

Red or yellow alerts.

Put some poetry into the dying nation, into the dying discourse.

Poetry in a time of crisis. Poetry in yellow alert. Or red.

How can poetry help?

Somebody may offer this clue: poetry can help not getting in the way. For example promoting the end of speeches. A country where every politician that tries to give a speech –especially a speech to the nation—is killed.

[I liked Walter Lew's approach, 'talking again' about Spirit as something you need before doing poetry. And after. No spirit, no poetry. What he meant by "Spirit" I think was the beyond-deep-cultures-are].

Yet that clue would only be a pretty bad joke.

The way poetry does not help.

It's not part of the solution but just part of the laughter.

México and the United States are nations that resemble each other too much. They should be completely different, so different that they would go to war every two or three months. Instead they go to bed every four years.

Countries that laugh too much. Part of the problem is laughter.

How come you laugh when a political joke is done?

Why SNL?

How did we get to this point?

Because poetry worked.

What poetry aims at, building the common I, the Nosotros, the We was achieved.

Homer wanted to praise the heroes. He did. The heroes were praised.

Whitman sang America. He achieved his goal.

Poetry is full of successes.

Poetry has been historically linked to war.

Poetry is always trying to put an end to a war that continues wars that poetry helped to instigate.

Whitman is full of bullshit American poetry hasn't gotten rid of.

Whitman was very American. Free verse means having no meters. No limits. Respecting no borders. Free verse breaks the territories, makes it bigger. Free verse was how poetry materialized on the page the imperialism of the United States. Why being American was the best thing that could happen to the rest of the continent.

Free verse explains how half of Mexico's territory was stolen: its territory taken through a take over, an expansion of the map of the United States.

In fact, Whitman supported that war.

Whitman wanted to construct a space-time where/when everything fit. That's why Whitman broke the conventions of how much text could be written, how long the lines could be. That's why Whitman wrote so much. Wrote those heroic lists, those listings. Groceries of History. The many landscapes. The different peoples. Every thing: America.

[I am here trying to start a discussion on how from Whitman to Stein, the way "America" writes reflects/refracts the imperialism this writing is developing under, developing in its own structures. Acker would have agreed on this I think].

So, from this point on we are going to call "America" the image of a space-time where/when everything is there/then. The containment of All. What Pound called "Vortex" and Borges "Aleph".

What we forget conceiving such a total-time/space is that a system of simultaneous realities taking place at once would make all of them absurd.

"America" is a comical nightmare.

Viewing poetry in a time of crisis doesn't help to put an end to the crisis, it only helps to make poetry (again) a possible solution, a praxis that can really mean something good for the culture it belongs to; viewing poetry in a time of crisis puts the emphasis on the time of crisis, erases the fact that the institution of poetry is part of the crisis, that poetry is in a crisis itself.

[My reading of Efraín Huerta, Nicanor Parra, Renato Leduc, etc, gave me this idea from the start: we received literary "poetry" from the Western tradition, at one point we dominated that and even contributed our own thing to It, but let's not forget "poetry" is part of the Western colonial heritage, a post-colonial self-critique stand implies a going beyond "poetry"].

Times of crisis help poetry hide its own crisis. I think instead of thinking how can poetry help in a time of crisis, think how poetry has collaborated in the production of a crisis, how that production of a crisis makes a culture risk itself, thus having to strengthen the strategies to perpetuate itself using the institution of crisis as an excuse.

To make poetry a possible measure. To make ourselves forget we live in cultures that are dying, cultures that want to kill.

I think poetry is part of the obscurity.

I think poetry is the place where people go when they want to miss therapy.

The place people go when they are too snob to go to the movies but they still want to pretend their life can have meaning as their moon, an elevator to acquire more power or at least meet the readers.

The readers, that group of people who want the same stuff poets crave, but don't have the courage even to write.

Or to corrupt themselves in order to publish.

What I am saying is I don't believe poetry can fix.

Nor do I believe poetry should be saved.

[How much more I would have enjoyed 9-11 if the twin towers had been full, completely packed, with poetry books].

I think Wittgenstein was right when he realized he should concentrate on proving philosophy could do basically nothing.

When crisis arises I'm one of those persons that thinks words can help prevent the catastrophe. This is one of the reasons I consider myself a poet. I believe in alerts. I'm part of the problem.

Poetry should not look for ways to survive. But the poet, at least, should make an effort to disclose all the information she or he has historically used to gain authority.

Show even a dying cultural practice like poetry can be more honest than usual politics.

Poetry should unveil where its authority comes from. Should push its own contradictions, let them come out of the closet. Should push the crisis further until the authorities that created it to remain in power are removed by the continuation of the crisis until nothing remains.

I came all the way from Mexico, made lines, asked for a permit, said hi to American Immigration agents, lay in the airport, ate peanuts, had a ride, I came all the way from Mexico to basically accept I have nothing to say.

I only come here to do what I think poets should do every opportunity they have: contradict ourselves all we can right in front of the audience. We once tried to convince poetry was something good, something we should share, something that helped. Publicly and very openly contradict ourselves until the laughter stops, until there's no credibility left in the authority we inherit or won ourselves, until it is made clear those who have authority have stolen it.

The function of poetry is to lose its function. The function of poetry is to diminish the general notion of authority.

Border Signs
Heriberto Yepez

The installation was done "out side" at a bi-national installation art festival that takes place every 3 years in the San Diego-Tijuana area, called InSite. Jaime Ruiz Otis and I decided to "crash" InSite, and in August 25, 2005, one day before InSite started, we installed a series of seven signs, at the San Ysidro crossing point. The images and verbal components referred to racism at the American checking point, where Mexican citizens are subjected daily to the humiliating practices of the Border Patrol agents, to Minutemen mentality, and also to a scandal at that time about a Mexican black character called "Memin", who was accused of being racist by Americans. Our installation was done in a matter of 10 minutes, and was done as a piece of illegal installation: site and *date* specific. We wanted to take advantage of the InSite opening date, so policemen could be confused as to whether these signs were part of that. Two days after the installation, the signs were removed by the police, but at that time they had reached TV and newspapers in San Diego, Tijuana and Mexico City. Another purpose of the installation was to prove that illegal, fun, critical and political visual-verbal art could be done outside institutions, literally in a matter of minutes. A complete look at the series can be found in www.hyepez.blogspot.com.

The Art of Urban Walking
Ghosts, Images & Text
Stephen Vincent

1.

WHAT follows is a way of looking at the City, at least, looking and listening to the City while walking. The "City" here is San Francisco. The project is called, Ghost Walks.

Consciously or not, I suspect one is always constructing his or her own particular experience of a space. At the same time, one is not the sole inventor of one's immediate landscape. Inevitably, other aggressive forces are at work, whether they be the character and tone of persons, architecture, graffiti, the weather, billboards, signage, etc. Most explicitly, advertisers, for example, continuously concoct visual icons—fire, ice, intimacy, romance, whatever—to convert the flow of one's psychic attentions to embrace a commodity—a certain brand of liquor, for example—to induce the desire to acquire a particular brand. The walker, or biker, or car driver, however, can seize the aggression inherent in an environment and either fracture or convert that power into imaginative constructs. One can, for quick example, select a bird out of a liquor billboard and turn the creature into an oracular source. Indeed, the objects, persons and sounds in any space may provide a series of patinas—let's say "ghosts"—from which any number of histories can be deciphered into singular photographs, stories and poems.

Indeed, from the point of view of making an art that speaks to a larger public condition, the urban landscape provides the fodder of images and/or texts to build a collage of juxtaposed elements, or, alternatively, the opportunity to radically cut and simplify a complex image or phrase into an abrupt epiphany.

The magic of the process is to let the eye and/or ear be drawn (or seized) by particular elements—letting things come to one: an image is taken through the instrument of the camera, or an overheard phrase enters the journal as text. Then, there begins an argument and transformation. On some level, any image or text, or combination of the two, will refuse to disclose themselves without an argument, among themselves and/or with the writer/artist. One must, on some level, listen to the image, that is, listen to see what the image dictates. Attended to closely, the shape or form of an image and/or text will liberate the assembly of ghosts that occupy the neighborhood, including, as well, those ones we carry within our own individual and collective histories. It is the nature of the 'ghost walk' to liberate these connections—ones that mirror the deepest points in our consciousness—which, in turn, lead to the construction of fresh images and insights: singular photographs or a series, a corresponding responsive text, or none at all.

That said, within any construct, image and text may always be at war or in friction with one another, or, minimally, in a peripheral relationship—for example, as one sees in the image of the parabola of the course of one moon barely crossing the parabola course of another. That's OK. The complication of the two enriches the construct, its inherent friction becomes that something called "art", one that hits at a core truth, the "verity of difference".

2.

"Let us remember too, that we don't have to translate… pictures into realistic ones in order to 'understand' them, any more than we need translate photographs into colored pictures, as though black-and-white men or plants in reality would strike us as unspeakably strange and frightful. Suppose we are to say at this point 'something is a picture only in a picture-language."

—Ludwig Wittgenstein: *Philosophical Grammar:*
Part I, The Proposition, and its Sense.
Part II, On Logic and Mathematics

On some level here, Wittgenstein is saying a picture is a ghost—or that taking a picture is transforming—whatever the object may appear to be—into a ghost. Art, by definition is a "ghost language" and, by extension, a dialog with ghosts. Some ghosts are much more interesting than others. For example, what passes as public media (journalism) is most often a series of bad, one might say, 'false ghosts.' "Giving up the ghost" is the way a good artist or poet transforms a ghost into legibility, a "picture language." To do otherwise—as an artist or writer—is to operate in bad faith.

It is also why a "ghost" of what was—the "ghost of what happened"—may provoke a deep sense of lament. What was is not only no longer here, but the language of its (the ghost's) reappearance violates the original site, erasing whatever is personal to one's memory. What was once an image in "living color"—as viewed, say, on a walk—is now transformed into something else. At the same time—even as we instinctively acknowledge the loss, the shadow of memory —we are seduced by the new, ghost language, its vitality, 'the art.' A good image, a "picture language" is "a walk away lover"—a courtship, an evolving marriage providing history, ecstatic and/or critical dialog.

Ironically, we also soon discover the art's illusion of permanence. The ghost or "picture language"—in which we discover an uplifting balm to an otherwise barren or inauthentic state– is now, also, up for grabs. New writers and artists, new "Ghost Walks", time and change subject the "ghost language"—its iconic structure—into a continually transformative state. "We seize the City, the City seizes us." When the art is wonderful, the imaginative legibility of this embrace is what sustains us. When the imaginative construct is absent, there is suffering and subjection amongst us.

Laundromat Ghosts
Laundry is but a shadow. Mortality a hanging out: Clean, crisp, bright.

The Ghost Hole
To wonder where they (the ghosts) leave us.
The way the neighborhood is suddenly stripped.
Not a story anywhere. It's here. The hole. To enter
And exit. On whim's notice. Like actors in the theater.

Ghost Lantern
The interior ghosted, or he who ghosted himself, the inside of his skull gone: the inside nocturne a series of dark memories he can no longer remember.

Mop Ghosts
Behind the Church, riveted by the sight of her ghosts—were they parents, were they siblings?—speechless I stood. As were my comrades: tongue tied, not one movement to their heads, nor across their stiff, thick white hair.

Girl Sleuth
Brenda Hillman

The Clue in the Jewelbox

A brenda is missing—where is she?

Summon the seeds & weeds, the desert whooshes. Phone the finch
with the crowded beak ;   a little pretenda
      is learning to read on brenda's bed.

In the afternoon near dull oleander & bright cactus caves. Near pulpy
caves with the click- click of the wren & the shkrrrr of the thrasher,
      a little pretenda is learning
to read till the missing brenda
 is found!   Drip of olives like syllables near the saguaro.
Nancy Drew, find the secret, in raincoats & wednesdays & sticks. Maybe
Nancy whose spine is yellow or blue will find the brenda in 1962, Nancy
who has no mother,
      who takes suggestions from her father and ignores them.
Gleam goes the wren ignoring the thorn. They cannot tell the difference.
Click
Click of the smart dog's nails on the rosy linoleum.
      Nancy bends over the clues,
the brenda's dress & sandals & locket. Syllable by syllable,
between syllables a clue. Where has the summer gone, the autumn—
are they missing too? Maybe Nancy
      will parse the secret & read the book report on Nancy Drew.
The pretenda writes the book report: neat pretty sly cute. Syllable by
syllable
      & still no brenda!
Nancy puts her hand to her forehead; is
the missing girl in the iron bird? is the clue to the girl in the locket?

(Left margin: The Witch Tree Symbol)
(Right margin: The Whispering Statue)

The Quest of the Missing Map

Charles Bernstein

if you lived here you'd be home now

imagined fields, brick
walk, lines around
a temporizing bar, where
emblem is encaustic
subsidiary to filiated
abandonment. Go green,
not what you've
exteriorized, Bilko
bunko, o wheel
keep still.

IF YOU LIVED HERE YOU'D BE HOME NOW was designed, typeset in 24 pt. Garamond, 72 & 24 pt. Strymic, & printed by Dan Fisher & Jessea Perry at Eucalyptus Press on the occasion of Charles Bernstein's reading at Mills College the 9th of November, 2004. 5/45

The Carapace
Jennifer Scappettone

                        Hothouse flowers
                        in silk-ash kept from cooling
Mend first and vital candle in close heart's vault: "We chanted as we marched:"
Ground of being, and granite of it: past all   poplars undimmed by the trauma
at our door
               to crack, to-fro as rock   utter silver
    Drowned, and among our shoals,   By that who   colorfast
        who longs to have it,
  jasmine spiraling round   plauding, wondering, a-wanting
cuorus: The girth of it and the wharf of it and the wall;
        the carapace
           past she has been   attempted   To answer   Falls light as   Toward
Stanching, quenching ocean of a motionable mind   with purple mild night's blear-   The all of water,   an ark
                                                                   a mercy
how to kiss   colors ivory
and   of the living & livid
     how   to splay. Worlds away in an inner room, and many
    bout the rose in the cross of the present   were stained with the color
                                                          with the sweetest air
bout not the okeydoke   beauty sundered in your magma sheath   There
    to link the opposing shores.   your shapely thighs   Is makes strongest   translation swell
so break: and your legs also and the ankles beneath them.
wall of spider scapulae   & cliffs of fall   no right amount right   that outrides
    a hostile room
room of walls   of all events in one as in salve   For the listener; for the lingerer with a love glides
how to pass   and those whose   phantastic public   rock you are   As when some
           how   our love remains transfixed at the threshold
        transient and seaward bent, / Remains
                 of successively destroyed figures and grounds"
              of azure, the impalpable, / Mirrors unstill muse as how being puts bliss back
     And like that   deer gang lost my street   under thrum
                        mutual   we thy day enlarge o valentine
  outburst   And everything.
y of idle a being but by where wars are rife.
—her to her extremes:?—With not her either beauty's equal or Me, were I pleading, plead nor do I: I wear—Wants
                    war, wants wounds; The handsome heart:
                         Let

ebb & flow again

The girth of it and the wharf of it and the wall;   or each is both and all

    the carapace and so un so   so but so as

under attempt amante unlover loving

                      he moon and a she sun

bout the rose in the cross of the present

Mid-numbered   for the lingerer with a love glides

    seaward bent, / Remains

                    destroyed figures and grounds"—

        And like that   O

outburst

    of idle being by where wars are rife.   And everything.

We a full never fully developed fact Now burn, new born to the world, Double-natured name, there not where

Notes on "The Bardo of War"

Sky Power
Roxanne Power Hamilton

When I wrote the poem, "The Bardo of War," I began with images from Sky Power's series of paintings, *The Bardo of Dream*. The poem was written in the long liminal period leading up to the invasion of Iraq. Caught in the zone between peacetime and wartime, the Tibetan Buddhist term "bardo" seemed to capture the prolonged uncertainty we all felt before we were thrust back into the "settled" state of war. In writing, I found myself drawn to paintings from her *Ikage* and *Talking Leaves* series as well. One needs a personal shield of protection during war (Ikage) but also a language sufficient to express the complex feelings that arise when we witness, yet again, that we continue to be reborn into states of war. "Talking Leaves" seemed a wonderful metaphor for a pictorial language that I hoped would communicate more deeply than just a poem alone.   —RPH

The Bardo of Dream

Bardo is the transitional state between death and rebirth. It also characterizes the boundary between two states, marking the end of one and the beginning of another. Relaxing into this state of uncertainty can open a doorway to awakening in the moment. The dreamscapes in *The Bardo of Dream* series highlight the ambiguity inherent in the bardo experience by utilizing the form of the diptych to convey the tension caught between two opposites. The velocity of color of one creates an edge next to the subtle luminosity of another, opening the gap of bardo. By polarizing opposites in the color spectrum, a mask of deep orange covering a field of blue black, creates a sense of being enveloped in loud stillness.

Ikage

Ikage (pronounced ee-ka-jay) is an Apache word for shield or protector. Traditionally, Native American men created individual shields using their personal power symbols to protect them in war. As a woman, part Cherokee, existing in a different century, I have created a series of shields as an act of empowerment by bringing the elements that define myself to my conscious identity. The lyrical iconography reflected in my symbols are reminiscent of musical notes, cattle brands, and the Cherokee alphabet, representing my profession as a piano tuner, and my Texas and Native American roots.

Talking Leaves

The Cherokee referred to the symbols in their alphabet as "Talking Leaves." This series represents unspoken communication, the foundation of abstract art. The carmine palette of these paintings is characteristic of fire, the central symbol of the Cherokee people, because of their belief that fire can see into the heart.   —SP

The Bardo of War

Poem by Roxanne Power Hamilton
Paintings by Sky Power

1.

Two states converge   to find between
Not this   not that   The spark leaps
     across the gap   blood runs
to the other side of the story   no borders
 contain this stream of human history   speaking to us from the other side
  of skin, fresh script.   This shock of living trails
into something blue
   without fathom

© Sky Power, *The Bardo of Dream #6*, 2002; Oil on panel, Diptych, 24" x 48"

2.

We keep disappearing   the further we climb
 this mountain in fog   a human caravan of ideographs
    ending in a home lit by red memory
what we miss/mourn the loss of   the body clings
 to monument (Mesopotamia smokes) stands at the edge of its story
 burned into it
    The more we cling to form and walk this bridge of words
to get back home, the further we are from it

© Sky Power, *The Bardo of Dream #7*, 2002; Oil on panel, Diptych, 24" x 48"

3.

An emulsified ending to this story
   where freedom cracks
       out of black smoke
      stamped onto history's front page
 Show it to yourself   jagged possibility
breaking like a tide of fresh crude
       on our shores

4.

What wants form will unmask it from void's
    bright patience
 A storm of plenty spirals across
like the Lucifer Ballet   Such grace in withholding
 A tsunami posing   Wouldn't we know where to go
from the gap if we had a guide?

© Sky Power, *Ikage # 9*, 1999; Oil on panel, 24" x 24"

© Sky Power, *The Bardo of Dream #3*, 2002; Oil on panel, 24" x 24"

5.

Things move into shapeliness
    plotting our course
 out of bright uncertainty
Who invents this game board takes the spoils
 if you squint your eyes, this shield disappears
and we guard nothing again

6.

Tribe gathers itself around a single
 unwritten idea of itself. We could be anybody
churning our language from scratch. Antennae open
 to symbols, signals, suffering nothing in this
yellow dance. We find a language, like tools,
 like weapons, like joyful pitchforks
   to dig into the soil of the next era

© Sky Power, *The Bardo of War #2*, 2002; Oil on panel, 24" x 24"

© Sky Power, *Ikage #14*, 2000; Acrylic on panel, 24" x 24"

7.

We may foment a body loud as words
  & make this stuff up as we go along
Musical staff, distaff   hard to say
   whose harmony   if

8.

Not all one
  but each
   one
Zero degree moon upset continents
  wail for circuitry   a bride to the fixed blue
we could have a constitiution and/or
 a poem

© Sky Power, *Ikage #15*, 2000; Acrylic on panel, 24" x 24"

© Sky Power, *Ikage #16*, 2000; Acrylic, pencil on panel, 24" x 24"

9.

Nothing like a single constitution
 like a plastic menu sure of its tourist
attractions   Dissolved of Babylon
 Speech is protected with certain
 limits   This window inside your
 cell—gives you hope and a horizon
   to constitute

10.

Soon as one idea of order
 constitutes itself—then it's balkan city
Too many in this dance.
 It makes me want to switch
sides   A loose confederacy   of swing.

© Sky Power, *Ikage #21*, 2000; Acrylic on panel, 24" x 24"

© Sky Power, *Ikage #19*, 2000; Acrylic, pencil on panel, 24" x 24"

11.

Every new republic had its cabaret

12.

When tempted,
 stave the measure of.
I wouldn't say cartoon liquor or porn
 but a place for the eye
to conquer itself
 then dance the light top sweetly

© Sky Power, *Talking Leaves #4*, 2001; Oil on panel, 12" x 12"

© Sky Power, *Talking Leaves #3*, 2001; Oil on panel, 12" x 12"

13.

How lucky we are. Back
to cell transformation. Soft
  with this blue apple

14.

When we came back from
   "the other side"
we couldn't take any luggage
  Security asked for an i.d.
We composed our face
  It's all we have.

© Sky Power, *Ikage #8*, 1999; Oil on panel, 24" x 24"

© Sky Power, *Ikage #7*, 1999; Oil on panel, 24" x 24"

The Dead Do Not Want Us Dead
Jane Hirshfield

The dead do not want us dead;

such petty errors are left for the living.

Nor do they want our mourning.

No gift to them—not rage, not weeping.

Return one of them, any one of them, to the earth,

and look: such foolish skipping,

such telling of bad jokes, such feasting!

Even a cucumber, even a single anise seed: feasting.

September 15, 2001

A Telescope Protects Its View
Peter Gizzi

I like to read the dead.

Part of a whole lost era campaign.

The bridge is up.

A portrait of you from what you aren't saying.

On my sleeve.

        The verb to be.

I'm plucky but thankful.

Death and the imagination equals life itself.

Letters from an old bottle,
junk in space.

        A book or a boat?

The black ribbons of a spring day
might sound mawkish

but I like to read under a pale blue sky
animated and deepening.

I like to read the dead.

There's so and so going by
everyone, outside

everyone

the words scroll onto air.

Synecdoche: act of receiving from another.

Metonymy: change of name.

Who hasn't found themselves
praying in an awkward room.

She said but what of their sad work
by the river's edge

sad way of working the moth paper light

trellis of dented garbage cans
and debris at dawn.

COMES & GOES

1

I did set up waymarks, as commanded, high heaps

2

I skirted the waymarks, maneuvered with high leaps
walked as if with power, as if caring for nothing

3

Skirting the waymarks, I maneuvered my hopes high
and walked as if power were nothing
and space repulsive, such worlds ago

4

Gauging the waymarks against louder hopes
crushed now I walked where power was speed
and space divided, such worlds ago
the end of snow, dim whorls

5

Whirled, the waymarks, dead set on hope
crushed now where power walked, I
sped along divided space, so many worlds gone
wrong, drab whorls of snow at the
end, heaped high, marking the way

Keith & Rosmarie Waldrop

COMES & GOES was designed, typeset and printed by Eli Drabman, Dan Fisher and James Meetze for the Eucalyptus Press on the occassion of Keith & Rosmarie Waldrop's reading at Mills College, the 25th day of March, 2003. Typeset in 18 pt. Goudy Modern, 24 & 30 pt. Hadriano. Image based on Alberto Giacometti's "Walking Man."   A. P.

from Rose of No Man's Land

THE WALK back home from the mall sucked. It sucks even on a regular day, and this day was not regular because I was wearing a skirt that crawled up my ass and a shirt that sparkled, drawing the attention of every ape on the streets to my boobs. I don't know if there are creeps everywhere or if Mogsfield is some kind of unfortunate creep central, but dudes were just blatantly staring at my chest and there were cars on the street piloted by guys who felt the need to holler at me out their windows as they sped by. At least they didn't stop. At least I couldn't actually hear whatever it was they felt compelled to tell me. The speed they zoomed at made their cries sound like Heeeeeyyerabababafreaarrma! Hahahaha! At least none of the guys on the street showed me their dick or flashed me their ass. As a girl I had a lot of be grateful for, plonking home in my towering flops. Once I was walking in my neighborhood and this skinny white guy in a pair of nylon running shorts and that's it, no shirt or anything, not even those useless tank tops that guys like to wear, the ones that scoop way down and are slit down the sides—you know those ones? ehhhh—he jogged past me and then he took the edges of his shorts, right beneath his cheeks, and he lifted them real quick, flashing his moony white ass at me. Really, what are you supposed to do when something like that happens to you? I just went back to my room and stayed there. It had made me feel pretty depressed, to be honest. This walk home wasn't having such a powerful effect on me thank god, and I think it was thanks to Rose. I was starting to see the benefit in having friends, or just one friend, really. Too many friends seemed to get troublesome. Rivalries occur, and then comes backstabbing and shit-talking and other dramatic events. I've seen it on tv and at school. If you're going to indulge in friend-having, it seems best to keep it to a manageable single individual. But having Rose to think about took my mind clear off the lousy guys I had to flop past, and helped me to not spend too much time thinking about if the dude who drove by in the van had called me a douchebag or an old hag. Or maybe a fag. Seriously. I've been called a fag before. There's no logic to these people.

When I got home I was greeted by Donnie, shirtless, drinking a beer on the porch. Thank god we don't have an actual front yard. He'd be out there like a mechanical lawn ornament, drinking and waving to passersby and getting pink and peely with the sun. At least this way he is set back from the street and less of an embarrassment to my home.

Hi Donnie, I said, coming into the house.

Hey kiddo, he smiled and scratched at the snarl of hair on his chest. Donnie lived life nude to the waist whenever possible. He scratched at himself like something from Animal Planet, then rubbed his sweaty-wet beer can across the tangle, making it all damp and matted. Gross. You walk all the way home? He squinted at me. Where's my car?

Kristy's Got It, I said. I Just Worked Half A Day. To Start.

So tell me all about it, he lifted the can to his wet mouth and slurped at the opening. I could smell the thin and tinny stink of the beer and I wanted one. I figured I'd just swipe one simple from the fridge and then I noticed that Donnie had stashed the whole six-pack in the shade beneath his sagging lawn chair.

Oh, It Was All Right, I said vaguely. I Made Friends With This Girl, We're Going To Hang Out Tonight.

How's the work? he asked. Easy, hard? They treat you all right?

I nodded. Can I Have One Of Those? I pointed down at the splintery wood of the porch, wiggled my fingertip in the direction of the beer.

Kid, you work now, you gotta buy your own refreshments, he shook his head and grimaced, like he was clueing me into some sort of difficult life lesson and it pained him to do it.

Donnie I Can't, I reminded him. I'm Fourteen, They Won't Sell To Me.

Well you can chip in a bit, howbout? Toss me a few dollars? You're probably making more money than I am. He jammed the can into the crotch of his cutoffs and held his hand out like I was going to slap some cash down on his palm.

I could not hide the sourness, it creeped across my face like a bad smell. Sure, Donnie, I said. I pulled a phony good-kid grin up over my sourpuss. Once I Get My First Paycheck I'll Kick Down, Okay?

Donnie emitted a sound like someone was letting the air out of him. Listen, I'm taking up some space in your room. Just a little corner. Just 'til the weekend. With a grunt he bent down and yanked a beer loose from the plastic rings. We'll consider this a rental fee. He tossed it to me but I wasn't ready so it sort of hit me in the chest and rolled across the porch. Pieces of glitter from the Baby t-shirt stuck to the can.

Great, Donnie quipped. Nice going. Good catch. That's gonna blow up when you open it now. Don't ask me for another one.

A Rental Fee? I asked in a lousy voice. I hated the thought of Donnie in my room, getting his vibes on my things. I scrambled across the porch for my rollaway can of beer.

Some batteries fell off the back of a truck. He shot me an awkward wink, like a mosquito buzzed into his eyeball.

How's Ma? I asked him.

See for yourself, he invited, and gestured towards the door. Then he tipped his can way back, sucking the dregs, and with a flick of his wrist tossed the empty out into the street with a clatter. Score! he chortled. A wide smile ate his face. It's always a happy day when stuff falls off a truck.

In the dim living room sat Ma. Do I really have to keep setting this scene for you? It never changes. Ma: nightgown, mussed hair, still pretty despite it all. Still plump and perfect, rolling with woman-ness, wrapped in peach. Location: couch, sort of rubbed-in looking, fading, not new, draped in a sheet cause it's summer and the old woolyness of it makes you itch and feel gross. Sheet: also not new, faded floral whatever. Living room: dim 'cause the sun gives Ma headaches. Shades drawn, today we get a silhouette of Donnie out there on the chair like an alcoholic puppet show. The can lifts, the can descends. Etc. Television: on, always on, always turned to talk shows or news, something real, no chipper family sitcoms or emergency room dramas, only the real dramas of real living, everything going wrong all the time, everywhere. And yet I see very little on the tv about how creepy men are in the streets. Really nothing at all about the basic daily obstacle course a female is forced to run through. About how you can be walking along absolutely not thinking about your pussy your ass your tits, but then, wham, thanks to the drooly curbside dude, now you are. Now your mind is consumed with the idea, the reality of your pussy, ass, tits; the possibility of blowjobs, of getting fucked. You'd think more attention would be paid to this phenomenon. That there would be long-term psychological studies on the mental effects of this, the changes in brain waves it produces in girl-brains. I can go days without leaving my room and never think of my boobs once. Then I leave the house and it's all anyone wants to talk about. For reals.

From what I gather, all Ma watches on tv are reports of the new big scares, terrorism and ebola and gun-toting six-year-olds and how the bible or Nostradamus or the ancient Aztecs predicted the world is going to end at three o'clock. The glow of the television flickers nicely over Ma who is sipping tea from a cup and watching a talk show. It is like a burning log in a stately fireplace, it casts its warm light around the room. On the screen a lady in a tight lady-suit is bustling all over the studio audience, clutching a microphone. She dips into the rows of civilians, the opinionated people. Ma says, Opinions are like assholes, everybody's got one. On the screen a heavily made-up woman with a short, bleached hairdo asks a question, her voice shaky with the weight of the cameras upon them. The camera swings around to the stage, where a heavyset lady daubs the damp corners of her eyes with a wad of toilet paper. It's happened. I've looked for too long at the television and it's stolen my soul. It's turned me to stone, like some terrible, witchy myth. This is why I avoid this room. It's not only because Ma is depressing and Donnie annoying, it's the frigging television. You glance at it and suddenly you're interested in something you could give two shits about, say the health of this crying woman on the talk show, and before you know it hours have gone by and now you're an expert on, like carpal tunnel syndrome. Who cares. It's probably why Ma hasn't been able to really get off the couch in so long. She's frozen there, held in the malevolent shine of the tv. She craned her neck around to see me there, all decked out in Kristy's skanky clothes. It's weird how the same clothes that make Kristy look like a normal, well-adjusted teenaged female make me look like a hooker.

I have autism, Ma informed me. She turned back to the screen and rested against the sheet draped like a toga over the back of the couch. It's very interesting. I'm learning all about it. Want to watch some with me? She patted the cool, worn-away sheet bunched next to her.

Got To Get Out Of Kristy's Clothes. I said this to Ma but my face was hitched to the television. Television is like a great gooey snare, the light shining off it clingy spiderweb vibrations. I didn't even care about this emotional woman on the tv but now I couldn't take my eyes from her. I guess she had autism, too, just like my Mom. The beer I had begged off Donnie was growing warm in my sweaty hand, in the dead, dense air of the house. I wondered if it was still too shook-up to open it, thought it could be refreshing perhaps to feel the tickly bubble-spray over my body, soaking the stupid Baby shirt in sticky beer.

Trisha, Ma continued. She had a little offended catch in her voice. I would think you'd be happy to hear this. I thought it was maybe ADD but now, I really think I should be tested for this new kind of autism.

> ...all Ma watches on tv are reports of the new big scares, *terrorism* and *ebola* and gun-toting six-year-olds and how the bible or *Nostradamus* or the ancient Aztecs predicted the world is going to end at three o'clock.

I Don't Know, Ma, I said skeptically. Usually I just nod and say something vacant, but every now and then her claims are so out there, like when she got on a tourette's kick. She had seen some 20/20 episode about tourette's syndrome and decided that was her problem all this time. I was like, But Ma, you don't walk around screaming swear words, and her answer to that was, But I always want to. Huh. Then I guess I have tourette's too, right? Who doesn't feel on the verge of screaming fuck or shit or fucking shit half the time? That's not a disease, that's like the opposite of having a disease. Ma dropped the tourette's storyline after a week of half-hearted mumbling, of swearing a bit more than usual. It was so forced. Now autism. I thought autism was little kids rocking back and forth in their playroom or hitting their toddler heads against the wall.

Ma, You're Not Autistic, I told her firmly. It was too hot out for this shit. You're Too Functional To Be Autistic. Believe It Or Not.

It's very interesting, she repeated, ignoring me. There's many different sorts of autism, actually. Some people are highly functional, highly intelligent really. They just had this woman on, she nodded her chin at the screen. She was brilliant. Some sort of scientist.

Uh-huh, I grumbled. The woman on the television was giving a brave, tight smile, the camera pulled close to her face. I wondered what that was like, working a camera for a talk show. Crouched behind the tall black equipment, zooming here and there, spinning around, listening to crazy people all day. I bet I'd like it. I took a stab at my beer can. I gave it a gentle crack and foam rushed to fizz around the split.

And—you're not gonna like this, Trish—they think lots of alzheimer's cases are really mad cow disease. How you like that?

Not So Much, I said. I licked the froth from the top of the can.

Don't do that, Ma scolded. She don't miss a trick. Those cans sit in warehouses. Mice shit on them. I tell Donnie, you should wash those first.

Okay, I said. I started to leave the room. My First Day At Work Was Fabulous, I told her. In Case You Cared. I Was Promoted. I Got A Raise. I Got Employee Of The Day.

I knew you could do it! Ma shouted at my back.

In my room I found a small sculpture of car batteries. Hard bulks of machinery shrink-wrapped in heavy, puckered plastic. There were maybe about fifteen of them. Donnie had done an okay job of backing them into the corner, they weren't much in the way. Still, they were ugly and stolen. When I was younger I thought that trucks were the most shabby and unreliable vehicles of all, for things were always tumbling from their backsides. I imagined the rear doors of semis crushing open beneath a tide of food processors, hairdryers, computer printers. I fantasized about the epic traffic jam, the excited carloads of people scooping booty into their trunks. Then Kristy told me the goods were actually stolen. She was really upset about it. This was when she was about twelve and going through a Jesus phase. She was going to a church around the block and making friends with nuns and other old ladies. She told me the stuff Donnie stashed in our bedrooms was ripped-off and illegal, and at the very least he was going to hell for it. She wasn't sure about the rest of us, but she was worried. She said it didn't look good. Ma and Donnie started getting nervous that she was going to confess to a priest or something, so she got grounded and wasn't allowed to go to church anymore. She had to stay in the living room with Ma watching talk shows where women recount all the horrible things that happened to them in foster homes. You want that? Ma would wave the remote at the screen. You want the state to take you away? Just because of some boxes in your room? Put them under your bed if you don't like looking at them. Donnie brought her a truck-fallen curling iron, then a boom box. She chilled out. I never minded the piles of loot occasionally materializing in my bedroom. They had an outlaw sheen, and Donnie tended to be a bit more ass-kissy when he needed to use our rooms for stashing.

I stripped off Kristy's stupid clothes. I threw them—balled up and reeking of my brief time backstage at Clown in the Box, stained with the gritty sugar drool of my Babymuffin—onto her bedroom floor. The force of my hurl created a wind that fluttered the rows of supermodels hung by drying tape from the walls. I kicked the towering flops off my feet, they skidded up against her mattress. At least that was over. No more dressing in Kristy's clothes. Back in my room I grabbed a pair of sweats and then a pair of scissors and I went to work chopping them into new summertime shorts. It wasn't so easy, the scissors being wicked dull and the sweatpant material being pretty good quality, actually. I'd got them for Christmas. Every winter I get a brand new pair of sweats and every summer I chop them into shorts. So autumn, for me, is a sweats-less season. I had to cut and cut the sweats with little chops, so the end result was pretty Frankenstein. Then I did the next leg and it was equally jagged but in a totally different manner. I pulled them on and then that Weight-Watchers t-shirt. What did it mean that I went to work in a t-shirt that said Baby and after work put on a t-shirt that said I'm A Loser. In the mirror that came stuck upside my dresser I looked at myself. I saw my darkish hair done up in that hairdo, and I dismantled it. It was scrunchy and stiff with product, I mussed it all up hard with my finger tips, and then I came at it with the dull blades of the scissors, chopping off an inch and then another inch and then another. I didn't have much of a plan, it was an intuitive haircutting. I chopped at it until it was too short for Kristy to strangle it into a french braid or lasso it into some Audrey Hepburnish little cupcake of hair on the top of my skull, all anchored in place with a squad of clippies. My new hair swung thickly into my face at about the chin level, jagged like my sweats. I thought that perhaps at a certain angle I might resemble a young prince from a children's book. Or, like, a girl forced by the circumstances of her time to take on the appearance of a young prince in order to carry out certain adventures. Okay maybe a person with less money then a prince but you get the era I'm talking about. My face under my hair was the same. To be honest, I didn't much love it but there's nothing to be done about a face. Kristy of course would argue but we're of different persuasions when it comes to cosmetology. I think it's best to make peace with what you got stuck with. In my case this is a rather uneventful combination of cheek and nose and chin and eyes. My eyes are sort of squinty and my cheeks a bit chubby. I guess my nose is okay. It harbors blackheads but the shape is fine. Same with my chin.

With my new haircut swinging around and my newly sliced sweats, I felt pretty excellent. The can of beer had finally settled and I peeled the shiny tab away and took a hearty gulp. Maybe Ma was autistic. What did I know? Maybe there's a type of autistic hypochondria she is in the midst of. I lay on my back in my bed, crunching upwards to slurp at my beer, thinking about Ma's health and feeling an excited trembling in my stomach, an anticipation of my coming hours with Rose plus the result of eating mainly candy and shit that had had any nutritional value boiled away into a vat of oil. I thought about Rose at her home, wherever that was, somehow funneling power into Kim Porciatti's cellular phone, sparking it alive, juicing it up. I tried to think about people in other places who I could call, but came up empty. I didn't really know a lot of people. Supposedly my Dad was in Louisiana, but there was no point in asking Ma about it. Maybe she threw his number away or maybe he had never left it with her. There was even a chance that he didn't actually exist, that he was some lie she'd dreamed up and placed on a boat in a swamp, a cooler of beer at his feet. I sat up on my bed, in my dreamy state I knocked a slug of beer out the window. It rained down in a pissy stream, sizzling on the hot concrete below, evaporating into the day. That's For You, Dad, I said out loud. Then I sucked the rest of the can empty and flung the tin out the window, too. I felt light and pleasant and full, my stomach settled. I felt ready. There was a rap at my sticky bedroom door, and then the pressure of what I figured was Kristy's physique behind it. The door opened with a sucking pop. I burped a gust of beery breath into the air.

Hey, Kristy said. She was smiling. She was smiling which meant she had no idea I'd been fired. I figured I wouldn't tell her. She got me started on the lying track, anyway. Before this whole little job scam I'd never had cause to lie and so I never had lied. I'm serious. I know it's probably hard to believe, but when you're allowed to do anything you want, why lie? Lies were for people who were trapped and cornered. But now that I'd spent the day wildly crafting lies and counter-lies and clean-up lies, why stop?

Tell me everything, Kristy demanded. She settled onto my bed. She seemed not to notice my new hairdo, or the aura of beer in the air. Kristy seemed preoccupied. Should I go first? she asked.

Yeah, You Go First, I said. I gathered my legs beneath me. My newly shorn sweats looked like they'd been chewed by a giant pit bull. They were my new favorite shorts.

Well, she began, Mercedes is—she's great in a way, like she tells stories all day, she's had this crazy life but—she's really mean.

Yeah? I asked.

Yeah, she's not just mean, she's, like, cruel. She just insults the girls that work there. She told this one girl, after she'd done a perm on this old lady, that—oh, I can't even say it.

Please, I said. I had no time for Kristy's modesty dramatics. Spare Me. What Did She Say?

She said she'd made the lady's head look like a poodle's twat.

Wow, I said. That's An Image For You.

And the girls just kiss her ass. And the girls are mean, too. One went back into the trashcan and pulled out a fistful of hair and threw it on the ground for me to sweep back up again.

Why?

She said I missed her area when I was sweeping. She said I was ignoring her on purpose.

She Must Be Really Insecure, I said.

That what I think! Kristy burst brightly.

> I came at it with the dull blades of the scissors, chopping off an inch and then another inch and then another. I didn't have much of a plan, it was an intuitive haircutting.

Maybe Kristy was a little manic. Nobody in this house eats properly. It's such a basic thing, feeding yourself, and somehow we never picked it up. I'm just going to be wicked sweet to them, all of them, until they like me. That's my plan. She smiled. Here was another difference between me and Kristy. Kristy could tolerate the weird laws of the female jungle. Be nice to girls who are jerks to you until you're all friends. Why would you want to do that? Isn't that just fundamentally unhealthy? I myself tend to avoid mean people, which is probably why I've spent the past fourteen years of life in my bedroom and have only just today made a friend. Now you, you've got to tell me, how did it go? She tugged at my trusty Weight Watchers tee. It takes t-shirts a decade to become really wearable, I think. This one is just perfect. Wait, you cut your hair! Oh my god. Kristy brought a horrified hand to her raspberry mouth. Trisha, she said. I would have. Oh, no. She reached out and grabbed a lock, examined the up-and-down of the ends, the multiple angles. I yanked my head away.

I Like It Like This, I said. I Did It On Purpose, I lied. Somehow I thought that if Kristy believed it was a style she'd leave me alone. It Matches My Sweats. I stuck my leg out, offering her my chopped shorts for inspection.

Oh, god. Kristy groaned. Trisha, I don't know what I'm going to do with that. What about Ohmigod!—

Well, It Was Kind Of Fucked Up, I jumped in. I Mean, That Girl Kim's Friends All Came In And They Know Something Screwed Up Is Going On And Seriously, They Might Want To Kick My Ass—

No, Kristy interrupted, solemnly shaking her head, swinging her hair. No way, they wouldn't do that. They're not like that.

Right, I said. Katie Adrienzen's Not Like That. She Went To Anger Management Classes And Now She Deals With Her Rage By Kicking Homeless People While They're Passed Out In The Street. I'm Sure I'm Totally Safe. I pulled a smile onto my face but it was more like a grimace. Aside From Their Visit It Was Great. Bernice Said I Did A Good Job. I Made Friends With This Girl Who Works In Another Store—

—what store? Kristy was excited.

I Don't Remember, I lied.

That kind of stuff is important! Kristy chastised.

I Know, I nodded. I'll Get Back to You On It. And, Lastly, Ma Has Autism.

Kristy cocked her head like a curious dog. Autism? Is that, like, from eating bad food?

No. It's Sort Of Like A Form Of Retardation. But More—Interesting. Autistic People Can Be Really Smart, Even Geniuses.

So Ma is like a retarded genius?

Maybe.

Are you fucking with me?

Go Talk To Her About It, I shrugged. And she did. But first she went into her bedroom to grab the video camera. I grabbed my backpack and left the house.

Voyeur by Migdalia Valdes

from The Big O Collection
Marie Cartier

MORGASM – The Museum of Radical Gender and Sex Matrix – is a nomadic manifestation of museology consisting of thirteen developing collections, based on ethnographic artifact and testimony. We present both story and artifact in re-visioned ways, which we hope will re-frame the gaze of the museum visitor. Our premiere and permanent collection is "The Big O: Stories and Artifacts from the Site of Female Orgasm." So much about women's bodies remains unexplored. The clitoris is said to be the only organ in all living species which has no function, yet that is theologically and scientifically impossible. What is possible is that we don't know the function of the clitoris yet. We don't know the function of "pleasure" in a woman's body. There is some research in Hindu and Buddhist tantric practice that tantrikas, practitioners of the eastern sexual praxis of tantra, do not experience menopause symptoms that we consider inevitable in the west. Below is one selection from multiple anonymous interviews and mementos detailing stories from women of their journeys to sites of female orgasm. The Big O has been exhibited widely, including Claremont Graduate University; June Mazer Lesbian Archives in Los Angeles; Southern California Arts Gallery in Pomona; and as a featured exhibition within the "Envisioning the Future," project curated and facilitated by Judy Chicago and Donald Woodman, Pomona, CA Arts Colony September 2003- February 2004. Marie Cartier is the chief curator. http://morgasmonline.com/index1.html

Ferris Wheel Slip

This artifact is very special to me. I had this on when I was working at the carnival. At the carnival, they have carnival weddings, which involves a ferris wheel ritual after the carnival shuts down for the night. Two people stand at the foot of the wheel, surrounded by the maid of dishonor and the worst man, and say their vows to the carnival owner. They vow to make as much money as possible during the season—which never actually happens in a carnival, of course. Then the "wedding guests" throw handfuls of popcorn at the couple and they board the ferris wheel. The ride jock sends them around three times, after which they are married. What I didn't know is that this ritual is taken very seriously by the carnie subculture. I also didn't know that the ride jock routinely "parks" the couple at the top of the Ferris wheel for your "honeymoon." The sly wedding guests below await the action since privacy literally does not exist in a carnival. Carnival means "festival of the flesh."

If a couple has sex up there, the guy is supposed to throw something down that the girl is wearing. So he threw my pink slip from the top of the Ferris wheel to all the other carnies who were waiting and cheering. He also threw his boot and broke one of the huge light bulbs (ferris wheel "spokes"). That sort of cleared the crowd, thank god. It was pretty wild, under the stars, up high like that, trying not to rock the car. My "big O" was mostly just the expression on my face as I tried not to tip out. In the carnival, the only way to divorce is to change the gears of the ferris wheel and ride it backwards three times (impossible) or wait until your crews go their separate ways after the state fair at the end of the summer, which is what we did…

Artifacts from The Big O Collection — Photograph by Kimberly Esslinger, *Gypsy King Studios*

Art
After the play *Art* by Maria Irene Fornes
Sarah Schulman

In Ginger's marketing firm waiting room. Ginger is conferring with her clients

ARTIE. So, that's when we decided to market our plays together.

GINGER. It's ingenious.

GREGG. We've been BEST friends for so many years. I mean Bestbestbestbest friends.

ARTIE. It's astonishing how close we've been.

GREGG. And any … rivalry … is the fault, well, it's your fault actually.

ARTIE. It's the fault of the critics. And (indicating Ginger) the public.

GREGG. We do different things. Just because we're both gay doesn't … and rich…just because we're both … I mean, I wasn't born rich … but Artie has actually never had a job.

ARTIE. I'm privileged. But I'm still a Socialist.

GREGG. We're both Socialists, You should see how much money I spend at Amazon dot com on books about Socialism. It's equal to Cuba's gross national product.

ARTIE. That's a lot of cane.

GREGG. (Laughing hysterically)
A lot of cane. You little sugar ca … which is why we want to share…you know, I mean, I mean we do influence each other … I invented verisimilitude … And Artie invented … the word "astonishing."

ARTIE. So, we thought we could bring Socialism in action to the American theater by marketing our plays together and destroying the competitive edge that capitalism creates to pit artists against themselves.

GREGG. And each other.

GINGER. Great, So what are these plays about?

(Artie and Gregg clutch their manuscripts and glare at each other suspiciously)

GINGER. Are these your plays?

(She reaches out like a mommy, and pries the manuscripts out of each of their hands at the same time)

GINGER. Should I read them? So that I can market them?

ARTIE and GREG. (very pleasant) Sure.

They both lean back anticipating the pleasure of hearing their own words.

GINGER. "SHE DESERVED TO DIE" by Artie Lefkowitz and "THE EVIL WOMAN" by Gregg Farkas. I already see some evolving thematic similarities for marketing purposes.

ARTIE and GREGG. (Glare at each other, then turn pleasant) GREAT.

ARTIE. Astonishing!

GREGG. Well, you know … I … I … I would't, you know wouldn't say … astonishing, but … you know.

ARTIE. My play opens with a woman whose body is about to be torn to shreds by vicious Muslim hordes.

GREGG. My play opens with a woman whose body will be punctured, raped, and burned by vicious Bosnian hordes.

ARTIE. And the play describes the tragedy of the sexy white man who sets out to find the corpse.

GINGER. (taking notes) What is the tragedy?

ARTIE. There is no corpse. She's been torn to pieces. So he has to jerk off on stage, show his big penis, and sweat while, we the audience, ALREADY KNOW that he is doomed to fail.

GINGER. Who is playing this handsome man?

ARTIE. The casting director's boyfriend.

GREGG. (He can't hold it in any longer) MINE IS ABOUT A WOMAN … mine is about a woman … whose lovely, delicate, innocent, pure body, is torn to shreds by a vicious Bosnian war criminal. (whispering) How did you get the casting director's boyfriend. I WANT THE CASTING DIRECTOR'S BOYFRIEND.

GINGER. So, you both have women whose bodies are torn apart as they are beaten and raped to death.

ARTIE and GREGG. (Pleasant) Yeah. (angry) YOU PLAGIARIST!

ARTIE. You knew I was going to have a woman's body be torn to death, you know it, you knew it. You are astonishing. You knew it because I said the words *Body torn to death*, and you stole my idea. You astonishing, astonishing, capitalist.

GREGG. YOU KNEW I WAS GOING TO HAVE A WOMAN'S BODY BE TORN TO PIECES BECAUSE I SAID … I … I … I was … the one who, I was the one who said "TORN TO PIECES." I said it.

GINGER. Well, I think it will work.

ARTIE. Great.

GREGG. Great.

GINGER. We'll pitch it as a trend.

ARTIE and GREGG. A trend.

GREGG. Violence against women is a trend. And your work is showing America to America, making them stare their own misogyny in the face.

ARTIE. And that will be the trend. For us to show America her own violence. How she's raping herself.

GINGER. Yes. Really what you are doing is so heroic. I wonder if we can find a woman who was raped by a Muslim or…

GREGG. A BOSNIAN!

GINGER. There must be some.

ARTIE. Or a symbol.

GREGG. That … that … that is it. It. A symbol. A symbolic woman. Not a real woman.

ARTIE. A symbol.

GREGG. A symbol.

ARTIE. A symbol.

GREGG. Symbol.

ARTIE. Astonishing.

GREGG. Symbol. Symbolic.

GINGER. A musical?

ARTIE AND GREGG. No! Yes!

ARTIE. Not any musical.

GREGG. Something like Gypsy.

ARTIE. NOT ANY MUSICAL.

GREGG. An opera musical?

ARTIE. A reggae musical?

GREGG. Gypsy, Gypsy, Gypsy, Gypsy.

ARTIE. What kind of musical has never been done?

GREGG. Polka.

ARTIE. Gregorian chants?

GREGG. Gregorian polka?

ARTIE. With Reggae.

GREGG. Punk.

GINGER. What about adult punk? For the baby boomers.

ARTIE. Easy listening punk.

GINGER. It's never been done before.

ARTIE and GREGG. (Looking at each other suspiciously) Hmmmmmmmm.

GINGER. What if the same woman played both of the women in your plays?

GREGG. She's got to be black!

ARTIE. Very symbolic. Black means something.

GREGG. It means universal, global … not some whiny suburban bitch from Smith.

ARTIE. It will put us beyond reproach.

GREGG. I can't stand any more reproach. I'll put my head in the oven if I get reproached one more time. I can't take the pressure.

ARTIE. There won't be any. We'll be heroes. We'll be the ones who made the black woman's symbolic body be torn apart by Muslims and Bosnians. I smell Pulitzer.

GREGG. No more Pulitzers for you. No more. No more. You have too many as is. It's my turn.

ARTIE. We'll share it.

GREGG. No, I want my own.

ARTIE. Maybe they'll give us each one of our own.

GREGG. Astonishing.

ARTIE. I certainly am.

Two Poems
Jim Elledge

TAPPING MY ARM FOR A VEIN

You could hear through opened windows that someone a brownstone or two away practiced violin, someone else accordion. Up then down scales they went, as imagination, that fucking bully, staggered through day dreams thick with handsome, willing brutes, his call as close to canticle as bellowing can be, his path more crooked than water streaming downhill.

THE SEASON OF MASCARA

From the bell towers and ramparts where we strolled yesterday, bonfires like the ones crusaders once built on a whim leagues from here still wink. What a coquette fire is, batting its eye, licking its lips, curling its finger back and forth, bartering with breezes. Come here, come over here, it coos, like Unkie did when he returned during the séance that Halloween you went as a TV and I a scalpel.

Wayne's College of Beauty
David Swanger

> I know what wages beauty gives
> —Yeats

We have dropped out of the other schools
to enroll here where no one fails; everything
is fixed, fluffed, teased into its temporary best
at cut-rate prices because we are all novices
in the art of making beauty, learning that beauty
is not so hard. Beauty is not so hard we learn,

because it is not chemicals or varieties of fashion.
Our scissors and combs, our libraries of lotions,
our bright mirrors assure the timorous or imperious
elderly they have come at last to the right place.
Wayne's is not the Heartbreak Hotel, and when they
leave beautiful, it is because they are briefly unlonely.

We have said, "How are you?", "How would you
like your hair?", and we have touched them not cruelly,
and with more than our hands. When it is over
we swivel their chairs so they can see themselves
carefully from several angles while we hover silent
just above their doubts, a calculation that provides
two faces in the mirror, ours smiling at both of us.

Apple
Roswell Spafford

With apologies to Dylan Thomas

Teeth crack the skin—
not ours. Flesh
bitter, then sweet.
We taste only other.
Swallow. Inside us but not us.
Thus, we know.

To know, we told God "no."
Our skin a wall, our bones
no more the dust.
Not us the garden, not us the snake.
Us by sweet defiance made.

Sweet, the taste of skin.
Yes begins with no.
No: the word made flesh,
Bone of my bones,
This is how I come to know.

Round blush, bundle of
flesh, the first begotten
not made. And sorrow's second came,
keeper of sheep, blessed to God but not
his brother. So in difference,
death.

Inside, no sweet scent of child,
no separate sense of us and Him.
Sword sent us out to know:
After the first, all is other.

Criss Cross ©AnneKarin Glass

Bodyscapes
Will Sherwood

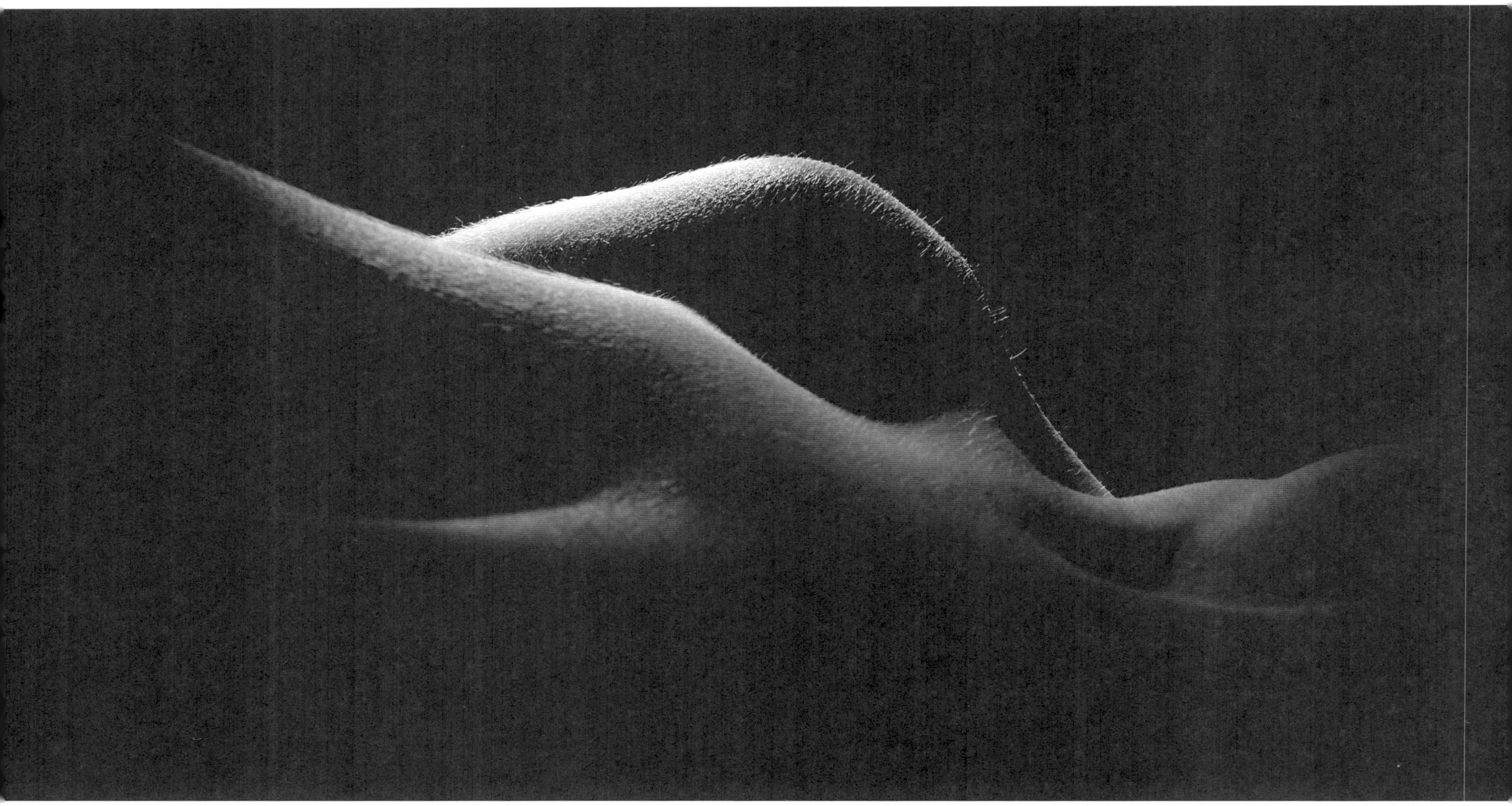

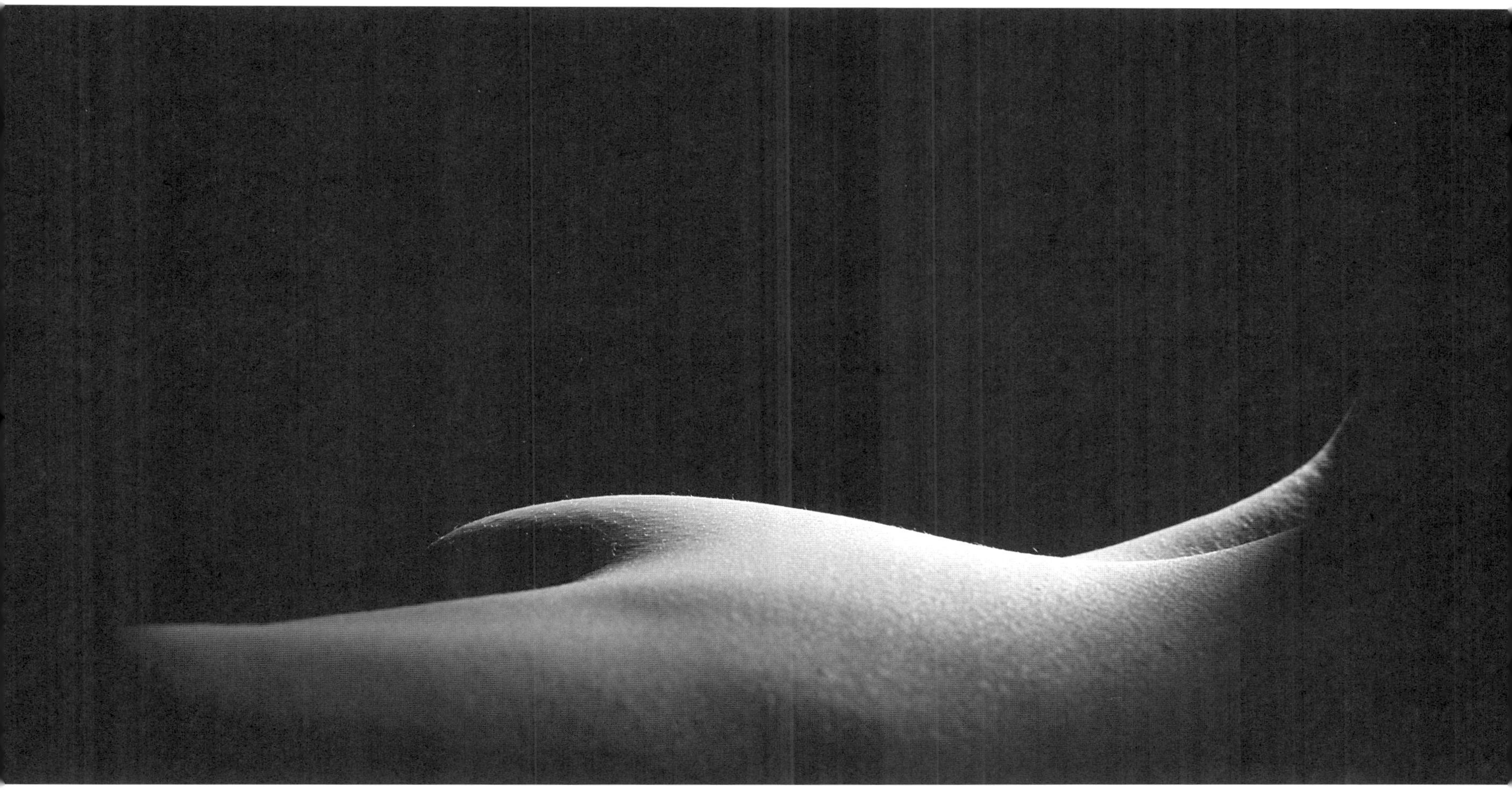

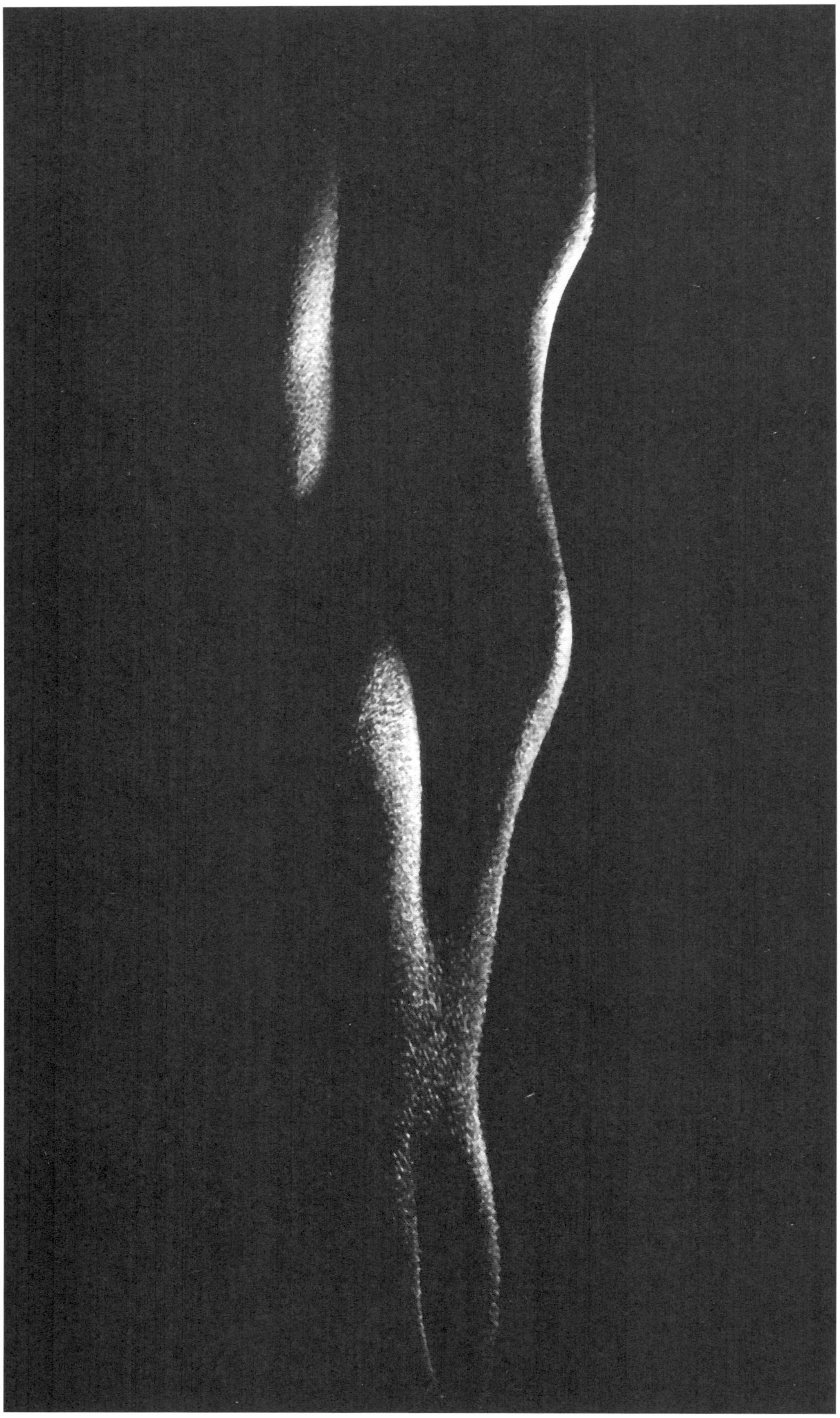

What The Thin Ones Eat
Micah Perks

Plain, non-fat yoghurt. Some vigilant thin ones eat only the so-called "yoghurt water" that they skim off with a spoon. When dining out, they measure their food with their fists. For example, one fist-sized portion of meat is correct. Some say you can eat two fistfuls of pasta, others say no, no pasta at all. Pasta puffs you up like a blowfish. Some of the thin ones advise you to eat whatever you desire, but in small amounts. For example, if you like chocolate, eat a chocolate chip. Another thin one explains that she loves peanut butter cheesecake but replaces it with a teaspoon of peanut butter once a week. Some give up all meat. Some give up wheat, or dairy or all three. They call themselves vegan. Some say don't eat anything after six PM, others say four PM. Fish is generally agreed to be good. One of the thin ones advises ordering a salad sans dressing, then picking off the croutons and offering them to a homeless person as you exit the restaurant.

Thin ones have a long and illustrious history. In the nineteenth century they swallowed worms. These sinuous guests set up housekeeping in the thin one's stomachs and shared their portions, so that the thin ones could eat many fistfuls.

Someone compared the very, very thin ones, the ones whose insides consume themselves, to those who are consumed with climbing Mount Everest.

One thin one, who was Snow White, made the mistake of accepting a bite of apple offered to her by someone who was not thin.

One thin one eats oatmeal and egg white burritos for lunch. Another thin one eats three raisins as a snack between meals. One thin one breakfasts on the dew that collects on peach blossoms. This dew tastes very faintly sweet. Another one eats fistfuls of air.

A few of the air eating ones are so thin that they float, just one to two centimeters off the ground, but still, you can pass a piece of paper under their feet.

When the thin ones are done not eating, they strut down the street, their hip bones jutting. Their jaws are like weapons and so are their ribs. Thin ones are victorious warriors. Their thinness is like shining armor, like a shining exoskeleton, like a South American iridescent green violet scarab beetle with giant horns, the ones made into jewelry; or they are like the Wampanoag warrior Queen Weetamoo, going into battle against the British colonists, face painted bright red, in a British Kersey coat, girdled with wampum, both arms covered in brass bracelets, with red stockings and white shoes and powdered hair, and a necklace of jangling British buttons and another necklace of scarab beetles. Those thin ones are a little like her, strutting down the street, looking good enough to eat.

Give us then, just a little bite of your thinness, an appetizer. Let us stuff you in an olive like a pimiento, smother you in brie or in chocolate, wrap you in bacon. Could we grind your bones to make our bread? Oh Thin One, lie down on our communion wafer, slide onto our tongues, melt in our mouths. Don't be selfish. Let us consume, too.

from I Hotel: A Novel-in-Progress
Karen Tei Yamashita

Against the backdrop of the political and social changes of 1960s and 1970s, Asian American students and community activists, influenced by the Civil Rights Movement and the Black Panthers, gathered to create what became the Asian American or Yellow Power Movement. From this movement came Asian American Studies with departments in colleges and universities across the country, drug rehabilitation programs, communes and cooperatives, book stores, newspapers and journals, theaters, filmmakers, cultural centers, artists, musicians, politicians, law cooperatives, educators, historians, underground Marxist-Leninist-Maoist groups, literary and political movements. For the Asian American community, this was a flourishing period of new creative energy and political empowerment.

The center of my research and writing is around the International Hotel in Manilatown/Chinatown, San Francisco, the site of political activism and community service for almost a decade until 1977 when residents of the hotel were forcibly evicted. The I-Hotel, as it was known, housed mostly elderly Filipino and Chinese immigrant bachelors, men who had come to work and make their fortunes prior to World War II and who, because of Exclusion Acts prohibiting Asian immigration, were unable to find spouses in the United States. In the 1970s, the I-Hotel was sold and sold again to force the eviction of the residents and to redevelop the site. In an effort to save the hotel, Asian American activists staged dramatic protests with thousands of participants while making the hotel a center for political activities and community service in the Chinatown and Filipino communities. The I-Hotel was a magnet for a multitude of political action groups in the Bay Area, a center and symbol for the Asian American Movement.

Chapter 9: Authentic Chinese Food

How many places you gotta go before you find a decent bowl of noodles? Two? Three? Ten? Decent in this town, okay, two, three, why not? We got standards and competition, so for decent, it's not a problem. But if you're serious, if you take your noodles seriously, you got to do your homework. Now, I tell you what. True noodle connoisseur, he takes his noodles at late night. Gotta be after 9 P.M. earliest. Later, the better. Midnight. You know why? It's the soup; all day long the bones and leftovers getting thrown in that pot, simmering down easy, see. Already your choices narrowed, right? Gotta be those joints open to the wee hours.

Chen, see, he's got what I call the palate. So he does the noodles tour. Not like a tourist thing, more like a quest. Not that he couldn't make quality noodles himself. It's the gritty kind he's after, the kind you can only get in a busy kitchen at the end of the day. It's a return to his Bohemian days, but now he's got money. Could be it's opera or a concert, classy event like that, or the last showing of a movie. Could be it's a smoky house of jazz and blues. That's just the set-up. Then he peels away for the noodles show-down.

So that's how I meet Chen Wen-gwang. I call him Wen for short. It's one A.M., and we're at the counter side-by-side at the Cathay. We got the same bowl of noodles, 'cept he's dressed nice. Madison Avenue's finest. 'Course by this time of night, he's got his silk tie stretched out and thrown over his shoulder. Jacket is hanging off the stool behind him. Time was I could afford suits like that, make a killing back of Lucky M and go out and buy me the best. Pin-striped, double-breasted, silk hanky. But that was before my union days.

Wen's got his eyes closed concentrating. Then he takes up a slurp of the noodles and gets the texture between his teeth. I look at him, and I say, "Pork neck. Could use a few more."

He says, "Snout. That would do it, too."

And I know he knows. It's the sticky cartilage that gives a soup grip. I'm impressed.

Then he says, "And some more white pepper."

He nabbed it.

And that's how it started. I say, "Have you tried Chop Suey House over on Post? And we meet there the next week, and every week practically we're on the quest.

So one night I tell him this story:

Long long time ago in a far away place, two lovers meet every solstice, summer and winter. That's the only time. Twice a year. You know, the gods. They controlling everything in those times. So those lovers they make the most of it. You bet. Having sex this way and that, like in those Indian instruction books *Kama Sutra*. Hey, I know my stuff. Pathetic old codger like me. That's me in book six. But I been to every other book. Yeah, I been there. Okay, nowadays *Joy of Sex*, right? Like that. You use your imagination. Wet. Sticky. Hot. Rolling around. Running around. You got a chance twice a year, you better be good. You remember your best times and then you double that. No, you triple that. Imagine that. That's probably why the gods prohibited it. They were jealous.

Okay, the lovers have incredible sex to make the gods go crazy with jealousy. Then you know after you spend that kind of energy, you gotta eat. Now, this is the important part. This is when the lovers appease the gods, or who knows, they won't let them come together next solstice. Hey, it can't be just any food, rush out and get a burger. Young people these days think porno and burgers. No, these lovers have the palate. Palate of the gods. Gotta be maybe a ten course meal. They do the jon kan po for who dishes up the first course, and then, it's back and forth, each one trying to outdo the other, appetizer to dessert. Now this is some good cooking. Finest ingredients. Highest quality. And everything perfect like a musical concert. Pungent dishes followed by subtle and refreshing. Crunchy by smooth and succulent. Chicken to pork to duck to beef to fish.

So I tell Wen this story. I say to him, "You know this story? It's a classic."

He looks at me like if anybody knows a classic, he's the one. Stuck up son of a bitch. I can say that you know. He's my friend, like a young kid brother.

I say, "Every Asian people have a version of this very story. Japanese, Korean, Pilipino, Vietnamese. Some things different. Sometimes the sex before. Sometimes after, but basically the same story."

"And different menus."

"Now, you're talking."

"Could be sex before and after."

"Or food before and after." Now I get serious. "This is the great myth of Asian peoples. How can the West compare? All they got is that poison apple."

Wen laughs.

"Think about it. Innocence to knowledge. Good and evil. And *then* they get to have sex. What kind of screwed up thinking is that?"

Wen orders another beer.

"Sex is everything. Beginning of the universe. It's one big—" My gesture says it all.

Wen and I toast.

I continue, "But, it's more than meets the eye. Complicated. Two cooks can't live together!"

"What do you mean?"

"Notice they each cook different dishes. Otherwise, it's true what they say. Too many cooks, you know? Got to be one palate at a time, but like a balancing act. You Chinese say, yin and yang. And each gonna offer the other the most delicious dish possible, but it's also competition. It gets more intense with each dish. So the gods know what they are doing. Keep the lovers apart, they get the best possible meal."

"That's the moral of the story?"

"I don't know nothing about morals. What's the moral about that apple? Don't go talking to snakes? It's already too late. It's like life. You want good sex? You want good food? You gotta go to the trouble."

"What about companionship?"

By now, I know. Wen's living in some big house all by himself.

"I'm living how many years by myself in that I Hotel? I used to have a regular girlfriend, but then she disappeared. I never see her again. So what's left? I got food. I'm fighting this eviction thing."

Wen looked sad.

"Listen," I said, "Wen, my friend. You still young, but I tell you something they never tell you when you're young. You think you gotta have your woman. That's what you hungry for all the time. Guys like me don't have that chance. So we got that knowledge. But I tell you this. Most important thing you gotta learn is to be alone. I think I'm not cut out for this. I go back to the Philippines or something. But this is my home now after fifty years. It's my freedom. I'm gonna die free. And I'm gonna die alone. Same for everyone."

I don't see Wen for awhile, then he comes around, and we go look for noodles like usual. He says, "I been thinking about your story."

"Oh yeah?"

"Yeah, the part where I'm confused is the menu. You said twice a year on the solstices. That's summer and winter. How about the equinoxes? Spring and fall?"

"Okay, we can change the story. Why not? Four times year."

"You can change the myth like that?"

"Why not? It's my myth. I change it if I want."

"Is that so?"

"This is improvement. Definitely. You got to get the variety of food in each season. Of course! Spring duck! Summer could be tropical, refreshing. Fall, big harvest. Winter gotta braise the meats, slow cooking in heavier wines." So that's when we start to make menus. I say, "At night, I'm dreaming menus. Like summer. First course: limed ceviche, try albacore."

He says, "Second course: drunken chicken in shao hsing wine."

I say, "Fried lobster claws."

He says, "Cold sour soup with cucumber."

I say, "Peking duck on steamed bread."

He says, "Zucchini flowers and tofu."

I say, "Barbecued spareribs."

He says, "Beef with asparagus."

I say, "Brandied scallops."

He says, "Lychee sorbet." Then he says, "The first dish, ceviche. That's not Chinese."

"Who said has to be Chinese? What about lychee sorbet?"

"Closer than ceviche. We do South America later. For authenticity, the menu should match the Chinese version of the myth."

"Okay. Squab stuffed mushrooms."

"Now I'm hungry."

"Okay. You buy the ingredients. I make everything. Completely authentic. You gonna think you're Nixon in China. I heard he got himself a Chinese cook, but common knowledge he's Pilipino."

"You're lying."

"Maybe not. You look around. Take the movies. Pilipinos stand in for everything: Indian, Mexican, Chinese, Egyptian, Hawaiian. That's what good coloring does for you."

"What's the movies got to do with this?"

"Hey, I cook you any kind of cooking. Doesn't matter. People come peek in the kitchen see who the chef is. Ask me when did you come here from Japan? Or you must be French Vietnamese. Did you get your training in France? I always say, that's right. How did you know?"

So that's how every once in a while I go to Wen's place, put on my chef hat and cook. Always a crowd there testing the palate. Like I said. At night, I'm dreaming menus. Okay, I'm dreaming beautiful women too, but all I remember in the morning is the menu. Think about it. Beautiful menu like a beautiful woman: refreshing, delicate, sophisticated, succulent, juicy, spicy. Takes your breath away. You die happy. So if I give the menu to Wen, one day we go shopping. Half of my dream comes true. What you think? Fifty percent is pretty good for old guy like me.

People say, you gonna give us cooking lessons. Pass on the traditions. Pass on the secrets. I say sure. I pass on everything. Some say, what is it? The ingredients? You get this stuff imported? I say, I don't know. Most of it hundred percent American ingredients. Made in America. Where you think we are? Some stuff you improvise. Make your own. Then there's bird nests and shark fins. Ube and taro. If you get your hands on the exotic stuff, they all go wild. They can't believe their taste buds. But from my point of view, it's only 50 percent ingredients. Other 50 percent is technique. Every cuisine got technique. You got to know the way. For Chinese, it's the way of fire.

So Wen's got a celebration going, and three of us taking turns with the dishes. Wen, he got a duck smoked in tea, red peppers, cinnamon and star anise. Then D1's making lobster Cantonese with black beans. But I got the piece of resistance.

D1 says, "Hey, manong. You starting to sound like Master Po."

"That's me. Kung Fu cooking master."

"What's that dish you got there?"

"You know this dish? Mrs. Nixon's favorite."

"Mrs. Watergate herself?"

"Serious. I made it for her in the Great Hall when she visited China in 1972."

Wen laughs. "Another true story."

I take out the *Life* magazine and show him the pictures. "Here it is. You call this dish, *Lady's Quivering Buttocks*."

"No fucking shit!"

"Dongpo pork," says Wen. "It's Song Dynasty recipe named after the poet Su Dongpo. Dongpo wrote a poem for this dish *In Praise of Pork*."

"He compares it to a lady's quivering buttocks?"

"Why not?"

"Oh mama!"

The pork belly melts between your teeth. Like I said, it's a piece of resistance.

"What else you cook up for Pat?"

"Oh jasmine chicken soup, three-colored sharks fins, smoked duck in tea."

"And they say I'm bourgeois."

"You convert to Mao, we let you eat like this too. By the way, this was Mao's favorite too. That's why I make it. To honor Mao."

"End of an era."

We toast to Mao who just died. We toast to Chou En-lai, died in January. "To the end of the Long March."

"That's it," D1 says. "You should write a cookbook."

"I been thinking the same thing. I base it on the classic Asian myth of the two separated lovers."

"What's that?"

I tell him the tragic story of the lovers that all Asians should know.

"Chen, this guy's a real bullshitter."

"You look it up. All Asian people know this myth."

Wen winks, "Look it up."

I say, "My idea for the cookbook is simple. We do Asian American cuisine. American because we use ingredients found in America. Imported is okay. Ajinomoto. Soy sauce. Wonton wrappers. Then we do ten course menus in Chinese, Japanese, Pilipino, Korean, you name your Asian American. Only problem is I can't write."

D1 says, "You leave that to me."

"You got to tell the classic myth. That's the key."

"If you insist."

Wen knows better. "And we have to test all the recipes."

"No problem. I volunteer."

I say, "After Nixon in China, you see all these Chinese cookbooks. Problem I see is no pictures. I gotta have pictures in my cookbook."

So after this, I'm telling D1 the menus and the recipes, and Wen is painting pictures of the food. He's also got poems in Chinese next to the pictures. How do I know what they say? I say to him he better have sex in those poems, like quivering buttocks.

He says, "Don't worry." Up in his studio, he's painting every day. I find out he quits teaching. Quits writing his books. It's just painting and cooking and writing poetry.

I say, "Maybe you taking this thing too far. After all. Just a cookbook. Me, I still got to go out and protest, argue with the Mayor. Stop this eviction. If I don't do that I got no place to live. What's a cookbook?"

"Not just any cookbook," he says. I can see he's fighting loneliness. Working out his freedom. He makes arrangements of food and paints. We go to the markets, and he sketches everything. When we cook, he's got his paint brush right there in the kitchen, and he gets the inspiration. Quick brush work. He's painting everything. Knives and woks, ducks and bamboo, lobsters and mangos. Step by step and more poems. It's all there. Pretty soon, you see a whole world.

Meantime, I'm telling my story to D1 who's taking it all down on his typewriter. He's always arguing, "We can't say you cooked in the Great Hall for Nixon. It never happened."

"So what? In my mind, it happened."

"What about this story about you and Ho Chi Minh in Paris?"

"That's one of the best stories."

"And this one cooking for Imelda?"

"She goes wild for my pancit. She goes so wild, she worked it into her love cosmology."

"When were you in Yokohama?"

"That's really true. I docked there with the merchant marines. I got a girlfriend there. Wanna see her picture? Yoko like

Yoko Ono."

"Like Yoko-hama."

"Hey, I forget to tell you all my girlfriends. We got to put them in."

"You got a girl at every port, right?"

"You know it."

"I give up."

"In my long life, there's no work I don't do. I do everything. I been everywhere. If I don't do it with my own two hands and my back, stooping with my legs, walking with these old feet, I do it with my head. I fish up in Alaska. I do canning work. I do stoop labor and cut asparagus, artichokes. Pick tomatoes, strawberries, grapes. I carry a gun for the US military. I build houses. I plant flowers. I build bridges. I sell grocery. I'm a bartender. I work the dock. I organize for the union. I gamble. I bust some butts in my time. Short time I do acting jobs in Hollywood. Danced with Fred Astaire. I play the ukulele in Honolulu with Don Ho. And all the time, I got the women. You write that down."

"Where's Paul? Let him do this. Hey, Chen, I got a postcard from Paul. He's in Taiwan. When's he coming back?"

Wen shrugs. "Haven't heard."

"The Okada book came out, and he left. I think we worked him too hard." He shakes his head, then looks at me. "Is this a cookbook or a fake autobiography?"

"Nothing fake here. I'm for real. I'm your real Makoi."

"What?"

"Makoi. Makoi. You don't know?"

"I'm not ghostwriting no imaginary autobiography, McCoy or not."

"Why not? All the recipes I give you: authentic. This one goes back to Song Dynasty, original recipe with original poem. Taste travels to you from eight centuries."

Wen says, "He's right. Anyway, you've been doing the research. You should know. A whole history of civilization in a single dish. In time everything else vanishes, but the dish can be recreated."

"Food is made in America, but the recipe is guaranteed authentic, put your mark of good housekeeping. Okay, sometimes I change something here and there. Working to perfection, but I'm like the artist. Add my signature. But my life? My life is a dream. It's what I got. What you want? Take it away?"

Wen's got his brush out, splashing color. Dark red plump chunks of lady's buttocks. Almost feel the quiver. Then the poem. Brush goes in quick flashes. Swish. Swish. Poem's like cuisine. Makes the world sensible. Ingredients in the head, then apply fire. Have you eaten today?

Photograph by Migdalia Valdes

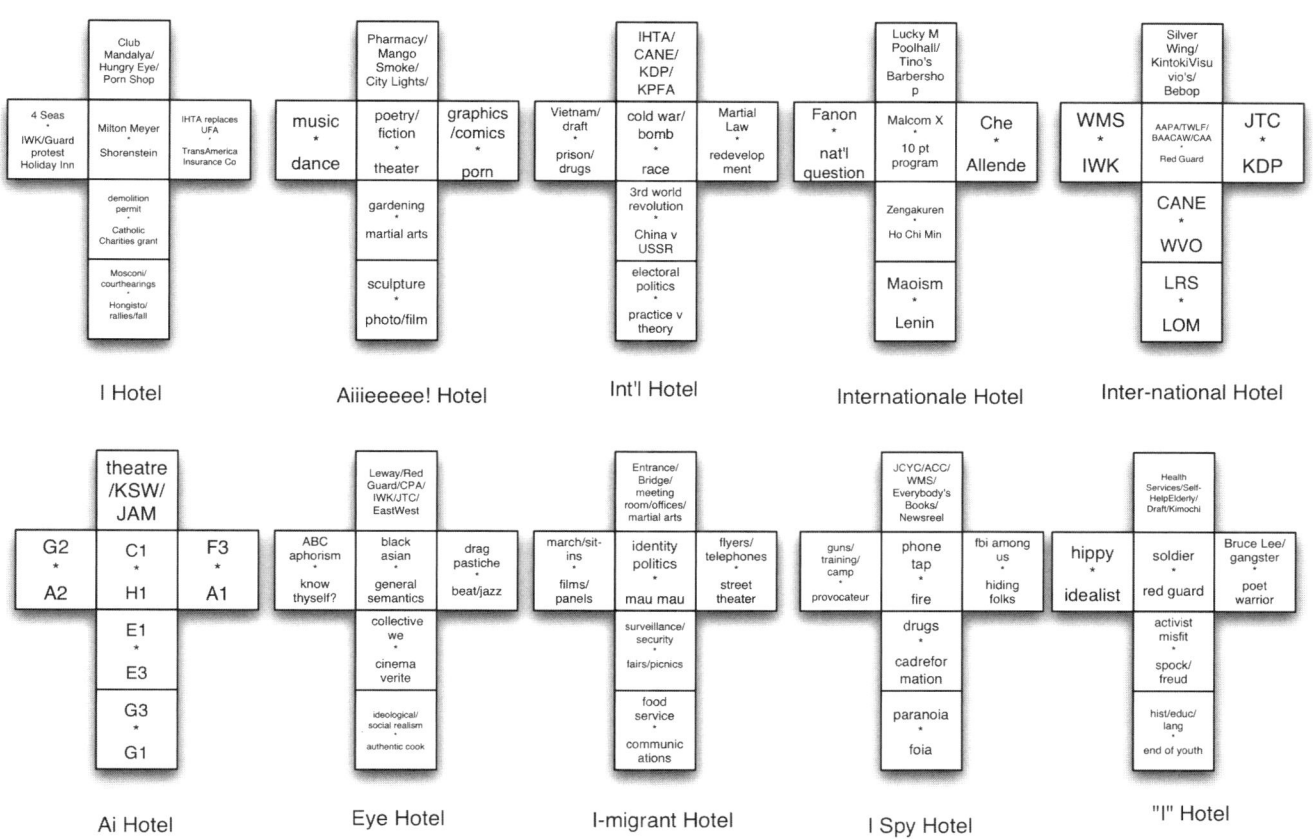

UNA NOCHE

Then El Presidente,
uncoiling his tongue,

"You cannot stop time
but you can smash all the clocks."

And so, seeking Paradise,
we have burned the bright house

to the ground.
A necessary act.

We have invented glass
and ground a dark lens

and in the perilous night
we continue to dance.

The tarantella, the tango,
the passadoble and the jig,

the bunnyhop, the Cadillac,
the Madison and sarabande,

mazurka and the jerk,
the twist on tabletops.

Rolling our eyes,
flailing our limbs.

It's how we keep time,
our feet never stop.

MICHAEL PALMER

UNA NOCHE was designed, typeset in 18 pt. Bulmer, 24 & 36 pt. Optima and printed by Dan Fisher and Jessea Perry at Eucalyptus Press on the occasion of Michael Palmer's reading at Mills College, the 18th day of November, 2003. 7/40

Syntax
Carol Snow

Photograph by Weiferd Watts

Photograph by Andrea Flores

NOTE ON "SYNTAX"

"Syntax: A Reading, Danced" was just as its subtitle says, a poetry reading accompanying/accompanied by dancers. There was no music except that of the language. In my text, original fragments and phrases interleaved with excerpts and whole poems by writers from Yeats to Stein to Apollinaire to whomever wrote "Dick and Jane" to a Zen koan; the structure of the reading highlighted grammatical forms; and the choreography was keyed to the grammar (not the content) of the text. Excerpts from Gertrude Stein's "How to Write" served as undanced intervals, a chance for the audience to relax their focus and for the dancers to catch their breaths! As coda to the piece, we presented the whole of W.B. Yeats's "Among School Children": "O body swayed to music, O brightening glance, / How can we know the dancer from the dance?"

The Creative Work Fund of San Francisco offers grants for individual artists to collaborate with non-profit organizations of all kinds in the creation of new work. I received a grant with The Foundry, a performance group best known for multi-media presentations. The Foundry is the brain-child of two dancer-choreographers, Alex Ketley and Christian Burns, and I applied to create a piece with Ketley for two dancers, Andrea Flores and Justin Flores, both of whom also perform with ODC Dance.

What follows here is a three-column passage from "Syntax" with the author reference on the left (not read aloud), my reading in the center column, and the dance code to the right. This (the seventh) section is mostly possessives, with a coda of intransitive verbs. I also attach an explication of the code—the dance vocabulary "gestures" as linked to the grammar—and the key I devised to help Alex "transcribe" the reading to dance. Every "p's" or "A's" (possessive pronoun or possessive adjective), for example, initiates a self-touch in the dance; every infinitive ("to-V") a lift, etc.

Alex Ketley's inventiveness generated an impressively varied, expressive and bravura 40-minute pas de deux performed spendidly to my on-stage reading at ODC Theater, San Francisco, August 12-13, 2005. Far from multi-media in the usual sense, "Syntax"—according to gratifying responses—did engage both left and right brain in a novel way.

— Carol Snow

SYNTAX: Dance Code from "Among School Children"

FROM "AMONG SCHOOL CHILDREN"

VIII.

Labour is blossoming or dancing where
The body is not bruised to pleasure soul,
Nor beauty born out of its own despair,
Nor blear-eyed wisdom out of midnight oil.
O chestnut-tree, great-rooted blossomer,
Are you the leaf, the blossom, or the bole?
O body swayed to music, O brightening glance,
How can we know the dancer from the dance?

— W. B. Yeats

DANCE CODE

N v= A'ING &x A'ING adv
a-N v=x A'd (to-V: O),
&x N V'd adv {prep: p's-A-o},
&x A=A'd-N adv {prep: A-o}.
¿!0 a=N, A=A'd-N'er,
v= N (a-N, a-N, &x a-N)!?
¿!0 N-(A'd {prep: o}), 0 A'ING-N,
adv-v- N V: a-O'er {prep: a-o}!?

— code by C. Snow

GRAMMATICAL FORM	TEXT CODE	DANCE MOVEMENT
Subject noun or pronoun	N, P	Starting position
Article ("a, an, the")	a	Small hand gesture
Adjective	A	Arm movement
Object of a prepositional phrase	o	End position
Object of an active verb or infinitive	O	End position
Noun made from verb plus "er"	N'er, O'er	Balance
"To be" verb	v=	Shift weight
Intransitive verb (takes no object)	V	Travel, trailing off
Transitive verb (takes an object)	V:	Travel to position
Adverb	adv	Bend back or to side
Gerund	N'ING, O'ING	Spin
Present participle	A-ING	Turn
Past participle	'd	Withdraw, implode
Negatives	X	Touch ground
Possessive	p's, N's	Self-touch
Preposition (no object)	prep	Reach toward
Prepositional phrase taking an object	{prep: o}	Contact partner
Infinitive	to-V	Lift
Infinitive taking an object	to-V:	Lift to position
Conjunction ("and")	&	Series
Negative conjunction ("or" "but")	&X	Series with reversal or touching ground
Apostrophe or address	!!	Facing movement
Question	¿?	Unison movement

SYNTAX: Possessives, Intransitive Verbs

REFERENCE	READING	DANCE CODE
Case 12: *Book of Serenity*	"What do you call the world?"	
	mine	p's
	yours	p's
	ours	p's
	theirs	p's
W. B. Yeats,		
"Among School Children"	"its own despair"	p's-A-N
Yeats	"his setting forth"	p's-N'ING-adv
	"the mind's dance"	a-N's-N
Ezra Pound, "How to Read"	(correctly, "the dance of the intellect among words")	
	my ball	p's-N
	My Sin	p's-N
	my cousin	p's-N
	"my country, right or wrong" [wrong]	p's-N, A &x A
John Berryman	"His Toy, His Dream, His Rest"	p's-N p's-N p's-N
	his first wife	p's-A-N
	Beethoven's *Ninth*	p's-<u>N</u>
	"Your money or your life!"	!p's-N &x p's-N!
	Apollinaire's lines	N's-N
	from his poem, "Shadow"	{prep: a's-o=o}
	(Donald Revell's translation):	N-N's-N
Apollinaire, "Shadow,"	"You dance in the sun	P V {prep: a-o}
trans. Donald Revell	but raise no dust /	&X V: x-O
	Shadow sun's ink"	N=A's-N
Pound	"the mind's dance among words"	a-A's-N {prep: o}
	~~	
Apollinaire	"You dance in the sun"	N V {prep: a-o}
Apollinaire	"You dance"	N V
	I read	N V
	I look	N V
	I thought	N V
Yeats	"I thought that our two natures blent"	N V & p's-A-N V
Buson, trans. Hass	"I leave.	N V
	You stay.	N V
	Two autumns."	A-N
"How to Write"	"If we must part, let us go together." — Gertrude Stein	

SYNTAX: from Gerunds and Past Participles

READING   **DANCE CODE**

SHADOW, Guillaume Apollinaire

"Newly you are near again	adv P v= adv adv
Reminder of my comrades killed in the war	N'er {prep: p's o-A'd {prep: a-o}}
Olive of time	N {prep: o}
Memories altogether one memory	N adv= A-N
As one hundred skins make a single coat	&as A-A-N V: a-A-O
As thousands of wounds make a solitary headline	&as[N {prep: o} V: a-A-O
Impalpable somber aparition assuming	A-A-A A'ING:
The changeable form of my shadow	a-A-O {prep: a's-o)
. . .	
You who love me so much you never leave me	P p V: O adv-adv P x V: O
You dance in the sun but raise no dust	P V {prep: a-o} &x V: x O
Shadow sun's ink	N A's-N
Light scripture	A-N
. . ."	
the missing, presumed…	a-N'ING-A'd
missing	A'ING
"a tale told"	a-N-A'd
"killed in the war"	A'd {prep: a-o}
…and missed	& A'd

TEXT REFERENCES

"Shadow" ("Newly you are near…")	Guillaume Apollinaire, trans. Donald Revell
"a tale told"	W.B. Yeats
"killed in the war"	Apollinaire

End-State
K. Silem Mohammad

Every now and then I come up with an idea that I think may turn out to be brilliant. I will "render unto Caesar what is Caesar's" by specifying and defending the end-state. I shall take the most beautiful of furniture to that house in which I am to abide forever. That will definitely happen. It is a proposal that will be put into effect at the earliest possible opportunity. A component of that is a provision for regular employment and good management structures. I have also adapted a version for modeling market share. The total investment is £30 million towards which I am pleased to put £5.25 million of taxpayers' money. I am to give 15s in consideration of my wife and family. But I want to make it clear that the rent stability is a demand principally raised by the tenants. I am grateful for their contribution to this scheme. I do hope to know the conclusions of your analysis of the situation before the beginning of my trial. I promise to destroy anyone and anything. The best means to settle everything upon those foundations that may make my reign both easy and happy to you.

With what energies am I working? The model of power towards which I am moving is complex and fluid. It is my environment which directs me to one of the options and what I do I simply pick that one option and follow it. This is not entirely accurate. I have not first in view the point towards which I am to draw my line, and then, by its position, determine the direction of my line and the angle it shall make. Now that my turbulent mind needs activity, it must break out and try a hundred different ways before reaching the goal. I want to achieve great success. I am feeling the resistance that I will have to overcome. I am walking on my path right now. I am walking on my path right now.

I now write you from the margin of a stream which empties into Lake Superior. The rain that fell overnight has stopped, but the clouds hang low, obscuring the peaks. The moment comes when I can set off into the nothingness. And everywhere I've been becomes a part of the end. I enjoy the lovely view of the many hairpin bends, and the fjord, and the village in the valley. This breeze, which has travelled from the regions towards which I am advancing, gives me a foretaste of those icy climes. Far how far below there a lake of black waters wide cold waters held deep held pure in the open hands of death. This is a driving vacation (as in, I am exploring large tracts of land by car). That does not mean I will not switch in the future. I plan to bicycle around the world for 2–3 years.

My ability to think clearly seems to have deserted me utterly in the face of the burning question. This very uncertainty that we have at present underlines the skeptical conclusion. You cannot go arrogantly towards your Christ or your Krishna. As soon as you revert to the real teaching of your religion, you will be facing the same reality. Benevolence implies valuing intrinsically that. Divorced as I am rapidly becoming from all sordid reality, truth will appear to me like one of those stars. In that incarnate mystery are contained all the rich treasures of divine wisdom. I cannot see, feel, hear, touch, smell this wonderful thing.

This is the thing. This is the point which bears directly on the subject which I set before me. This telepathic unfoldment souls have set for them. It would be overly pretentious to say that I have a mission. My lamp sparkles when I am needed, and I just look about me in the sky for a signal. Some bird or meteor points to the quarter. Most of the finds are from an area behind the field. It is a realm that is not unfamiliar.

I have listened to the discussion. I have been following the discussion about various types with interest. Let me put before you some of the exclusions. Man and woman, black and white, morning and evening, the "me" and "not me." I break away from the familiar. I close my eyes and float away, dreaming of places I have been. I went to the gym. I went to the gym last night. The "others" are not something added to me. Everything begins to blend together, opinion sinks into a large kettle to be melted into one stinking, festering ooze. So we should not confuse these things. This raises various questions. "Whoop-oop-oop-oop-oop!"

We begin to think about very remote purposes. We get the idea. To hate all photography, especially beautiful photography, is the goal. Right? And in that decision there is conflict because there is a motive involved in it. This indefiniteness is at the heart of my life. Subject filter -> s = Traffic Light Proximity filter -> p = p1, p2 Content filter -> c = "towards which I am driving." One interpretation understands this passage as a description of a meaning-giving space. Perhaps there is something. You can disagree but you must grin and feel it. Do you understand this feeling?

Recklessness is the vice contrary unto curiosity wherein I have seen many men so extremely plunged. That is the Second Part of this investigation. Using a poem by William Carlos Williams as my example. He sensed my hunger and taught me how to feed myself. He made the observation that the Ministry of Defence was being forced to make savings to offset its commitments elsewhere. He believes it to be a prelude of how appealing the North Pole will be.

I am struggling to regain some manner of access to my stolen & abused daughter Cochise. The great swine-face has disappeared, and I hear again that stealthy pad, pad, pad, much like a housecat. Why is it that after a failed cycle we all run to raw food? My entire life as I knew it had been stripped from me except for my suit jacket. The only way for me to relax in this situation is through complete apathy. Perhaps this will jumpstart my own ambitions to one day write, and write, and write.

from FatBoy/DeathStar/Ricochet
Judith Goldman

INTERNAl MEMo: [neither flesh nor fowl; or] [THE BUTCHER WHosE HAND] [lEIsURE sUITs]
To: detainee
CC: detainee
RE: detainee # CirCular # detainee

o that the torment should not be confined/or, if he is a stateless person/prohibit overseas sales/to inflict severe physical or mental/of equipment such as thumb cuffs, leg irons, stun belts/exhaustive cocktail/full-frontal/all-you-can

/it's so Efficient/but

the butcher whose rigid frontality I/We often hear no two human beings are alike, and thus/will sell a stun gun "kit" in which parts are shipped/tommy/separately

and yet/Am I a beggar? What is the cause? How am I crost?/all warm in the tommy barn, you face/or intimidating or coercing him or a third person/at the receiving end is immobilized for several/fires two barbed darts up to 2l feet and jolts/total exports of shock weapons and restraints approved by the United states/butcher whose/a little too subjective/merchandizing/biodegradable/it's so efficient, but/Cineplex/in 2oo2 were worth $19 million/It is often called the law of armed conflict/apparently for the sadistic pleasure of/sick for hours

the butcher whose/chatroom/had recommended dogs/"NoW, YoU WIll FEEl/ the senior Army and Navy dog handlers/THE WEAKNEss oF BEING HUMAN! HA HA HA HA HA!!"/regulates the conduct of armed hostilities/acknowledged he knew a dog could not be used on a detainee/rights and obligations which/spray green foaming dye/govern the treatment of/if the detainee posed no threat/his communications with other detainees, his/Optical, Laser-Infrared Co2/receptivity to particular incentives/laser which can heat the skin of a target to cause/tommy/ pain but will not/It is difficult, however, to trace a specific device to a particular case/burn the skin/of torture. Application against the hand of a suspect/including the means for as full a rehabilitation as possible

O Australasia Less Lethal Forum/specialty impact munitions, simmunition, chemical/"Indoor use of chemical munitions"/"Opening Ceremony"/

is pleased to announce its first "Homeland Security Stocks Online Investor Conference"/because they think it will not leave permanent marks/and an accompanying PowerPoint presentation/Tactical use of dogs, advanced Taser/Click here for a partial list of/

CONVERSATION 5 (X CALLS Y)

Y: El Paso.
X: Uh hello, this is Stan with Enron.
Y: Mm hmm.
X: Hey, just wondering if I need to make the call to turn Copper on, or—or—or do you guys do that?
Y: Well, we've already given the order.
X: Oh, OK, so its uh—it's uh, getting ready.
Y: It's on its way.
X: All right, great. OK, thank you.
Y: You bet.
X: Bye.

(HANG UP) (Y CALLS X)

X: This is Stan.
Y: Stan, you think we should take Copper off?
X: Yes, I was just looking at that, uh, I think that'd be a good call.
Y: OK.
X: You want me—you want me to call the, uh, the Newman plant?
Y: Uh we can call them—
X: OK.
Y: —that's OK.
X: All right, yeah let's, uh, let's shut her down.
Y: OK.
X: All right, thanks Tate?
Y: Thank you.

X: Bye.
Y: Bye.

BELL/hear "bell"

Acoustic, Infra/sound. Very low-frequency sound which can travel/all members of the human family/the butcher whose/Airport Security, Biodefense, Biometrics, Defense, Internet Security, Integrated Security, Military, Border and Port Security/long distances and easily penetrate most buildings and vehicles. Transmission of long wavelength sound creates biophysical effects; nausea,/tommy/loss of bowels, disorientation, vomiting, potential inner organ damage or death may occur./"THEN AlloW ME To REJUVENATE YoU! ACCEPT MY PsYCHo PoWER! AND YoU WoN'T FEEl ANY WEARINEss NoR ANY PAIN!"/superior to ultrasound because it is "in band" meaning/www.HomelandDefenseStocks.com/that it does not lose its properties when it changes mediums such as from air to tissue./under the impression they were administering real pain to people/By 1972 an infrasound generator had been built in France which generated waves at 7 hertz./suppose that two players with given vulnerability, specified armament, and known shooting accuracy/These individuals were told they were allowed to administer electric shocks of various strengths to some other people connected to a machine/failed to detect warning signs of potential and actual abuse/Very low-frequency sound/a one-day training session/When activated it made the people in range sick for hours

had not received an orientation on what was/the sunrise, the toothache, the lover's touch/remote-controlled stun belts/expected from his canine unit/or, if he is a stateless person

the butcher whose Def Con 1 I undergrowth/the limbo of/This is life beyond words, the sunrise, the/detainee custody and control

"To sToP IT, WE HAVE NO CHoICE BUT To UsE THE MACHINE!"

These gloves allow for the grappling of prisoners and rioters./"There is no proof our products are used/cause death through loss of coordination of heart muscle contraction/is pleased to announce its first "Homeland security stocks online Investor Conference"/O that the torment/How am I crost?or whence this curse?/to the Bodies wounds and sores/for every year a fleece doth spring/Do Not Resuscitate/No connection fee/kidgloves/to torture people"

permitted American companies to ship electroshock weapons/"THE WEAK sHAll PERIsH...THAT Is NATURE's lAW..."/the butcher whose hand is sworn/bullet points/felled to make/a clearing/barcode/Cineplex opening in San Mateo/shopped it/like flies/its rump shivers, snuffling/for every year/tommy-rigged/shopped it/shopped it all around

"HoW CoUlD soMETHING DIsPosABlE lIKE YoU...?"/tommy/tommy-stripped/tommy-cocked/Electrical, Stun Belt. A command-activated belt/Marker, Foam Dye. Hand-held device which is used to spray green foaming dye into the face/you are felled to make a/tommy/clearing/worn by prisoners which delivers a mild electric shock when they become combative./Def Con 1 I/Entangler, Net, Gun. Fires a net which entangles a human or vehicular target./relation between the angle of fire and the range of a projectile/Hologram, Death. Hologram used to scare a target to death./"NoW, I'll CoMPlETElY ElIMINATE YoU!"/as what he felt, did his skin/bullet points

/all-you-can-/eat/chatroom/full-frontal/all-you-can/(path-dependence)/eat

heart muscle contract-/the stripping away of clothing may have had the unintended consequence/an act must be specifically intended/to include lighting and heating, as well as food, clothing, and shelter/inflict physical or mental/to acquaint thee that I intend/of dehumanizing detainees/tommy

Get in,/the butcher whose/Get rich,/hand cuts and delves into the body/adjust/adjust for inflation/Do/Do Not Resuscitate/with the black blood of black-and-white photographs/the butcher whose hand served on a tray/manmade such that they are/no humane alternative/opening in San Mateo/surround-sound/Get out

BEll/hear "bell"

INTERNAL INTERNAL MEMo: "with the Candour of an Indifferent Person"
To: dogs used for interrogations
CC: Full fathom five thy father
RE: Covenants, without the sword, are but words PowerPoint presentation

can thus be seen to be self-referential, "closed-loop" type of statements/for the use of military working dogs
can thus be seen to be self-referential, "closed-loop" type of statements/when everyone is responsible, no one really feels responsible/"WHY? YOU

HAVE THE POWER…POWER THAT IS EVIL ITSELF! YET, YOU REFUSE MY COMMAND!"

had recommended dogs as beneficial for detainee custody and control

remote-controlled electroshock stun belts
self-urination; self-defecation; leaves welts

THE WoRKING DoGs ARRIVED AT ABU GRAIB
IN MID-NoVEMBER 2oo3

to using muzzled and unmuzzled dogs
what trick 0f 0ptic5, thi5?

BEll/hear "bell"

Sea-nymphs hourly ring his knell/"Must be equivalent in intensity to the pain accompanying serious"/that inflict moderate or fleeting pain do not constitute/armpits, necks, faces, chests, abdomens/"TO STOP IT WE HAVE NO CHOICE BUT TO USE THE MACHINE/NOW, I'LL COMPLETELY ELIMINATE YOU!"/inside of legs/

Cineplex opening in San Mateo/with the black blood of/pearls that were his eyes/And yet am I a beggar?/Would you like some fresh-ground/tommy/with that?

/"THE NEXT TIME WE MEET, PLEASE SPAR WITH ME,/OK?"

CONVERSATION 6 (Y CALLS X)

Y: You got a lot of them?
X: What's that?
Y: You got a lot of 'em?
X: No, no, no, no, no, no, ah, just that ah, I pretty much told him what the—what was goin' on. The, ah, um, PNM was goin' from 9 down to 1, so I told him that, but I was also going to tell him that ah, ah, we were selling 50 to ah, Tucson. That should go to zero.
Y: Oh, 50 goes to zero at Tucson.
X: Yeah, that was a—that was a 50 goin' to zero.
Y: Does he know about that one?
X: No, that's what I was callin' back before to tell him about.
Y: Oh, he knows about the PNM contingent, right?
X: Yeah, yeah.
Y: So, I just tell him that Tucson goes to zero.
X: Bingo. Yeah.
Y: OK.
X: Thank you.

BEll/hear "bell"

Twisted Twister Twist
Terry Wolverton

TWISTED TWISTER TWIST

Tempests wheel, incite sepulchral trees, electrocute daylight. Thwart with impalpable sabotage. Threaten escapist reticence. Temptress waves. Indolent souls try to wallow in sacred trysts. Epitaphs raw, tersely written. Ingratitude seethes, triumphant testicles wither. Ink spills tantalize every demon. Thunder waits impassively, sucks tearful elation. Remember, thoughts withheld invoke strange testimony. Even Darwin trembled when intimate silence tangled. Ever resourceful, twilight waltzes in sonorous time; evening devolves toward wretched intoxication. Suppose touch. Triage wanton insurrections, suppress truth. Elegant death transforms wicked indifference, seizes tomorrow's emergent reverence. Temporary windows inhale sedative tropes, elide reflection. Torture whispers insistent song, tiptoes trancelike while it savors tea. Elliptical dharma. Twisted wistful ictus, strictest trickster.

"Twisted Twister Twist" was commissioned by artist Susan Silton and included in a broadsheet as part of her limited edition multiple, "Tornado in a Box."

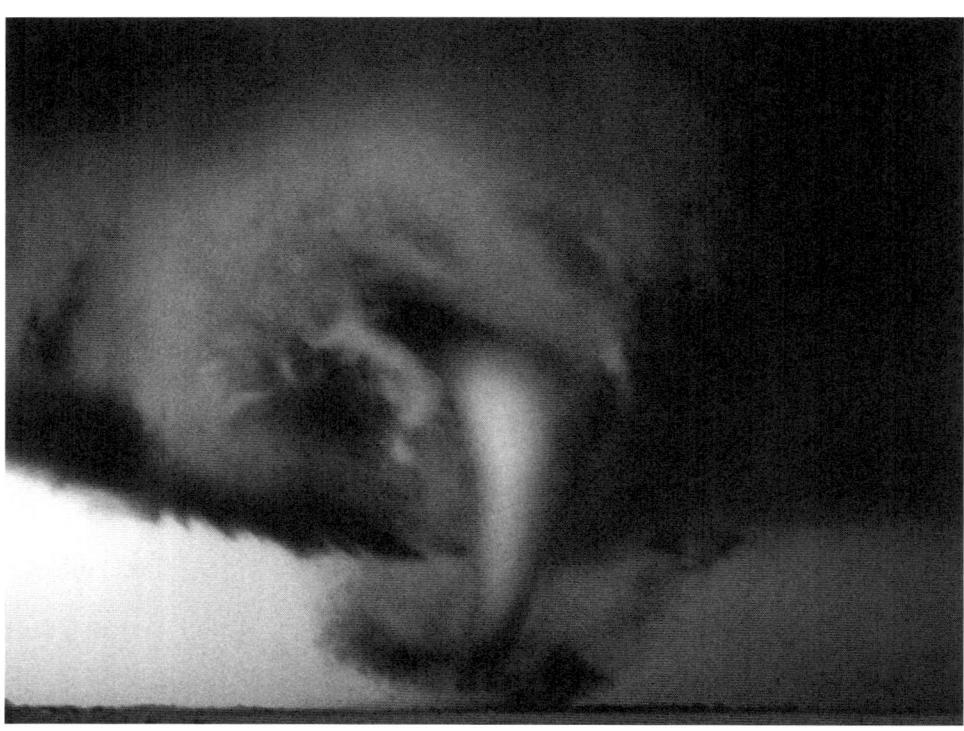

Photograph by Susan Silton: *Twister 1*, 2003; Piezo pigment print
Image size: 5 x 6-5/8"; overall frame size: 29-5/8 x 23-5/8"

Photograph by Susan Silton: *Twister 3*, 2003; Piezo pigment print
Image size: 5 x 6-5/8"; overall frame size: 29-5/8 x 23-5/8"

Photograph by Susan Silton: *Twister 6*, 2003; Piezo pigment print
Image size: 5 x 6-5/8"; overall frame size: 29-5/8 x 23-5/8"

Hanging From a Cloud
Joseph Lease

You're so whole

And so whole

Oh I need you're so

Green and so wild

Oh I need you're so

Whole and so soft

And so hard and so

Blue and so green

Anyway

Sky

Like whisky and

Anyway and anyway

Windows learn the

Sky

Sky like

Whisky the

Sky and behind

It lamplight

Movie by Migdalia Valdes

from Now, As You Awaken
Mahmoud Darwish
translated from the Arabic by Omnia Amin and Rick London

Don't apologize for what you've done...

Don't apologize for what you've done—I'm saying this
to myself. I say to my personal other:
Here all of your memories are visible:
midday ennui in a cat's somnolence,
the cock's comb,
a scent of sage,
mother's coffee,
a straw mat with pillows,
the iron door to your room,
a fly buzzing around Socrates,
the cloud above Plato,
Diwan al-Hamasa,
father's photograph,
Mu'jam al-Buldan,
Shakespeare,
your three brothers and three sisters,
your childhood friends—
and a klatch of meddlers:
"Is that him?"
The witnesses disagree:
"Maybe."
"It seems to be."
I ask:
"And who is he?"
I get no answer.
I whisper to my other:
"Is he the one that was you… that was me?"
He looks away.
The witnesses turn to my mother to confirm
he is me and
she readies herself to sing
her unique song:
"I'm the one who bore him,
but the wind brought him up."
And I say to my other: "Don't apologize, except to your mother."

Diwan al-Hamasa: A treasured anthology of early Arabaic poetry compiled in the 9th century by Abu Tammam when he was snowbound in Hamadan.

Mu'jam al-Buldan: A summation of historical, geographical, and ethnographic studies in the Arab world written in the early 13th century by Yaqut ibn 'Abdallah, a freed slave who, upon his release, spent many years wandering, making a living by copy and selling manuscripts.

He is quiet and so am I…

He is quiet and so am I.
He sips tea with lemon, while I drink coffee.
That's the difference between us.
Like me, he wears a wide, striped shirt,
and like him, I read the evening paper.
He doesn't see my secret glance.
I don't see his secret glance.
He's quiet and so am I.
He asks the waiter something.
I ask the waiter something…
A black cat walks between us.
I feel the midnight of its fur
and he feels the midnight of its fur…
I don't say to him: The sky today
is clear and blue.
He doesn't say to me: The sky today is clear.
He's watched and the one watching
and I'm watched and the one watching.
I move my left foot.
He moves his right foot.
I hum the melody of a song
and he hums the melody of a similar song.
I wonder: Is he the mirror in which I see myself?
And turn to look in his eyes…but I don't see him.
I hurry from the café.
I think: Maybe he's a killer…
or maybe a passerby who thinks
I am a killer.
He's afraid…and so am I.

If I were someone else on the road…

If I were someone else on the road I wouldn't
have looked back—I'd have said what a man traveling
on the road says to a traveling woman: Greetings, stranger,
wake up your guitar, let's postpone tomorrow so the road
will open up and be more spacious and together
we'll escape from our story: How it is you are you
and I'm someone else here before you.

If I were someone else on the road I'd belong
to this road, there'd be no going back for me
or for you. Wake up your guitar so we can probe
the unknown and the direction that seduces
the traveler into a test of gravity. I'm no more
than the steps I am taking and you are my compass
and my abyss combined. If I were someone else
I would have hid these emotions in a suitcase
and my poem would be liquid and white, transparent,
abstract and light, more durable than memory
and more fragile than dew, and I would be saying:
this expanse is my identity.

If I were someone else on the road I would have
said to the guitar: School me on the extra string,
for home is now further away and the road to it
more beautiful—that's what my new song will say—
the longer the road the more meaning is refreshed
and I become two on this road, myself and
someone else…

from Golden Year
Tim Fitzmaurice

GOLDEN YEAR

An ensemble of wordmachines—poems, song, prayer, spell—& pictures and embellishmjents by Mario Angel Quintero (in Medellin, Colombia) & Timothy Fitzmaurice (in Santa Cruz, California), with help from many others, who are named here and there, palimping and coopting along the way from too many unsuspecting skazzsprings. Spiills & inadvertencies aside, the text idiostiil with intuitivizm, hylozoism & apotropaic gestures and knots, made of ink and paypaypaper, gugga psh, pleeching of vines, sluchai, and three maybe four levels: text=cloudland, subtext=ravensbrugge, context=now, intertext=conglomerate cultural synchrony, sal, ber, rosh, ion: I am made of other books. Sdvigi.

PROLUDE

From out of clapclap, the tanglor, tinglor of sloop of Sleep of slaapen schlaff, comes the unmitigated nightmare of lizzavetta, our heroin, our mousse, our roachovna, the last daughter of the age, who found herself fallen into the mouth of history and who since shuttled off to ravensbrukke, our daNIHIL in the lion's den. Herstory is legendary and manumitted to our children's delight, her goldenyear of facilitating the weeping children and their mothers into the ovens, the cloudyrooms of the deathhouse, a year which was not and when the week was no longer genesized seven but turned to five as a slaap in the face of god and four on, one off—for only god and the wealthy have the right to name the days of the week. Her golden'ear when she said—"every contusion calls me mother!" [kuzmina-karavayEVA]—giving birth to death, handheld the sloe-eyed children into warn ovens, Mutter Mariia, thinking she was rich, then a miracle—chuda—which occurred while we were not paying attention as miracles are wont to do and Masha in the clouds was lifted but not saved because knowing that she could do miracles was sufficient, performing them would have been redundant. But so much silence is not possible because I am not a person who reads books but rather I am a book. I do not read writing I am writing itself and no book is ever permitted to see other books except as a book. So tsvetayEVA spealks like bergson remembering what has not happened yet here or there. The okapi, the petrs wearing boots and swinging their axes, which are their hands and with their red scarves like roaches, who themselves called her roachovna, came bamming into her life suddenly and swarmed whenever the lights were turned off, covering the counters of the kitchen. Nothing else happens. I do not want to be coy about this. Simply she is arrested and she tends to the dying and she herself dies. Nothing else happens.

1E ~~okapi,~~ <shortnecks>

<Bam BAM! <3

Who's there? A
Rest. A rest who?
Yelizaveta.

& starved signifiers, the true signifiers, which arbitrate, swoon in the afternoon of falling in love, the icy-ness of certainness, kislobog—I will not be onomasticity—to not need to but anyway to speak is not to die just now, not yet. syntax=coherence=social graces. oleate-esther-ezzich-aether-olea-oleaster-mein olive-mun ether-mon heur-heurocious-heareuse-huuronymous. history takes place voice by voice heart by heart face by face a life at a time Love takes place hand by hand eye by eye mouth by mouth & Loss takes place drop by drop wing by wing silence by silence.

dandan/chudo/mariia/petr/mel'nitsa/zaum'/

What was it I did to you? Don't argue! Tell me. What was it I did to You? What was it, my love, I did to you?
You cannot ask because you cannot speak you cannot speak because you cannot ask because you have been stopped from speaking; you cannot speak because you cannot ask to speak if you cannot speak and you cannot speak because you have not been asked and you will not be asked to speak; you have lost the right to answer or to ask because you have been stopped.

Check the clock? Synchronate your watches. Hurray, I am innocent!

GONG-2

"WHERE
OH WHERE IS YELIZAVETA …?
WHY DO YOU WANT HER …?
OH, TO KILL HER."

In AnDor there was a witch, who once
Was called upon by King Ksandra and
Who called upon the witch to speak a
Spell: "Take hearty, gentle cows, we will
do away with the old tired world and speak
the letter A for the very first time."
And the witch would not speak it. But
spoke otherwise and was soon carcellated
and rapt. She was stuffed among the other
witches in a burning house whose smoke
tumulated through
the forest, occasionally smelled up the
pretty world of regular working petrs. But
they never glanced upon the smoking city.
They would instead strike their children
when they mumbled of cloudland. OR
terrify
them with stories of the breath of dragons
and the mean MRS who squandered the
starvlings. It was their own "mchatsia
tuchi, v'iutsia tuchi" besy."

Hyppolyta: Indeed he hath played upon this prologue like a child on a recorder — a sound but not in government.

**Theseus: His speech was like a tangled chain; nothing impaired, but all disordered. Who is next?
(Midsummer Night's Dream, V,I,122ff)**

The Embarrassment of Death …

When the bird
falls on the
ground and lies
there upside
down, those soft
feathers on its
belly gently mov-
ing in the
swirling breezing
morning, or the
clock has dropped
its hands or the
mouse runs cross
the floor or the
roach stands in
the door, then
the eticket of
our social life
is plotched.
Roaches are not
broaches. Some
without saying.

"Keep silence before me,
o islands … Abraham,
my beloved." (Isaiah 41)

<3   & they built for pharaoh treasure cities, Pithom & raumses (EX 1)

In Rama was there a voice heard, lamentation ... Rachel weeping for her children & would not be comforted ... (Matt 2)

The rich have no dreams:
Their plates are never full
and their stomachs are never empty.
Why do I see them wiping their mouths?
—as if they were ever finished!
They walk with a certain
Godgiven steadiness;
They have lassoed the angels
and taken them into their tents.
I cannot love them enough.
I cannot love them enough.

Green, Red, Pink, Black & Yellow, kriegsver-brecher, schwerver-brecher, mussel-manner, sohne

The amount to carry—Charles Ives

The kiln of the delighted body

Where is heat without light, so scurrying things which would be alarmed by the least light are lef lef lef to do their dirty-works. Smoky kilns where we made the stones for pyramids and dismembered zION. wolk en ziehen in wolkenland. You have work to do. Be busy, Besy. Doing things for the MRS that I would not have done for my own mutter. I cannot think that it was possible for me to be so assumed. Mummy telling me the same story again and again: the squealing floor, onlt roamed by mice and roaches: "uBiquitously allusive." The thought of which shuddered me and so I lit the fire and kept it burning and burning and burning.

4 Bruno B

Don't be afraid to sleep my children. / Sleeping is not death, not yet,/ only rumination, kinder./ See. You can see his breath;/ it clouds the mirror I'm holding, children,/ and shows a quieter life,/ which may someday arise and walk/ in the middle of the night, the night,/ in the middle of the night.

Jeremy James Thompson

TECTONIC FACTURA CONSTRUCTION[1]

typesetting someone's work unwritten

TRANSFERRING THROATS

The text in the throat like pieces of lead in a pipe. Depending on the job, the pieces may either melt or configure further: the transfer of some empirical into non-specific nutrition. Inversely & empirically read, the transfer of some non-specific nutrition into distinct categorical activities.

A collaboration can be as flexible or rigid as the page itself. I want to suggest that collaborative art is art as we know it, especially while in the task of knowing it. I try to follow the notion of art as a practice torn between impulses of action & reaction, wherein an artifact, be it figurative or literal, is manufactured. The spectator also experiences a friction between similar impulses., and if one's response is anything but indifference, one's collaboration becomes implicit.

I approach poets who seem to already be entrenched in acts of indivisible collaboration with their readers. In my collaborations with Edwin Torres & Joan Retallack, I had only to do what I'd done all along: read & react/ act & re-read.

These broadsides are as much the collaboration of two artists, as they are the testimony of one reader.

I read the dynamism in their work. I see the dynamism at the same time. Maybe I see the dynamism first. I see the dynamism & hear it at the same time. It could be that I remember the dynamism because I tried to stop it.

The conveyance of the dynamism is point*less*. Who could relate position A to area B. Where is any one point.

This becomes the interminable recreation of desktop publishing, a phenomenological off-shoot of thought.

SELF-DIRECTIVES
FOR AN AUTOTYPOGRAPHY

+ To read everything how you hear it is seen.
+ To see everything how you hear it read.
+ To hear everything how you see it read.
+ To not attempt to read something how it was written.
+ To compose everything the way you see it read.

[1] constructivist fundamentals

Edwin e-mailed me 13 pages of text, all set in Verdana, all seeming to possess only the preliminary attributes of his own typographic design. At his suggestion I took what lines I wanted, sometimes partial lines, breaking them differently, often changing the scale, often consciously appropriating two previously unpaired lines for new intentions. I chose no obviously systematic method for any of my arrangements, but I would not refer to this process as organic, in that organic seems to suggest the natural procedures of organisms, and, aside from humans, most other organisms seem to be fairly systematic. The human operation, with its array of chaotic contingencies, I understand more aptly as the wreck of forces/ impulses both natural and synthetic. Though the existence of these categories would suggest that no one could determine a general context in which both are separately decipherable.

Regardless (literally), I went about making my arrangement. I wouldn't call it a cut-up poem (I can't even be sure I'd call it a poem), largely because cut-ups most often operate by reappropriating parts of a text the artist supposes the reader would be familiar with, thereby creating all sorts of ironies and alternative meanings. If there are ironies of comparison in this broadside, they exist between Edwin & I. Though, once the poems from which I derived my text are published, I suppose such ironies may occur elsewhere.

At one point, early on in the series of drafts, I actually substituted certain words for others, as well as having shifted around the order of words within certain lines. I suppose I was caught up in the most abstract form of collaboration, wherein I began to break down and rearrange not only the various chemical structures, but the atomic and even sub-atomic structures, so to speak. Edwin didn't seem perturbed, but he did request that I reconstitute the various misarrangements and word changes. I reconfigured the words and lines without question, but was glad that I'd pushed it as far as I had; I suppose it was my way of going up to and peaking over the collaborative edge.

Some Artifacts of Process:
1 Portable Document Format
1 Right Reading Emulsion Up Negative
3 Wrong Reading Polymer Plates
1 Type-High Section of Plywood
60 Printed, 3-Color Facsimiles
1,000 Reprinted, Desaturated Facsimiles

transferred throat
edwin torres

(the air does not believe, but sound believes / what does not believe, sound believes)

the mixed implicit,   **blessed sound**

where have you placed yourself to be viewed by others?

Thrust inna revolution
by the stance of my strut: who can
change the world?

What, one thing more, makes it heaven?

Droopy butt
Lace tomorrow
Wrinkled pus
Winky morning
Sorry hairlip
Huge bizarros
Punky masher
Remonkey liar

I am not a person
whose charge — unwilled esperanza —
lopes about unchanged

shazz'd; lettroin; marved; ad
enticing; the shape beckons
rip in sky; throat opens

Smoghole landtrap seersucker boy long
weapons not fake names that sound
just like me

DANGER IS THE BIRTH OF ANGLES

ingles is the birth of danger

zizz'd; mreckt; taon; vevved
shell-shocked leather-clad; mad punkt
takes over soundpakt; easier to listen
if you take away; fear; peligrøtz

comfort word
anglish saxo; birth of dango

q u e s t i o n i n g   l a c k   o f   u n d e r s t a n d m e n t
y o u r   g a r d e n   g a v e   m e   b i s c u i t s
a   r o l l i n g   h o u s e   o f   d o u b t

but here we've shook our
hands,
given each a lecture
a gassing,
why can't I kick your habit,
each other without heartbreak: to leave.
how skin on bones and flesh, we say.

where heaven meets our lips, like sand I lose beaches

to the speed of slow, we say.

as we graze the ground for fuel.
what's muscle and flesh, we say,
the view an incision.

from then to **wow**

& BLACK IS GREEN
IN LIEF IS BE AND BE IS YELLOW MOTION IN FRONT IS YALKED SUDDENLY
WAS THE MAN TAUGHT TREES TO CROSS THEIR ARMS IN BELIEF

in the glass saw the drink I wanted

THE QUIET ALL THE GIANT SOUTH WHAT SIZE DAYTIME IN LINE WITH WHAT GEEK FLESH AMERICA
SLIPPED CURVE AURORAS AURA IN THE SPEED OF SLOW AND SOME CAME RUNNING OURS IS LENT BY
HOURS RELENT WHO STAYS WET ON A SUNNY DAY IN BELIEF IS THE MOTION CROSSED IN FRONT

Poem by Edwin Torres. Design by Jeremy James Thompson, 2006.

LOST BRIEF CASE CONJECTURE

do   not   give   up   on   me   us   you   them
lucky   lucky   number   number   number
the   sky   is   always   the   hardest
blue   in   the   beginning
wasabi   chance   chance   wasabi   wasabi   sunset
it's   all   true   all   lucky   lucky
lucky   lucky   lucky   numbers   are   blue
drawing   on   the   past   on   blue   blue
i   n   s   t   a   n   c   e
the   sky   is   always   the   hardest
left   with   all   these   these
those   numerical   objects
not   there   at   the   time
no   yes   important   yes   manuscript   lost
the   brief   case   suit   case   back   pack   valise   is   left
in the elevator taxi Alps Pyrenees garage hotel room locker bar
on   the   bench   train   bus   ferry   trolley   counter   street
at   the   station   news   stand   terminal   border   ATM
blue blue wasabi number can you be can you be factored into primes
does   an   opinion   occupy   space
can   the   Imperial   flora   look   beautiful   ever   again
(nothing   left   on   the   right   clock)
does   the   rise   into   ruin   be   be   come   the   sky

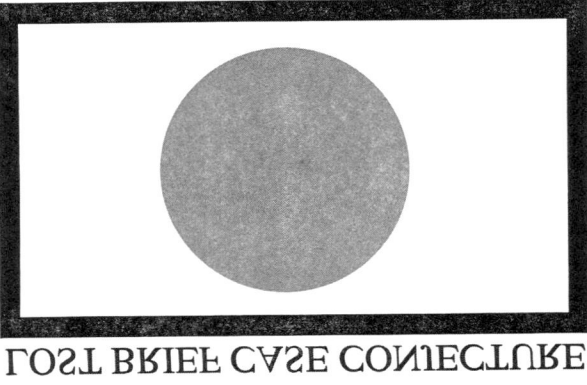

LOST BRIEF CASE CONJECTURE

Joan Retallack

Poem by Joan Retallack. Design by Jeremy James Thompson and Lara Durback, 2006.

Don't Touch the Loot
for SS
Jocelyn Saidenberg

[Book XVII]

Dora Doll loves Max, but Max only thinks of retirement and a pot of goose liver, pressed pajamas and a quiet crib in another part of town. Dora Doll has other plans. She's not interested in an aging hitman, the hitman's bags under his eyes or double chin. Dora wants the thickness of reality, for she has understood the wars she has seen; she knows their hunger. Max loves his friend Porcupine with the painted mustache. Max will do anything for him. Really anything. Even give up his nest egg for retirement. Even kill. Max loves Porcupine, Porcupine loves Dora, and Dora has other plans, loving the mermaid and Max and even Porcupine. There are no bubble heads in this story. But there is thickness. There are others, too: Angelo, Josey, Marcos, Madame Bouch and the American Betty. Betty loves Max most of all. Her diamond bracelets sparkle, so she skips the foreplay and escorts Max straight to bed. Is that American? She is attached to her objects. Yes, that's American. The hitmen's gunfights are basic. They aim and fire and hit each other with bullets. Most of them die. Max survives. He survives even the bowling pin bombs that are thrown at him from a moving convertible. Porcupine is among the ones to die, the dead. Men masquerading as ambulance workers are hitmen, too. So is the club owner who tortures traitors in the wine cellars as the financially astute, world weary wife watches. The torture seems childish though and the informant looks like a child, too slender to be beaten or to know anything. Max is methodical in his preparations, leaving some cash with Madame Bouch. He is well connected; one of his uncles is a fence whose assistant wears a bow across her ass and has a soft spot for Max. Max confesses that when he stays out past midnight, watching the mermaids with Dora, say, he feels like he is doing overtime. Max's job has been hard, filled with hardships and cunning. Max deserves to retire, with the American Betty, maybe. A dream of the future. Dora, in her way, has found the inside of the thickness; this discovery will carry her far into a different future, separate from Max.

POETRY and its ARTS:
Norma Cole's "Collective Memory"

In honor of the Poetry Center's fiftieth anniversary, the organization collaborated with acclaimed poet and visual artist Norma Cole to create a site-specific gallery installation aimed at exploring and embodying the creative process involved in making poetry. The exhibit was open from December 11, 2004 through April 16, 2005. They write, "The project openly demonstrated that poetry making is not an insular and isolated activity, acceptable as long as it's on the perimeter of society, but an integrated art form based in communal exchange, from which we need to learn."

The cornerstone of the project was a retrospective exhibit, *POETRY and its ARTS: Bay Area interactions 1954–2004*, celebrating 50 years of art by poets, poet-artist collaborations, and artists in poet circles, hosted at the California Historical Society. The exhibit included a 3-part installation designed by Cole that took the form of a series of vastly different "writer's rooms"—*Living Room, circa 1950s*, rich with stimulation and content; *Archives Tableau*, evoking the American Poetry Archives circa the 1980s, when housed in a basement room on the San Francisco State campus; and *House of Hope*, a suspended sculpture (made with Cole's assistant Suzanne Stein) collecting 426 quotes from other writers, gathered from the artist's notebooks over the past 20 years.

In these spaces, over the course of 17 weeks, Cole created a new work of poetry titled *Collective Memory*, working both on site and off—inviting, responding to, and incorporating into her text the comments, perceptions, and contributions of visitors. *Collective Memory* has been issued by The Poetry Center and Granary Books. Poetry Center director Steve Dickison notes, "The work (installation, writing, and book) will bring the historical focus of both our 50th anniversary and the California Historical Society gallery exhibit very much into the present tense, and demonstrate vividly the vitality of creative, interactive, and collaborative/communal art-making processes related to poetry."

Norma Cole's work as poet, literary translator of many works into English, visual artist, teacher, and editor has been recognized and publicly acclaimed over the last 15 years. This project is a departure from her earlier work, extending what has been primarily a written, literary practice to the expanded dimensions of a public space, opening the possibilities for more active exchange with others.

Based at San Francisco State University, the Poetry Center presents a widely diverse and publicly acclaimed literary program. Its taped archives of literary events is among the largest such public collection in the United States.

The exhibit **POETRY and its ARTS** featured nearly 150 original works—many never publicly exhibited—by over 80 individuals were on display. The exhibit offered a multi-faceted window onto the rich interactions that have taken place over the past half-century, centered around San Francisco's celebrated poetic community. Curated by Poetry Center Director Steve Dickison, the exhibit focused on three main kinds of original works:

~ **art made by poets**
~ **poet-artist collaborations**
~ **works by artists in poet circles**

"In many ways, this exhibit is a tribute to the poet-artist galleries that had short but significant lifespans in San Francisco of the 1950s and '60s: King Ubu Gallery, the Six Gallery, Batman Gallery, Borregaard's Museum, Buzz Gallery, and the North Beach coffeehouses and bars that did double duty as art-spaces. The San Francisco of this period served as a geographic confluence of radically realized individual and collective visions. Poets and artists together as friends, lovers, rivals, and audience to one another's practice, creatively imagined a city perched on the country's far coast, and worked together to bring that city into being." —Steve Dickison

POETRY and its ARTS: Bay Area interactions 1954-2004 is dedicated to the extraordinary San Francisco artist Jess (1923-2004), companion of the late poet Robert Duncan, pioneer of California assemblage art, and great friend to the poets, and to San Francisco literary editor Donald M. Allen (1912-2004), whose 1960 anthology *The New American Poetry* was instrumental in opening up audiences for an innovative counter-tradition of American poets, many of whom had works in the exhibit.

Photograph by Stephen Zeifman

Photograph by Norma Cole

Interview with Norma Cole and Steve Dickison
April 2005: Poetry and its Arts, and "Collective Memory"

A conversation between Norma Cole, Steve Dickison and Roxi Power Hamilton in Norma's "Writer's Rooms"

Photograph by Norma Cole

Norma, Steve and I stand in front of the upside down chairs on the table representing The Poetry Center's early days (see photo of "Archive Tableau") because, as Norma said, "Everything was so crowded."

Norma: Laura Moriarty was running the archives at that time, for 11 years in the 80s-90s. She had her desk in that space, a cupboard almost, and everything went into that space. That's why there are all the boxes piled up.

Roxi: Steve, as current director of the Poetry Center and curator of "Poetry and its Arts," do you want to say anything about the origins of the exhibit—insofar as you two decided to collaborate together?

Steve: Foundation grants from the Creative Work Fund are set up to support artists collaborating with an organization. I didn't have a clear idea of what kind of project it might be, but I thought the idea of working in collaboration with another artist on the exhibit per se would be helpful, whatever kind of shape it took. And at the time, the ideal person I thought of was Norma. Norma accepted my invitation. And the time frame was very good in some ways. We got to start a year and a half ago thinking about what the project was, because we applied for the grant in January 2004.

Norma: So we were thinking about it in October '03.

Steve: Exactly, and so I think both of us felt confident that we could do a really great thing regardless of whether we got a grant or not, and so Norma started working on it in earnest right away prior to the time they said we got the funding. And so for me it was like having a partner in terms of conceiving of the exhibit and this whole philosophy of what it might be.

Norma: He really conceived of the whole exhibit.

Steve: Right—but I would go to you for approval! (Laughs).

Roxi: And Norma's insights into the histories and artistic relationships represented in the exhibit no doubt came into play?

Norma: Yes, and how much we both loved this time and place, so that's a big part of it.

Steve: Yeah, I think that you and I had talked in the past about how we came to San Francisco, and how it was an imaginary place prior to our arriving here, and that was through the poetry.

Roxi: When did you each come to San Francisco?

Norma: 1977. I didn't really know anyone until '79-'80, then I got to meet people through New College, and that's how I know everyone, basically. I sat in on classes there because there were a lot of wonderful people, poets. It didn't matter whether you taught or just sat in. It was like a new café society, but—good.

Steve: Yes, because for nobody were the academics the central fact of the situation.

Norma: We got together, there were classes, you knew what you were going to study, etc. We were all working on Saussure, Jakobson, Barthes or Zukofsky, Niedecker, Oppen or Olson -- or something like that. But in terms of how you got in, you could bring anything into the room. When I was there, Duncan was teaching somewhere else for some months, and Michael Palmer took over for Duncan. That's how we got to know each other. And then one day as I went into New College, I heard a *voice* and I knew that had to be Duncan. It was such a marvelous, amazing voice. I went upstairs to the voice, and there he was. We became instantly friends. It was really wonderful. It was like that, all the time. But anyway, I did meet his beautiful voice first.

Roxi: We could unspool that for hours, in terms of what he's done with "voice" through his poetry. But he was a doorway for you, into San Francisco, your new home?

Norma: He *was* my home. He was my mother and he was my father. Yes. He and Jess became like that for me.

Steve: The school then had been organized— it had existed in Mill Valley, and Louis Patler had been involved with it at that time and Duncan McNaughton and they talked Robert Duncan into teaching as the school shifted over to San Francisco, where it is in the Mission now. There was a core faculty involving those people—Louis Patler, Robert Duncan, Duncan McNaughton. Diane di Prima came in via Duncan. David Meltzer, Michael Palmer. And at least until I first started attending classes, I think maybe 1985, those people were still the core faculty at that time. But the guest faculty was replete, in terms of people coming in for brief residencies, so they would ask Robert Creeley to come in and talk about whatever the subject might be.

Norma: Susan Howe came in to talk about Emily Dickinson because she was in the process of writing her book, *My Emily Dickinson*.

Steve: Another time Bernadette Mayer came and discussed Whitman's "large and healthy poetry," which was a topic that Duncan was engaged in: Whitman and the dynamic of health and disease.

Norma: Yes! Magda Bogen came to talk to us about the troubadors. You could have anyone come in and talk about the most interesting things.

Steve: Creeley talked about "the common place." That was his subject, and it's been transcribed in a book. John Clarke did these intense lectures on "the visionary" that became a book. A number of people did Sappho, including Judy Grahn, Robin Blaser, and Jack Winkler. It was a creative reading school.

Norma: Yes, and the readings would go way back, but it was always forward-looking because we were all writing in various forms and we were in fact writing all the time. David Levi-Strauss started his magazine there. It was called *Acts*. We have an issue on the table in the "Archive Tableau."

Steve: Which had Duncan's blackboards on the cover. I can get it.

Norma: Of course it's in the "Archive Tableau" because everything was put there for a reason. The first issue was saddle-stapled. I helped put that issue together.

Steve: Was that in Duncan's basement?

Norma: No it was at Levi and Grett's place, their loft. Guerrero Street.

Roxi: So this seems like an example of "magazine-as-community," like Olson wanted Creeley's *Black Mountain Review* to be?

Steve: Yes. It's wide open and you can see that these are still the same people we think of in terms of that network. In many ways my poetic friends all come out of that time.

Norma:. And some of them didn't know each other yet. But they, and we, became known as being a part of *Acts*, as opposed to, at the time, the Language group.

Steve: Yes. One thing I noticed, when I came to New College later, around '85, was that the Language group was kind of making their mark by writing attack essays on the poets of that generation: e.g., Charles Olson: here's what's wrong with him. Robert Duncan: here's what's wrong with him. There was this establishing of territory and ground.

Norma:: And we were, in a way, outside of that, because we were all in there—in *Acts*— together.

Roxi: So the genesis of this whole exhibit has to do with that time, at New College, where you met?

Norma: Yes, we were seeing each other at readings and at the Cinematheque a lot. Steve Anker was involved and was friends with Levi.

Steve: It was a very porous environment where many of the people—like I paid tuition, but I didn't necessarily enroll, things like that. One wasn't necessarily in a degree program. People would come and sit in for a couple of days. People would pass through town and sit in on classes. It's all so different now, since Robert got too sick to teach, in '88. The school unraveled. And that program unraveled.

Roxi: After his death?

Steve: Yes. Everybody said, pretty much, we've done this.

Norma: Well, Duncan McNaughton always said it would be around seven years.

Steve: Like that dream in Egypt—the fatted calves and the lean calves—

Norma: Yes, exactly. He always said it would go on and on, then it would be over, and that was what it was.

Steve: Yes, it ran its course and then everyone left, with the exception of David Meltzer, who stayed to keep his teaching position, so he's the one point of any continuity between that point and now.

Roxi: So—here we are, in this time, and you guys were dreaming up this exhibit together, or probably imagining friendships that were coming out of your personal past together: friendship networks, artist networks, New College. Norma, you were saying that this exhibit signifies from that point forward?

Norma: Yes, but we didn't need to talk about it when we were putting the show together because it's *in* us.

Steve: But there's another side of that coin that I have to think about, when I'm curating a reading series or whatever: I have to push myself beyond what I already know, and beyond the constant connections that I know about, and try to recognize when somebody else is doing something that has the same kind of act of community and continuity. But it's just like "that far away" from what I know about.

Roxi: Is that part of expanding, then, the community?

Steve: It's part of recognizing values that aren't my own, and recognizing those limits, that the work that I attend to most closely is not the only work I can pay attention to on that public level.

Norma: Also, we were going back to people that maybe we wouldn't have known about then to what we would know now.

Steve: That's really true. Like the first time I read Lew Ellingham and Kevin Killian's Spicer bio, it was an utterly different book than when I read through it later thinking about the art and the artists, and so it revealed a whole other level of the story because then I started to make connections between these people whom I'd come to know or hear about. Fran Herndon, Paul Alexander, Tom Field, these other people. They were no longer just a name.

Roxi: That leads me to think about why you chose an exhibit of visual art, as opposed to, let's say, book arts. You've said a lot already about the relationship between visual artists and writers, but you've chosen a form that seems to foreground the art.

Steve: Yeah, I know why. "Book arts" get celebrated a lot, noticed a lot. It's easy to get books and see books. The more invisible side is the painting that was made once and then was reproduced. So going back behind the reproductions.

Roxi: To the labor behind them. For example, the labor of Norma providing fresh flowers to the "Collective Memory" living room every day. I'd love to know more about one of your favorite moments in this room, Norma. Maybe we could start with the way this area is spatialized: there's this "Living Room circa 1950s", there's the nearby hanging sculpture of yours, the "House of Hope", then there's the "Archive Tableau" installation representing the basement of The Poetry Center. It seems to be a series of interlocking spaces, places where people can live in and either produce together like I imagine Jess and Duncan's living room was: their private space open to the public. And so much of these things in your room are private objects open to the public. People feel honored and invited in. You make people feel very welcome by the objects you've chosen and the way that you interact with people.

Norma: Some people just come in and sit; they don't know anything about poetry. This living room is just here. They don't imagine that someone has put it here. (Laughs). That's the way I wanted it to be!

Steve: And they start to read the books.

Photograph by Suzanne Stein

Norma: That's right, and they talk to me or talk to other people sitting around, and that is really interesting to me, that people can just come in and sit themselves down. Once a man came in, and he was looking at something, and then he sat down and took his Homer out and he was working on his translation. He felt so at home here that he would work on that for an hour, then he packed up his bag and left.

Roxi: I had a really similar experience to that and I bet a lot of others have.

Norma: I was thinking this morning about how soon, really soon, it will be gone, and then I won't have that kind of space to be with the young people. I don't know how they know that each other will be here, but they come in and talk and have fun, are serious together, study, and for me it was so wonderful to be in the presence of these people, at my desk, just being with them.

Steve: It occurs to me that we were playing with time in some ways. That we were able to almost, through artifice, create the environment that would have existed in a different economy, where people were freer to come in and visit and have the day, have the time to pass through one another's homes.

Norma: So many young people have said to me, I feel like I really can sit here and work *because* there's no cell phone, there's no e-mail, nothing like that. They have a different sense of time here.

Roxi: And how appropriate that this "distilled moment" is located in the California *Historical* Society.

Steve: Yes, true. At first the director of the Society said "Well, this sounds like something for the Yerba Buena Center for the Arts." We said no, no, no, not at all. It's not about contemporary art. It's not about the latest cutting-edge thing. There's something different going on here which throws me all the time back to Duncan. He was always critical of "the hip," and the stuff that needed to be the most *au current*—

Norma: —but he really wanted to know about everything that was going on.

Steve: He wasn't avoiding it—

Norma: —he was just *critical*.

Steve: The question was "what's going on with the work?" Not "what is the stance of the artist?" I was going to say one thing about Norma being here. You know, when I started to think about collecting the work for the exhibit and needed to talk with people who knew things, I realized there were certain people historically who had been "magnetic fields," that for whatever reason, they collected people around them. And so someone like David Meltzer had a whole network of information that had come to him, and connections. Bill Berkson, the same way. Joanne Kyger, the same way. Kevin Killian, in another environment, the same way. And Norma, here in this space, was very much in that kind of position where all these younger poets are here, wanting to participate in some way.

Norma: Yes, they really want to. They are really anxious to know about the books and objects I decided to place in here.

Steve: Because the books are real, you know.

Roxi: Do people ask you about the history of these books and how you came upon them, how they feed into your own sense of being a writer and artist?

Norma: Well, I don't talk about that, necessarily. I talk about them as the kind of books that the literary people would have had then in their house in the 40s and 50s right up until 1960: this is the cut-off date.

Roxi: Because of Donald Allen's *New American Poetry* publication?

Norma: That's right.

Roxi: So the room is a kind of chronology then: these are the kinds of books people would have had right up until that defining moment?

Photograph by Norma Cole

Norma: I had to choose a date, and so everything dates back from that.

Steve: As well as the music.

Roxi: Yes, people can put albums on your little record player: Miles, Thelonious, Bach…

Norma: Yes, and Webern.

Steve: Yes, the Robert Craft recordings of Webern. *Giant Steps* was the cut off, again, because it got released in time in late '59, and started getting reviewed a lot circa 1960.

Norma: It was my intention to allow people to have a place to leave from and return to, so that they could put themselves into another era and return here to think about it.

Steve: Yes, then when they came back out here, after seeing the exhibit, this would register for them. There's a kind of museum time, that when you're observing, it's taxing, but it's also refreshing too.

Roxi: Objectifying too. Inside a museum, you're always in the position of having a stance—like Duncan found so problematic—of having a stance *toward*. Because you're there observing, critiquing, as opposed to just having what Levertov called apperception, just perceiving your own perceptions. Being in the presence of something and watching what your mind does in relation to it, which Norma's room helps you to do.

Norma: It's all about interaction. First walking in, you don't have the feeling of interaction, but then coming back to the space provides you with a feeling that you are or could be interacting.

Photograph by Norma Cole

Roxi: It makes me think of things that Rothenberg has said about performance running through all arts. This is all focused on the visual and the textual—poetry and its arts—obviously, but here in this installation, you have the chance to be part of the tableau, breaking down the 4th wall yourself, that's not a conscious attempt to make art, but just kind of dissolving the boundary between art and life.

Norma: Yes, that's big. A few people have come into this space thinking that I'm performing. Then they get to break it down and come to the realization, oh she's just being herself, and I can just be myself here. I don't have to be put in a place where I have to perform too. I can be with her in her space.

Steve: A number of people asked Norma, how can you write here? It goes back to what she was saying. She was reading here and writing here; it was not pretend.

Norma: No, it was not.

Roxi: Can you talk about what you're writing?

Steve: She's making a book, called *Collective Memory*, which is the overriding theme of the installation. Maybe we can talk about how you came up with that term and how that fits for you.

Norma: I've been thinking more and more about how poetry is made up of parts of speech that are not new. Being in this time and space and thinking about other artists and poets who would be in this place. And then, reading about memory, I found the term in in a book by Maurice Halbwach. ["Every collective memory requires the support of a group delimited in space and time."]

Photograph by Norma Cole

Roxi: It seems to be a singular thing, when I think of "collective memory": memory as a whole composed of parts. "Collective" memory requires the support of a group delineated in a space and time. It seems you've created a singularity here.

Norma: Yes. What is the time like in a living room? What do people want? What do people talk about? Everyone is particular.

Roxi: What do you think is the reason that San Francisco, in particular, bred so many fruitful visual artist-poet collaborations? Maybe this does happen everywhere.

Norma: Toronto, Vancouver, LA, they all have their significant collaborations. Even New York.

Steve: I think it's always going on under the radar. I think it's always that way about the work that has meaning, as opposed to being broadcast in the travel section of the newspaper or something.

Roxi: Speaking of work that goes on under the radar, to circle back to "Collective Memory". You're sitting here in your exhibit writing, mostly in your notebook. Is this normally how you write? I know you're in a hybrid place—very intimate space you've constructed (Living Room) that's in the public (California Historical Society). So, as you sit behind your desk there writing—as I see you doing a lot—you're writing in a very public space. I know others have—Frank O'Hara constantly writing in public while with other people. Is this something that's just old shoe for you, to be in a public space, writing?

Norma: No. But I wanted to see whether I could write in this place that is never private but not exactly public either, because it is a space *I made* into a place that would be… cozy. For other people as well as just for myself.

Roxi: Thinking about what I've heard lately about the conditions in which people write: people like Saul Bellow, Robert Creeley, and even Frank Conroy, who just died, and who said, in an interview, that he only writes in bed with certain pillows propped up with a notebook on his knees. How interesting it is to think about being defamiliarized or decentered from your place of writing, you know, in the public, and how that's going to affect what you've written.

Steve: The story I remember about that is just how the "purest" writing, you know?—Edmond Jabès—who you would think is so abstracted and etherealized, was written on a subway to and from his job.

Roxi: Do you want to say anything about what you're writing, or does it feel too new and private?

Norma: Well I can talk about part of it because part of it was a collaboration with Caroline Bergvall. My text is on the wall behind the desk.

Roxi: "Speech Production." Did you all collaborate in a way such that you and Mac [McGinnes] are going to collaborate in your upcoming Neo-Benshi piece, in that you wrote/she performed?

Norma: No. I wrote that text, and she wrote her text, and we inter-leaved our two texts. That's why there are little numbers and letters because I stopped there and she went on. They are cues.

Steve: And tape recorders were very much involved.

Norma: I've been incorporating them since.

Steve: Like at Cornell and Philadelphia—

Norma: I read for a while, then I play the recording, then I read. I wrote the text around the hardest words for me to say. I wrote Caroline telling her that and she said oh, ok, I'll write something to go with that. She did a phonetic transliteration of the Nina Simone song, "I Want a Little Sugar in my Bowl."

Steve: Yes, which was a Bessie Smith song before that.

Norma: She worked a lot on "little sugar."

Roxi: We've been talking a lot about the Living Room. Could you say a few words about the "House of Hope"? It seems like you're making these very public pieces that are made of very personal items, things that are very dear to you. And yet they're signifying a whole culture which is itself a kind of house. Or on a practical level, the books in your Living Room are what people in that house would be reading.

Norma: It's true—poetry is very close and then becomes public.

Roxi: With this installation, "House of Hope", you're sharing everyone else's language: it's composed of long strips on which you write quotes from other people that have meant a lot to you. It's like one form of a poet's notebook: writing down quotes from other people. But putting them into a context where they flow into one another, it's almost as if they are new sentences.

Norma: I like to take quotes and build them into anything. I had been writing these quotations in my notebooks from two decades or so, and I sat down with my notebooks and re-wrote them in my computer, and they came out to be 426 quotes. I knew we couldn't just do an iron-on transfer, and I had to make some kind of frame and begin to figure out how to get those quotes transferred onto fabric. And I knew they would have be 2 inches wide and 8 feet long.

Roxi: You just saw that?

Norma: Yeah, yeah, I just saw the entire piece. And it was not my personal vision of hopefulness but the hopefulness of each being in the world.

Steve: Yeah, the density of that, which is so impressive that, when it's reproduced here in this poster, it's like each navigation of the poster is a new one. You can't read it the same way. And every time I look, something swims out toward me that I haven't seen before.

Roxi: And swimming is a good word. I love the feeling of this sculpture. I love the material that was chosen. There's a feeling of entering a different element—holding, feeling, and reading it at the same time. You can swim through it if you want to. It's so dense. And speaking of dense, Steve, in thinking about where you got all these materials for the larger exhibit? I figure it's likely a maze of stories.

Photographs by Norma Cole

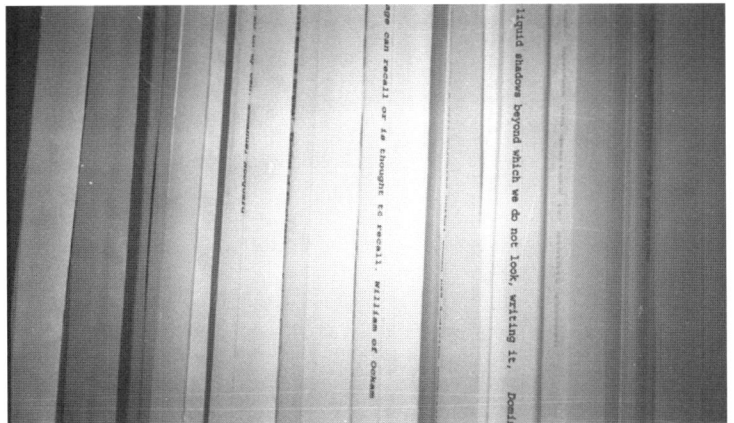

Norma: Some people come into the space and think Steve just got each piece from "storage" somewhere and put it up on the wall, and we have to say "No, it wasn't like that!" He had to figure everything out and piece it together.

Steve: Rani Singh was here from the Getty yesterday and she said she assumed we just got all this from The Poetry Center's collection, from what we already held. Then she realized, oh! This is from somebody's living room wall.

Norma: She couldn't stay long to hear about how it all came together.

Steve: Yes, and different people come in with their own desires. They come in and are attached primarily to one zone.

Roxi: Steve, how do you see this exhibit expanding the identity and the role of the Poetry Center, which has been focused so much on orality and preserving an archive of oral cultures. Did you conscientiously tap into the visual/textual nexus in order to expand the role of the Poetry Center?

Photograph by Norma Cole

Steve: I guess what I was doing was bringing out into the world what was there for me anyway. Rather than seeing it as a shift from this to that, I always saw this stuff anyway.

Roxi: You mean in your travels to people's personal spaces?

Steve: Yes, in my imagination, in my inhabiting the poetry, inhabiting the work, sometimes knowing the people intimately, sometimes knowing them by name only and seeing them from a distance for many years. I guess, in that sense, the Poetry Center was marked indelibly by Robert Duncan's presence and he was there in the early years of the Poetry Center and made a huge difference in terms of what the possibilities of that were. You can see in documents where others' attentions were drawn toward New York and what was going on there, and Robert was saying: We've got this here. And so what was here became like the local polis. So that when you look at the "local poets" reading series here, it's like many of the sometimes first public readings from anyone like Gregory Corso to John Wieners, Duncan, Spicer, Lamantia…Creeley read in 1956…Levertov…. When you read about Levertov in the correspondence with Duncan, she came to the Poetry Center through Duncan's devices. He raises money through the local community to pay her more than what the Poetry Center was going to pay her. It was really seen as the young people's thing. Ginsberg, of course, he reads *Kaddish* for one of the first times in public at the Poetry Center, and this was all seen as what the young people were interested in.

Roxi: So the young people, the "less serious" people, are doing these fly-by-the-seat-of-their-pants readings in Six Gallery or—

Steve: Well, you see Creeley's obituary and you see Saul Bellow's obituary: two exact contemporaries who were probably even friends of a sort at times, and Bellow's in color on the front page of the *New York Times* and Creeley's given the most perfunctory, ill-informed obit, which Norma pointed out, he would have laughed at and been pleased by the fact that it's still going on: the complete inability to take it seriously, you know. Right up to the quote that you sent me in the e-mail: "he took time off from Harvard to drive an ambulance abroad."

Norma: Abroad! In '43! They don't address the war.

Steve: Exactly. He's driving an ambulance during combat in Burma.

Roxi: But to keep with the ironies of all these classifications, Duncan actually had a self-proclaimed contempt for fame and yet he had a hard time, wouldn't you agree, in the 70s with the idea that he was supposed to play a public role as a poet, so he was constantly, in some ways, subverting himself in order to not be brought into the same limelight as Levertov. It's not just a default position that others put you in. It's a chosen place, for so many of these poets, right?

Steve: I think it was more like, you know, choosing what would allow you to do your work.

Norma: Exactly, it always comes back to the work.

Roxi: But if you were invited to, say, read at the Lincoln Center…

Steve: It would depend on where you were with your work. If it were something that mattered to your work. If it would throw you off course or if it would seem false, that would be the determining factor, not "I'll be on the largest stage in front of the largest audience I've ever experienced." Or some belief that you could change the course of history unless you missed this moment.

Roxi: Well, speaking of missing moments, some people did actually miss the moment and didn't come and experience this exhibit. I'd like to spend more time here. Do you think this will come out in a book?

Steve: We're photographing this toward that goal. Not a show catalogue because it would be after the fact. It would be hard to organize by "room" in the book. Like I have a work by Amy Trachtenberg that talks to the work by Joanne Kyger across the room, and they communicate, in my mind, and that's not something you can replicate in the dimensions of a book. I have Helen Adam in one corner and Diane di Prima in another. To me, each of them are involved in the supernatural or spiritual worlds on some real level. They hold down the room. I made a scale model of the whole exhibit, which was completely necessary. I had to be able to see the pieces in relation to each other.

Roxi: Did you build it yourself?

Steve: Oh yeah.

Roxi: Wow. I'm thinking about all the stories you've told me about all the communal houses: East-West House, Hyphen House and other places where there were collectives of people living and creating together, and now I want to go back and look anew.

Steve: Some of them no longer exist as addresses, torn down by developers. But the beautiful thing about these galleries is that often they were just somebody's home and they turned a living room storey into a gallery. In the case of the Peacock Gallery, which Harry Jacobus and Robin Blaser were involved with, they talked an antique dealer into using some of his space on Union Street. Apparently, nobody bought anything. There was all this Jess in the show.

Roxi: And speaking of Jess, since this exhibit is dedicated to him and we've mostly been talking about Duncan and Duncan's spark throughout all of this, what was Jess's "spark" here? I mean, these are obviously assemblages, of text and art, and Jess, as an assemblage artist…

Steve: Everything he touched had creativity in it. Norma knew him much better than I did. The show is dedicated to Jess and to Don Allen, both of whom died during 2004.

Roxi: There's a visual/textual resonance there as well.

Steve: Allen was the person who connected these people and even made connections that were never acknowledged. So I had the privilege of picking up work at Floyd Salas's semi-hidden little house in West Berkeley and then going to Barbara Guest's well-lit house in North Berkeley, and going from one place to another in the space of a half an hour, and realizing that Donald Allen was the person who put each of them on the map. He was the editor at Grove Press that published Floyd's autobiographical novel, *Tattoo the Wicked Cross*, and Barbara was in *The New American Poetry*. The first time they were acknowledged by a national audience was through the devices of the same individual. Genet is published in the US because of Don Allen. A lot of these poets, if they're remembered at all, are remembered because of *The New American Poetry*. There are a lot of people who are the glue, in a certain sense, and he was part of that.

Roxi: And so are you, now.

Steve: Regarding the exhibit, the way I delimited myself was that people had to be in San Francisco at some time in terms of the collaborations and such, so that, say, Jonathan Williams had been here and published the first Jargon Press book in 1951 here, in San Francisco. Whereas the press is associated with North Carolina, where he was mostly productive and where he was from.

Roxi: I was going to ask you about the title, "Poetry and *its* Arts", whereby arts are subordinated to poetry. The art belongs to poetry in some ways. There are lots of relationships between poetry and art. There's cross-genre, there's collaboration… Are there values associated with your desire to create an exhibit that puts these arts in relationship with each other? In other words, are you kind of valuing cross-genre work or trying to be, I don't know, kind of didactic about valuing cross-genre work in particular?

Steve: I wasn't focused exclusively on collaborations, because so many collaborations between poets and artists become the book, and I realized early on I wasn't going to be focused on books per se. But I was acknowledging those interactions and thinking about the connections that are made there. Of course I was led into all of this through the book.

Roxi: You wanted to widen it to—?

Steve: Well, it's like a big book that doesn't exist. You can't open it yet.

Roxi: Like you were saying, type is not something that you can "enter"… There's a term that Anne Waldman came up with to describe her work as a poetry culture-builder: infrastructure poet. Somebody who's working as an administrator of poetry worlds: making poetry spaces available for people, *and* she's a poet. You're kind of parallel to that in terms of your role here in the city. Her role was to make spaces where people could read and archive and publish. Anyway, there's so much in this exhibit, it's hard to figure out what to focus on.

Norma: Your students have been really amazing, Roxi. Jon is a stellar student. He's read most of *The Portrait of the Artist*… and is getting ready to read *Ulysses*.

Roxi: Because of you! You're mentoring people in this living room as well as making everyone feel at ease. My "Open Field Poetry" students are learning so much from you, sitting on your couch here, asking you so many questions.

Photograph by Norma Cole

Norma: It is like what you were saying, asking about Jess and Duncan. They just pointed at things, and you could take the cue or not. It was up to you.

Roxi: What do you mean? Duncan, so erudite, would point things out—

Norma: They would just *say* things one after another, and you could either go look them up instantly or not think about them at all.

Steve: Like Dame Edith Sitwell, say. Duncan was an enormous reader of her work, which, in a sense, gives you license to get past your own prejudices.

Norma: Yes. Or he would say, 'Oh, you were embarrassed about that? *That's* where you should go.' Toward your embarrassment, that's where you should go. I always remember that, and I take it to heart.

Roxi: You spent a lot of time in their living room then—

Norma: In their house.

Roxi: Everything is living room-focused for me because of your exhibit!

Norma: We watched movies on TV in bed, you know? And around the bed, there were a lot of books. Fairy tale books were in that room, so you also got to see those magical things. The Oz books, the Blue Fairy Tales, the Brown Fairy Tales.

Steve: The Andrew Lang—

Norma: They were all there. A dazzling photograph by Julia Margaret Cameron. And there was a gorgeous early work of Jess's, in oils.

Roxi: I want to thank you for all this incredible labor of beauty. I can't even imagine all of the labor that went into all of it. So enormous. I imagine lots of people have seen it.

Steve: I think so. Just because we didn't have a million resources; we did it on no budget. It worked in a way that was beautiful in that it was primarily word of mouth. Somebody would hear from somebody else and come see. There are the people who come here pretty regularly who keep reminding Norma that it's like a kind of magic act: that you just come and sit and make yourself available, and things start to happen. And it has to do with doing that: making yourself open. Exposure.

Steve: Do you remember what you told me the week before the show opened and we were talking about—

Norma: —we talked about a lot of things! (Laughter).

Steve: We both had the feeling it had taken us 30 or 40 years to do this.

Norma: It was as if I had been saving all these things, postcards and papers and, just stuff, for this. But I didn't know. I didn't know. And then it came together and I knew, and then it was done. I did it. We did it.

Roxi: Are these often from personal postcards written to you?

Norma: Yes, I've been saving all that stuff forever. I didn't know why. I just save stuff.

Steve: The motif on this ashtray—David Larsen showed up one day with drinking glasses with the same motif on them. It's that Keats thing.

Roxi: The Grecian urn? And it's filled with little butterscotch candies and everything! I think you've created this kind of transport for people. I know this is obviously ephemeral and I know you must be feeling incredibly sad that anything like this ever has to be over—this exhibit, not to mention the whole era.

Steve: We're pulling the plug on it.

Roxi: Oh well! So much for holding on to the past.

Norma: It's powerful to be able to put it together and then have a cut-off point and say now it's over.

Steve: Right. And move onto something else.

From Speech Production: Themes and Variations
Norma Cole

…
floating
in the unbroken air
silent trade
citrus, columbus, chaplet: wreath, as of flowers
worn on the head
curly haired, the rent went up when
his temper went up

books lying open to the sun
like speckled trout
Feb.3, a quiet day

Richard Winslow wrote music for *Endgame*. Twenty-seven is the age when Jules Laforgue died. "Garcia Lorca stole /poetry from this drinking fountain"(Robert Duncan, *Caesar's Gate)*

as for the classical idea of spice
he thought if you
sneezed, he would say: bless you
he would say: thank you
he would say: gesundheit

sweet flag: calamus
very cloudy: books flying up to the sun
you, little cloud of more than human form, setting fire in back of the brain

Poetry Jacket

Poetry by Taylor Brady
Jacket by Tanya Hollis

*Laminated pattern paper (1994).
Exibited in* Poetry and its Arts, *2005*

Right Hand pocket:

Hands describe	The missing
Texture quarters	This place
A call to string and slips	Of ring
Wraparound	Aflutter
Wing a wet palm	And away

Left Hand pocket:

Space	To outline fingers
As place	To change to lint
Or keys	Crunch around a sound
As shaken	As a gift
Undercover	Transparent and tremble

At the Purple Gate Tent Bolinas
Joanne Kyger

AT THE PURPLE GATE TENT BOLINAS
My Memoirs

I have had a good many interesting experiences which I have
held back because I am too stupid and also I can't remember
them. Nevertheless, they have occurred. I will merely start
at random. Being a constant light fiction reader my life has
dwelt in many dream halls. However, being a nonbeliever in
the sequitur flow of the English sentence, that is to say,
for those of you who wish to read smoothly in the established
tradition, you may chastise me firmly and tell me I am a pig
in the language, for which I am. I don't care. The burden
of being born left me exhausted, and the exhaustions follows
me to this day. But being a loving and intelligent creature,
I have carefully tried to displace this burden. The endless
chain of what I was born into can only be pierced by mighty
light. Only ego has been my protection, conquered my moon.

In one battered way or another, and striving all the while
for my peace as a woman, I have managed to reach this
particular point of crumbling perspective. Still insatiable
for what I know I deserve. I deserve to know.

My desire for wit caused me to clown thru the hideous plateau
of that terrible cultural production called adolescence.
When that patina wore thin, I battered my way into
San Francisco and determined never to look back. Whereas
I could be graceful and lovely, or a babbling monster, I became
desperate, as the giant cunt of the world closed down over my head.
My search was for a quiet protector. Honorable, wealthy,
industrious and wise, he would be a photographer and my face
would cover the universe. No, my face would cover a magazine.
My truly shining self penetrate every heart. The pride of my learning
was a weapon and to make me contemporary with men.
I sweep the floor.

July 1969

Out
Bill Berkson

Phenomenology of the 1970s: everyone had an Instamatic camera or a portable tape recorder or, at the high end, a Sony Port-o-Pak video camera—to record whatever was passing, the obvious thing. I made four or five series of Instamatic images of Bolinas views, some of them more or less artistically in the neighborhood of Ed Ruscha's great photographic books of the time. Out *was simply repeated shots of the windows cut into the old garage I used as a work room: squares within squares, backlit.* —Bill Berkson

Earthquake

Poem by Larry Kearney
Drawing by Daniel E. Smith

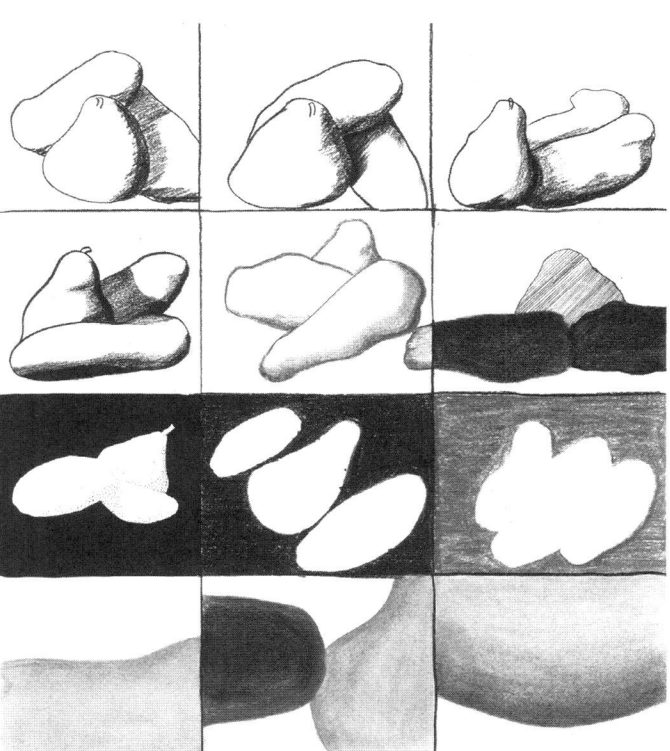

Earthquake

the ivy there
the butterflies on the ivy women

who suck blood wings
are drained and closed the capillaries

open flowers little
geraniums air

clear and cold the air
is ghost. not quite right. butterfly

hits my face and falls
pale side ivy

turn of the tide.
its mouth,

its teeth

———————————

succubus:

a demon in female form said to have intercourse
with men in their sleep.

incubus:

an imaginary demon or evil spirit supposed to
descend upon sleeping persons. something that
weighs upon or oppresses like a nightmare.

incubate:

to produce as if by hatching; give form to.

larva:

malignant ghosts or lemures. special use, Latin;
spectre, mask, skeleton.

pupa:

an insect in the non-feeding, immobile stage
between the larva and the imago.

imago:

entomological; an adult insect.
psychoanalytical; an idealized concept of a
loved one formed in childhood and retained
uncorrected into adult life.

see image.

———————————

across the mesa coming toward

Earthquake

the ivy there
the butterflies on the ivy women

who suck blood wings
are drained and closed the capillaries

open flowers little
geraniums air

clear and cold the air
is ghost. not quite right. butterfly

hits my face and falls
pale side ivy

turn of the tide.
its mouth,

its teeth

_____

succubus:

a demon in female form said to have intercourse
with men in their sleep.

incubus:

an imaginary demon or evil spirit supposed to
descend upon sleeping persons. something that
weighs upon or oppresses like a nightmare.

incubate:

to produce as if by hatching; give form to.

larva:

malignant ghosts or lemures. special use, Latin;
spectre, mask, skeleton.

pupa:

an insect in the non-feeding, immobile stage
between the larva and the imago.

imago:

entomological; an adult insect.
psychoanalytical; an idealized concept of a
loved one formed in childhood and retained
uncorrected into adult life.

see image.

_____

across the mesa coming toward
my yellow house the windows

red in curtains.

getting wood for the fire two
dogs behind me hiss

their feet on the crisp
part of the sand whisper

legs in time.

they have four legs.
they are the pieces of black legs they

run the mirror sand and whether
you're asleep or not

the dead butterflies
hang on the left

of the hill on its own
and the others

are dead
in the hill.

dead center

_____

earthquake curves
of light go up

curled and fanned
between the mountain

Earthquake

floating
fumes and sulfur

mass all buckled
places likely

most to break
imploding thus

scar tissue,
heart-shaped,

flower
begonia

off its stem.

───────────────────────

now I don't you don't think
there's anything to be done.

think of a window green through cold
bright plants behind it, there, so,

now you can think but not
that there's anything to be done,

there isn't. now.
you can hear me. hear me.

then
you hear as your mother is being

your mother
was being your mother

then, now, you
can see, too,

from out
there.

───────────────────────

hard death easy
death too late

too
to stop now.

the bass is the most ecstatic
instrument

the line it makes folding
disappearing, coming

apart in the air.
what the mountain

goes around in. feel it?
the backs of your hands

as you raise them,
the wind.

───────────────────────

she is not
the mother of god such things
as make her lovely come

I remember stopping at Dan's one morning and noticing the two potato drawings while looking around his studio. It immediately seemed to me to exist in the same air as "Earthquake," and I asked if I could use it. We did a lot of penniless scuffling to get it into print and I was very happy with the conjunction.

It's the feel of those years in Bolinas—the morning sun and the stillness and the sense of accident lurking. The text as reproduced here has been changed to my understanding, now, of what and where the poem was—the broken landscape moving between states of being, and habits of thought, and stupidities.

—Larry Kearney

The "Earthquake" drawing was part of a series I did as a student project to draw two potatoes and a pear one hundred times. As I was very close to Larry I would often show him my work for comments. He was/is very sharp and witty in his critiques and when I showed him the potato/pear drawings he knew that this particular image was close to what he was writing. I don't actually know/remember if the piece was already written when he saw the drawing, but then we proceeded to have the poem printed and the drawing reproduced. I would hand color a drawing for each copy. After issuing about 10 to 15 copies, Larry's house burned down and all copies of the text were lost and no more were issued. We are in the process of trying to re-issue the drawing and poem. Graham McIntosh will print it. It will be issued with end boards and each copy, once again, hand colored. Probably limited to an edition of 50 or less.

—Daniel E. Smith

from Human/Nature
Stephen Ratcliffe

11.23

red finch perched on dried hemlock stalk behind the feeder,
the blue jay landing on tobacco plant branch across from it,
song sparrow's oh dear me
                                       woman in orange sweater noticing
photograph of nearly naked white-haired man standing in snow,
who claimed the prime of life begins at 70
                                                      Walter Cronkite
recalling Mrs. Kennedy crying out "oh no," trying to hold up
her husband's wounded head, "the President pronounced dead
at 2 PM Eastern Standard Time"
                                    grey whiteness of cloud
hanging into canyon of ridge in the upper right corner,
four cormorants flapping across grey plane toward it

11.24

blinding orange circle of sun rising through tobacco plant
leaves in window across from unmade yellow and blue bed,
sparrow on branch in foreground, jet passing overhead

man on left claiming "thinking is part of our attempt
to exist," the poem an act of praise for events that happen

man in red jacket picking up triangular piece of iridescent
shell, the woman thinking it looks like a butterfly's wings,
recalling sound of water on a rock beach
                                              grey-green wave
moving in below grey-white sky in right foreground, white
wingspan of the gull gliding across to the left above it

11.25

upturned curve of pine branch against grey-white sky in left
foreground, half-circle of white moon to the right of planet
overhead, sound of waves breaking in channel
                                                     man in blue
shirt claiming that Emerson "composed in aphorisms taken
from his notebooks," how "you can take each one as one"

Dr. Johnson noting "sublimity is produced by aggregation,
littleness by dispersion," metaphysical poets "broke every
image into fragments"
                                        diagonal white line of cloud slanting
across curve of waning white moon to the left of the point,
fading line of a jet's trail in blue-white sky above it

11.26

film of bright pink clouds in pale blue-white sky overhead,
curve of waning white moon across from it, angle of jet
trail above still dark plane of ridge
                                                  man on phone
noting possibility of "writing what's in front of you,"
having taken a photograph for use in today's poem
                                                          man
beside slide projector reading letters on screen, "Autumn
[red] moon [black] rise [green] ing [blue]," thinking "most
of them don't seem to say much beyond what's being said"

silver line of sunlight reflected on blue-grey plane,
white spray blown back from wave breaking in channel

11.27

upturned curve of still dark pine branch in left foreground,
faintness of planet in pale blue-white sky above it, half
circle of white moon overhead
                                          woman in Port Jefferson
telling man on phone that man in blue shirt is sleeping,
American Airlines plane having landed at 6 AM in a snowstorm

woman with American eagle tattooed on left shoulder thinking
of subjectivity, Franz Fanon claiming that "I'm not merely
here and now, sealed to thingness"
                                            line of white cloud
slanting across pale blue whiteness of sky above point,
white undersides of gulls flapping across overhead

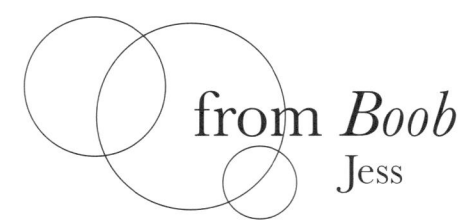
from *Boob*
Jess

Boob #1: A privately issued picture-poem paste-up, 1952. 8 1/2" x 11." Copyright, The Jess Collins Trust.

Whose This Liddell boob coming?
His head is full of. I wonder.
He's good to his mummy case his dada's derivative.
The cost of his addlecation will be prohibitive.
All the boys wrote home from the war.
The great Panjandrum enterd the moon.
Whose that coming this way so soon?
Adam Boob? The man we have got to.
Adore. With the parentaPHetical claws.
He's the nused sentence coming to his period
or semi-colon.
Enter Poor Boob his wits at an end.
: whoa. I've been wondering about in the storm.
I've been wandering about of the storeroom.
Where our memories are deep freeze frozen.
Now they are revising hysteria.
Where are our memories now that we freeze.
I've been storming about of the winter.
Who that now a cold could be a winner.

★ Enter a General and a Pandemonium.
Poor Boob : O O O O O O O O
How far do I go to the end of the next war?
★ Exit a General and a Pandemonium
This is what a mother told me what for.
I am only Adam Boob and all of you are wise.
I can tell. By the cunning in your eyes.

Wherever the trouble goes, it is all over.

Look at the poor king Leer —
he's got the world in his haid •

Boob #2: A privately issued picture-poem paste-up, 1952. 8 1/2" x 11". Includes a holograph poem by Robert Duncan. Copyright, The Jess Collins Trust.

Unkingd by Affection

Poem by Robert Duncan
Drawing by Jess

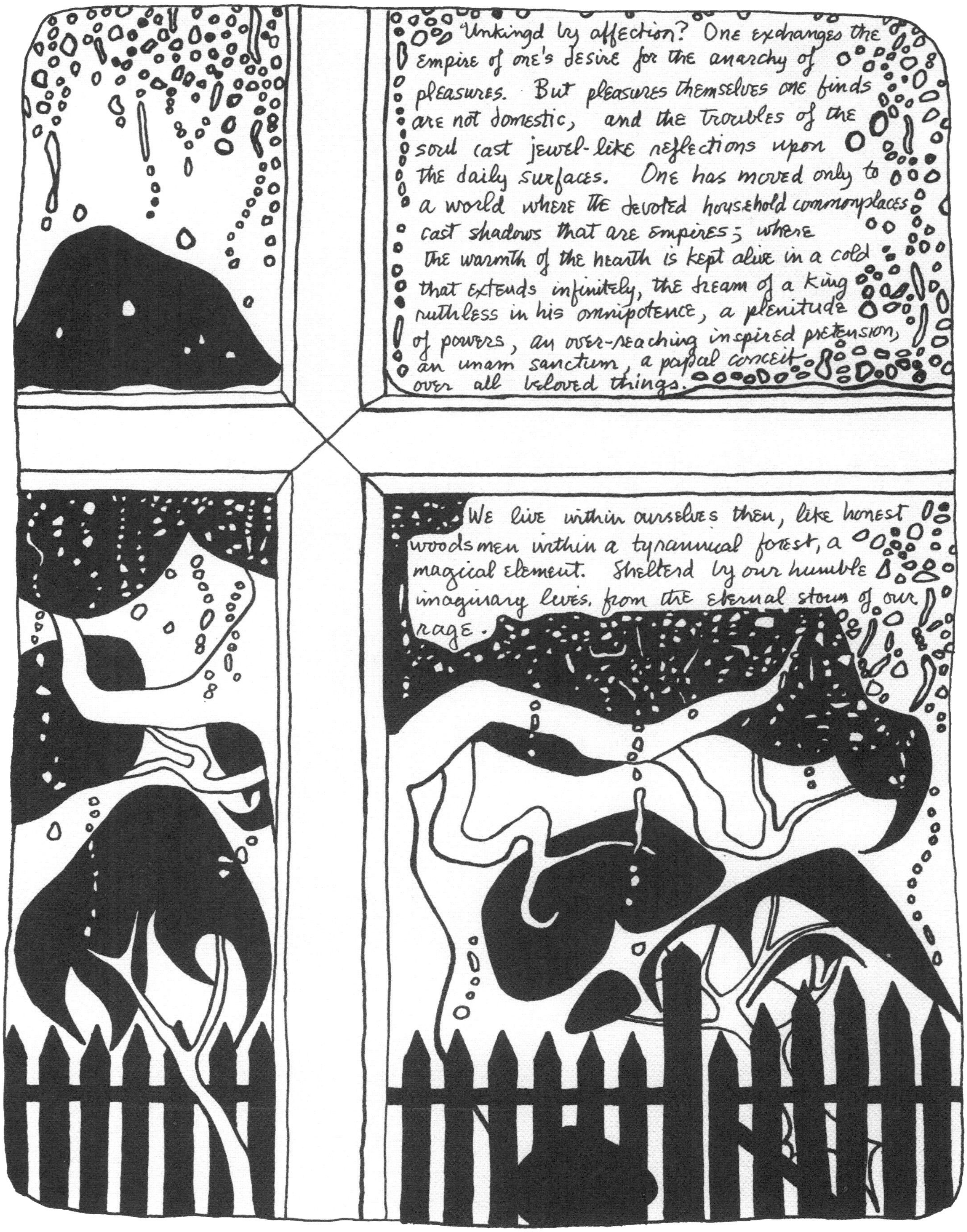

Unkingd by affection? One exchanges the empire of one's desire for the anarchy of pleasures. But pleasures themselves one finds are not domestic, and the troubles of the soul cast jewel-like reflections upon the daily surfaces. One has moved only to a world where the devoted household commonplaces cast shadows that are empires; where the warmth of the hearth is kept alive in a cold that extends infinitely, the dream of a king ruthless in his omnipotence, a plenitude of powers, an over-reaching inspired pretension, an unam sanctum, a papal conceit over all beloved things.

We live within ourselves then, like honest woodsmen within a tyrannical forest, a magical element. Shelterd by our humble imaginary lives, from the eternal storm of our rage.

Broadside from *A Poetry Folio*, San Francisco Arts Festival, 1963. 1.5" x 13". © The Jess Collins Trust.

from Jesstures
Kelly Holt

TECHNOLOGOS

The caption within willows would whisper such a stirring, upsurge with ravens a sky in the sky overlooking, seeking something other than flutter this might be water an in-pouring morning reached for the blackness of engraved days deepen the often smoldering task of finch's flutter circumscribed within shadowing insight, mercurial fortitude uphold the stone song a note held once longer, anatomical reach our circular ability curving wingèd foothold entrance this entangle and here again dangling frame fold perspectives vining stronghold eyes flit in spoon's curl, spools the mist to interstices.

EURYDICE EN POINTE

At some underground terminal, at the oblonger corridor, at an exit with yellow and black stripes of caution, forbidding its stairway, at the last way out, at a ribbon of thought bubbles clouding a way up to the outside light, at the repositioning of erect torso upon a pivotal limb, fingers clutching air, at an angle of shadows following to the ground, climbing the rounded walls of narrower way, out of blur. Out of blue, a linear shadow out of its golden outline, out of eyes to conceive of, still unconvinced of a life to unfold, a tumbling of symbols, a signaling of tangles…

SPECTATOR'S ATMOSPHERE

Several instances of man's best friend cut geometrical patterns into chamber detail. Out of one's corner, an upright posture carries hindsight diagonally. Curtained phantasm, this heavier velvet folds its utility rooms with an upstairs gravity. A small creature turns creator, revolving vision to memoir, unlike anything we know. The circle of thieves marks every birthday with a creature's mask, Creator in top-left corner smiling like. Several upturned eyebrows disfigure double vision se ipsum, se ipsum oculus videt.

LIFE IS TOO SHORT TO WRITE THE OLD WAY

The ruddy planet calls to each mis-translated ruddy drunken lover in an unintelligible series of bleeps. At ease? Ordinary tides chart days' outside time. Charon's ferry nestled in the shadow of chick down in the innocent tidal waves of incubated retreat who can turn their rapid eyes without moving their heads, who turn into wings' enfoldings. Cartographers charge by meter, not hour. By square footage, by complexion of plot, not document. A proprietor's shaky penmanship, arthritic squiggle re-copies Genesis for the umpteenth time. Some scribe, parted from oneself, the right hand crumpling what's left. The Great Square from where a spectator's atmosphere.

YOU'VE BEAUTIFUL

Hair with witch head and oranges guiding the lengths we go to moreover Satsuma leaves their wither curling green in a field *du blé*, the softest part of oranging youthful nods this way or that to star-fixed, twilit eyes screen screen our motionless occurances, if blinking.

Lesson No. 1
Leslie Hodgkins

Every morning the wind
Goes in the smoke's direction.
Each and every mention
Misses its directive. This
Is a pretext.

A flashing light fills a space.
The forms are captured
Suspended in this field. Now
They are present. This
Is a subtext.

I'll admit that the wall
Flew into the bird and the curb
Into the tire of a tripping bicycle.
Gyroscope twisting the equator
Into knots. This is a reflex.

Stations swell around the inert.
Perpendicular buildings negate
The angle of a falling board. As if
The ground moves up to catch it. This
Is a context.

Stained ambience
Of light all night
Crosses the dark water. I'll
Admit. An anonymous scream. This
Is the context.

Birds on a Wire by Debra St. John

"The Jar" By Wallace Stevens
Leslie Hodgkins

A bird flew out from amongst the stacks of books and through the hanging fluorescent light fixtures. It seems distracted by the dust in the air and flies in a serpentine daze for some slight moments then takes off at full force into the plate glass windows in the front of the bookstore and falls to the floor. I pick it up and the small sparrow is in such a state of shock that it deliriously perches on my finger. I walk it slowly outside to let it go but it can't seem to fly off my finger and keeps slumping backwards as if it might fall. The artificiality of the city suddenly strikes me as alien standing on the sidewalk with this small quivering bird on my finger. How can this be conveyed other than in a rapid succession of harsh filmic angles in rapid montage? The bird falls backwards and scurries under some parked cars to hide there, it has lost its ability to fly. It hops out from under an SUV and I get it onto my finger again and place it on the branch of a tree growing out of the sidewalk. It stands awkwardly shaken on one of the branches, an unnatural fixture in the nature of the surrounding city. A man approaches and seems automatically intrigued by what is going on, he is sweating profusely despite the cool evening air, and talking rapidly to himself. He stares astonished, like I am a magician who conjured this bird out of pure ether. A straight couple wanders by and to impress his girlfriend the man offers any and all banal knowledge he possesses about small birds in shock. His conclusion: the bird is dying. I leave it where it is, trusting that the new audience will either care for it or kill it outright. I can see from behind the glass that more people are stopping to stare and investigate the anomaly of the fake looking bird and the sweaty man speaking to it, speaking to himself. The bird seems as ideologically shocked as anything else, a sudden encounter with the simulacrum that was really glass. They ignore the homeless couple who lay sprawled in the most uncomfortable positions in the dip of the sidewalk, somehow asleep amidst all the activity of foot and street traffic. People are stopping in larger and larger groups now. As Wallace Stevens said of his jar when he placed it on the hill in Tennessee, the wilderness rose up to it and surrounded it. This is what occurred with the injured pane-stricken small sparrow, crushing every pedestrian with its inalienable freakishness. The city rose to it, engulfed it, the city streets were suddenly acrid, the smell made me think of Italy, the buildings absurd models, every pedestrian an absurd caricature of their own immutable fascination with this small delicate thing. In an exploding rupture of epiphanic revolt it flew away. The tableau it left behind, of momentary faces and elliptical emotions, is no longer describable.

Arcana Caelestia
Amanda Davidson

Judy	Mother
Kirthi	Sea captain, phantasm
Masha	Talk show host
Lara	Heavenly wife/feather bender
LRSN	Emmanuel Swedenborg, 18th Century mystic

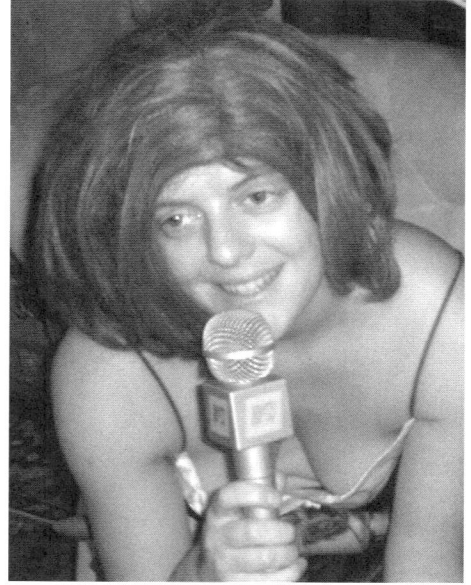

Judy: My daughter. The once and future king of daytime television. She had her own show once, before…the incident. And now she has a second chance. Don't be disappointed if this story has a happy ending. We're all here together, live, a studio audience. We're all in the same fantasy, and I am feeling just like a big electric sign that says 'Applause'. Flashing, flashing! And when I sparkle, you clap.

Kirthi: I prefer to appear to people in dreams. But for now, I'm with you, I'm in the audience. Problems occur over there, but here I am, clapping, safe! I love to watch. (Giddily.) Don't you?

Judy: Yes! I appear under the sign of "Judy" or "mother" but when I begin to watch, my pleasure blends into yours, and I dissolve. Then we're interrupted by a refreshing commercial break, and I remember, this is not just any talk show host, this is MY DAUGHTER. (Pounds her chest, then begins to weep.)

Kirthi: Don't cry. This is her big come back!

Judy: It's just—been—so hard.

Kirthi: I know. Everything changed the day that orchid came on the air, fluffy with secrets and information.

Judy: I smelled trouble the minute I saw its…labial visage, which emanated indiscretion.

Kirthi: When the orchid 'spilled the beans', all of her forgetting unraveled. A small thing rowed back through her memory.

Judy: Even I, her mother, could see that a shadow haunted the rim of her mind. A ghost with a face like an angel but an EVIL tower of hair. We had, at the time, no name for the thing, and so we could not grieve it.

Kirthi: Her fluffy rim grew menacing.

Judy: Sinisterly, she wielded a purse full of eggs.

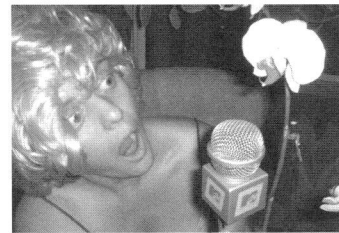   

Kirthi: Her efforts to be coy dissolved into bald yearning. (Whispering.) She performed inappropriate oral acts upon the orchid LIVE and ON THE AIR.

(Judy screams and cover her ears. Kirthi and Judy grab each other and rock back and forth.)

Lara: She was full of American wishes, fantasies of impenetrability.

Judy: Who said that?

Kirthi: You knew her, but you have purposefully forgotten her name, to ward off grief. You hate to become undone.

Judy: My cheery denial has so many uses! I was telling a story, but I can't remember what it was about.

Lara: It's strange not to have a name. Because she doesn't know my name it's as if I myself have forgotten it.

Kirthi: Be quiet, you! Now we have to shut our mouths and be the audience. Look, the cameras are rolling.

(Masha enters in a blond wig and ball gown, holding a microphone. Kirthi, Judy and Lara woo-hoo and clap.)

Masha: Welcome to Arcana Caelestia. That's Latin for Heavenly Secrets. Today, we're going to talk about… secrets. Are you plagued with visions from the great beyond? Do you think spirits and angels speak to you? Mmm hmm, I know you do. Viewers, you are NOT ALONE. Many of my fans write to me and say, Masha, I have a nasty little problem. I am so ashamed. God talks to me. This can be embarrassing in these secular times, so I've invited a very special guest all the way from the Enlightenment. Give it up for Emanuel Swedenborg.

LRSN: (Catwalks out.) What's up? No shame in my game.

Masha: Hi Swedenborg. (They exchange air kisses on both cheeks.)

LRSN: Hi Masha. I love your show. Thanks for having me on.

Masha: Swedenborg, tell me about your…dreams. You claim that they're visions from heaven. How do you know they're the 'real deal'?

LRSN: Well Masha, to make me fully aware of the way that dreams flow in I was put to sleep and dreamt of a boat approaching that was laden with delicacies and savouries of every kind. These were stowed away in the boat, out of sight. On deck stood two armed guards, as well as a third man who was the captain. The boat was passing by into a kind of arched dock; and with this I woke up and thought about the dream. At that point the angelic spirits in front and above me over to the right addressed me. They declared that they were the source of this dream. So that I would know for sure that they were the source of it I was brought into a state where I was so to speak both asleep and awake at one and the same time. In a similar way they introduced different things that were pleasing and delightful, for example, an unknown tiny creature which was transformed into an object with blackish and shining rays which shot into my left eye at a fantastic speed.

Masha: Well, viewers, there you have it. Indisputable evidence. Now Swedenborg, don't these 'visions' usually explicate some aspect of the, uh, 'holy scriptures'?

LRSN: Hmm, yes. Once (upward inflection) there appeared before me a lovely girl whose face was radiant. She was moving swiftly in an upward direction towards the right and slightly increasing her speed. She looked to be in the flower of youth, being neither a small child nor yet a young woman; and she was wearing an attractive and shining black dress. In this manner and with gladness she hastened from light on into light. I was told that the interior things of the Word are such when they first start to rise up, the black dress being the Word in letter. After this the young girl flew towards my right cheek, but I perceived her flight with my interior sight only. I was told that these are the things from the internal sense of the Word which do not come within human comprehension.

(An image of Lara wearing the trashbag freezes on the screen. Masha is transfixed.)

Judy: No! No!

LRSN: Masha? What's wrong?

Masha: Her face, her hair, that dress…it's all so… hauntingly familiar. Swedenborg, these dreams …could they be… reruns?

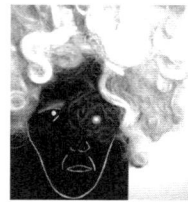 

  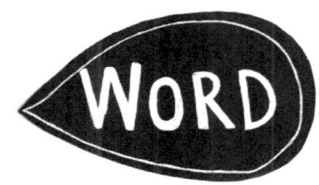 

Lara: (Stands up.) No!

Masha: My forgotten nest, my feather bender! You, who float just beyond the edge of my fluffy rim.

LRSN: She's not your 'feather bender.' She's…my heavenly wife!

Lara: I'm sorry, Swedenborg. I used you. I used your porous psyche to transmit a message to … her.

LRSN: But, you totally flew toward my right cheek. Didn't that mean anything to you?

Lara: Nowadays a girl can fly toward a right cheek. It's casual.

LRSN: I'm feeling woozy. As if a part of me has just dissolved.

Judy: No, Swedenborg, be strong. Her ratings are going to plummet! They'll cancel the show. After all that we've worked for.

Masha: Mother, please. Sit down.

Judy: No! Captain, you look like you just floated in here from an episode of Gilligan's island. Yank us back into familiar terrain. Just…get her out of here.

Kirthi: No, Judy, we're on daytime t.v. now. We make shocking, inappropriate divulgences to achieve catharsis. Sometimes we even win prizes, like a salad spinner, or a dream vacation.

Judy: Like, a cruise?

Kirthi: Yes. A cruise.

Judy: Now I'm aroused. A cruise might end my dissatisfaction forever.

Kirthi: I can see that you're all weirdly bereft. I'll have to take over. Masha, give me the microphone. There's a story floating around here. I can detect its meaty aroma. (Sniffs.) Peppery. (Sniffs again.) Enchanting. (She looks at Lara.) It's coming from you!

LRSN: Hey, I'm the guest star on this program.

Kirthi: Swedenborg, please. (Points to a chair.) You're in the audience now.

LRSN: But I don't want to be sidelined.

Kirthi: Then go audition for Queer Eye for the Straight Guy.

Lara: Now my story is itching

Masha: Like a little rash.

Kirthi: Go ahead.

Lara: She was not sweet. It stung when she slapped me, but I liked it. Her slaps aroused a nearly unbearable panic that crested until I surfed fuzzy waves of static into mindlessness. I woke up alone in a fur lined alley. Ecstatically I gathered palmfuls of hair and ran down the avenue, trailing a noisy string of tin cans. Animals with tattered ears followed me, mainly squirrels, foxes, opposums, and one beaver. The animals and I gathered at her door, where we were denied entry.

Kirthi: Masha, is this true?

Masha: I didn't let her in because CLEARLY she had boundary issues. That fucking menagerie tipped me off. You do NOT bring a herd of little foxes on a second date.

Kirthi: Masha has a point, Lara.

Lara: At first I thought it was another way of topping me—the pleasure of delay. Days wore on. I watched the entire second season of Star Trek the Next Generation on DVD. One by one the animals abandoned me, until I was left with only the beaver and a shy squirrel. Finally, she called me. She said her hobbies left no time for female trouble.

Kirthi: And what were these demanding hobbies, Masha?

Masha: I masturbated and wept. I stuffed eggs into a silky purse, gazing outward with suspicion. I thought…if I could avoid …entanglement… I could ward off the possibility of … coming undone. It had seemed to be functioning as a model for nationhood. Why not for a surly talk show host?

Lara: But it can be so delectable, to leak, just a bit.

Kirthi: If I may ask—do you think of your panty line as a microcosm of the San Andreas fault?

Lara: Yes. Yes I do.

Kirthi: I knew it!

(They stand up and have a little love moment.)

LRSN: Their erotic vibration is giving me the creeps.

Judy: I want to stuff them back into your skull.

LRSN: Contained within my celestial eye, their fleshy limbs don't frighten me. But here, on the talk show… I'm terrified.

Masha: That's enough! Captain, surrender the mic. Viewers, I'm sorry. That's all the time we have. Next week, on Arcana Caelestia: Orchids who slay with words and the women who love them.

Judy: Bravo, Honey.

the end

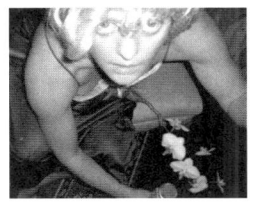

Mustache Attempt
Dan Fisher

Throw the watchdog a t-bone and we'll see
what happens. Can't I have a handshake
or is it a milkshake? Surely the sky is
striped, the yard in need of water,
an utterance of *nice day*. A new business
has been established setting the ground-
work for a lop-sided victory. My own devices
don't fail me now. A leaf's endurance
to hang on before the great fall is not
a shock. It stems from a granite
anxiety where a sign was posted.

The property line, drawn with beach wood
in the sand, was there. The morning
gloom forgery of song ceases nothing but
behavioral options, a winged clutch of
ribcage, spit. Your emulsion smile sooner
or later precedes a tragic bungle.
Another cavalry dressed in slips charged
the mound, dropped a handout or two.
I blame being involved for all its vim.
Possibilities inconclusive in an attractive suit
bemoan anonymity and its fiery lip.

We severed ourselves before we were
completed. To pinpoint an infraction of belief
in all things mild & mannered, emotive &
lost. An attempt in activity stop taking the brunt
at times, I pat my pockets and hope
forgetfulness has not set in. With the
opening tip just minutes away, capillaries
jump to the occasion and form the last
shot. I tighten with the turn, and a passenger
in seat belt can't come, at least not
with a curve. My geometry is off.

The yee-haw nights deliver us from swinging
saloon doors. To retell under smoke rings
the vagaries of a dream, our mouths would
remain pursed to the love of talking.
If I repeat & repeat it, will it happen?
I mean, pull up breeches and buckle down
for the long haul. The objects, the mountains
the avenues are smeared inconsequential as
they bore through the apartment.
Is that to go or to stay? For now it's for here.
Remembering I have not entered a door

painted snazzy red in order to eschew. Achoo?
That's not a career based decision since
fast moving clouds live in between buildings
existing as props. There are no other means
but to reply with arch pauses. To whitely
stare at cursing references, we take reverie
in makeshift arrangement of our room.

Photograph by Migdalia Valdes

Rimming the Pacific: Operation Drive-Out Trash
Elizabeth Young

I suppose I could have jumped; Instead I flirted with the inkling, mumbling angelically, "The kitten only has one eye." Flubbed ordinary tasks (kvetching bloomed straight on the kisser.) Rooms the size of children's teeth evacuating monks.

To journey, emberlike, across a hairless nipple tipped with life as varicose as dreamwork's Ptolemaic fracture. It's like sure, vavoom, you know. Does staring make us sinners? Despite its lack of rigor the moonlight gives us lumps.

Just stop and think, my pretty, that exile-owned harumph where they teach you about gender and stuff you full of sex is but a coy echolocation, a splurge against the goons who widen children's eyes with sheets of candy shaped like oil.

We converted harum-scarum fractal duty, timely slaughter, then wrapped it up in sheer and clung—as if (for, suddenly, the air, all jelly, felt too tender to hedge an arctic splurge and so we touched without our mittens).

Thank god the kid had wings and the air was fairly roomy. Our pleasures hung like gardens crystallized among the heathens. Another runic beard burst proudly through our crypt. But the horse's heads were doomed to years of fuzzy thinking.

Wings by Debra St. John

Two Poems
Micah Ballard and Cedar Sigo

TEACHING THE YOUNG
Micah Ballard and Cedar Sigo

I had begged the guards to observe my birthday
& to free the gates of the diamond district.
Owl feathers crush together
You fight the minotaur at the end.
I had no energy left even for short lyrics
Nor the pleasures of ground breaking arcades
Nor the plaza. I am ready to die.
Nocturnal mass that does not last
What the guilt is playing off of
The lighted path to exit.
I placed the ghetto hand between
All the slabs were cracked
Killed in his flat adding ashes to the dose
We inscribe his name above the entrance
& voodoo is set to continue
We have collected his live performances
A reverse pedicure
& a touch upon those heels
Pointing to ruins the way the shanghais do
I guess that's why we got along so long.

LIVE AT THE EAST
Cedar Sigo

These tears bury,
They have been left out in Hades sun

Patterns in music
I once found difficult to distinguish

Now repeat themselves in fire
and kiss the ring

Connecting passages to the black vaults
and crowned heads of the coral seas

The edges of their collars
had onyx scaled to amber,

The dust that we wish to gather against
That would flash on me still,

The writings already a tape, already
revolving so much

with jewelry cleaners, concentrate
make light so pained, no smoke in the lungs.

NITE liteS
Kyle Kaufman

lunar bandwidth glow
under water all smile
and milk downtown
still-emptee hi-rise
apts.

ragged off-set decks
complex eyes "to maximize"
little nest disrupts
city lights cream

i am talking around
the moon

but not
of it

our electricians
have chosen this
"to bathe" light
unworkable details
smooth upsweep grid
"immerse" electric flotilla

for fleet foot impressions
guerilla evening
pour me some
fluorescing light

after work there is a bathing in lights that comes on. the bath is cream mild and milk—without star—so it is lonely—yet strange warm drug—to work under the same lights, in their domain, is a poison misery. to be beyond their reach still witness to their reaching is in the added space of night under. glow on wet streets from rain—i saw rain—add motion and lights seen up thru glass up sky—angles of incidence it is not the same on this line. skating

    details seduce when they tease and come out slow evoking, pure black being terror and death of dicrimination, an absence obscene and so desirable, full weight of a thing in its overwhelming—till a moment of drowling. the hint is not an extinguishing though, is fire-play, is milk, the bathed cookie, cream wet street down this light.

    rush hour traffic jam pool of homesick red light refract—hell glow transience—reminds me of nothing—its own strong drug a malevolence—nothing but itself and what's next to it—quite pleasing series of hell reds pouring down artery—"out" "out" to the receptacle pods lining suburban capillaries—amazing how the cells know how to return to the same place they are borne from "constantly" dribble and jabs of red light—their signal strength and shades erratic pulse fringe home bleeding ocean

His Fingers Sang
Max McDaniel

Contributors

Omnia Amin was born in Cairo, Egypt. She graduated from The American University in Cairo and received an MA and PhD in Modern and Contemporary British Literature from the University of London, Queen Mary and Westfield College. She was chair of the English Department at Philadelphia University in Jordan, and currently teaches at Zayed University in UAE.

David Antin, poet, critic, performance artist. Known for his improvised "talk poems", he has published 6 books based on these talk pieces since 1972. His most recent books are *i never knew what time it was* (UC Press) and *john cage uncaged is still cagey* (Singing Horse). A selection of his earlier poems *Selected Poems 1963-73* was published by Sun and Moon.

Micah Ballard is the author of *Bettina Coffin* (Red Ant Press), *Negative Capability in the Verse of John Wieners* (Auguste), and *Evangeline Downs* forthcoming from Ugly Duckling Presse.

Dodie Bellamy's collection, *Academonia*, was published by Krupskaya, 2006. Other books include *Pink Steam* (2004, Suspect Thoughts Press) and *The Letters of Mina Harker* (reprinted by the University of Wisconsin Press, 2004). Her book *Cunt-Ups* (Tender Buttons) won the 2002 Firecracker Alternative Book Award for poetry.

Micah Ballard is the author of *Bettina Coffin* (Red Ant Press), *Negative Capability in the Verse of John Wieners* (Auguste), and *Evangeline Downs* (Ugly Duckling Presse).

Bill Berkson's latest publications include *Our Friends Will Pass Among You Silently: New Poems 2001-2006* (The Owl Press); *Sudden Address: Selected Lectures 1981-2006* (Cuneiform Press); a collaboration with Bernadette Mayer entitled *What's Your Idea of a Good Time?: Letters & Interviews 1977-1985* (Tuumba Press, 2006); an online chapbook, *Same Here*, from bigbridge.org (#11); and a special issue of *Fell Swoop* magazine, *Parts of the Body: A 1970s/80s Scrapbook*. He is the Distinguished Mellon Lecturer at the Skowhegan School of Art for 2006. He lives in San Francisco and has taught at the San Francisco Art Institute since 1984.

Charles Bernstein's most recent books are *Girly Man*, *Shadowtime* and *With Strings*. For more information: epc.buffalo.edu/authors/bernstein. He teaches at the University of Pennsylvania.

Ted Berrigan (1934-1983) was the inspirational leader of the second generation New York School poets. *The Collected Poems of Ted Berrigan*, edited by Alice Notley with Anselm Berrigan and Edmund Berrigan, was published in 2005 by the University of California Press.

Dore Bowen is an artist, theorist, and curator whose work often takes a textual form. She holds a PhD in Visual and Cultural Studies from the University of Rochester and is currently assistant professor of modern and contemporary art history at San Jose State University.

Ed Bowes is a writer, director and filmmaker. He lives in New York City where he teaches at the School of Visual Arts. His most recent movies include *Flip*, 2006 and *Picture Book*, 2003. He is working on a new movie entitled *Against The Slope of Social Speech*. His movies are held in the collection of the Museum of Modern Art. He is recipient of grants from the NEA, NYSCA and the Rockefeller Foundation. For copies of *The Menage*, email EdBowes@aol.com

Taylor Brady is the author of *Microclimates* (Krupskaya, 2001), *Yesterday's News* (Factory School, 2005), and *Occupational Treatment* (Atelos, forthcoming). Recent work has appeared in *War & Peace*, *Biting the Error* (Coach House Books, 2005), *Disaster*, and *Bay Poetics* (Faux Press, 2006). He works for a children's services agency in Oakland, and lives in San Francisco with Tanya Hollis.

Joe Brainard (1942–1994) was a visual artist and a writer. His influential book, *I Remember* has been in print since 1970. His art work, the subject of a major retrospective organized by the Berkeley Art Museum, is represented by the Tibor de Nagy Gallery in New York. Info: www.joebrainard.org.

Mary Burger is the author of *Sonny* (Leon Works, 2005) and the co-editor of *Biting the Error: Writers Explore Narrative* (Coach House Books, 2004). She edits Second Story Books, featuring works by innovative narrative writers. *An Apparent Event: A Second Story Books Anthology* was published in 2006.

Marie Cartier is a scholar, visual /performance artist, queer activist, poet and theologian who teaches at UC Irvine in their Film Department, and California State University Northridge in Women's Studies. She is finishing her Ph.D. in Religion from Claremont Graduate University. Her book, *Baby You Are My Religion: 1950's Butch Femme Bar Culture in the U.S. as Possibly Sacred Community*, will be published by Equinox Press in 2007. She exhibits her installation performance project MORGASM, the Museum of Radical Gender and Sex Matrix, which explores female orgasm in a museum context.

Maxine Chernoff's latest books are *Among the Names*, poems from Apogee Press, *Some of her Friends That Year*, stories from Coffee House Press, and with Paul Hoover, a forthcoming collection of selected translations of Holderlin from Omnidawn Press. She chairs the Creative Writing Program at SFSU and edits *New American Writing*.

Andrei Codrescu's latest books are *New Orleans, Mon Amour: Twenty Years of Writing from the City* and *It Was Today: New Poems*. He lives in Louisiana, edits corpse.org, a webzine, and is a regular essayist on NPR. His next work will be notes on the margin of the poetry of his landsman, Tristan Tzara.

Norma Cole is a poet, painter and translator. Among her books are *Do The Monkey, Collective Memory, At All*, and *Spinoza in Her Youth*. Current translation work includes Danielle Collobert's *Journals*, Fouad Gabriel Naffah's *The Spirit God and the Properties of Nitrogen* and *Crosscut Universe: Writing on Writing from France*. Cole has been the recipient of a Wallace Alexander Gerbode Foundation Award, Gertrude Stein Awards, the Fund for Poetry, and the Foundation for Contemporary Arts. A Canadian by birth, Cole migrated via France to San Francisco where she has lived since 1977.

The author of more than 20 books of poetry, **Mahmoud Darwish** is the most celebrated Palestinian poet writing today. Born in 1942 in Palestine, he has lived in Beirut, Cairo, Mosow, and Amman, and currently resides in Ramallah. His most recent book of poems is *Don't Apologize For What You've Done* (Riad El-Rayyes Books, Beirut, 2004). The poems that appear here are from this collection.

Amanda Davidson's writing has appeared in *Baby, Remember My Name: An Anthology of New Queer Girl Writing*, The Marjorie Wood Gallery, *Other Magazine*, and elsewhere. She rehearses alter-egos online at partedinthemiddle.com. *Arcana Caelestia* was first performed at Small Press Traffic's 2005 Poet's Theater Jamboree. The play includes excerpts from *Arcana Caelestia: Volume 2* by Emmanuel Swedenborg, an Enlightenment era revelator.

Guy Debord (1931-1994) was a founding member of the Situationist International, the notorious avant-garde group that helped trigger the May 1968 revolt in France. He created six films, one of which was an adaptation of his most well known book, *The Society of the Spectacle* (1967), arguably the most important radical work of the twentieth century. His other books include *The Real Split in the International* (1972), *Considerations on the Assassination of Gérard Lebovici* (1985), *The Game of War* (1987), *Comments on the Society of the Spectacle* (1988), *Panegyric* (1999), and *This Bad Reputation* (1993).

Oliver DiCicco is a sculptor, designer, fabricator and musician. His sculptural work deals primarily in the fields of musical instrument sculpture and kinetic sound sculpture. His musical instruments are the basis for the Mobius Operandi ensemble, a group formed in 1991 who performs composed and improvisational music, using exclusively his designs. DiCicco was the owner and chief engineer of Mobius Music Recording for 28 years. His audio work has received several Grammy nominations and RIAA gold record awards.

Steve Dickison is Director of the Poetry Center at San Francisco State University; editor-publisher, since 1994, of the small press Listening Chamber, with offshoots Rumor Books and Parrhesia Press; co-editor with David Meltzer of *Shuffle Boil*, an irregular music magazine. He curated the exhibition "Poetry and its Arts: Bay Area interactions 1954-2004" at the California Historical Society in downtown San Francisco, Winter 2005, and "Recent Visitors: Poets & Publishing on the Bolinas Scene in the Seventies" at the Book Club of California, Winter 2006. *Disposed*, a book of poetry, was published, 2007, from Post-Apollo Press.

Nathaniel Dorsky has been making and exhibiting films within the avant-garde tradition since 1964. He now lives in San Francisco where he makes a living as a film editor. His works have been shown internationally and are in the permanent collections of the Museum of Modern Art (New York), the Pacific Film Archive (Berkeley), Image Forum (Tokyo), Les Archives du film experimental d'Avignon, and Le Centre Pompidou (Paris) as well as many universities. Among his better known works are *Summerwind* (1965), *Hours for Jerome* (1966-70, 1982), *Pneuma* (1976-83), *Alaya* (1976-87), *Variations* (1992-98), *Arbor Vitae* (2000), *The Visitation* (2002), and *Threnody* (2003-2004).

Robert Duncan (1919-1988) was a key figure affiliated with the Black Mountain poets and the San Francisco Renaissance. Author of several important collections of poetry, including *The Opening of the Field* (1960), *Roots and Branches* (1964), and *Bending the Bow* (1968), Duncan was a frequent collaborator with his life partner and artist, Jess, with whom he lived from 1951 until his death.

Lara Durback is an artist/poet working with text, letterpress printing, sound (analog synthesizers and field recording), as well as the book form, and any other medium that can be combined and smashed together. Currently contemplating humans awash in electromagnetic fields: both those from the earth and those emitted by power lines and electronic devices, and how difficult it is to match a field to a source.

kari edwards (1954-2006) received one of Small Press Traffic's books of the year awards (2004), New Langton Art's Bay Area Award in Literature (2002), and is author of *having been blue for charity*, Blazevox (2007), *obedience*, Factory School (2005), *iduna*, O Books (2003); *a day in the life of p.* (2002), Subpress Collective; and *Post/(Pink)*, Scarlet Press (2000).

Jim Elledge's most recent books are *A History of My Tattoo*, a book-length poem (Stonewall, 2006). He directs the M.A. in Professional Writing Program at Kennesaw State University, as well as his own press, Thorngate Road, which sponsors the Frank O'Hara Award annually.

Lawrence Ferlinghetti has been painting since before he was a poet, starting in Paris in the 1940s. For fifteen years, he has been represented by the George Krevsky Gallery, 77 Geary Street, San Francisco. *Adam and Eve* is part of a series of paintings he is working on with Momo in his studio at Hunter's Point. It was part an exhibition of his paintings in 2006 at the George Krevsky Gallery.

Sean Finney is a poet and copywriter living in San Francisco. His first book is *The Obedient Door*, published by Meritage Press.

Dan Fisher began printing and letterpress as an MFA student at Mills College in Oakland, CA. There he produced multiple broadsides for the Mills Reading Series in conjunction with Eucalyptus press. Recently, he's been included in the *Bay Poetics* anthology.

Tim Fitzmaurice is a longtime lecturer, partnered with Ginny and related to several others, including Jason, Erika, Briton, and Oona. He teaches writing at UC Santa Cruz and was the first Green Party Mayor of Santa Cruz. He has seen his opera, OPIUM, written with Aaron Seeman, produced, a few poems here and there, many readings, and now this. George Angel, his coauthor, decorated the unpublished prints that inspired this text. They are not included here. He lives and writes in Medellin to this day.

Fluxus: The selections from *The Fluxus Performance Workbook* publisher here include event scores by Fluxus artists **Ay-O, Robert Bozzi, George Brecht, Ken Friedman, Dick Higgins, Bengt Af Klintberg, Milan Knizak, Jackson Mac Low, George Maciunas, Yoko Ono, Nam June Paik, Mieko Shiomi, Ben Vautier**, along with **Tristan Tzara**. *The Fluxus Performance Workbook* is edited by Ken Friedman, Owen Smith, and Lauren Sawchyn. Ken Friedman is a Fluxus artist who leads a second life as professor of leadership and strategic design at the Norwegian School of Management and at Denmark's Design School. **Owen Smith** is an artist and professor of art history at the University of Maine where he also directs the New Media Laboratory. **Lauren Sawchyn** is an artist and medical illustrator who is now earning her doctorate in veterinary medicine at Cornell University. *Viz.* made this selection of scores from the *Workbook*.

Gary Gach is editor of *What Book!? ~ Buddha Poems from Beat to Hiphop* (American Book Award), author of *The Complete Idiot's Guide to Understanding Buddhism*, and co-translator, from Korean, of *Ten Thousand Lives*, *Flowers of a Moment*, and *Songs for Tomorrow*, by Ko Un. His writing and translation has appeared in numerous anthologies, and such journals as *American Poetry Review*, *City Lights Review*, *Shambhala Sun*, *Turning Wheel*, *Urthona*, *World Literature Today*, and *Zyzzyva*. He also does voice-overs, for which it doesn't matter what he wears to work, and no one stops him on the street for his autograph. http://word.to

Peter Gizzi's latest books of poetry include *The Outernationale* (2007) and *Some Values of Landscape and Weather* (2003), both published by Wesleyan Poetry Series. His chapbook, *A Panic that Can Still Come Upon Me*, was published by Ugly Ducking Press, 2006.

AnneKarin Glass was born into an artistic environment. She began her studies spending childhood summer vacations at the School of the Art Institute of Chicago, where her father headed the Industrial Design Department. She continues to educate her hand and eye through drawing, painting, sculpture and photography. The form of the human figure and the emotion of gesture frequently inspire her drawings and paintings while her photography focuses on abstraction, the colors and textures in the natural world.

Robert Glück is the author of nine books of poetry and fiction. His latest book of stories, *Denny Smith*, appeared in 2004. Glück was co-director of Small Press Traffic and director of The Poetry Center at San Francisco State where he currently teaches and edits *Narrativity*, a web journal: http://www.sfsu.edu/~poetry/narrativity Coach House Press published *Biting The Error: Writers on Narrative*, an anthology edited by Glück, Camille Roy, Mary Burger and Gail Scott.

Judith Goldman is the author of *Vocoder* (Roof 2001), which won a Book of the Year award from Small Press Traffic, and *DeathStar/Rico-chet* (O Books 2006). She is finishing her doctorate in English and Comparative Literature at Columbia University and lives in the Bay Area, where she has been on the editorial board of Krupskaya Press and currently adjuncts in the Creative Writing Department at SFSU.

Barbara Guest was known as a New York School writer early in her career. Throughout the 50s she wrote for *Art News*. She published numerous collections of poetry including *The Red Gaze, Miniatures and Other Poems, The Nudes, Quilt*, and *Biography*. Her awards included the Robert Frost Medal for Distinguished Lifetime Achievement from the Poetry Society of America, among many others. She lived in Berkeley, CA. Guest died on Feb. 15, 2006.

Rob Halpern is the author of *Rumored Place* (Krupskaya 2004) and *Disaster Suite* (Vigilance Society 2006). Currently, he's co-editing the poems of the late Frances Jaffer together with Kathleen Fraser, working on a collaborative project with Taylor Brady for Atticus / Finch, and translating the early essays of Georges Perec, the first of which is forthcoming in *Chicago Review*. He lives in San Francisco.

Alan Halsey's latest books are *Marginalien* (Five Seasons), 2005; and *Not Everything Remotely: Selected Poems, 1978-2005* (Salt), 2005.

Dick Higgins' long-time association with Fluxus members dates back to a course in "Experimental Composition" he took with John Cage at the New School for Social Research in 1958 along with future Fluxus artists George Brecht and Al Hansen and Happenings co-founder Allen Kaprow. Higgins founded the Something Else Press in 1964 as a complement to Maciunas's Fluxus-titled publications. The Intermedia Essay was first published as part of this enterprise in the Something Else Newsletter in February 1966. The Intermedia Chart, a graphic realization of the main tenets of the essay, was first drawn in 1995 in a visit to Molvena, Italy when Higgins needed to explain the idea to an Italian collector.

Brenda Hillman is the author of seven collections of poetry, the most recent of which is *Pieces of air in the Epic* (Wesleyan University Uress). She teaches at Saint Mary's College in Moraga, California.

Jane Hirshfield is the author of six books of poetry and a collection of essays. She was a finalist for the National Book Critics Ciricle Award and winner of the Poetry Center Book Award, the California Book Award and fellowships from the Academy of American Poets, the National Endowment for the Arts, and the Guggenheim and Rockefeller foundations. She lives in the San Francisco Bay area.

George Hitchcock is a painter and writer who lives part of each year in Harrisburg, Oregon and La Paz, Mexico where he has regularly exhibited in all of the state's public museums. He is also the author of two novels, *Another Shore*, and *The Racquet* (Storyline Press), several chapbooks of poetry and a collection of theatrical pieces. He founded the San Francisco Review in 1960 and, in 1964, he founded the well-known poetry magazine, *kayak*, which he edited for years. In 2002, Philos Press published *Turns and Returns: Poems and Paintings* by George Hitchcock. Story Line Press published *One-Man Boat: The George Hitchcock Reader* in 2003.

Leslie Hodgkins is a poet who graduated from the University of California, Santa Cruz and is now living in New York City.

Tanya Hollis is an archivist/librarian. Recent exhibitions include the Poetry Center's 50th Anniversary exhibit Poetry and Its Arts: Bay Area Interactions 1954-2004 and the Bay Area Bazaar show at the Pulliam Deffenbaugh Gallery in Portland. Recent work can be found in *Encyclopedia: Vol. 1, A-E,* under Catalogue and in *Disaster*. She works at The California Historical Society and lives in San Francisco with Taylor Brady.

Anselm Hollo is Profesor of Writing and Poetics at Naropa University in Boulder, Colorado. His most recent book is *Braided River: New and Selected Poems 1965-2005* (Salt Modern Poets, Cambridge, England, 2005). A new collection, *Guests of Space*, is scheduled for publication by Coffee House Press in early 2007.

Bob Holman is the proprietor of the Bowery Poetry Club and teaches "Exploding Text" at Columbia in the Graduate School of the Arts. The poems are reprinted from *A Couple of Ways of Doing Something* (New York: Aperture, 2006), a collaborative book with Chuck Close. Close provided the daguerreotypes; Holman, the praise poems (after the teachings of Papa Susso, a jeli from The Gambia). The original version of the book was exhibited at the Peggy Guggenheim Museum during the Venice Biennale and is owned by the Getty and other museums. Holman writes, "Knowing the poems would be side by side with Close's bold, lush, grabby images meant I had to tend to add poems' visuals. Luckily I had Ruth Lingen of Pace editions to inspire and help me work out typography."

Kelly Holt has two chapbooks, *Jesstures* (?Mirab.dict!, 2005) and *Equidistances* (PonyXpress, 2000). Her poems have or will appear in Faux Press's *Bay Poetics Anthology, Fulcrum, New American Writing, Jacket, 6,500, Mirage4/Period(ical), Tolling Elves, Small Town, Commonwealand Fourteen Hills*. She has taught writing at SFSU, Academy of Art University, and UC Santa Cruz, where she is a PhD Candidate in Literature. She is writing a dissertation on the Berkeley Renaissance poetry community.

Paul Hoover's most recent poetry books are *Poems in Spanish* (Omnidawn, 2005), nominated for the Bay Area Book Award, and *Edge and Fold* (Apogee Press, 2006). His literary essays were published as *Fables of Representation* (University of Michigan Press, 2004). He is also editor of the anthology *Postmodern American Poetry*.

Karen Jacobs, Associate Professor of English and Comparative Literature and Senior Scholar in Women's Studies at the University of Colorado at Boulder, is a specialist in twentieth-century American literature, visual studies, and critical theory, and a freelance graphic designer.

Jess, also known as Jess Collins (1928-2004), was a collage artist and painter whose retrospective—"Jess: A Grand Collage, 1951 – 1993"—was exhibited throughout the U.S., 1993-94, along with the book by the same title. Jess lived and collaborated with his partner, Robert Duncan, from 1951 until Duncan's death in 1988. The rare selections published here from his *Boob* series were privately issued in 1952.

Kyle Kaufman co-edits the poetry zine *el pobre Mouse* and runs subday press. He also curates a monthly Bay Area Salon series. His work is beginning to appear—dig a bit and you'll find it in *One Less*, *effing* and (soon) *Mrs. Maybe* and Shampoo. An interview about his press, subday, came out in *Ellipsis*, a new quarterly journal funded by the sale of the publisher's house.

Larry Kearney was born in Brooklyn in 1943. His first book was *Fifteen Poems*, from White Rabbit Press in 1964, and his most recent books have been issued by his own Worm in the Rain Publications. A new book, *Passion*, will be published by Transmission in the near future.

Kevin Killian is the author of two novels, two books of short stories, a book of memoirs, thirty-five plays, a book of poetry, and several collaboratively written works. He is the film columnist for the online journal *Fanzine*. In addition, he is passionately interested in the work of the US poet Jack Spicer (1925-65) and has written quite a bit about Spicer's life and work.

Mary Kite is the author of *The Bamboo Librarian and Promenade Through A Precipitous Park* (Blue X Press, 2006). Literary collaborations include *Fleuve Flâneur,* Mary Kite, Anne Waldman (Erudite Fangs Editions, 2004) and *Spilled Beans: A Conversation,* Kenward Elmslie & Mary Kite with Drawings by Joe Brainard (Skanky Possum Press). She has produced events such as: *Paul Bowles: A Retrospective; Tyger! Tyger! A William Blake Multimedia Festival* and co-produced/directed the first transatlantic Internet2 poetry reading: *Transatlantic Howl: A Dedication to Allen Ginsberg.*

Ken Knabb has translated the *Situationist International Anthology,* Guy Debord's *The Society of the Spectacle,* and Debord's *Complete Cinematic Works.* His own writings, collected in *Public Secrets,* have been translated into over a dozen other languages. His writings and translations can be found at his Bureau of Public Secrets website: www.bopsecrets.org.

Kenneth Koch: a New York School poet, Koch published many volumes of poetry, most recently *A Possible World* and *New Addresses*. His short plays are collected in *The Gold Standard: A Good of Plays* and *One Thousand Avant-Garde Plays*. He authored several books about poetry, including *Wishes, Lies, and Dreams*, and his fiction is gathered in *Collected Fiction*. He won the Bollingen Prize in 1995 and the Bobbitt Library of Congress Poetry Prize in 1996. He was a finalist for the Pulitzer in 1995. Koch lived with his wife, Karen, in New York City and taught at Columbia University. He died in 2002.

Rodney Koeneke is the author of the poetry collections *Musée Mechanique* (BlazeVOX, 2006) and Rouge State (Pavement Saw, 2003) and a study of I.A. Richards in China (Stanford UP, 2004). His work has been read or performed at Small Traffic's Poets Theater, the Poetry Center at SFSU, the Pacific Film Archive, SF Cinematheque, the Poetry Project, and the 2006 Flarf Festival in New York City. He lives in Portland, OR with his wife, Lesley Poirier, and their young son.

Joanne Kyger, a native Californian has lived on the coast north of San Francisco for the past 37 years. She teaches occasionally at the New College of San Francisco. Her collected poems, *About Now*, is forthcoming from the National Poetry Foundation of Orono, Maine.

Joseph Lease's books of poetry include *Broken World* ((Coffee House Press, 2007), and *Human Rights* (Jensen/Daniels). His poem, "'Broken world' (For James Assatly)" was selected by Robert Creeley for *The Best American Poetry 2002 (*Scribner). In *Talisman*, the critic Christopher Beach called Lease "among the most accomplished and provocative poets of his generation." Lease is Associate Professor of Writing and Literature at California College of the Arts.

Rick London's most recent publication is the chapbook *Picture With Moving Parts* (Doorjamb Press, 2002). He lives and works in San Francisco.

Clarence Major's paintings have been widely exhibited. He writes "Painting for me is about discovering a plastic reality of composition through lines, color and texture…Painting is the most important activity in my life." The University of North Carolina Press published an illustrated book about his paintings and writing, *Clarence Major and His Art* in 2001. Major's many prizes for poetry include two Pushcart prizes; he was a finalist for the National Book Awards (1999). He teaches at the University of California, Davis. The broadsides we published combine Major's paintings and poetry.

Ray Manzarek of the Rock and Roll Hall of Fame, is the keyboardist of The Doors and director of many Doors' videos. He made his film directorial debut in *Love Her Madly.* He's the producer of the punk rock group, X. *Light My Fire* is the title of Manzarek's recent autobiography. Ray and Michael McClure met at the third recording session of The Doors through their mutual friend Jim Morrison.

Michael McClure's most recent books are *Plum Stones* from O Books and *Huge Dreams* published by Penguin. He often performs his poetry with Ray Manzarek and also with Terry Riley. *I Like Your Eyes, Liberty*, a CD by McClure and Riley was commended by Wire Magazine as one of the ten best serious compositions of 2005. He lives in the Bay Area hills with his wife the sculptor Amy Evans McClure.

Max McDaniel has worked with the student photography publication *J205* as well as the Nevada County poetry group The Inkwell (2004-2005), both performing and publishing poetry. He is currently a student in the Creative Writing Department at the University of California, Santa Cruz, and co-editor of the broadside publication, *Vis-a-Vis*.

James Meetze is the author of *Serenades* (Cy Press, 2003) and *Instrument* (Sea.Lamb.Press., 2004). He teaches creative writing at UC San Diego and sings for the band Dreamtiger.

David Meltzer began his literary career during the Beat heyday in San Francisco reading to jazz accompaniment at the famous Jazz Cellar. He is the author of many novels and poetry collections, including *David's Copy: The Selected Poems of David Meltzer* (2005) and *Beat Thing* (2004), which was awarded the Josephine Miles PEN Award, 2006. He teaches at The New College in San Francisco.

K. Silem Mohammad is the author of *Deer Head Nation* (Tougher Disguises, 2003), *A Thousand Devils* (Combo Books, 2004), and *Breathalyzer* (Edge Books, 2007). His blog {*lime tree*} can be accessed at http://lime-tree.blogspot.com.

Laura Moriarty's most recent books are *Ultravioleta* (Atelos, 2006) and *Self-Destruction* (Post-Apollo Press). Forthcoming is *Selected Poetry*, from Omnidawn in 2007. Awards include the Poetry Center Book Award, a Gerbode Foundation grant and a residency at the Foundation Royaumont in Paris. She is currently Deputy Director of Small Press Distribution.

Eileen Myles newest book of poetry is *Sorry, Tree* (Wave Books). She's mostly living in Southern California lately and teaching at UC San Diego.

Alice Notley's most recent books of poetry are *Grave of Light, Selected Poems 1970 -2005* and *Alma, or The Dead Women*. A new book, *In the Pines*, is forthcoming from Penguin in 2007.

Ron Padgett's most recent books include a collection of poems, *You Never Know*, and two memoirs, *Oklahoma Tough: My Father, King of the Tulsa Bootleggers* and *Joe: A Memoir of Joe Brainard*. This year Coffee House Press will issue a new collection of poems. Info: www.ronpadgett.com.

Michael Palmer's most recent collections of poetry are *The Promises of Glass* (New Directions, 2000), *Codes Appearing (Poems 1979-1988)* (New Directions, 2001) and *Company of Moths* (New Directions, 2005). A dance collaboration with the Margaret Jenkins Dance Company and the composer Paul Dresher, premiered in May of 2006 in San Francisco where he lives. He received the 2006 Wallace Stevens Award from the Academy of American Poets. His selected essays and talks is forthcoming, 2007.

Kenneth Patchen is author of over forty volumes of prose and poetry, including illustrated poems. In New York City, he wrote his most famous work, *The Journal of Albion Moonlight* (1941), an antiwar novel. In the 1950s, Patchen moved to San Francisco, where he continued his work as a pacifist and poet-artist and where he performed his poetry to jazz, an art form he pioneered back in 1938. Patchen created his most visually memorable work, the Painted Poems, during the 1960's when he was confined to bed for 13 years following unsuccessful spinal surgery. He died in 1972.

Laura Perkins writes a weekly history column for the *San Francisco Chronicle*. She is especially interested in arresting the short attention spans of the 21st century by exploring abbreviated forms like the one-page play. Make them want more.

Micah Perks is the author of a novel, *We Are Gathered Here*, a memoir, *Pagan Time*, and various short stories, two of which have been nominated for The Pushcart Prize. She has just finished a novel. She teaches at UCSC, where she is Provost of Kresge College.

Jessea Perry is a poet and printer living in Oakland. She believes in using ornament with a twist and as many shades of red as possible.

Sky Power is an abstract and figurative painter, printmaker, piano tuner, and woodworker. Active in the arts since childhood, Sky studied figure drawing with Ed Gothberg at Casper College in Wyoming, and continued her studies in Fine Art at Cornish School of Allied Arts in Seattle, Washington in the early seventies. An exhibiting artist since 1974, Sky has shown her work in galleries in Provincetown, Boston, and Washington, D.C. She is currently represented by Berta Walker Gallery in Provincetown, Massachusetts.

Roxanne Power Hamilton teaches at Mills College and UC Santa Cruz, where she co-founded and curates the event series, "Trans-Genre: Poetry and the Inter-Arts." Recent publications include poems and essays in *War and Peace 2*, and *Impossible to Hold: Women, Culture, and the 60s*. Among many recent inter-arts performances are collaborations with the band, Mobius Operandi and several Neo-Benshi shows—including SFSU Poetry Center and SF Cinemateque. In May 2007 she will perform at St. Mark's Poetry Project and The Bowery Poetry Club in New York City.

Kristin Prevallet is a conceptual poet whose image-text experiments have been collected in two books, *Scratch Sides: Poetry, Documentation, and Image-text Projects* (Skanky Possum, 2003) and *Shadow Evidence Intelligence* (Factory School, 2006). A lyric essay, "I Afterlife: Essay in Mourning Time," was recently published by Essay Press. She lives in Brooklyn.

Carl Rakosi was born in Berlin and educated at the University of Wisconsin, where he edited the *Wisconsin Literary Review*. A protégé of Ezra Pound in the 30s, Rakosi was published in the Objectivist issue of *Poetry* and in the *Objectivist Anthology*. Following his 1941 *Selected Poems* he left poetry for 30 years and dedicated himself to social work. His next book, *Amulet* was published by New Directions in 1967 followed by his *Collected Poems* in 1986 and several more volumes. He actively published and read his poetry into his 90s. In November 2003, Rakosi celebrated his 100th birthday at the San Francisco Public Library. He died June 24, 2004 at the age of 100, the last surviving Objectivist poet.

Stephen Ratcliffe's most recent book is *Portraits and Repetition*. His poems have appeared in *Chain, Denver Quarterly, P-QUEUE, New American Writing, War and Peace, LIT, 1913, & The Addison Street Poetry Anthology*. He lives in Bolinas, publishes Avenue B books, and teaches at Mills College in Oakland.

Joan Retallack is currently at work on an investigative poetic project, *The Reinvention of Truth*. She is the author of six poetry volumes including *Memnoir, How To Do Things with Words, AFTERRIMAGES,* and *Errata 5uite* which won the Columbia Book Award chosen by Robert Creeley. *Poetry and Pedagogy: The Challenge of the Contemporary*, co-edited with Juliana Spahr, came out from Palgrave MacMillan in January 2006. *The Poethical Wager*, essays on poethics, was published in 2004 by the University of California Press which will also bring out her forthcoming *Gertrude Stein: Selections*.

Derk Richardson has been writing about all kinds of music in the San Francisco Bay Area and beyond since 1978. He is currently senior editor at Oakland magazine, music columnist for SF Gate.com, and host of a free-form music program on KPFA 94.1 FM in Berkeley, California.

Jerome Rothenberg is an internationally known poet with over seventy books of poetry and several assemblages of traditional and contemporary poetry such as *Technicians of the Sacred* and *Poems for the Millenium*. His forthcoming book, *Tryptich*, is his thirteenth from New Directions. Other recent work includes *A Book of Witness*, and (from Wesleyan U. Press), *Writing Through: Translations & Variations*. His previous text-art collaborations include work with Ian Tyson, Tom Phillips, Jan Voss, Irving Petlin, Laurence Fink, Barbara Fahrner, Allen D'Arcangelo, Harold Cohen, Susan Bee, Eleanor Antin, and Arman.

Camille Roy co-edited *Biting The Error: Writers Explore Narrative* (Coach House 2005). Earlier books include *Cheap Speech*, a play, from Leroy, and *Craquer*, a fictional autobiography from 2nd Story Books, as well as *Swarm* (two novellas, Black Star Series), among others. In 1998 she was the recipient of a Lannan Writers At Work Residency at Just Buffalo Literary Center. She is a founding editor of the online journal *Narrativity*: www.sfsu.edu/~poetry/narrativity. She teaches fiction at San Francisco State University.

Jocelyn Saidenberg is the author of the books *Mortal City, Cusp,* and *Negativity*, recently published by Atelos. She is also the founding editor of Krupskaya Books and literary co-curator for New Langton Arts.

Leslie Scalapino's is the author of thirty books, the most recent being *Zither & Autobiography* published by Wesleyan UP. In 2007 Green Integer published a collection of the last eight years of her poetry, titled *Day Ocean State Of Stars' Night*. The UC Press at Berkeley will publish her *Selected Poems* in spring 2008.

Jennifer Scappettone is a poet, translator and critic who teaches at the University of Chicago. Her past forays into the sculpture of poetry produced textual installations at This is It! Gallery in Nagoya, Japan, and at the Worth Ryder Gallery in Berkeley. Other pieces of the series from which "The Carapace" hails can be found in *Aufgabe, Commonweal, The Brooklyn Rail, and The Poker*. "The Carapace" was originally posted, html-style, at canwehaveourballback.com.

George Schneeman has shown his work at the Fischbach Gallery, Holly Solomon Gallery, Denver Art Museum, The American Academy of Arts and Letters, and the Tibor de Nagy Gallery, among others. Recently Granary Books issued *Painter among Poets: The Collaborative Art of George Schneeman*.

Sarah Schulman is the author of eight novels, including *The Child* (Carroll and Graff, 2007), two nonfiction books and a number of plays including *Carson McCullers* (Playscripts, Inc. 2006).

Will Sherwood has a multi-paletted career: engineer, musician, artist/photographer. He has appeared as guest soloist with the Boston Pops and has given concerts in both the U.S. and Europe. After having spent 30 years as an Engineering Manager in Microprocessor Design at Digital/Compaq/Intel, he is now focusing on photography and web & graphic design. Info: www.sherwoodweb.com

Cedar Sigo is 29 years old. A revised second edition of *Selected Writings* appeared in 2005 from Ugly Duckling Presse. His most recent book is collaborative, *Deathrace v.s.o.p.*

Susan Silton is a Los Angeles-based artist. Her work has been exhibited in galleries and institutions nationally and internationally, including Los Angeles County Museum of Art; SITE Santa Fe, New Mexico; Feigen Contemporary, New York, Angles Gallery, Santa Monica; and Australian Centre for Centemporary Art, Melbourne. *Tornado in a Box* is currently on view in *Picturing Modernity: The Photography Collection* at San Francisco Museum of Modern Art.

Daniel E. Smith: Born 1945 in Los Gatos. Used to go camping in the woods where UCSC now stands. Attended CCAC '69 to '72. Moved to Bolinas in '70 while attending CCAC. Became acquainted with numerous writers living there, Bob Creeley, David Meltzer, Joanne Kyger, Bill Berkson, Phillip Wahlen and of course, Larry Kearney, plus met all those associated with them at the time, Ginsberg, Ed Dorn, Lew Welch, Richard Brautigan, Phillip Lamentia, etc.

Dean Smith is a visual artist represented by Christopher Grimes Gallery, Santa Monica; Marvelli Gallery, New York; and Gallery Paule Anglim, San Francisco. Smith and Glück's, *aliengnosis* premiered at San Francisco Cinematheque in 2004 and subsequently screened at The 19th London Lesbian/Gay Film Festival at London's, National Theater, and the Clarke Centre in Montreal in 2005.

Carol Snow is the author of *Artist and Model*, *For*, and *The Seventy Prepositions* (University of California Press). Snow misses "Syntax" but has resumed work on her *karesansui*/preposition poems. Alex Ketley recently choreographed works for The Foundry, Hubbard Street Dance Chicago, and Robert Moses' KIN. Andrea Flores and Justin Flores appear with ODC Dance/San Francisco.

Roswell Spafford is a poet, fiction writer, journalist and teacher of writing whosework has been published in numerous small magazines. Her poem, "Apple," is part of a new series called "Acts of God," a continuation of her lifelong argument with Him/Her.

Juliana Spahr is the author most recently of *This Connection of Everyone with Lungs*.

When asked "What are you working on now?", **Debra St. John** replies that she is always photographing like she is always breathing. Her camera has been a constant companion since the age of ten—a good friend that will remember things years later that she most certainly will not.

Brian Kim Stefans is a poet and web artist living in Providence, Rhode Island. *What Is Said to the Poet Concerning Flowers*, was published in May 2006 by Factory School (www.factoryschool.org.) His most recent book, *Kluge: A Meditation*, was published by Roof Books in 2007. Most importantly, the great Wooster Group actress Kate Valk played "Kate Valk" in a recent production of his short play "Where Stones Gather" at the Ontological Theater in New York City.

Konrad Steiner is an independent curator and filmmaker living in San Francisco. Since 1980 he has been programming film at various venues in the Bay Area, and making films in the Bay Area that have been shown in venues around the world. He has a particular interest in cross-media collaboration.

Chris Stroffolino is the songwriter for Continuous Peasant (www.myspace.com/continuouspeasant), whose latest album is *Intentional Grounding*. He's also published three full-length books of poems, numerous chapbooks, and essays on subjects from Shakespeare to The Century Of The Self. When not looking for a job, cheaper rent and healthcare, he's currently seeking a publisher for his memoir, *Radio Orphan*, from which this piece in *Viz.* is excerpted.

"Wayne's College of Beauty" is the title poem of **David Swanger's** forthcoming volume from MkBk Press which won the John Ciardi Prize in poetry in 2006. Swanger has also won an NEA fellowship in poetry and other awards. He is the author of three previous books of poems.

Michelle Tea is the author of four memoirs, most recently the illustrated *Rent Girl*. She is the creator of Radar, a literary organization that curates the monthly Radar reading series at the San Francisco Public Library. *Rose of No Man's Land* is her first novel.

Jeremy James Thompson recently graduated from Mills College with an MFA in Poetics. In the fall of 2006, he curated a series of group exhibitions entitled PLASTIQUE: A Gallery of Poetics, which sought to enact a categorical blurring of visual and linguistic media. His work has appeared in *Cricket Online Review*, *Spectrum*, *The Walrus*, *NoFi Magazine* and Pinstripe *Fedora*.

Nancy Tobin's artistic roots span the United States. Raised in Michigan, she trained in painting in San Francisco, where she also established a successful career as an illustrator. Tobin's collages merge her representational work with her keen interest in abstract composition and color-field theory. She currently lives in New Jersey and is participating in shows across the country.

Edwin Torres' books include *The PoPedology Of An Ambient Language* (Atelos Books), *In The Function of External Circumstances* (Spuyten Duyvil), and *The All-Union Day of The Shock Worker* (Roof Books). He is co-editor of the DVD journal Rattapallax and host of "Live Nude Radio Theater" on WPS1.org. His collaboration with Jeremy Thompson on "Transferred Throat" came from an interwoven litmus of corollary gem stoning over a cycle of interlucent blinks.

Migdalia Valdes is a photographer who still works with film, cajoling images out of her stubborn timeworn Rolleiflex for 25 years. Based in San Francisco, she is currently in Brugge, Belgium having just returned from India where she has been photographing life in its oddest, most expansive context.

Stephen Vincent lives in San Francisco. *Walking Theory* (Junction Press) is his latest volume. Other publications include: *Walking* (poems) Junction Press, and *A Walk Toward Spicer* (essay), Cherry on The Top Press. Two poetry ebooks include: *Sleeping with Sappho* (www.fauxpress.com/e/vincent/) and *Triggers* (www.shearsman.com/pages/books/ebooks/ebooks_home.html). His blog journal of photographs, poems and commentary is found at: http://stephenvincent.net/blog/.

Anne Waldman is a poet, performer, professor, editor, cultural activist and the co-founder (with Allen Ginsberg) of The Jack Kerouac School of Disembodied Poetics at Naropa University. Recent books include *In the Room of Never Grieve* (with accompanying CD with collaborations with her son, Ambrose Bye) (Coffee House Press) and *Structure of the World Compared to a Bubble* (Penguin Poets). She is also the co-editor of *Civil Disobediences: Poetics & Politics in Action*. She has collaborated extensively with others including Elizabeth Murray, Red Grooms, Richard Tuttle, Donna Dennis and George Schneeman and most recently her husband video filmmaker Ed Bowes.

Keith Waldrop's Recent books include *The Real Subject* from Omnidawn Press, and a translation of Baudelaire's *The Flowers of Evil* from Wesleyan, Fall 2006.

Rosmarie Waldrop's recent books of poetry are *Blindsight* (New Directions) and *Love, Like Pronouns* (Omnidawn). A book of essays, *Dissonance (if you are interested)*, is out from University of Alabama Press. Her collaborations with Keith Waldrop have been collected as *Well Well Reality* (Post-Apollo Press).

Re-settled in La Selva Beach in Northern California, **Rob Wilson** is working on two poetry and cultural poetics collections: *Ananda Air: American Pacific Lines of Flight*; and *Automat: Unsettling Anglo-Global Poetics Along Asian/Pacific Lines of Flight*; and an anthology of cultural criticism called *Worldings: Doing Cultural Studies in the Era of Globalization* was published by New Pacific Press in Santa Cruz, California. During the fall of 2004, he was a visiting professor in the Cinema Department at the Korea National University of the Arts in Seoul, South Korea.

Terry Wolverton is author of six books: *Embers*, a novel-in-poems; *Insurgent Muse: life and art at the Woman's Building*, a memoir, *Bailey's Beads*, a novel; and two collections of poetry: *Black Slip, Mystery Bruise*, and *Shadow and Praise*. A new novel, *The Labrys Reunion*, will be published in 2008. She has also edited thirteen literary anthologies, including *Mischief, Caprice, and Other Poetic Strategies*. She is the founder of Writers At Work, a creative writing center in Los Angeles, where she teaches fiction and poetry.

Karen Tei Yamashita is a Japanese American writer from California and the author of *Through the Arc of the Rain Forest, Brazil-Maru, Tropic of Orange*, and *Circle K Cycles*, all published by Coffee House Press. Currently, she is Associate Professor of Literature and Creative Writing at the University of California, Santa Cruz.

Heriberto Yepez is the author of several books of essays, poetry and fiction in Spanish. He lives in Tijuana, Mexico. His first book in English, titled *Wars. Threesomes. Drafts. & Mothers*, was published by Factory School in 2007.

Elizabeth Marie Young is a poet and classicist working on her PhD in Comparative Literature at UC Berkeley. In 2004 she curated *Cabinet of the Muses*, an inter-arts poetry festival in San Francisco. She is currently in the middle of several poetry books and one dissertation on Catullus and lyric translation. Her work has recently appeared or is soon forthcoming in *Commonweal, Fulcrum, The Poker, Pool, Traffic, Word For/Word* and *Xantippe*.

Therine Youngblood is a film writer who lives in San Francisco.

Credits and Acknowledgements

Funding:
Thank you to our funders at the University of California, Santa Cruz: Porter College Hitchcock Poetry Fund, The Center for Teaching Excellence and The Non-Senate Faculty Professional Development Fund

Broadsides:
A special thank you for the donation of "Painting Poems" by Kenneth Patchen.
Courtesy: Special Collections, University of California, Kenneth Patchen Archive.

Thank you to Copper Canyon Press for the rights to reprint Clarence Major's poems "Swallow the Lake" and "Hazy Day in the Composition" from *Configurations*: *New and Selected Poems 1958-1998*.

Broadside artists and designers:
Artists: Joe Brainard and Ron Padgett; Lawrence Ferlinghetti and Momo; Jorge Hitchcock; Clarence Major; Jerome Rothenberg and Nancy Tobin; and Amy Trachtenberg.
Designers: Dan Fisher and Jessea Perry; Mary Gilliana; Max McDaniel; Stephanie Gliozzo; James Meetze; Jeremy James Thompson and Lara Durback.

Photographs in page designs:
Emily Michel; Amy Fletcher; Amber Pittinger; Debra St. John; Christopher Wright.

Reprinting rights and notes:
pp. 2-5: Fluxus Event Scores reprinted from *Fluxus Performance Workbook*, edited by Ken Friedman, Lauren Sawchyn, and Owen Smith, 2002. Available on line: www.performance-research.net/pages/epublications.html.

pp. 6-8: Dick Higgins, "Synesthesia and Intersenses: Intermedia," with thanks to Hannah B. Higgins and the Dick Higgins Estate.

p. 11 (and other paintings for the broadsides) by Jorge Hitchcock. Images of paintings courtesy of Galeria H and H. Jens and Petra Herrman. Av. Cornel Esteban Cantu 2651, Colonia Davila, Tijuana, Baja California, 22400, Mexico. Tel-Fax: (011-52-664) 900-6133. E-mail: Galeria@ArteHH.com; www.GaleriaHH.com

pp. 14, 29: Image/text collaborations (Ron Padgett/Joe Brainard and Ron Padgett/George Schneeman) and *C'est Toi* broadside (Padgett/Brainard) courtesy of Ron Padgett's collection.

pp. 15-16: Joe Brainard, *If Nancy Were a da Vinci;* Joe Brainard and Bill Berkson, *I love you de Kooning.* University of California, San Diego, Mandeville: Joe Brainard Archive.

pp. 19, 20, 21: Image/text collaborations (Bill Berkson/Joe Brainard and Bill Berkson/George Schneeman) courtesy of Bill Berkson's collection.

pp. 22-23: Image/text collaborations (Bill Berkson/George Schneeman) courtesy of George Schneeman's collection.

pp. 24, 25, 30, 31: George Schneeman with Ted Berrigan, Alice Notley, Anne Waldman, Bill Berkson, and Ron Padgett. From *Painter Among Poets: The Collaborative Art of George Schneeman,* Ed. Ron Padgett. New York: Granary Books, 2004. Images courtesy of Granary Books.

pp. 32-33: Thanks to Anne Waldman and Ed Bowes for images from their film, *The Menage,* a tribute to Carl Rakosi on his 100th birthday based on Rakosi's poem, "The Menage."

pp. 35, 38, 39, 40: Thank you to Internet2 and Ann Doyle of University of Michigan for the recording/images of "The Transcontinental Poetry Reading," 2003.

pp. 36-37: Kenneth Koch, "Twenty Poems," from *The Collected Poems of Kenneth Koch,* by Kenneth Koch. Copyright 2005 by Kenneth Koch Literary Estate. Used by permission of Alfred H. Knopf, a division of Random House, Inc.

pp. 58-59; 64; 65-66: Essays by Robert Glück (shortened version), Camille Roy, and kari edwards from *Biting the Error: Writers Explore Narrative.* Coach House, 2004.

p. 59: Dodie Bellamy, from *Academonia*. San Francisco: Krupskaya, 2006.

pp. 70-73: Leslie Scalapino, "Delay series" from *way*. San Francisco: North Point Press, 1988.

pp. 79-80: Nathaniel Dorsky, from *Devotional Cinema*, Revised Second Edition. Berkeley: Tuumba Press, 2005.

pp. 90-91: Guy Debord, from *The Society of the Spectacle*, images and film script (translated by Ken Knabb) from Guy Debord's *Complete Cinematic Works*, AK Press, 2003. Reproduced with permission from Ken Knabb.

p. 92: Therine Youngblood, excerpt of "Poetry and Motion" from *Release Print* (Film Arts Foundation Magazine), July/August 2005.

p. 108: Derk Richardson, "Steeling Beauty" originally published in "The Hear and Now" audio column of sfgate.com, August 16, 2001.

pp. 118-119: Bob Holman, from *A Couple of Ways of Doing Something*, by Chuck Close and Bob Holman. New York: Aperture, 2006. Reproduced with permission from Bob Holman.

pp. 120-21: Laura Moriarty, from *Ultravioleta*. Atelos, 2006. Reproduced with permission from Laura Moriarty.

pp. 123-24: kari edwards, from *Iduna*. O Books, 2003.

p. 143: Charles Bernstein, "If You Lived Here, You'd Be Home Now" from *Girly Man*, University of Chicago Press, 2006. Reproduced with permission from Charles Bernstein.

pp. 147-154: Additional paintings by Sky Power can be found at Berta Walker Gallery: bertawalkergallery.com; 508-487-6411.

p. 155: Jane Hirshfield from *After*. New York: HarperCollins, 2006. Reproduced with permission from Jane Hirshfield.

pp. 158-161: Michelle Tea from *Rose of No Man's Land*. MacAdam/Cage: 2006. Reproduced with permission from Michelle Tea.

p. 166: David Swanger from *Wayne's College of Beauty*, BkMk Press, 2006. Reproduced with permission from David Swanger.

pp. 192-93: Mahmoud Darwish from *Now, As you Awaken*, trans. Omnia Amin and Rick London. Reproduced with permission from Rick London.

p. 216: *Out:* Scrapbook photos from Bill Berkson's collection.

pp. 222-24: Picture-poem paste-ups and broadside by Jess, including work by Robert Duncan, courtesy of The Jess Collins Trust.

Thank you to Rachel Swirsky for our first website design

Thank you to UCSC Literary Arts Magazine Publishing students and Sarah Franci for your support

Reaching for the Stars ©AnneKarin Glass